Formative Assessment, Learning Data Analytics and Gamification

Formative Assessment, Learning Data Analytics and Gamification
In ICT Education

Edited by

Santi Caballé and Robert Clarisó
Universitat Oberta de Catalunya, Barcelona, Spain

Series Editor Fatos Xhafa

AMSTERDAM • BOSTON • HEIDELBERG • LONDON
NEW YORK • OXFORD • PARIS • SAN DIEGO
SAN FRANCISCO • SINGAPORE • SYDNEY • TOKYO
Academic Press is an imprint of Elsevier

Academic Press is an imprint of Elsevier
125 London Wall, London EC2Y 5AS, UK
525 B Street, Suite 1800, San Diego, CA 92101-4495, USA
50 Hampshire Street, 5th Floor, Cambridge, MA 02139, USA
The Boulevard, Langford Lane, Kidlington, Oxford OX5 1GB, UK

Notices
Knowledge and best practice in this field are constantly changing. As new research and experience broaden our understanding, changes in research methods, professional practices, or medical treatment may become necessary.

Practitioners and researchers must always rely on their own experience and knowledge in evaluating and using any information, methods, compounds, or experiments described herein. In using such information or methods they should be mindful of their own safety and the safety of others, including parties for whom they have a professional responsibility.

To the fullest extent of the law, neither the Publisher nor the authors, contributors, or editors, assume any liability for any injury and/or damage to persons or property as a matter of products liability, negligence or otherwise, or from any use or operation of any methods, products, instructions, or ideas contained in the material herein.

Library of Congress Cataloging-in-Publication Data
A catalog record for this book is available from the Library of Congress

British Library Cataloguing-in-Publication Data
A catalogue record for this book is available from the British Library

ISBN: 978-0-12-803637-2

For information on all Academic Press publications
visit our website at https://www.elsevier.com/

Working together
to grow libraries in
developing countries

www.elsevier.com • www.bookaid.org

Publisher: Todd Green
Acquisition Editor: Brian Romer
Editorial Project Manager: Amy Invernizzi
Production Project Manager: Punithavathy Govindaradjane
Designer: Victoria Pearson

Typeset by SPi Global, India

To our families

Contents

PART 1   FORMATIVE e-ASSESSMENT

PART 2   LEARNING ANALYTICS

List of Contributors

K. Aoki
The Open University of Japan, Chiba, Japan

J. Arnedo-Moreno
Open University of Catalonia, Barcelona, Spain

I. Balasooriya
Universitat Oberta de Catalunya, Barcelona, Spain

D. Baneres
Open University of Catalonia, Barcelona, Spain

X. Baró
Open University of Catalonia, Barcelona, Spain

Z. Callejas
University of Granada, Granada, Spain

M.M. Chan
Galileo University, Guatemala, Guatemala

P. Compañ-Rosique
Universitat d'Alacant, Alicante, Spain

J. Conesa
Open University of Catalonia, Barcelona, Spain

M. Drlík
Constantine the Philosopher University in Nitra, Nitra, Slovakia

A.A. Economides
University of Macedonia, Thessaloniki, Greece

M. Elena Rodríguez
Open University of Catalonia, Barcelona, Spain

N. Escudero-Viladoms
Autonomous University of Barcelona, Barcelona, Spain

M.F. Farghally
Virginia Tech, Blacksburg, VA, United States

M. Feidakis
University of Aegean, Mytilene, Greece

E. Fouh
Virginia Tech, Blacksburg, VA, United States

F.J. Gallego-Durán
Universitat d'Alacant, Alicante, Spain

D. Griol
Carlos III University of Madrid, Madrid, Spain

A.-E. Guerrero-Roldán
Open University of Catalonia, Barcelona, Spain

C. Guetl
Graz University of Technology, Graz, Austria

I. Guitart
Open University of Catalonia, Barcelona, Spain

S. Hamouda
Virginia Tech, Blacksburg, VA, United States

E. Hettiarachchi
University of Colombo School of Computing, Colombo, Sri Lanka

M.A. Huertas
Universitat Oberta de Catalunya, Barcelona, Spain

F. Llorens-Largo
Universitat d'Alacant, Alicante, Spain

V.I. Marín
University of the Balearic Islands, Palma, Spain

R. Molina-Carmona
Universitat d'Alacant, Alicante, Spain

E. Mor
Universitat Oberta de Catalunya, Barcelona, Spain

M. Munk
Constantine the Philosopher University in Nitra, Nitra, Slovakia

Z. Papamitsiou
University of Macedonia, Thessaloniki, Greece

A. Pérez Garcias
University of the Balearic Islands, Palma, Spain

D. Riera
Open University of Catalonia, Barcelona, Spain

R.H. Rizzardini
Galileo University, Guatemala, Guatemala

T. Sancho-Vinuesa
Open University of Catalonia, Barcelona, Spain

R. Satorre-Cuerda
Universitat d'Alacant, Alicante, Spain

C.A. Shaffer
Virginia Tech, Blacksburg, VA, United States

U. Tudevdagva
Mongolian University of Science and Technology, Ulaanbaatar, Mongolia

C.J. Villagrá-Arnedo
Universitat d'Alacant, Alicante, Spain

Foreword

D. Whitelock

Professor of Technology Enhanced Assessment and Learning,
The Open University, Institute of Education,
Walton Hall, Milton Keynes, MK7 4AA, U.K.

In recent years a number of changes to the design and delivery of ICT Education have taken place. These include the growth of e-assessment, together with an emerging focus on learning design and gamification, a greater interest in a student-centred approach and an institutional desire to find efficient and effective ways to deliver feedback and assessment support. In fact, assessment both impacts on and is influenced by broader curriculum and societal changes. Rowntree (1987) draws our attention to the role of encompassing assessment by stating:

> if we wish to discover the truth about an educational system, we must look into its assessment procedures
>
> **Rowntree (1987, p.1)**

The pace of change in the assessment area has been slow, yet there is increasing agreement across the sector that changes are necessary. Chris Rust (2013) in a recent review of the international state of research on assessment and examinations in higher education concludes that there appears "a fairly high degree of consistency and homogeneity [...] both in terms of its criticisms of current practices and outcomes, and in the proposed solutions [...]. And the need to do something appears to be gaining recognition and perceived importance. So despite the enormity of the culture-change needed, we may actually be close to approaching the point when the collective will to engage [will reach] critical mass." Many commentators, including Whitelock (2009), have argued that such change must be accompanied by a greater emphasis on pedagogically driven models for e-assessment. These modules should facilitate the blending of e-assessment and e-feedback into a holistic dialogic learning framework. Chapter 15 of this book supports this argument with a discussion of the use of conversational agents in educational games.

In order to effect meaningful changes in assessment and curriculum design with ICT institutions must understand the role of innovation in this area and, more importantly, elicit how well this is working for students. This book illustrates the benefits and some of the problems in moving the ICT agenda forward with the assistance of Learning Analytics to promote a "Students First" approach to learning.

Formative assessment is stressed in Chapters 8 and 12 with illustrations of its use for cognitive support as well as skill development. Chapter 3's authors highlight its use for online engineering education. Formative assessment has gained substantial ground in the last 10 years with its potential to promote student learning. Hattie and Yates (2014) emphasize the role of feedback for learning, illustrating that technologies have shown a positive effect on learning achievements. Tamin et al. (2011) report an average effect size of 0.33 while Hatie's meta-analysis of computer-assisted education over the past 30 years revealed a positive effect size of 0.37. These findings all point to the need for vigorous evaluations of technological innovation in education and Chapter 4 points the way with its structure oriented evaluation model (SURE).

One of the questions raised in many of the chapters in this book is, how can ICT assist with student retention and progression? Chapter 5 offers some insights from the teaching of mathematics, while Chapter 6 suggests that moving towards a more personalized learning model can assist with this process. Chapter 7's authors emphasize the role of tracking and measuring student progress with Learning Analytics, which again can lead to a more personalized approach to teaching and learning.

Rienties and Toetenel (2016) have employed Learning Analytics to analyze students' online behavior linked to the learning designs of a substantial number of courses at the OUUK. They linked 151 modules, which contained 111,256 students with the different learning designs for these modules. Then using regression models they found the primary predictor for success was the time that students spent on communication activities, ie, where students were working together and learning from each other. They suggest that well-designed communication tasks that align with the learning objectives of the course may be a way forward to enhance academic retention. This work illustrates how large data sets are influencing recent evaluation studies and Chapter 7 proposes an Assessment Analytics Framework (AAF) for enhancing students' progress, while Chapter 9 stresses the importance of Learning Analytics and Chapter 10 presents a methodology for the predictive modeling of students' behavior. We should not, however, neglect the increasing interest in emotion-aware systems for e-learning in Virtual Environments as described in Chapter 11. They describe the challenges and benefits of self-awareness.

Massive Open and Online courses (MOOCs) are also referred to in Chapter 14. MOOCs have been growing in popularity since 2008. The main recent drivers have come from the Open Educational Resources movement in Canada and the 2008 event on Connectivism and Connective Knowledge, led by Stephen Davies and George Siemens through the University of Manitoba. Through these processes MOOCs were constructed so that participants could use the technologies of their choice and interact freely with the content and each other. The theoretical premises for the construction and delivery of MOOCs were those of connectivism (Siemens, 2004), described as a Learning Theory for the Digital Age. This modern theory takes into account the use of social networking and the availability of a plethora of information on the web, which can be shared around the world almost instantaneously.

MOOCs, however, have been termed as an "uncourse" by Hirst (2009) since anyone can contribute anywhere and, in fact, some learners do not use the course tools but prefer to collaborate using wikis, blogs, Facebook or Twitter (Beetham, 2008; Guldberg and Mackness, 2009). This presents a number of challenges, especially with the design of appropriate learning tasks. The use of educational games can support learners in MOOCs and Chapter 14 compares learning in a MOOC with and without a gamified learning method. The latter was shown to motivate and improve student participation in the course.

This book illustrates how technology can enrich student learning with its focus on information technologies and computational methods. A huge range of applications are being used in higher education; however, a wide extent of choice brings its own challenges for students and teachers alike. Feedback is highlighted in many chapters and providing electronic feedback when no other support is available for example on draft essays (Whitelock et al., 2015) can support learning when it is most needed. More importantly, these types of feedback systems can also encourage students to believe that they can improve their academic attainment. This is no small feat for learners who may often feel isolated and stretched trying to squeeze study into a day filled with other commitments and demands on their time.

The chapters in this book support the idea that there is a need for a "second-look" at the whole assessment process while, more importantly, "closing-the-loop" through effective institutional learning and dissemination. They describe some recent innovations and point the way to evaluation frameworks that assist with the development of new pedagogies for the 21st Century.

REFERENCES

Beetham, H., 2008. Learners' experiences of e-learning: research from the UK. http://www.networkedlearningconference.org.uk/past/nlc2008/abstracts/PDFs/BeethamIntro_464-466.pdf (accessed 27.02.16).

Guldberg, K., Mackness, J., 2009. Foundations of communities of practice: enablers and barriers to participation. J. Comput. Assist. Learn. 25 (6), 528–538.

Hattie, J., Yates, G., 2014. Visible Learning and the Science of How We Learn. Routledge, New York, NY.

Hirst, T., 2009. Non-Linear Uncourses—Time for Linked Ed? http://ouseful.wordpress.com/2009/01/30/non-linear-uncourses-time-for-linked-ed/ (accessed 27.02.16).

Rienties, B., Toetenel, L., 2016. The impact of learning design on student behaviour, satisfaction and performance: a cross-institutional comparison across 151 modules. Comput. Human Behav. 60, 333–341.

Rowntree, D., 1987. Assessing Students: How shall we know them? Kogan Page, London.

Rust, C., 2013. The International State of Research on Assessment and Examination in Higher Education, Symposium of Assessment Research, University of Hamburg, Germany, 20 August 2013.

Siemens, G., 2004. Connectivism: a learning theory for the digital age. elearnspace. http://www.elearnspace.org/Articles/connectivism.htm (accessed 27.02.16).

Tamin, R., Bernard, R., Borokhovski, E., Abrami, P., Schmid, R., 2011. What forty years of research says about the impact of technology on learning: A second order meta-analysis and validation study. Rev. Educ. Res. 81 (1), 4–28. http://dx.doi.org/10.3102/0034654310393361. (accessed 27.02.16).

Whitelock, D., 2009. e-Assessment: developing new dialogues for the digital age. Br. J. Educ. Technol. 40 (2), 199–202.

Whitelock, D., Gilbert, L., Wills, G., 2013. Feedback generators: providing feedback in MOOCS. In: International Computer Assisted Assessment (CAA) Conference, Research into e-Assessment, DeVere Grand Harbour Hotel, Southampton, July 9–10, 2013.

Whitelock, D., Twiner, A., Richardson, J.T.E., Field, D., Pulman, S., 2015. OpenEssayist: a supply and demand learning analytics tool for drafting academic essays. In: The 5th International Learning Analytics and Knowledge (LAK) Conference, Poughkeepsie, New York, USA, March 16–20, 2015. ISBN: 978-1-4503-3417-4.

Preface

S. Caballé, R. Clarisó

Universitat Oberta de Catalunya, Barcelona, Spain

Education in the field of Information and Communication Technologies (ICT) includes very practical competencies, which can only be acquired by means of experience, exercises, designing, projects, etc. In addition to the challenge of motivating students to solve activities, lecturers face the problem of assessing and providing suitable feedback for each submission. Receiving immediate and continuous feedback can facilitate the acquisition of the competencies, although this requires support in the form of automatic tools. The automation of the assessment process may be simple in some activities (eg, practical activities on programming) but it may be complex in activities about design or modeling.

Monitoring the use of these tools can reveal very valuable information for the tracking, management and continuous improvement of the course by the teaching team. However, in order to leverage all its potential, this information should be complemented with data from other sources (eg, the student's academic file) and historical information from previous editions of the same course.

To this end, formative assessment (e-assessment) is an appropriate teaching strategy for learning procedural competencies, such as those in the scope of ICT. Previous studies combine formative assessment tools with Learning Analytics and gamification, in order to design algorithms for automatic feedback as well as improve the formative assessment fed back to students. However, these studies explore all these axes separately and thus have less impact on the learning process. Therefore, the integration of these approaches will create beneficial synergies with relevant e-learning scenarios.

The contributions of this book have a relevant impact on students, lecturers, managers and academic coordinators. This impact results in students' greater participation and performance while lowering drop-out rates and improving satisfaction and retention levels. In addition, tutors, academic coordinators and managers are provided with tools that facilitate the formative assessment and feedback processes. As a result, educational institutions can benefit from an improvement of their academic outcomes, improved student satisfaction with the ICT courses and provision of complete information on the students' activities for decision making (from prediction to estimation). Society at large will leverage the generalization of this approach in the long term through the improvement of the perception of ICT courses and a more efficient ICT higher education, resulting in a better response to the great demands of ICT professionals.

The ultimate aim of this book is to stimulate research from both a theoretical and practical point of view into resources such as open source tools, which allows other educational institutions and organizations to apply, evaluate and reproduce the book's contributions. In this way, industry and academic researchers, professionals and practitioners can leverage the experiences and ideas found in the book.

This book consists of 15 chapters organized into three major areas:

- *Formative e-assessment.* The chapters in this area are concerned with the provision of immediate feedback by means of automatic assessment. The scope of the research focuses on knowledge areas with high cognitive or modeling levels, such as the design or modeling of software and hardware.

- *Learning analytics.* In this area, the chapters present solutions to monitor the activity and progress of the student by analyzing the learning outcomes, identifying the critical points and defining actions of improvement, among others. These analytics also incorporate other sources of academic and historical information to facilitate the course tracking and decision making processes by the teaching team.
- *Gamification.* The chapters covering this area propose incentive schemes to motivate students to solve new activities and increase their engagement without sacrificing the academic rigor.

The chapters in the first area of **Formative e-Assessment** are organized as follows:

In Chapter 1, Marín and Pérez-Garcias present a collaborative e-assessment activity as a strategy for promoting self-regulated learning. This activity uses the workshop plugin of the institutional virtual learning environment (VLE) based on Moodle and is applied in a pre-service teacher training course at the University of the Balearic Islands (Spain). Experimental data were collected through the use of student questionnaires and written reflections and the teachers' observations of the co-assessment results. The findings confirm the positive effects of co-assessment for students' learning and improving self-regulated learning abilities, and that the workshop tool is valid for developing this type of e-assessment strategy in other university courses. As another relevant result of the study, a model of the co-assessment strategy using the Moodle workshop plugin is proposed. The ultimate goal of the chapter is to face various the challenges raised by the European Higher Education Area regarding the use of didactical strategies centered on the learner, including learning assessment and improving self-regulated learning skills in students in preparation for lifelong learning.

Bañeres et al. in Chapter 2 aim to deliver personalized resources and activities based on the competencies and knowledge that the learner has to acquire. The authors claim that the feedback provided by the assessment activities helps to evaluate the next step in the formative process of the learner, though classical approaches do not take into account other evidences to guide the formative process. To overcome this limitation, the chapter focuses on the adaptive e-assessment systems needed to select the next assessment activity to be deployed. In addition, to help the learner to acquire knowledge, a trust-based e-assessment system is proposed to ensure a secure environment and authorship validation in online and blended learning environments while avoiding the time and physical space limitations imposed by face-to-face examinations.

Chapter 3 by Hettiarachchi et al. presents a literature review addressing the general areas of e-assessment in online higher education with special focus on skill acquisition in engineering education. The authors' premise is that knowledge and understanding gained from studying learning materials is not enough without having the higher-order cognitive skills needed to solve practical problems. Moreover, assessment can be used to evaluate whether students are capable of achieving the required skills as well as continuously improving their engineering education. Under these premises, the chapter specifically addresses aspects of engineering education, such as assessment, skill and knowledge assessment; e-assessment; supporting students' learning process through formative e-assessment; standards, specifications and models that should be followed to design and develop e-assessment systems, which are interoperable and secure; general trends and positions associated with e-assessment; and previous research based on skill assessment in engineering education.

Chapter 4 by Uranchimeg Tudevdagva discusses a structure-oriented evaluation model named SURE. The SURE model is reviewed first for evaluation of e-learning and then for evaluation of robustness of complex systems and self-assessment of faculty. Advantages of this model are highlighted, such as the visualization of evaluation goals by logical structures and the structure-related score calculation rules for collected data. The logical structure of evaluation goals and the clearly defined calculation rules of this model are presented forming the basis for the development of e-assessment software. The chapter describes the main steps of the SURE model, the theoretical background, examples with simulated data, as well as the architecture and functions of e-assessment software supporting the SURE model.

Escudero and Sancho in Chapter 5 address the student dropout rates and, particularly, the percentage of students who fail mathematics in online higher education, which is very high. The main aim of this chapter is to study the relationship between an online student's mathematical confidence and mathematics learning. In order to achieve it, the authors characterize and analyze both variables in a Basic Mathematics course at the Universitat Oberta de Catalunya. The methodology used is qualitative based on an in-depth analysis of the learning process of a few students using a set of indicators. The chapter shows three main findings: first, the mathematical confidence level is found to be similar for the students studied and is quite high; second, the level of learning through mathematical reasoning, communication and math skills tests varies depending on the topics and depends on the student; and finally, the three profiles outlined for mathematical learning and mathematical confidence are found to be stable and they remained stable over the entire academic term.

In Chapter 6, Kumiko Aoki illustrates the case study of a distance education university in Japan in terms of its struggle to ride the tidal wave of formative assessment and learner-centered learning. The chapter provides an interesting general discussion on traditional methods of teaching and learning, especially those conducted at a distance, where formative assessment has not been the main focus, but teaching, in terms of content delivery, has been the focus of duties teachers must fulfill. The discussion is backed up with a review of literature on online formative assessment that states that embedding formative assessment within online courses fosters a sense of interactive and collaborative online learning communities. However, based on the author's personal experience in the Open University of Japan, the chapter concludes with the assertion that the shift to online learning requires a drastic change in the perceptions of teachers as well as students, not to mention in the administrative and organizational structure of formal educational institutions.

The chapters in the second area of **Learning Analytics** are organized as follows:

Chapter 7 by Zacharoula and Economides addresses the topic of assessment analytics for revealing the intelligence held in e-assessment systems and provide accurate methods to track and measure students' progress. However, the authors claim that a framework that is capable of organizing empirical assessment analytics results is missing. To this end, they propose a theoretical framework for assessment analytics aiming at: (a) developing a conceptual representation that will act as a reference point for the discussion of the literature, (b) developing a theory that could be used to move beyond descriptions of "what" to explanations of "why" and "how," and (c) providing a structure that could act as a useful guide to understanding, evaluating and designing analytics for assessment. The authors follow an inductive and deductive inquiry methodology for conceptual mapping for sense making during construction of the framework. Overall, the chapter discusses the main concepts involved in the proposed theory, explaining how former research papers fit in the suggested framework.

Fouh et al. in Chapter 8 are concerned with how to provide appropriate feedback to students on their level of knowledge and supply a sufficient number of practice problems, which are major concerns for many courses. For this purpose, the authors explore how an eTextbook can be used to address these issues and improve learning outcomes by providing feedback from student analytics data in the form of logs to record keystrokes, mouse clicks, and timestamps, as well as higher-order information, such as performance on practice problems. Overall, the chapter discusses how the information gathered from user interaction logs can be used both to understand student behavior and to improve the system. In addition, the chapter explores the deployment of basic gamification techniques within an eTextbook to motivate students and to encourage them toward more learning-oriented behavior.

Chapter 9 by Guitart and Conesa aims at creating analytic information systems in order to make universities more competitive. The authors claim that analytical systems, when applied to universities, have been less successful than when they have been used in enterprises, since these systems do not cover the main activities of universities (mainly teaching and research). To overcome this limitation the authors propose the creation of Analytical Information Systems for Universities, which bring together two approaches: one based on management with institutional support and the other based on university activities without institutional support. The authors state that the idea of developing analytical information systems in universities is a grand challenge for information systems research and then show the benefits of integrating both approaches. The chapter first reviews the characteristics and benefits of analytical systems in the context of enterprises and universities, then discusses the differences between them, and finally proposes how universities can benefit from industries' experience.

The aim of Chapter 10 by Munk and Drlik is the provision of a methodology that can be used for modeling the behavior of virtual learning environment (VLE) stakeholders with reference to time. The presented methodology allows the probability modeling of stakeholders' accesses to the different web parts (activities, e-learning courses, course categories) with reference to time. For this purpose, a multinomial logit model is used. The contribution of the presented methodology consists of the data preparation and data modeling. Data preparation covers the design methodology and recommendations for acquiring reliable data from the log files of the VLE, while in the data modeling the chapter brings a detailed model description and methodology of modeling of stakeholders' behavior with reference to time. Moreover, the description of the possibilities of how to use this obtained knowledge also represents a valuable contribution by this chapter.

Feidakis et al. in Chapter 11 discuss the limitations of current emotion-aware systems, which still strive to provide means that effectively deal with important issues in e-learning, such as students' lack of self-confidence, high dropout rates, low motivation and engagement, self-regulation and task performance. Consequently, many learning systems have been produced from current research work in the areas of adaptive and personalized learning, which need to consider and incorporate emotion awareness features to enhance their ways of adapting to the real internal world of each student and to be capable of providing effective personalized feedback to a varied spectrum of needs created in student's life. The authors conclude the discussion stating that the integration of emotion awareness can greatly advance the frontiers of educational technologies and provide an added value to enhance and improve the overall distance-learning experience as well as discover new opportunities for the cost-effective delivery of training programs.

The chapters in the third and last area of **Gamification** are organized as follows:

Chapter 12 by Llorens-Largo et al. addresses the topic of gamification as a promising line of research providing many benefits to education, based on motivation, progressiveness and instant feedback. The authors claim that motivation and the active role of students are key points to enhance learning, and are two of the main challenges in education; the ultimate aim being a customized student-centered learning model, in which the student may have some autonomy. To achieve this goal, the chapter proposes an innovative and adaptive gamified training model, called LudifyME, which takes advantage of the benefits of gamification and has a strong technological component as a basis. Finally, as a case study, the chapter shows an online gamified system based on the proposed gamified training model in which a progressive prediction system of students' performance has been developed.

Riera and Arnedo-Moreno in Chapter 13 analyze how video-games have taken a relevant place as a medium in society and how this has led to the rise of a generation who has grown up playing them and feeling comfortable in a daily life where game-like mechanics have become increasingly prevalent. The result is a breeding ground for tools that use such mechanics to improve learning experiences, such as serious games and gamification. To this end, the chapter presents the design and implementation of kPAX, an open learning environment that may cater to this new generation. Specifically, kPAX is described as a technological platform for the distribution of serious games, where each game may be added as a pluggable independent module. The platform relies on gamification and integration with existing social networks as its main engagement and feedback mechanisms.

In Chapter 14, Hernández-Rizzardini et al. address the Massive Open Online Courses (MOOCs), which have dramatically expanded online learning opportunities, and many institutions have made considerable efforts to develop and promote such courses. However, the authors claim that MOOCs have failed to produce evidence of their influence on the future of higher education as one of the major recurring issues is the consistently high dropout rate of MOOC learners with completion rates under 10%. The chapter reviews the existing literature on MOOC dropout rates and analyzes the attrition and retention factors, the open online learner group classification and the funnel of involvement in an open learning setting. Furthermore, the chapter provides results from two courses given by the Telescope Project (an initiative with a similar objective to Coursera or EdX) at Galileo University. Finally, the chapter makes a comparative analysis between the conventional learning method used in the first MOOC, and the gamified strategies as a learning method used in the second MOOC to motivate and improve student participation.

The last Chapter 15 by Griol and Callejas discusses the wide variety of applications for which multimodal conversational systems are being used in education within the context of gamification. The chapter also describes a modular and scalable framework to develop such systems efficiently for mobile devices and virtual environments. To show its potentiality, the authors present two different agents created with the framework for two pedagogical systems corresponding to different educative domains, and show the results of their evaluation with students of different age groups. The results show that the generated agents provide a natural and user-adapted human–machine interaction with educative applications, which adapts to the progress of each student, and that students find motivating.

FINAL WORDS

The book covers scientific and technical research perspectives that contribute to the advance of the state of the art and provide better understanding of the different problems and challenges of current e-learning in general education. In particular, the book addresses the application of automatic techniques for assessment of ICT learning activities; strategies to provide immediate and useful feedback to students' activities; methods to collect, analyze and correctly present the information and extracted knowledge in educational environments; and the application, benefits and challenges of using gamification techniques in an academic context.

Researchers will find in this book the latest trends in these research topics. Academics will find practical insights into how to use conceptual and experimental approaches in their daily tasks. Meanwhile, developers from the e-learning community can be inspired and put into practice the proposed models and methodologies and evaluate them for the specific purposes within their own work and context.

Finally, we would like to thank the authors of the chapters and also the referees for their invaluable collaboration and prompt responses to our enquiries, which enabled completion of this book on time. We also thank Professor Denise Whitelock for her excellent contribution to the foreword of this book. Last, but not least, we gratefully acknowledge the feedback, assistance and encouragement received from the Editor-in-Chief of this Elsevier Book Series, Prof. Fatos Xhafa, and Elsevier's editorial staff, Amy Invernizzi and Punitha Govindaradjane.

We hope the readers of this book will find it a valuable resource in their research, development and educational activities in online teaching and learning environments.

FORMATIVE
e-ASSESSMENT

COLLABORATIVE e-ASSESSMENT AS A STRATEGY FOR SCAFFOLDING SELF-REGULATED LEARNING IN HIGHER EDUCATION

1

V.I. Marín, A. Pérez Garcias
University of the Balearic Islands, Palma, Spain

1 INTRODUCTION

The need for didactical student-centered strategies has been made explicit since the European Higher Education Area and its premises were introduced. Students become the central focus of the teaching-learning process, including the organization of the learning process, teaching period, contact time, and learning assessment and accreditation (Ferrão, 2010), and developing self-regulation skills for lifelong learning life are essential in this endeavor.

Assessment clearly has a key role in teaching and learning since students define the curriculum according to how their work is evaluated; thus, evaluation is one of the most important elements of motivation for studying and an integral part of the learning experience for students (Keppell et al., 2006; Moccozet and Tardy, 2015). Assessment can be used to evaluate students' outcomes and to support student learning; therefore, assessment techniques must also consider students' participation (Ibarra Sáiz and Rodríguez Gómez, 2014; Reinholz, 2015) and should be used to empower students as self-regulated learners (Nicol and MacFarlane-Dick, 2006; Reinholz, 2015).

A key issue for assessment in higher education is formative feedback. This form of feedback is the main element of the learning process since learning from feedback offers the tools to students for building meaning and self-regulating their learning (van den Boom et al., 2004; Clark, 2012). However, previous studies have reported that students are less satisfied with formative feedback than other elements in a course (Nicol et al., 2014). Thus, considering alternative assessment strategies that include and improve formative feedback is important (Whitelock, 2010).

With these aspects in mind, the aim of this chapter is to propose a formative feedback strategy using a virtual learning environment (VLE) in the University of the Balearic Islands (Spain). This strategy promotes and scaffolds self-regulated learning in the future primary education teachers.

RESEARCH QUESTIONS

Our main interest in the experiment introduced above is to enhance the development of self-regulated learning competencies related to assessment and self-evaluation in the students.

In this sense, we aimed to develop and evaluate strategies that encourage students to be more active in the formative assessment processes.

The research questions posed in this experiment were:

RQ1: Is scaffolded student participation in assessment activities—co-assessment—a good learning strategy for the development of self-regulated learning competencies within preservice teacher training?

RQ2: Is the workshop plugin of Moodle a supportive tool that facilitates the development of assessment strategies based on the participation of students together with the teacher?

Considering these research questions, this chapter is structured into five differentiated sections. First, the framework for the study including the main concepts for the experiment is introduced: the concept of self-regulated learning; different strategies for formative assessment such as self-assessment, peer assessment, and collaborative assessment; and e-assessment with Moodle. Next, we move onto our study, its context, the characteristics of the learning activity and the phases in which the collaborative e-assessment activity was carried out. In the third section, the methodology of the study is outlined including the data collection procedures. In the fourth section, the results of the study are described and discussed in comparison with previous studies. Finally, some highlights of the study, in addition to some suggestions, are covered in Conclusions.

2 FRAMEWORK
2.1 SELF-REGULATED LEARNING

Self-regulated learning can be defined as the ability of a learner to actively monitor and control his or her own learning processes, such as setting learning goals, controlling the products produced, managing the effort involved, interpretatiing external feedback, creating strategies to reach the goals, providing self-feedback, etc., while maintaining a high level of motivation (Nicol and MacFarlane-Dick, 2006; Zimmerman and Schunk, 1989). Self-regulated learners are metacognitive, motivational, and behaviorally active participating in their own learning process (Zimmerman and Schunk, 2001, cited in Liaw and Huang, 2013). The notion of self-regulated learning involves reflection as a cognitive and affective activity that requires the active engagement of the individual and involves examining one's answers, beliefs, and premises in light of the situation at hand (Rogers, 2001). Self-motivation, self-efficacy, interaction, and environment management are the influencing factors in self-regulated learning (Liaw and Huang, 2013).

Self-regulatory processes detail the self-regulation process as follows, in three cyclical phases (Zimmerman, 2002, pp. 67–69):

- *Forethought phase.* This refers to the cognitive activities carried out before learning. It consists of two major processes: task analysis, which involves setting goals and planning learning strategies, and self-motivation, which is related to students' perceptions of their own self-efficacy and their expectations about learning results.

- *Performance phase*. This refers to the processes carried out during the implementation and involves two main operations: self-control and self-observation. The former is about implementing the strategies planned in the previous phase. The latter is about self-recording their learning performance, and self-monitoring is another related process that consists of tracking learning.
- *Self-reflection phase*. This comprises the processes carried out after learning and involves two main cognitive tasks: self-judgment and self-reaction. The former can be carried out as self-evaluation, which consists of comparing the self-observation with standards, and causal attribution, which involves attributing causes to one's own mistakes. The latter is about feelings such as self-satisfaction and the consequent response, for example, adaptive, such as increasing learning effectiveness, or defensive, such as protecting one's own image by avoiding further learning experiences.

In addition, external self-regulatory feedback—peer and instruction feedback—is needed to inform the learner of how to adjust his or her learning approach to accomplish the academic goals effectively (Kitsantas, 2013). In this respect, Clark (2012) points out that formative assessment facilitates the acquisition of self-regulated learning strategies. Peer assessment or co-evaluation is an instructional strategy that enables self-monitoring and self-evaluation. Learners acquire the skills to use learning and assessment tools. As Sadler and Good (2006) note, formative assessment strategies consisting of self-assessment, peer-assessment, or student-grading make learners more aware of their own progress, gaps and strengths, and enable higher order thinking, such as, for instance, critical thinking skills, to make judgments about others' work.

Also, Zimmerman and Kitsantas (2005) and Zimmerman and Tsikalas (2005), both cited in Beishuizen and Steffens (2011), present a social cognitive model of development of self-regulated learning in four levels: (1) observational of an expert model, (2) emulation, (3) self-control, and (4) self-regulation. Students improve their self-regulatory skills at each level.

2.2 ALTERNATIVE ASSESSMENT AND FORMATIVE FEEDBACK

Alternative assessment is linked to providing good opportunities for formative feedback and encouraging discussion between students and teachers. The most important characteristic of alternative assessment is the student-centeredness (in traditional assessment, the student is excluded from this process), the idea that the students are empowered and allowed to actively construct their learning while their confidence increases.

Formative assessment includes peer assessment, collaborative assessment, as well as self-assessment strategies. These strategies help the students in playing a more active role in their own learning and promote the ability of self-correcting (Gikandi et al., 2011; Whitelock, 2010).

Therefore, formative assessment is linked to two assessment objectives: assessment for learning and assessment as learning. Whereas the assessment for learning focuses on monitoring the progress of the learner toward a desired goal, the assessment as learning is considered a process of collaborative and individual reflection on the evidences of learning (Clark, 2012).

There are numerous studies available on formative assessment in higher education, in which the assessment strategy is considered differently from the teacher's unilateral final decision about the student's work, and understands feedback as a dialogue. For instance, Álvarez Valdivia's (2008) work explores the correlations between different kinds of assessment (peer assessment, self-assessment, and assessment by the instructor) and reports that co-assessment encourages self-management, self-regulation, and positive interdependence. Nicol et al. (2014) analyze how students construct and receive feedback, and report that peer feedback enable students to acquire the skills and abilities to evaluate, make informed judgments and improve their own work based on this process. Ibarra Sáiz et al. (2012) refer to these alternative methods as assessment oriented toward learning and based on the active participation of the students, authentic tasks and feedforward. Whitelock (2010) calls them "Advice for Action" since feedback will be given to students that they will use in future learning tasks and assessment. Black and William (1998, cited in Webb, 2010) in their review and meta-analysis, report that students' learning gains are greater when formative assessment strategies are used than when traditional assessment strategies are used. Nevertheless, as Liu and Carless (2006) highlight, both summative and formative assessment approaches can be combined in order to provide marks and feedbacks, respectively. In addition, this mixed approach provides an opportunity to review weak learning areas and more trial and less error in student learning, preparing the students for the lifelong journey of learning (Orsmond, 2004; Rodríguez Gómez et al., 2011).

2.2.1 Self-assessment
Self-assessment is one type of formative assessment in which students are involved in assessing their own learning. It includes the appraisal of their own skills and performance during the learning process against a standard and results in increases in the students' knowledge of their own learning (Falchikov, 2003; Rodríguez Gómez et al., 2011). Therefore, students not only grade their own work but also determine what is considered good work in a given situation (Boud, 1995; Nicol and MacFarlane-Dick, 2006). This process has been closely connected to self-regulation, especially monitoring one's performance on a task (Reinholz, 2015; Zimmerman, 2002), as will be detailed later.

In addition to self-assessment, assessment strategies based on participation among students are well-known more specifically, peer review, or peer assessment, and collaborative assessment.

2.2.2 Peer assessment
Peer assessment or peer review is viewed "as an arrangement whereby students evaluate and make judgements about the work of their peers and construct feedback commentary" (Nicol et al., 2014, p.103). This dialogue is a learning process that increases students' opportunities to construct meaning because they analyze, discuss with others, and connect it to previous knowledge while providing feedback for others (Nicol et al., 2014). This strategy involves a collaborative learning process because students assess the learning process or the product of a classmate, or of a group of peers (Ibarra Sáiz et al., 2012). Peer assessment can also help students to learn how to regulate their own learning processes and support learning related to peer interactions and communication skills (Reinholz, 2015). It has been identified as a good form of feedback practice that might involve the development of self-assessment and reflection in learning (Heinrich et al., 2009). The benefits of peer assessment are as follows (Álvarez Valdivia, 2008; Fraguell et al., 2014; Gil Flores and Padilla Carmona, 2009; Ibarra Sáiz and Rodríguez Gómez, 2014; Ibarra Sáiz et al., 2012; McConnell, 2002a,b; Nicol et al., 2014; Yu and Sung, 2015):

- It involves not only giving a grade, but also providing an opportunity for students to learn how to assess.
- It is a tool for developing students' abilities to assume responsibilities in the assessment and to think more deeply about how to set their learning goals. Thus, it might be a strategy for self-regulated learning.

- Students perceive feedback from peers as more understandable, helpful, and comprehensive than the teacher's feedback, because student feedback is composed in a familiar language and their learning status is similar. In addition, in this way students receive more feedback on their work than if the teacher is the only evaluator.
- This practice allows students to apply the feedback they receive to improve their learning process and products.
- It helps improve collaborative work and autonomous learning skills.
- Students' self-efficacy in terms of academic competence and self-esteem tends to be affected more by evaluations by peers than by teachers.

Falchikov (2003, 2005, cited in Ibarra Sáiz et al., 2012) proposes different stages to set up a self- or peer-assessment strategy:

- *Preparation*. The assessment strategy is designed carefully considering the provision of clear instructions for the task and the criteria for assessment.
- *Implementation*. In this phase, students follow the instructions for peer assessment and give feedback to their peers using the criteria previously set and justifying their evaluation.
- *Follow-up and evaluation*. The feedback is collected and analyzed by the teacher. In addition to this phase, the whole process might be repeated with the same cohort and the development of student self- or peer-assessment skills could be monitored over time.
- *Self-evaluation*. Students receive feedback from their peers and self-assess the experience. These reflections may result in variations of the process to start the strategy again from the preparation phase.

2.2.3 Co-assessment

Collaborative e-assessment or co-assessment (or cooperative assessment) provides students with the opportunity to participate in the assessment of their peers' work in an active way, and the teacher is also involved in the process by reviewing each participant's assessment. In this case, the teacher controls the assessment process and the final decisions; nevertheless, he or she shares the responsibility for the assessment with the student (Álvarez Valdivia, 2008; Gil Flores and Padilla Carmona, 2009; McConnell, 2002b).

One particular case of co-assessment is group assessment, which usually includes peer assessment and/or self-assessment, and focuses on the assessment of products of student group work—assessment of products from students in other groups (inter-peer assessment)—or assessment of the product of group work by students within a group (intra-peer assessment) (Race, 2001). Inter-peer assessment within collaborative assessment is the strategy carried out in this experiment.

The benefits of collaborative assessment in e-learning are supplementary to those of peer assessment (Álvarez Valdivia, 2008; Fraguell et al., 2014; Gil Flores and Padilla Carmona, 2009; McConnell, 2002a,b; Yu and Sung, 2015):

- It reduces the effects of the students' subjectivity or inexperience in peer assessment since the teacher also participates in the assessment.
- Students obtain a more realistic opinion of their own abilities, and co-assessment helps them make judgments about their own work.

Although peer assessment and collaborative assessment have many benefits for learning, they require a good design and planning to reduce difficulties that may appear in these types of assessment (Ibarra Sáiz et al., 2012; Sánchez-Vera and Prendes, 2015). These difficulties, which are mitigated in collaborative assessment, might be, for instance:

- that students tend to consider the effort more than the quality of the academic activity in the assessment, thus students may create their own rules for assessment,
- the influence of the personality of the student being assessed, the effect of friendship or leadership (Yu and Sung, 2015), the fact that the student may be considered an "expert" among his or her peers, or an instance where a student does not carry out the assessment,
- a lack of assessment criteria or inexperience on the part of the assessor (Race, 2001), which can result in poor quality peer feedback, especially in peer assessment strategies (Li et al., 2010).

Results from previous research showed that (a) there is a correlation between the score given by the students and the teachers and among the students, and (b) peer assessment requires that students have a clear and real expectation of the assessment activity.

To deal with the importance of providing assessment criteria, rubrics can help students develop a better sense of the assessment criteria if they are actively involved in applying the rubrics (Cebrián et al., 2014; Reinholz, 2015). Assignment criteria must be clearly linked to learning outcomes so that they make sense to the students, and "analytic or holistic scoring rubrics should be developed and made available to students before an assignment is due to give students a clear idea of what is expected of their work" (Heinrich et al., 2009, p. 470). Providing comments and feedback has been found to bring cognitive and learning gains; hence, being more efficient for assessors than simply assigning a mark (Moccozet and Tardy, 2015). In addition, having clear criteria with the support of rubrics can counteract the possible subjectivity that students infuse the evaluation of their peers' work with (Arcos et al., 2010).

2.3 SELF-REGULATED LEARNING AND FORMATIVE ASSESSMENT

As can be observed from the process by Zimmerman (2002) detailed previously, self-assessment is closely related to self-regulation (Reinholz, 2015), and its phases (Falchikov, 2003) can be identified in the process. Since peer assessment and self-assessment are part of co-assessment strategies, Sadler (1989) mentions three components of self-assessment in a constant interplay that provides focal areas for how peer and co-assessment can help students develop self-assessment skills (Reinholz, 2015):

- *Goal awareness*: an understanding of what one is trying to achieve
- *Self-awareness*: the ability to accurately judge the quality of one's own work
- *Gap closure*: achieved by reducing the discrepancies between actual and desired performance.

Nicol and MacFarlane-Dick (2006) and Butler and Winne (1995) propose a model of self-regulated learning (Fig. 1.1) and feedback principles that support and develop self-regulation in students, which are useful for our study.

These authors suggest that self-regulatory processes are carried out during the entire assessment process, since the task is set by the teacher until external feedback (from the teacher, peers, and/or

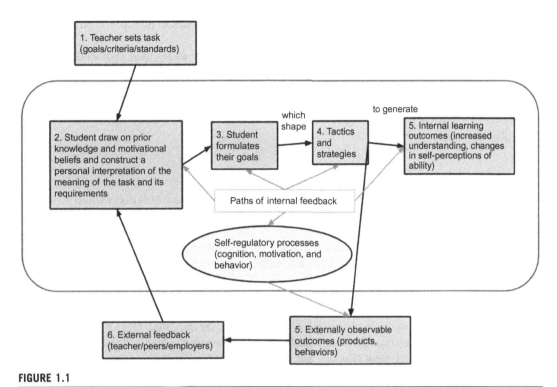

FIGURE 1.1

Model of self-regulated learning (Butler and Winne, 1995, p. 248; Nicol and MacFarlane-Dick, 2006, p. 203).

others) is given, shaping the students' learning goals, strategies, and outcomes (internal and external). Nicol and MacFarlane-Dick (2006, p. 203) propose the following feedback principles:

1. Clarify what a good performance is
2. Facilitate self-assessment
3. Deliver high-quality feedback information
4. Encourage teacher and peer dialogue
5. Encourage positive motivation and self-esteem
6. Provide opportunities to close the gap
7. Use feedback to improve teaching.

Reinholz (2015) proposed an assessment cycle to make a connection between peer and self-assessment, which includes six activities, or only a subset, which are suitable for collaborative assessment as well:

- *Task engagement*. Students begin by engaging with a task similar to the one that they will assess afterwards.
- *Peer analysis*. It supposes any attempt to make judgments about the quality of a piece of work, to generate feedback, or assign a grade.

- *Feedback provision*. In this activity, students describe their analysis to their peers, providing written and/or verbal feedback.
- *Feedback reception*. Students receive feedback that allows them to see their own work from another's perspective.
- *Peer conferencing*. Students can discuss their feedback by explaining and discussing their ideas more broadly.
- *Revision*. This activity closes the feedback cycle and is the moment when students can use the feedback to revise their work.

2.4 e-ASSESSMENT WITH MOODLE

Information and Communication Technology (ICT) can be viewed as a set of skills or competencies, a vehicle for teaching and learning, or as an agent of change (Keppell et al., 2006). e-Strategies for assessment cover the four characteristics of technology-enhanced learning environments pointed out by Wang and Kinuthia (2004, p. 2725): "using technology to motivate people, using technology to enrich learning resources, using technology to implement learning and instructional strategies and using technology to assess and evaluate learning goals."

e-Assessment has also been called computer-assisted assessment, online assessment, and computer-based assessment, and is usually linked to test generation (Ferrão, 2010), which can create different types of questions such as multiple-choice questions, short-answer questions, true-or-false questions, etc. Computer-assisted assessment has considerable potential to ease the load and provide innovative and powerful modes of assessment (Conole and Warburton, 2005). For instance, other contemplated possibilities are posed as sophisticated e-assessment tasks and might include intelligent tutors, microworlds, simulations, media-rich stimulus material, and so on (Boyle and Hutchison, 2009). There are also specific computer-mediated assessment tools for supporting peer assessment, such as the Self- and Peer Assessment Resource Kit (SPARK) (Freeman et al., 2006), the OpenAnswer system (Sterbini and Temperini, 2013), and other tools for peer review (Luxton-Reilly, 2009). Recently, Assessment 2.0 has started to be considered by using, for instance, e-Portfolios (Zubizarreta, 2009), instant surveys or polls or other specific tools, such as the "open-book, open web" from U21 Global or the WebPA tool from Loughborough University (Whitelock, 2010).

Learning management systems (LMSs) have many possibilities related to the generation of tests for assessment (Butcher, 2008). However, they also consider other forms of e-assessment that might be more interesting and applicable to the improvement of self-regulated learning and critical thinking in students. In this sense, the possibilities that LMSs offer for carrying out alternative and formative assessment should be considered in e-assessments.

Students traditionally use an LMS to deliver a task and receive feedback by using the assignment submission. This type of e-tool frees up the time that teachers spend on administrative tasks such as accepting assignment submissions, managing deadlines, recording submission details, managing the distribution of assignments for grading, and returning grading sheets, commented-on assignments, and grades to students to focus on quality feedback (Heinrich et al., 2009). Other methods are presented in Keppell et al.'s (2006) study, involving the use of Blackboard LMS tools such as groups, discussion boards, or reflective journals, among others.

The open source LMS Moodle (http://www.moodle.org) offers an integrated plugin called Workshop, which makes conducting different e-assessment strategies possible. This tool has its own method for assessing activities, leaving a broad margin to decide how to evaluate the rubrics, percentages, importance of activities, etc. (Arcos et al., 2010). In addition, several studies have reported on the advantages and benefits of this specific tool (Arcos et al., 2010; Puente et al., 2012). For instance, the possibility to self-correct, evaluate, assess, and receive feedback online; assign the percentage of the appraisal made by the teacher, peers, and the student him- or herself; or organize an anonymous system so that only the teacher knows who is correcting which work.

Puente et al. (2012) reported an improvement in academic results in a telecommunication engineering course that used the Moodle Workshop plugin for formative assessment. They also highlighted that students developed analytical skills and critical thinking skills by using the Workshop tool.

By using this tool in our study, included in our institutional LMS based on Moodle, we aimed to take advantage of these benefits and boost self-regulated learning skills in preservice teachers for primary education, and to test its potential for co-assessment.

3 THE STUDY
3.1 CONTEXT

The experiment took place during the mandatory course Technological Means and Resources in the teaching-learning process in primary education in the third year of the primary education degree with 2 groups of a total of 149 students and 2 teachers at the University of the Balearic Islands (Spain).

The main objective of this course is to develop technology skills that will aid teaching and learning processes at school. The methodology of the course is based on learning principles centered on the student and collaboration and social construction of knowledge (Salinas et al., 2008), fostering skills related to managing information, sharing resources, and creating educational materials using ICT tools that connect various learning contexts (Marín et al., 2014a,b). Although the course is mainly face-to-face, it has virtual support (submitting tasks, disposing of materials, communicating, reporting qualifications) in the institutional VLE of the University, which is based on Moodle.

During the course, different activities for creating ICT educational resources and their didactic guides took place: interactive activities, posters, podcast, etc. The co-assessment activity was carried out during the video creation activity.

In this activity, students in groups of two, three, or four had to design and develop a 3- to 5-min didactic video with some minimum requirements. The design of the video included writing a technical and literary script and creating a didactic guide for educational use of the video, while the development involved recording video and sound and assembling the elements.

Finally, the students had to publish the video on their public learning e-portfolio of the group using an online embed video player. After this task, the co-assessment activity was introduced.

3.2 THE CO-ASSESSMENT ACTIVITY

The activity was conducted in several consecutive phases, following the stages proposed by Falchikov (2003, 2005, cited in Ibarra Sáiz et al., 2012). Reinholz's assessment cycle (2015), which connects with elements of self-regulated learning, was also taken into consideration. The process was supported by the Workshop plugin of the VLE based on Moodle.

This tool was selected because it enabled us to work in an integrated way within the institutional VLE and conveniently allowed us to manage the process of co-assessment in different phases.

The first phase was the preparation. This stage included a preliminary phase and a setting up subphase. In the preliminary phase, students were trained to assess a previous class activity face-to-face. They received the assessment rubrics, each student group presented their work, and the others put in common items of assessment. During the task, the students explained their ideas by being aware of their performance and made revisions during the process, working toward closing the gap.

In the setting up subphase, students received instructions that were explained during the class and given the criteria in a rubric for assessing another classmate's work electronically. In the plugin, this phase is the configuration phase.

The second phase was the *implementation*. First, one student from each group had to submit the group's video for assessment through the plugin. The academic task set by the teacher triggers self-regulatory processes for the student, first drawing on prior knowledge and motivational beliefs, and constructing a personal interpretation of the meaning of the task and its requirements. Then the student shaped his or her learning goals, strategies, and external and internal outcomes (Nicol and MacFarlane-Dick, 2006). After the submission deadline, all students in the course had to provide formative feedback by applying a rubric and a grade (maximum 10) to video, which had a weight of 8% of the final grade. Therefore, each group video received three student assessments. In the plugin, the first part of this phase is the submission phase, and the second part is the assessment phase. This latter includes peer analysis, in which students become aware of the goals by analyzing various examples, and provide feedback. In the latter, students become aware of their performance by explaining ideas and receiving feedback on the explanation and by developing constructive feedback to improve the video and not just critique it, which supported closing the gap. The instructions for the task and the basic rubrics are in Annex 1.

The next phase was the *follow-up and evaluation*. After the peer e-assessment, the teachers revised each assessment and made the final decision on each group work. This phase also included grading the assessment activity itself for each student according to the quantitative and qualitative assessment. In the plugin, this phase is the rating assessment. The score for the assessment activity was calculated automatically by the system through comparing each grade given by the three students to a peer and averaging the three grades, which is useful in detecting who is overscoring or underscoring. However, in some cases, teachers modified this automatically calculated grade for the assessment activity so that students received the maximum grade for this task if they had completed it and had justified their grade for their peers' work. The highest grade for the assessment activity was 5 and had a weight of 2% of the final grade.

The last phase was getting the *results*. In this phase, the students received their grades and comments on their work and the students' self-assessment on the collaborative e-assessment experience through the final questionnaire and a final written reflection on their e-portfolios. In the plugin, this phase is the closure of the activity. Students who received feedback improved their performance awareness by being able to view their own work from others' perspectives'.

See Fig. 1.2 to view the correspondence between the different phases that results in a model for co-assessment in the Moodle LMS, which boosts self-regulation skills.

The process in the plugin is shown in Figs. 1.3 and 1.4.

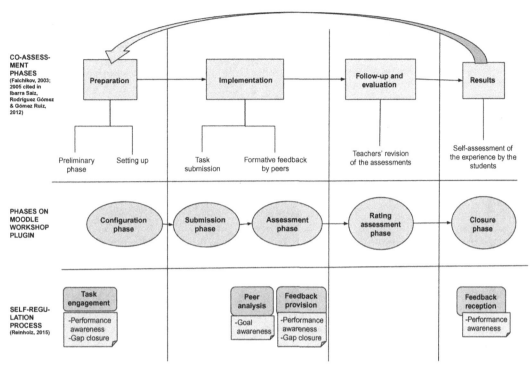

FIGURE 1.2

Co-assessment process carried out.

Adapted from peer assessment phases by Falchikov (2003, 2005, cited in Ibarra Sáiz et al., 2012) and the assessment cycle by Reinholz (2015).

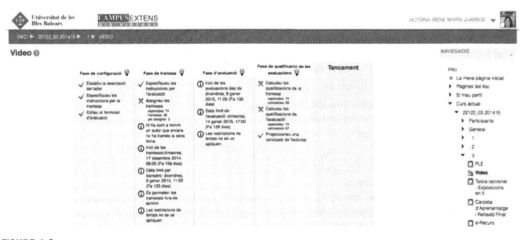

FIGURE 1.3

Workshop plugin on the virtual space of the course on the institutional virtual learning environment of the University of the Balearic Islands.

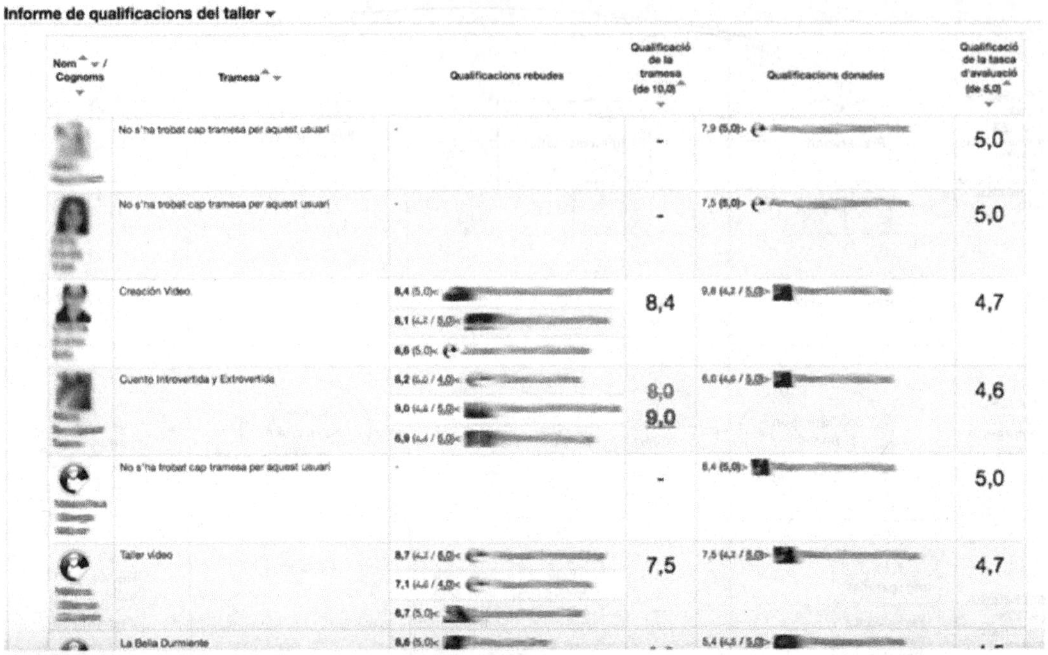

Informe de qualificacions del taller ▾

Nom ▲ ▾ / Cognoms ▾	Tramesa ▲ ▾	Qualificacions rebudes	Qualificació de la tramesa (de 10,0) ▲ ▾	Qualificacions donades	Qualificació de la tasca d'avaluació (de 5,0) ▲ ▾
	No s'ha trobat cap tramesa per aquest usuari	-	-	7,9 (5,0)> (⊕ ▬▬▬	5,0
	No s'ha trobat cap tramesa per aquest usuari	-	-	7,5 (5,0) (⊕ ▬▬▬	5,0
	Creación Video	8,4 (5,0)< ▬▬▬ 8,1 (4,2 / 5,0)< ▬▬▬ 6,6 (5,0)< (⊕ ▬▬	8,4	9,8 (4,2 / 5,0)> ▬▬▬	4,7
	Cuento Introvertida y Extrovertida	8,2 (5,0 / 4,0)< (⊕ ▬▬ 9,0 (4,4 / 5,0)< ▬▬▬ 6,9 (4,4 / 5,0)< ▬▬▬	8,0 9,0	6,0 (4,8 / 5,0)> ▬▬▬	4,6
	No s'ha trobat cap tramesa per aquest usuari	-	-	6,4 (5,0)> ▬▬▬	5,0
	Taller vídeo	8,7 (4,2 / 5,0)< (⊕ ▬▬ 7,1 (4,6 / 4,0)< (⊕ ▬▬ 6,7 (5,0)< ▬▬▬	7,5	7,5 (4,2 / 5,0)> ▬▬▬	4,7
	La Bella Durmiente	8,6 (5,0)< ▬▬▬	-	5,4 (4,5 / 5,0)> ▬▬▬	-

FIGURE 1.4

Report of the workshop assessments on the workshop plugin.

4 METHODOLOGY

Data from the experiment were collected through qualitative and quantitative means.

In relation to RQ1 (Is scaffolded students' participation in assessment activities—co-assessment—a good learning strategy for the development of self-regulated learning competencies within preservice teacher training?), the perceived effectiveness related to the co-assessment activity by the students was analyzed. Students were asked to answer specific questions about their appraisal of the collaborative assessment activity on a questionnaire, but they also had to individually write a personal reflection on this activity in their e-portfolio at the end of the course. Teachers' observations about the final grades of the activity were also considered.

The questionnaire data were averaged and compared to the central value (2.5). The students' responses were coded by using the procedures for qualitative thematic analysis (Braun and Clarke, 2006) and presented in percentages.

In order to find response to the RQ2 (Is the workshop plugin of Moodle a supportive tool that facilitates the development of assessment strategies based on the participation of the students together with the teacher?), the learning activity was designed and developed using the Moodle's workshop while being monitored. This way, teachers could analyze the procedure related to its effectiveness in co-assessment. This procedure was designed according to the co-assessment model described previously (Fig. 1.2) and included the connection with the workshop plugin phases.

5 RESULTS AND DISCUSSION

Overall, the results of the experiment highlighted a positive feeling and satisfaction with the co-assessment activity from the perspective of the students and the teachers.

5.1 STUDENTS' QUESTIONNAIRE

The questionnaire was answered by 134 students, who represented 89.9% of the total ($n = 149$), and included different items in categories related to the course. One item regarded the co-assessment activity and was used to ask the students to rate different statements choosing their perception of the activity with a 4-point Likert scale: completely disagree (1), disagree (2), agree (3), or completely agree (4). The statements, which relate to aspects identified in previous studies on self-regulated learning and formative assessment (Clark, 2012; Liaw and Huang, 2013; Nicol and Macfarlane-Dick, 2006; Sadler and Good, 2006), were the following:

– It has helped me self-assess my work.
– It has helped me to learn how to evaluate a piece of work with these characteristics.
– It made me put myself in the teacher's place.
– The assessment I received from my classmates seemed fair to me (numerical rating).
– The assessment I received from my classmates seemed useful (comments as an assessment report).
– I found it a useful task for my future.

Students rated the usefulness of the co-assessment very highly, which can be transferred to self-assessment of an activity and to their professional future. They also thought their peers' assessments were fair (the numerical rating) and useful (the comments provided), with a slight difference in agreement (higher in usefulness than in fairness), as can be observed in the ST values as well.

Fig. 1.5 shows the distribution of responses in percentages and Table 1.1 the main descriptive statistics.

5.2 CONTENT ANALYSIS OF THE WRITTEN REFLECTIONS

Eighty-six individual written reflections on the e-portfolios were collected, and 84 were accepted (56.4% of the total students) for coding according to different categories regarding the students' evaluation of the co-assessment activity.

When students were asked to report their reflections on the activity, they wrote about (a) the value of participating in the assessment task (Fig. 1.6). They pointed out the usefulness of the task for their own professional future ($n = 46$, 54.7%) and the contribution to developing critical thinking ($n = 20$, 24%).

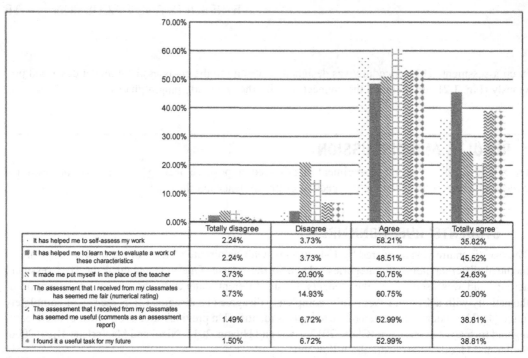

	Totally disagree	Disagree	Agree	Totally agree
· It has helped me to self-assess my work	2.24%	3.73%	58.21%	35.82%
▒ It has helped me to learn how to evaluate a work of these characteristics	2.24%	3.73%	48.51%	45.52%
﹨ It made me put myself in the place of the teacher	3.73%	20.90%	50.75%	24.63%
¦ The assessment that I received from my classmates has seemed me fair (numerical rating)	3.73%	14.93%	60.75%	20.90%
⁄ The assessment that I received from my classmates has seemed me useful (comments as an assessment report)	1.49%	6.72%	52.99%	38.81%
⬥ I found it a useful task for my future	1.50%	6.72%	52.99%	38.81%

FIGURE 1.5

Results of the students' questionnaire on the co-assessment activity in percentages.

Table 1.1 Descriptive Statistics of the Students' Responses on the Questionnaire

	Average	Median	Mode	ST	Variance	Percentile		
						25	50	75
It has helped me to self-assess my work	3.28	3.00	3.00	0.642	0.412	3.00	3.00	4.00
It has helped me to learn how to evaluate a work of these characteristics	3.32	3.00	3.00	0.656	0.430	3.00	3.00	4.00
It make put myself in the place of the teacher	3.37	3.00	3.00	0.668	0.446	3.00	3.00	4.00
The assessment that I received from my classmates has seemed me fair (numerical rating)	2.96	3.00	3.00	0.779	0.608	3.00	3.00	3.25
The assessment that I received from my classmates has seemed me useful (comments as an assessment report)	2.99	3.00	3.00	0.715	0.511	3.00	2.75	3.00
I found it an useful task for may future	3.29	3.00	3.00	0.658	0.433	3.00	3.00	4.00

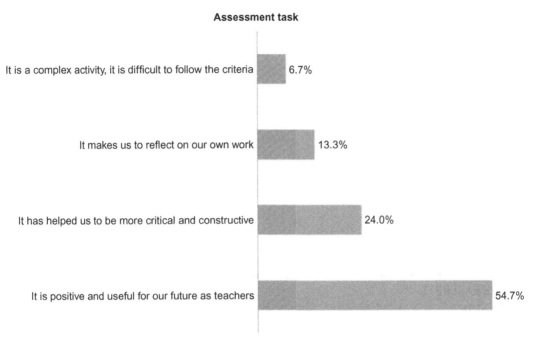

Assessment task

It is a complex activity, it is difficult to follow the criteria — 6.7%

It makes us to reflect on our own work — 13.3%

It has helped us to be more critical and constructive — 24.0%

It is positive and useful for our future as teachers — 54.7%

FIGURE 1.6

Values of the categories extracted from coding the reflections on the assessment task with more than 5% ($n = 4$).

SOME EXCERPTS

I considered the co-assessment activity useful because we could see our peers' work, the way in which they have carried out the task, and we became aware of the weaknesses of our own work.

It has been interesting since I could see the practical part of what an assessment really is. When we do didactical units or some activity and we had to determine how to assess, we did it at a theoretical level but few times at a practical level like in this case.

It has been useful to know which aspects to assess and how to do it. In addition, we had to take the role of the teacher and practice the assessment task, which I will have to do in the future many times.

I think that the co-assessment activity has been an interesting task and approaches us to the role of the teachers regarding assessment and constructive critical sense. It gives us the possibility to see and make explicit the aspects that our peers have been done well and others that should be improved, and provide feedback to complement or enhance the work if it is necessary.

The students also reported on (b) the quality of their peers' feedback (Fig. 1.7). They considered having received good feedback ($n = 30$, 36.1%) useful to let them know the weaknesses and strengths of their work ($n = 23$, 27.8%). They also liked receiving different views of their peers about the work ($n = 21$, 25%). However, several students ($n = 9$, 11.1%) pointed out a certain degree of dissatisfaction with the feedback and argued that it was not constructive or was poorly documented.

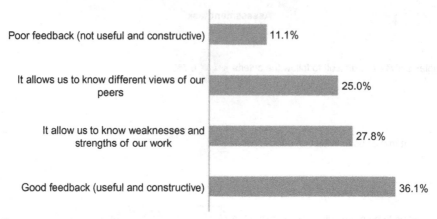

FIGURE 1.7

Values of the categories extracted from coding the reflections on the quality of the feedback.

SOME EXCERPTS

The feedback received by our peers has been useful for me to know which things were done poorly or can be improved, and if the peers liked the task.

I would appreciate that once a grade was given brief feedback was provided justifying it or at least detail the criteria that the teacher would use to assess our evaluations.

It helps us to see different points of view and self-reflect on the way that we have worked. You see that it is a colleague that tells you their evaluation, and maybe their constructive critics help you to do a better task the next time.

From the data obtained, we can observe the results related to the effectiveness of the co-assessment strategy as a learning and assessment strategy for preservice teacher training.

As in Moccozet and Tardy's (2015) study, the students seem to feel that they engage in the peer-assessment process. Similarly, our study confirms that peer assessment is beneficial for the development of critical and reflective skills, and useful in the transfer of the process (Heinrich et al., 2009; Ibarra Sáiz et al., 2012; Moccozet and Tardy, 2015; Reinholz, 2015).

Even if the peer assessment was not completely anonymous, since the names of the students who performed the group work were in the video credits, the use of anonymity did not have a significant effect on the students' targeted behavior during the online peer assessment, as Yu and Sung (2015) reported in their study. Training for the assessment task before the activity was useful since some students noted informally in class that they had done nothing similar before in their studies (Gil Flores and Padilla Carmona, 2009; Ibarra Sáiz et al., 2012; Sluijsmans et al., 1998). The use of rubrics was also praised by the students as a method for learning how to self-assess and have a clear criteria to assess another's work (Arcos et al., 2010; Heinrich et al., 2009; Sluijsmans et al., 1998). This appraisement coincides with Hafner and Hafner's (2003) study, which concluded that rubric-based assessment seems to be a valid and reliable tool for peer-group assessment.

The results coincide with other studies that concluded these types of alternative assessment are effective and good strategies for learning and assessment, which consider the participation of the learner, and thus, they are didactic strategies centered on the learner (Álvarez Valdivia, 2008;

Gil Flores and Padilla Carmona, 2009; Guessa, 2011; Ibarra Sáiz et al., 2012; Nicol and MacFarlane-Dick, 2006; Nicol et al., 2014; Rodríguez Gómez et al., 2011; Sluijsmans et al., 1998). This is applicable to preservice teacher training as well, which confirms RQ1.

5.3 QUALIFICATION OUTCOMES

Concerning the qualification outcomes of the assessment, the observation of the teachers on the students' evaluations showed that, in most cases, the average grade from the three students who assessed each group work was close to the grade that the teacher would have given or thought that the work deserved.

In six video activities (out of 47), the final grade for the group work had to be modified to a great extent due to visualization problems with the video and/or the didactic guide (students who had to do the review did not have access to one or any of them, so they graded it negatively). In these cases, the teacher added a comment to justify the grade change. In other cases (10 out of 47), the final grade for the video work was rounded up slightly (up 1 point); while in eight cases, the final grade was rounded down slightly (down 1 point). This confirms Falchikov and Goldfinch's (2000) observation that peer grades generally agree with teachers' grades.

Concerning the evaluation of the assessment activity, some students did not do the task (11 out of 149), and eight did not justify the grade they gave to their peers (or they did it poorly), so they were given a lower grade for this activity by the teacher.

In the whole process of co-assessment, the Moodle workshop was a facilitating tool to deploy the learning activity, as previous experiments have shown for other formative assessment strategies (Arcos et al., 2010; Puente et al., 2012). Also, the workshop plugin phases have combined well with the ones of the co-assessment strategy, which confirms RQ2. An improvement for the plugin could include a better management of the feedback between the different agents involved.

6 CONCLUSIONS

We focused on the strategy for scaffolding students' self-regulated learning and provide insights into and ideas for carrying out and improving the collaborative e-assessment process.

The co-assessment model linked to the self-regulation processes based on Falchikov's (2003, 2005, cited in Ibarra Sáiz et al., 2012) and Reinholz's (2015) work was useful for developing this process online and could be utilized and enhanced in each new implementation. We consider the model, shown in Fig. 1.2 and described in previous sections, to be a relevant result of our experiment for the purposes of co-assessment with the Moodle workshop plugin and a contribution to the field of formative assessment strategies.

Concerning the plugin, it was considered a powerful tool for carrying out and supporting this process. It would be interesting to consider another phase in the Workshop plugin to support the peer conferencing activity proposed by Reinholz (2015), in which students can discuss their feedback by explaining and discussing their ideas more broadly and resolve possible disagreements on the feedback provided during peer review (Falchikov, 2003). Also, the possibility of actually working with the separated groups option of the plugin.

The skills in self-, peer-, and co-assessment are required for lifelong and autonomous learners to use in different contexts, such as continuing learning, performance appraisal, team building, etc., where learners must take responsibility for their own learning by communicating with others, and providing and receiving feedback (Keppell et al., 2006; Sluijsmans et al., 1998). For future teachers, similar to our preservice primary education teachers, who will need to be familiar with "assessing each other's work and contribution fairly, sensitively and appropriately" (Race, 2001, p. 6), developing these skills acquires special relevance. And, if peer learning, group work, and collaboration in teaching and learning are valued, peer assessment must be included within the formal assessment for the course, assigning a weight for the task in the total of the qualification of the course (Keppell et al., 2006; Sadler and Good, 2006).

As for future work, we consider it important to explore other new ways of including students' participation within the assessment processes.

ACKNOWLEDGMENTS

This work is framed within the research project EDU2011-25499 Methodological strategies for integrating institutional virtual environments, personal and social learning, developed by the Educational Technology Group (GTE) of the University of the Balearic Islands since 2012 and funded by the Ministry of Education and Science of Spain, within the National Programme for Fundamental Research. It is also part of a teaching innovation project funded by the University of the Balearic Islands in the academic year 2014/15 called Learning and assessment strategies centered on the student with the use of ICT as nexus for knowledge transfer and connecting formal and informal learning.

ANNEX 1 INSTRUCTIONS FOR THE CO-ASSESSMENT TASK ON THE MOODLE WORKSHOP

Delivery of the video activity and co-assessment. Only one member for each group has to send the task. Deliver through an online video player and a link to short didactic guide of the video.

Assess the video workshop assigned to a group following the evaluation criteria listed and adding comments to it. Grade according to the scales indicated.

Item	Description	Maximum Grade
Formal presentation	The information is organized well; the information is clear; it provides the video and a short didactic guide published through an embedded video player and active links.	5
Reflections	It provides conclusions about the activity in the form of criteria to create or to work with videos in primary education. It provides conclusions/assessments about the video created. It provides conclusions about the educational value of videos in primary education.	15

Quality of the video	Duration (3–5 min) Visual quality (image quality, not pixelated images, style consistency of the images) Quality visual of the editing (appropriate transitions, adequate visual continuity) Quality of the sound elements (narrative quality of the sound files, good integration of the sound elements) There is a good audiovisual integration (sound and image) The material is structured: title, development, and full credits The contents and their treatment are suitable for the target The proposal is original and creative It makes good ethical and responsible use of others' ideas It is published under a Creative Commons license	45

Quality of the short didactic guide	It provides a short didactic guide with:
	   a. General data of the video: title, authors, target, objectives, types of educational use, content, duration
	   b. A description of the video and its script
	   c. The basic teaching guidelines to work with the video in the classroom (before, during, and after) and planning interventions for the teacher and the student before, during, and after.
	 Is the educational proposal perceived clearly and well-articulated?
	 Is there consistency between the curricular elements: objectives, content, activities, target?
	 Is it sustainable? Is it replicable?
	 Do you think it is a good practice to use a video for primary education?
		35

REFERENCES

Álvarez Valdivia, I., 2008. La coevaluación como alternativa para mejorar la calidad del aprendizaje de los estudiantes universitarios: valoración de una experiencia. Revista Interuniversitaria de Formación Del Profesorado 63 (22,3), 127–140.

Arcos, F., et al., 2010. La autoevaluación y la evaluación por pares en el taller de Moodle como parte del blended learning o aprendizaje mixto. In: VIII Jornadas de Redes de Investigación en Docencia Universitaria: nuevas titulaciones y cambio universitario. Alicante, Spain, 8–9 July. Universidad de Alicante, Alicante, pp. 1471–1489.

Beishuizen, J., Steffens, K., 2011. A conceptual framework for research on self-regulated learning. In: Carneiro, R. et al. (Ed.), Self-Regulated Learning in Technology Enhanced Learning Environments. A European Perspective. Sense Publishers, Rotterdam/Boston/Taipei, pp. 3–20.

Boud, D., 1995. Enhancing Learning Through Self-Assessment. RoutledgeFalmer, New York.

Boyle, A., Hutchison, D., 2009. Sophisticated tasks in e-assessment: What are they and what are their benefits? Assess. Eval. High. Educ. 34 (3), 305–319.

Braun, V., Clarke, V., 2006. Using thematic analysis in psychology. Qual. Res. Psychol. 3 (2), 77–101.

Butcher, P., 2008. Online assessment at the Open University using open source software: moodle, openmark and more. In: Khandia, F. (Ed.), 12th CAA International Computer Assisted Assessment Conference: Proceedings of the Conference. Loughborough University, Loughborough, pp. 65–78.

Butler, D.L., Winne, P.H., 1995. Feedback and self-regulated learning: a theoretical synthesis. Rev. Educ. Res. 65 (3), 245–281.

Cebrián, M., Serrano, J., Ruiz, M., 2014. Las eRúbricas en la evaluación cooperativa del aprendizaje en la Universidad. Comunicar 43, 153–161.

Clark, I., 2012. Formative assessment: assessment is for self-regulated learning. Educ. Psychol. Rev. 24, 205–249.

Conole, G., Warburton, B., 2005. A review of computer-assisted assessment. Res. Learn. Technol. 13 (1), 17–31.

Falchikov, N., 2003. Involving students in assessment. Psychol. Learn. Teach. 3 (2), 102–108.

Falchikov, N., 2005. Improving Assessment Through Student Involvement. Practical Solutions for Aiding Learning in Higher and Further Education. RoutledgeFalmer, London.

Falchikov, N., Goldfinch, J., 2000. Student peer assessment in higher education: a meta-analysis comparing peer and teacher marks. Rev. Educ. Res. 70 (3), 287–322.

Ferrão, M., 2010. E-assessment within the Bologna paradigm: evidence from Portugal. Assess. Eval. High. Educ. 35 (7), 819–830.

Fraguell, R.M., et al., 2014. Percepció dels estudiants de la coavaluació del treball en equip a la Universitat de Girona. CIDUI. 2. Available at: http://www.cidui.org/revistacidui/index.php/cidui/article/view/689 (accessed 30.11.15.).

Freeman, M., et al., 2006. Iterative learning: self and peer assessment of group work. In: Proceedings of the 23rd Annual Ascilite Conference: Who's Learning? Whose Technology? Sydney, Australia, 3–6 December. Ascilite, The University of Sydney, Sydney, pp. 257–266.

Gikandi, J.W., Morrow, D., Davis, N.E., 2011. Online formative assessment in higher education: a review of the literature. Comput. Educ. 57 (4), 2333–2351.

Gil Flores, J., Padilla Carmona, M.T., 2009. La participación del alumnado universitario en la evaluación del aprendizaje. Educación XX1 12, 43–65.

Guessa, A., 2011. La coevaluación como metodología complementaria de la evaluación del aprendizaje. Análisis y reflexión en las aulas universitarias. Revista de Educación 354, 749–764.

Hafner, J., Hafner, P., 2003. Quantitative analysis of the rubric as an assessment tool: an empirical study of student peer group rating. Int. J. Sci. Educ. 25 (12), 1509–1528.

Heinrich, E., et al., 2009. Recommendations for the use of e-tools for improvements around assignment marking quality. Assess. Eval. High. Educ. 34 (4), 469–479.

Ibarra Sáiz, M.S., Rodríguez Gómez, G., 2014. Modalidades participativas de evaluación: un análisis de la percepción del profesorado y de los estudiantes universitarios. Revista de Investigación Educativa 32 (2), 339–361.

Ibarra Sáiz, M.S., Rodríguez Gómez, G., Gómez Ruiz, M.A., 2012. La evaluación entre iguales: beneficios y estrategias para su práctica en la universidad. Revista de Educación 359, 7–10.

Keppell, M., et al., 2006. Peer learning and learning-oriented assessment in technology-enhanced environments. Assess. Eval. High. Educ. 31 (4), 453–464.

Kitsantas, A., 2013. Fostering college students' self-regulated learning with learning technologies. Hell. J. Psychol. 10 (3), 235–252.

Li, L., Liu, X., Steckelberg, A.L., 2010. Assessor or assessee: How student learning improves by giving and receiving peer feedback. Br. J. Educ. Technol. 41 (3), 525–536.

Liaw, S.-S., Huang, H.-M., 2013. Perceived satisfaction, perceived usefulness and interactive learning environments as predictors to self-regulation in e-learning environments. Comput. Educ. 60, 14–24.

Liu, N.-F., Carless, D., 2006. Peer feedback: the learning element of peer assessment. Teach. High. Educ. 11 (3), 279–290.

Luxton-Reilly, A., 2009. A systematic review of tools that support peer assessment. Comput. Sci. Educ. 19 (4), 209–232.

Marín, V.I., Negre, F., Pérez Garcias, A., 2014a. Entornos y redes personales de aprendizaje (PLEPLN) para el aprendizaje colaborativo [Construction of the Foundations of the PLE and PLN for Collaborative Learning]. Comunicar 42, 35–43.

Marín, V.I., de la Osa, T., Pérez Garcias, A., 2014b. A methodological strategy focused on the integration of different learning contexts in higher education. In: Proceedings of the 3rd Workshop on Design in Educational Environments. Albacete, Spain, 9 June. ACM, New York, pp. 64–69.

McConnell, D., 2002a. Collaborative assessment as a learning process in e-learning. In: Proceedings of the Conference on Computer Support for Collaborative Learning Foundations for a CSCL Community—CSCL '02. Association for Computational Linguistics, Morristown, NJ, pp. 566–567.

McConnell, D., 2002b. The experience of collaborative assessment in e-learning. Stud. Contin. Educ. 24 (1), 73–92.

Moccozet, L., Tardy, C., 2015. An assessment for learning framework with peer assessment of group works. In: Proceedings of the 14th International Conference on Information Technology Based Higher Education and Training (ITHET'15). Caparica, Lisbon, Portugal, 11–13 June.

Nicol, D.J., Macfarlane-Dick, D., 2006. Formative assessment and self-regulated learning: a model and seven principles of good feedback practice. Stud. High. Educ. 31 (2), 199–218.

Nicol, D., Thomson, A., Breslin, C., 2014. Rethinking feedback practices in higher education: a peer review perspective. Assess. Eval. High. Educ. 39 (1), 102–122.

Orsmond, P., 2004. Self- and Peer-Assessment: Guidance on Practice in the Biosciences. Centre for Bioscience, The Higher Education Academy, Leeds.

Puente, L. del V. et al., 2012. Uso de la herramienta Taller de Moodle para la mejora de resultados académicos en una asignatura de Ingeniería de Telecomunicación. In: Santamaría, M., Sánchez-Elvira, Á. (coord.), Innovación Docente Universitaria en Entornos de Aprendizaje Enriquecidos: I Jornadas de Redes de Investigación en Innovación Docente, UNED, Madrid, pp. 100–103.

Race, P., 2001. A briefing on self, peer and group assessment. Report of LTSN Generic Centre. Available at: http://phil-race.co.uk/wp-content/uploads/Self,_peer_and_group_assessment.pdf (accessed 30.11.15.).

Reinholz, D., 2015. The assessment cycle: a model for learning through peer assessment. Assess. Eval. High. Educ. 2, 37–41.

Rodríguez Gómez, G., Ibarra Sáiz, M.S., Gómez Ruiz, M.Á., 2011. e-Autoevaluación en la universidad: un reto para profesores y estudiantes. Revista de Educación 356, 401–430.

Rogers, R., 2001. Reflection in higher education: a concept analysis. Innov. High. Educ. 26 (1), 37–57.

Sadler, D.R., 1989. Formative assessment and the design of instructional systems. Instr. Sci. 18 (2), 119–144.

Sadler, P.M., Good, D., 2006. The impact of self- and peer-grading on student learning. Educ. Assess. 11 (1), 1–31.

Salinas, J., Pérez Garcias, A., de Benito, B., 2008. Metodologías centradas en el alumno para el aprendizaje en red. Editorial Síntesis, Madrid.

Sánchez-Vera, M., Prendes, M.P., 2015. 'Más allá de las pruebas objetivas y la evaluación por pares: alternativas de evaluación en los MOOC. RUSC Univ. Knowl. Soc. J. 12 (1), 119–131.

Sluijsmans, D., Dochy, F., Moerkerke, G., 1998. The Use of Self-, Peer- and Co-assessment in Higher Education. A Review of Literature. Open University of the Netherlands, Heerlen, The Netherlands (Otec report 98/R04).

Sterbini, A., Temperini, M., 2013. Peer-assessment and grading of open answers in a web-based e-learning setting. In: Proceedings of the Information Technology Based Higher Education and Training (ITHET) 2013 International Conference. Antalya, Turkey, 10–12 October. IEEE, pp. 1–7.

van den Boom, G., et al., 2004. Reflection prompts and tutor feedback in a web-based learning environments: effects on students self-regulated learning competence. Comput. Hum. Behav. 20, 551–567.

Wang, C.X., Kinuthia, W., 2004. Defining technology enhanced learning environments for pre-service teachers. In: Ferdig, R. et al. (Ed.), Proceedings of Society for Information Technology and Teacher Education

International Conference, 2004. Association for the Advancement of Computing in Education (AACE), Chesapeake, VA, pp. 2724–2727.

Webb, M., 2010. Beginning teacher education and collaborative formative e-assessment. Assess. Eval. High. Educ. 35 (5), 597–618.

Whitelock, D., 2010. Activating assessment for learning: Are we on the way with Web 2.0? In: Lee, M.J.W., McLoughlin, C. (Eds.), Web 2.0-Based-E-Learning: Applying Social Informatics for Tertiary Teaching. IGI Global, USA.

Yu, F.-Y., Sung, S., 2015. A mixed methods approach to the assessor's targeting behavior during online peer assessment: effects of anonymity and underlying reasons. Interactive Learning Environments. Available at: http://www.tandfonline.com/doi/abs/10.1080/10494820.2015.1041405?journalCode=nile20   (accessed 30.11.15.).

Zimmerman, B.J., 2002. Becoming a self-regulated learner: an overview. Theory Pract. 41 (2), 64–70.

Zimmerman, B.J., Schunk, D.H. (Eds.), 1989. Self-Regulated Learning and Academic Achievement: Theory, Research and Practice. Springer-Verlag, New York.

Zubizarreta, J., 2009. The Learning Portfolio: Reflective Practice for Improving Student Learning, second ed. John Wiley & Sons, San Francisco, CA.

TOWARDS AN ADAPTIVE e-ASSESSMENT SYSTEM BASED ON TRUSTWORTHINESS

D. Baneres, M. Elena Rodríguez, A.-E. Guerrero-Roldán, X. Baró

Open University of Catalonia, Barcelona, Spain

1 INTRODUCTION

Nowadays, many virtual learning environments (VLEs) are being proposed in the literature. They are being used in fully online education, partially in face-to-face education or even in blended approaches. Many frameworks assume the following: the learner enrolled in the course is the genuine learner who will learn and follow the code of honor of the program. However, unfortunately, this statement is not always true.

In case of face-to-face or blended approaches this statement can be fulfilled by performing some assessment activities on-site. With this approach, we can assume that at least on some occasions the learner will perform an assessment activity on-site and the identity will be checked with an identity card and his or her authorship will be implicitly checked since the assessment activity is performed by him- or herself. However this solution cannot be applied on fully virtual environments.

Moreover, in recent times, the mobility of learners and professionals has increased. Together with the boost of internationalization processes, it leads to a situation where maintaining the face-to-face requirement in the assessment model becomes difficult. Current technology enables a direct translation from face-to-face to a virtual environment, for instance, via proctoring services. However, this approach lacks scalability and quickly becomes unfeasible, especially when we are talking about tens of thousands of learners. Therefore, a cost-effective compromise must be reached.

In this case, commonly, some authentication measures are currently used in order to identify the learner when he or she is accessing the environment. Less effective (login) or more sophisticated (biometric) techniques can be used or combined to identify the learner assuming that, when the learner successfully accesses with this authentication system, we can assure that the learner is really the learner. However, with this security system, we cannot verify the authorship of the assessment activities. In this case, plagiarism detection techniques should be used in order to verify the authorship of the assignments.

In this chapter, we propose a different approach in order to verify the identity and to check the authorship of the learner by designing a trust-based virtual assessment system. The system measures the level of confidence between the learner and the institution (virtual or on-site). The measurement is performed by analyzing evidences collected from the learner through different activities, interaction within the VLE and success in the authentication systems.

Formative Assessment, Learning Data Analytics and Gamification. http://dx.doi.org/10.1016/B978-0-12-803637-2.00002-6

Evidences stem from analyzing the behavior of the learner during his or her studies. The security mechanisms placed in the VLE, in the assessment activities, and in the authentication systems provide automatic evidences. Note that, not all evidences must come from automatic systems. Instructors could also provide manual evidences.

The system cannot be deployed in a straightforward manner throughout a program. The assessment activities, the final exams (FEs) of individual subjects, the authentication systems, and the authorship detection approaches should be globally and strategically designed to deploy different security mechanisms in the whole program. Furthermore, each activity may deploy a different set of security mechanisms, which may also be selected for a learner depending on his or her current trust level. For instance, an activity may be assessed using an interview (eg, Skype) for learners with a low trust level, but just as a deliverable document for learners with a higher trust level. Therefore, the trust-based assessment system is basically an *adaptive* trust-based assessment system, since the activities are adapted based on the trust level of the learner.

Moreover, this information also can be transferred among VLEs, taking into account privacy and legal issues. Similar to the previous knowledge of a learner, the trust level can be shared between VLEs in order to discover the behavior of the learner in the previous institution. This is an important additional contribution to the system since this information can be used in the new VLE to continue adapting the assessment of the learner based on his or her previous trust score.

The outline of the chapter is described below:

- *State of the art*: This section defines some fundamental concepts needed for this chapter and it also analyzes previous work in trust-based and adaptive assessment systems.
- *Design of the trust-based model*: In this section, a trust-based model that measures the level of confidence between a learner and the educational institution is presented.
- *General adaptive e-assessment system*: In this section, a general adaptive e-assessment system is described. The objective is to present a fully parameterizable adaptive system well-fitted to be used as a trust-based e-assessment system.
- *Trust-based e-assessment system*: This section explains how the general adaptive e-assessment system can be configured to be used as a trust-based e-assessment system. Moreover, an analysis of the security mechanism that can be deployed and the type of activities that can be used to evaluate the learners and to collect evidences is performed.
- *Simulation of a trust-based e-assessment system*: This section shows a simulation of a trust-based e-assessment system based on collected evidences from a real setting.
  Results are correlated with a non adaptive e-assessment system to see whether the results are sound.
- Some discussion and challenges related to the topic presented in this chapter are provided.
- Finally, conclusions of the chapter and future work are described.

2 STATE OF THE ART

In this section, some fundamental concepts required for the following sections are described. Next, some previous work on trust-based adaptability and adaptive e-assessment is outlined.

2.1 **FUNDAMENTAL CONCEPTS**

The large volume and variety of information that can be found and accessed through Internet has far exceeded the ability of users to select and choose it according to its relevance. Personalization (Riecken, 2000) implies receiving only the information that is relevant for an individual or group of individuals. Note that, this term is different from customization, which refers to the selection of the options under the direct control of the user who explicitly chooses to include or exclude them. Thus, the information, services, or products can be offered based on the needs, actions, and preferences of users. Although there is not a consistent set of terms for describing the different ways in which personalization can be achieved, authors in Smith et al. (2006) identify the adaptive personalization type. Adaptive personalization (also known as inferred personalization) is where the availability of options is based on the gradual acquisition of knowledge about the user. Such knowledge comes from tracking the user's activity as well as from the analysis of other information sources (eg, user profiles). In this case, the system supporting adaptation identifies the items that are potentially interesting for the user and the controls that are eventually available to them. The adaptive personalization is usually based on one of the following two approaches:

- Adaptive personalization based on user activity: This kind of service allows the identification and recommendation of information or a product for a particular user, based on the preferences of users who have similar characteristics or a similar activity log. One example is the Amazon recommendation system.
- Adaptive personalization based on data extraction, such as ruled-based filters, or systems that exploit different data sources about the user. For example, in an educational context, data can be extracted from the learner record in the educational institution.

As discussed in Hammond et al. (2008), there is an extensive literature review of personalization, including the development of adaptive systems as well as the methods and techniques that need to be considered from both computer science and artificial intelligence. However, the main objective of an adaptive system is to support each individual learner to reach his or her full potential (Green et al., 2005). The personalization is not a benefit in itself. On the contrary, the benefit should be considered in the context of specific developments and in relation to the learning process, rather than a desired goal. A personalization system is an application that adapts its behavior to the objectives, interests, and tasks of a users or group of users (Quarati, 2003).

In the field of education, different personalization systems have been designed such as Mampadi et al. (2011), Tsolis et al. (2012), and Baig (2013). These systems are being continuously improved to emphasize promoting the needs of learners and the reuse of resources. As discussed in Ashman et al. (2009), the key for personalization is that education is a very personal experience, because everyone learns in a different way. Without personalization, there is no chance of establishing different learning models centered on the learner. The development of adaptive systems helps to solve the negative effects derived from the traditional position of one size fits all (Brusilovsky and Maybury, 2002). In this sense, adaptive learning (Chen and Magoulas, 2005) should be understood as the ability to modify learning resources, activities, and assessment processes, using different parameters or a set of predefined rules, in order to provide learners with the most suitable options.

Beyond the different types of adaptive options aforementioned, other types of adaptive learning, tailored to the educational context are provided in Brusilovsky (2001), Chin (2001), He et al. (2002), and Bra et al. (2004): learning process adaptation (or adaptive learning), adaptive content, and adaptive interface. These three types reflect the adaptation of the learning process at different levels. The first and second levels are the relevant ones for the work presented in this chapter. These levels allow dealing with the activities and the assessment process depending on the learner profile and the activities that the learner delivers during his or her learning and assessment process. These levels also include the provision of feedback for the activities delivered for each learner as a crucial factor for establishing the adaptive level that the system has to support in each step of the learning and assessment process. Therefore, the work performed by the learner should be taken into account, as well as the evaluation done by the teacher and the set of methods and technologies that will help on the process of decision making.

Mostly the decision is reflected on the selection of a learning path. An adaptive learning path is understood as a set of sequential learning resources and activities that are followed by the learner in an irregular manner (Guerrero and Minguilln, 2007). The term adaptive refers to how the resources and activities are shown and evaluated according the learner performance. A learning path is triggered at the beginning of any training action and it ends when competencies are acquired. Through activities and final examinations the learner is assessed so an adaptive system has to propose the most suitable methods and techniques for developing a model which takes into account the existing assessment models.

If we focus on the assessment part of the learning process on a VLE, we can define e-assessment as the process where information and communication technologies are used for the management of the end-to-end assessment process (Cook and Jenkins, 2010). In other words, e-assessment deals with methods, processes, and web-based software tools (or systems) that allow systematic inferences and judgments to be made about the learner's skills, knowledge, and capabilities (Crisp, 2007). Adaptive e-assessment (or simply adaptive assessment) is commonly defined as a particular feature in adaptive learning. The learning path of the learner is adapted and, at the same time, the assessment activities are also adapted since they belong to a specific learning path. Adaptive e-assessment tends to analyze prior the cognitive level of the learner, and based on this analysis it proposes the next appropriated assessment activity. In this case, from a computerized point of view, the system evaluates a set of indicators to select the next activity to be presented to the learner.

2.2 TRUST-BASED ADAPTABILITY

In this section, the previous work related to trust-based adaptation is described. The literature discusses different models and platforms for virtual automatic assessment such as the work of Ala-Mutka (2005) and Ihantola et al. (2010). However, most of this literature focuses on an educational or a technological description without taking into account any security measure.

In this context, we define security measure as how the learner is authenticated on the system when a learning activity is performed or submitted, how the authorship of the activity is verified, and how the system protects the integrity of submitted activity. These security requirements have been previously considered in Weippl (2005) and Neila and Rabai (2014) in the attempt to cover all the possibilities of cheating. However, the counter-measures to mitigate these issues are not always easy to implement.

Authentication in a VLE has been addressed using different levels of security. The simplest and most commonly used method is login authentication using a password. A more secure approach would be using a digital certificate, such as the platform designed in Lu et al. (2013). Digital certificate is more secure assuming that the user will never share his or her certificate. However, even though these approaches may be acceptable to access services, when authorship also must be considered, their usefulness is questionable.

Levy and Ramim (2007), Flior and Kowalski (2010), and Kambourakis and Damopoulos (2013) propose using other authentication systems based on biometric recognition, which involves keystroke detection (Choraś and Mroczkowski, 2007; Monaco et al., 2013), face recognition (Zhao et al., 2003; Wagner et al., 2012; Wechsler et al., 2012), voice recognition (Kinnunen et al., 2006; Sumithra and Devika, 2012), or fingerprint detection (Uz et al., 2009). By using this approach, the level of security increases significantly, since this information cannot be just handed over to a third party, and these methods even can be combined to reduce the possibilities of cheating. Currently, implementations of biometric authentication are also used in MOOC platforms like Coursera to verify the identity of the learners for earning certifications of completion.

Integrity is also a critical issue in a VLE. Several works describe platforms based on secure data transfer protocols (Herrera-Joancomarti et al., 2004; Bella et al., 2014) or specific secure platforms (Fluck et al., 2009; Modiri et al., 2011). The main objective of these platforms is to secure data exchanges between the learner's computer and the VLE and to securely store the submitted activities. In this regard, integrity can also be considered as an added value, since it guarantees that the correct data reach the VLE.

Authorship is another important objective, addressed as plagiarism detection in some works. Previous secure mechanism also stands for preserving this last objective and simplifying the process of validation of the authorship. If the user is securely identified and there is a guarantee of the integrity of the activity, the authorship is reduced to check if the content of the activity has been performed by the user. There is a relevant discussion about which type of method would be sufficient to refute the authorship of an activity (Graven and MacKinnon, 2008; Simon et al., 2013).

Basic semi-automated tools have been proposed based on proctoring. Companies such as ProctorU (https://www.kryteriononline.com/) or Kryterion (https://www.kryteriononline.com/) offer a system where a person monitors online, via a webcam, the progression of an activity performed by a learner. The system is scalable assuming than the company is able to provide infrastructure and any number of proctors. In order to create more scalable systems, tools such as Secure Exam (http://www.softwaresecure.com/) or Safe Exam Browser (http://www.safeexambrowser.org/) have been proposed. They offer a secure environment via the computer for the user during the realization of the activity. These systems are intrusive by blocking undesirable applications and connections to online resources and monitoring all the actions of the user.

If we focus on plagiarism, there are many tools that help to automatically detect its existence (Alzahrani et al., 2012). However, some authors consider techniques based on forensic linguistics preferable (Koppel and Schler, 2003; Stamatatos, 2009), since the authorship of a text is assessed exclusively through comparison of different creations from the same author. Other models also have been proposed to check authorship based on the trustworthiness level of the user. In these models, the user is evaluated based on the reputation acquired in the VLE by analyzing his or her behavior or evaluating the opinion of other learners and instructors by peer-assessment. For instance, authors Liu et al. (2011) proposed a quality assurance and trustable e-learning environment with quality certification and trust evaluation. Another approach (Champaign and Cohen, 2012) was based on trust, similarity, and knowledge gains, providing support to peer-based information sharing within web-based contexts.

Note that all these works try to solve some of the described security measures. However, they only partially solve some of the measures without covering others. The objective of the trust-based model proposed in Section 3 is to take advantage of the benefits of all of these measures to obtain evidences for the trustworthiness of the learners in the context of a VLE.

2.3 ADAPTIVE e-ASSESSMENT

The integration of a trust-based adaptive model on a conventional adaptive learning system will generate new learning paths based on a trust-oriented selection. Note that this adaptation will also select different assessment activities, since the adaptive e-assessment system will be also modified. This section focuses on related work on adaptive e-assessment.

An adaptive e-assessment is commonly used as a part of an adaptive learning system. There are different ways to perform the adaptation. One option is to associate a unique learning activity to a learning path. Thus, the adaption is based on the selection of the learning path. Another option is to associate multiple learning activities to the same learning path. In this case, the level of knowledge and competences of the learner within the learning path should be analyzed in order to select the best suitable individual assessment activity. These approaches are based on the principle that the assessment activity is a part of the learning path and, therefore, it helps to acquire the concepts and skills within the path, and it does not merely serve as an activity to obtain a mark.

Different systems have been developed based on this principle. Wang (2004) proposes a system to provide personalized assessment activities based on the cognitive level of the learner. The proposed system learns and memorizes good learning assessment activities for different learners, and accordingly provides a personalized learning sequence for other similar learners. A similar system was introduced in Armendariz et al. (2014) where the assessment questions were triggered based on the expertise proved by the learner. Nacheva-Skopalik and Green (2012) described a different system where learning and assessment were totally adaptable based on knowledge, competences, preferences, and needs of the learner.

Research on this topic mainly focused on automatic generation of computer adapted tests (CATs) based on the proficiency of the learner. These approaches tend to develop a large set of banked questions categorized by concept and level of difficulty, and they are triggered based on the learning conditions met by the learner. There has been considerable research attention focused on Item Response Theory (IRT) (Baker, 2001) where the objective is to design systems to automatically provide and score questionnaires to measure abilities, attitudes, or other variables. Among others, systems such as PARES (Marinagi et al., 2007), ITSAS (Maqsood and Durrani, 2011), IRTT (Vega et al., 2012), and AAS (Rajamani and Kathiravan, 2013) have been proposed using variations of the IRT approach.

Note that, the previous systems rely on the construction of a profile for the learner, the quality of the collected information, and the ability of the model to predict the knowledge and competences to be assessed. Based on the prediction model, Bayesian (Ueno, 2001; Chika et al., 2009; Rajamani and Kathiravan, 2013) and Fuzzy (Stathacopoulou et al., 1999; Wang, 2004; Nebot et al., 2010) methodologies have been used. These methodologies help to evaluate hypotheses based on some prior collected evidences.

However all these approaches are focused on adapting the assessment based on prior acquired learning, without taking into account other evidences that also may be relevant to the selection of the next assessment activity. Moreover, the presented approaches have several difficulties that are relevant to a trust-based adaptive e-assessment system. In this chapter, after defining a novel trust-based model in Section 3, we describe in Section 4 a more general system that takes into account evidences of different types in order to generate the next assessment. This general system can be fully parameterizable to be used as an adaptive trust-based e-assessment system as we show in Section 5. Finally, a simulation of a trust-based system from a real setting and challenges of this type of systems are presented in Section 6 and Section 7 respectively.

3 ADAPTIVE TRUST-BASED MODEL

In this section, we define an adaptive trust-based model that measures the level of confidence (or trust level) of the learner. The measurement is performed by analyzing evidences collected from the learner through different activities and interactions. Such trust level is basically represented as a score, dynamically updated according to the collected evidences during the period of time the learner is in the university.

Evidences stem from analyzing the behavior of the learner during his or her studies. The security mechanisms placed in the VLE, in the assessment activities, and in the FEs provide automatic evidences to update the trust score. Note that, not all evidences come from automatic systems. Instructors could also provide manual evidences from his interaction with the learners.

The model cannot be applied in a straightforward manner throughout a program. The assessment activities and the FEs of individual subjects should be globally designed to deploy different security mechanisms, from on-site face-to-face to fully virtual activities, throughout the program. Each activity may have multiple designs and each design may deploy a different set of security mechanisms. Note that, this adaptation of an activity to multiple designs may be difficult, and one fundamental objective is that the evaluated knowledge and competences should be equivalent for all designs. These designs will be triggered depending on the current trust score of a learner. For instance, an activity may be evaluated using an interview for learners with a low trust score, but just as a deliverable document for learners with a higher trust score.

Fig. 2.1 shows the flow of the model on an assessment activity. During the pre-process activity phase, the score dynamically decides which design of the activity should be performed by the learner based on the security mechanisms that need to be raised depending on the trust level of the learner.

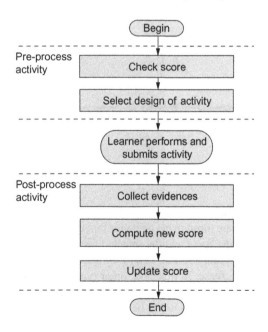

FIGURE 2.1

Model flow.

At the end of each activity, during the post-process activity phase, each security mechanism outputs different evidences. In the most common scenario, the system cannot definitely decide that an infraction has happened. Often, automated security mechanisms can only provide a probability of infraction depending on the collected data. This probability depends on the learner's actions, since some of them might be flagged as suspicious, but with reasonable doubt. The final probability is used to calculate a partial trust score, which will impact the learner's global score. On the other hand, it is possible that the mechanism detects an infraction beyond any reasonable doubt. In this scenario, there is no partial trust score. A penalty is inflicted on the learner and his global trust score is automatically lowered to 0. Collected evidences are used to justify the penalty to the learner.

Fig. 2.2 illustrates an example of the model behavior through a program. Let us assume a learner starts a program under this model. Therefore, assessment activities have been designed including a broad set of different security mechanisms. The chart shows the evolution of the trust score through different semesters where the Y-axis denotes the learner's global score and the X-axis denotes the semesters. We can observe that each semester has different assessment activities (represented by a dot).

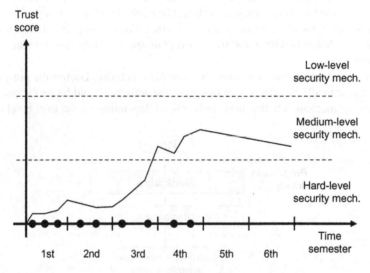

FIGURE 2.2

Example of application of the model.

When a learner starts the program, the score is set to 0. There is no evidence of confidence. Therefore, the learner should demonstrate through his behavior that the institution can trust him. The subjects of the first semester set up the trust score and the selected security mechanisms through the design of the activities will tend to be strict, that is, an on-site FE or interviews. Given the partial activity scores, at some point, the score could increase. In this case, other types of mechanisms may be used for new activities (see fourth semester in Fig. 2.2), adapting the assessment activities to the learner's behavior.

Note that, the objective of this model is not to penalize learners with a low level of confidence, but rather to benefit learners with higher levels. The designs defined as hard are the default assessment activities in a program without this model. If a learner does not demonstrate any evidence of trust, the standard process of evaluation is followed, whereas a learner with a higher level benefits from other less exhaustive evaluation activities. Based on this idea, this model needs constant information to maintain the score, that is, the score decreases on semesters where the learner is not enrolled in any course (see fifth and sixth semester in Fig 2.2).

4 GENERAL ADAPTIVE e-ASSESSMENT SYSTEM

As mentioned above, the previous trust-based model should be integrated into an adaptive e-assessment system. In this section, we define a general system that can be parameterizable to be trust-based. Note that, we focus on the assessment part of the learning process and, therefore, the general system is oriented to support adaptive e-assessment.

The main properties of the general adaptive e-assessment system are (1) to collect any type of evidence and analyze it to update the learner profile; and, (2) to create the next assessment activity to be delivered to the learner based on the information gathered and the objectives and competences associated to the assessment activity.

Note that, a system with these characteristics is general enough to be applied to on-site or virtual learning. However, a VLE has some advantages, since most of the evidences can be obtained automatically without any intervention of an agent (instructor, administration staff, etc.) using learning analytics frameworks.

The aim of a general adaptive e-assessment system is extended to be able to do more than just adapt the assessment process according to the knowledge and competences that need to be acquired. Other objectives can be taken into account related to the instructional and assessment process. We have detected, at least, the next objectives:

- *Knowledge and competences acquisition*: This is the main objective of an adaptive learning system and, consequently, of an adaptive assessment system.
- *Trust assurance*: Some systems (not only in e-learning environments) evaluate the reputation of the user. In a VLE, the assessment process of a leaner with a high level of trustworthiness can be adapted to be more flexible, that is, an exam (which consists of a set of exercises and evaluated with a quantitative grade) can be transformed into a final test validation activity (which could be composed of exercises to validate the assessment activities delivered by the learner and evaluated as pass or fail, that is, a qualitative mark is issued) since the learner constantly proves his or her knowledge and proficiency through interaction with the VLE and collaboration with other learners.
- *Security assurance*: It is crucial that the assessment process performed by a learner has been conducted without any infraction, as would be the case in plagiarism. Some security issues such as authorship sometimes has a high level of uncertainty. The instructor suspects that the learner may not be the author, but he cannot prove it. In this case, the next assessment activity can be personalized to refute or confirm the teacher's suspicions.

It is important to note that the adaptation can be done at different levels of granularity (the coarser levels subsume the finest ones). The top level refers to the personalization of the assessment model and, therefore, all the assessment activities within the model. In addition more than one assessment model can coexist within a subject. The intermediate level adapts individual assessment activities.

Here, an assessment activity is personalized with all its internal exercises. At the finest level, several exercises within the assessment activity are personalized.

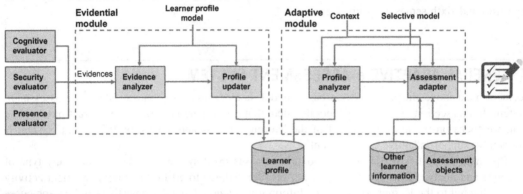

FIGURE 2.3

General adaptive e-assessment system.

A general adaptive assessment system, as Fig. 2.3 shows, is composed of two main modules:

1. *Evidential module*: This module is focused to analyze the gathered evidences and detect which evidences are relevant to update the profile of the learner.
2. *Adaptive module*: This module is responsible for adapting the next assessment activity to be delivered to the learner.

Note that the modules have different scheduling. On the one hand, the evidential module is continuously analyzing evidences, since they are collected from the learning process and assessment results of the learner. On the other hand, the adaptive module is only used when assessment activities are delivered. This module will personalize the activities according to the evidences collected by the previous module. In the next subsections, we describe each module in detail.

4.1 EVIDENTIAL MODULE

The objective of the evidential module (see left part of Fig. 2.3) is to analyze the evidences generated during the learning experience of the learner.

The module has inputs from different data sources. There are different evaluators that provide evidences from the learning process and interaction of the learner within the VLE system. Additionally, the module requires that all the outcomes and information related to the learner are collected and stored in the learner profile. According to be a general system, the module can be configured with a parameterizable learner profile model that specifies the particular information that should be stored for each learner. Thus, the learner profile and the required stored information related to the learner could vary from one learner to another: information about knowledge, competences, activity on the VLE system, reputation, interaction with learning resources, etc. The learner profile model helps to reduce the amount of data included in the learner profile. Some systems create large profiles with all the characteristics and information of a learner. On the other hand, a VLE system works and produces massive data sets of different types and a large number of evidences in a continuous way. Therefore, optimization issues should be taken into account when designing new systems. Processing only the relevant data needed to perform the adaptation will significantly decrease the computation and analysis time, thus improving the overall throughput of the system and facilitating data management.

The evidential module is composed of the following components:

- *Evidence analyzer*: This component is responsible for processing the evidences and generating the internal indicators for updating the learner profile. Depending on the information stored in the learner profile specified by the learner profile model, the evidences will be evaluated in different forms (ie, they will generate different indicators) and some of them should be even dismissed since they will not have an impact on the profile. The component should specify which type of data sources are acceptable and how the data should be sent. A good review of different models for the collection of information based on learning analytics can be found in Lukarov et al. (2014).
- *Profile updater*: This component updates the learner profile based on the indicators generated by the previous component. The learner profile model should be as extensible as possible in order to be able to gather all the relevant information related to the learner (Ramandalahy et al., 2009; Guerrero-Roldan and Rodriguez, 2014) and, therefore, create a sophisticated personalized assessment models in the adaptive module.

The evidence generators supply the set of evidences that the evidence analyzer needs. We have identified three evidence generators:

- *Cognitive evaluator*: This component evaluates the knowledge and proficiency level of the learner during his or her learning and assessment process. The evidences collected are the ones needed for adaptive systems focused on knowledge. Information such as a score of an activity, an achievement, acquisition of a competence, among others, can be transformed into an indicator of the progression of the learner.
- *Security evaluator*: Security information is highly significant in VLE systems. Learner actions should be analyzed to check if any infraction has occurred. The results of checking security properties (authorship, integrity, non repudiation, authentication, and presence) are transformed into indicators to see whether the learner cheats during the learning and assessment process. Note that this information may have a high level of uncertainty in some cases.
- *Presence evaluator*: Presence information is also important in some type of activities such as peer assessment or collaboration activities. This system evaluates the learner's reputation and the trust and confidence the VLE system has in the learner. Techniques to collect information regarding trust and reputation in general systems (not specifically in VLE systems) can be used (Jøsang et al., 2007; Artz and Gil, 2007).

It is important to note that more generators may appear in the future. The system will be able to use them as long as they fulfill the specification to send the evidences to the Evidence Analyzer.

4.2 ADAPTIVE MODULE

The adaptive module (see right part of Fig. 2.3) provides support to the creation of the adaptive assessment.

In this case, the module uses several storage components. The learner profile is shared with the Evidential Module. This module only reads the profile built for the learner since the Evidential Module is responsible for updating it. Next, the module also uses other relevant information of the learner such as his or her learning preferences or accessibility needs. In some systems, this type of information is merged within the learner profile. In this case, we split it into two different data sources (the learner profile and other learner information), because the other learner information is more static (ie, less frequently updated), related to learning preferences and accessibility needs, and not based on evidences from the Evidential Module. Finally, the assessment objects are stored in data banks. We assume that the assessment objects have been created previously. In the case that a particular system needs to create new assessment objects, an additional module should be created to add assessment objects in the data banks. However, this is out of the scope of this chapter.

Additionally, the module can be parameterizable providing the context in which the assessment activity will be deployed and the selective model. The selective model describes which information is used from the learner profile to create the assessment activity, the level of granularity of the assessment adaption (model, activity, or exercise) and the procedure used to select the assessment objects.

The module is composed of the following components:

- *Profile analyzer*: This component will process the learner profile to evaluate the level of knowledge and competence of the learner. The context (Yaghmaie and Bahreininejad, 2011) in which the assessment activity will be deployed and the selective model to be applied should be known, since the analysis will be based on this information. The set of assessed indicators (knowledge, competence acquisition, reputation, etc.) is transferred to the next component. This information will be used to build the adaptive assessment activity.
- *Assessment adapter*: This component collects the previous data and, using the procedure to select the assessment objects, taking into account the level of granularity, will create the assessment activity to be delivered to the learner. Note that the component reuses the assessment objects stored in data banks. The assessment objects could be tests, open questions, or any type of exercise that can be assessed automatically (preferred) or manually by the instructor or, even, in a peer-review basis. The component also uses other information about the learner that is relevant to the building of a fully fledged personalized assessment.

5 ADAPTIVE TRUST-BASED e-ASSESSMENT SYSTEM

After defining the trust-based model and explaining a general adaptive e-assessment system, we are ready to define the trust-based e-assessment system. The aim of this section is to describe this novel system.

The flow of the model (see Fig. 2.1) perfectly fits in the proposed system. The pre-process activity phase is performed by the Adaptive Module, meanwhile the post-process activity phase is performed by the Evidential Module.

The parameterizable components can be configured to transform the general adaptive e-assessment system into a trust-based e-assessment system:

- *Learner profile model*: This system stores the basic information required in typical adaptive systems such as performance, progression, competence acquisition, etc. Additionally, the system also stores information based on the applied security mechanisms (see Section 2.2) such as security access log, biometric information, or keystroke model, among others. This information will depend on the security mechanisms enabled in the VLE. Additionally, the learner profile defines the function to compute the trust-level score and how the evidences are combined to compute this score. This score will be added as a new indicator in the learner profile.
- *Context*: The context gathers all information related to the program, subject, and type of activity (continuous assessment activity, FE, groupwork, etc.). This information is needed to best select the design of the activity.
- *Selective model*: The selective model supplies information from the learner profile that is used to select the assessment activity. In addition, the selective model provides the different intervals of the trust-level score where designs with hard-, medium-, and low-level security mechanisms are triggered depending on the granularity of the adaption. Thus, with a unique selective model, different types of adaption can be carried out using the same system.
- *Assessment objects*: The assessment objects are categorized. Metadata such as the subject, activity, design of the activity, security mechanisms deployed, or the classification of the design (hard-, medium-, low-level activity) will help to best select the object.

The cognitive evaluator (see Section 4.1) needs to be connected with the record system of the learner to extract information about the learning progression of the learner. However, the security and presence evaluators need to identify which security mechanisms will be deployed in the VLE and which evidences will be collected. Currently, we have identified five basic security requirements: Authorship (Autho), Integrity (Intg), Non-Repudiation (NoRp), Authentication (Authe), and Presence (Pres). As far as we have analyzed, no single security mechanism has been found to produce evidences for all five requirements. Next, the list of security mechanisms that have been taken into consideration are described:

- *Digital signature*: The learner digitally signs his or her work before submission, using a digital certificate issued by a certification authority accepted by the education institution. The chosen authorities must guarantee minimum identity checks before issuing such certificates to learners.
- *Timestamp*: The learner's work is digitally timestamped upon completion. Therefore, the learner is able to prove that his or her work was completed on time, regardless of when it was actually submitted (for instance, because of network outages).
- *Forensic analysis*: The learner's work content is analyzed a posteriori, once the submission is accepted. Aspects such as writing style are analyzed to determine the content's author.
- *Plagiarism detection*: Looking for similarities in the activities of different learners, or even looking up online available resources.
- *Real-time monitor*: Learner actions are monitored while he or she is working on the activity. There are basically three approaches to this technique: fully automated (using biometrics techniques such as keystroke analysis or computer vision), fully manual (a human is watching), or a hybrid method (automated, but some alerts lead to human intervention).
- *Real-time identification*: This is a similar approach to monitoring but, instead of monitoring the whole activity, is just enough to identify the learner. We have separated this approach into a different category, because the identification process may be used independently.

- *Instructor feedback*: The instructor evaluates the learner's confidence given his or her own perceptions throughout the course (strange circumstances, learner behavior not aligned with his grades, etc.).
- *Peer feedback*: The learner is evaluated by his or her peers, as far as his or her trustworthiness is concerned. Has he or she been a valuable team member? Has he or she actually made contributions? Has he or she cheated?
- *Proctor monitor*: The learner is controlled all the time by an instructor (or proctor) during the realization of the activity. The control can be on-site or online via a proctoring service.
- *Learning analytics*: This mechanism can help in the evaluation of the learner's presence at the university. The data is collected in a progressive way from different learning tools and resources. Subsequently, we consider that this system can include information about the learner's impact at the university.

We have analyzed which type of activities can exist in a virtual assessment setting. The different designs have been classified on a classical approach of synchronous (S) or asynchronous (A) in space (S) and time (T). Nevertheless, activities synchronous in space but asynchronous in time (SS-AT) are not considered, since they are unfeasible on a virtual setting. In the following section we provide a brief description of each type of design that we have considered for the system. Note that the list is not exhaustive.

- *Deliverable*: This is an individual work in which the learner produces a document that must be submitted for its evaluation. This document may contain any kind of data and the answers are not necessarily limited to prose text, that is, video or audio recording, programming code, etc., are possible options.
- *Exposition*: The learner solves a problem or exercise under the direct supervision of the instructor. Assessment is on the spot. However, interaction is basically unidirectional, that is, a presentation or a demo.
- *Interview*: Similar to exposition, but in this case a conversation occurs between the learner and the instructor, who may make further inquiries depending on the learner's answers. Interaction is fully bidirectional.
- *Discussion*: Different learners work together (in a collaborative or antagonistic manner) to discuss a topic proposed by the instructor.
- *Groupwork*: This is similar to deliverable, but work is not individual in this case, but produced by a group of learners. Learners will be assessed as a whole, not individually.
- *Internship*: A learner works at a company for some time and his or her performance is evaluated on site by a supervisor.

Finally, Fig. 2.4 provides a general summary about how types of designs of activities are aligned with the different security mechanisms. The first column classifies each possible design as being synchronous or asynchronous in space and time. Also, in the top row, the figure shows which security property is evaluated by each mechanism. We can observe that many designs have some security mechanisms always activated due to their low cost of activation and scalability, meanwhile others have mechanisms that can be optionally activated due to their higher cost of utilization or lower reliability.

Type of activity/ Mechanism		Authe Intg NoRp Autho Pres	Digital signature	Timestamp	Forensic analysis	Plagiarism detection	Real-time monitor	Real-time identification	Teacher feedback	Feedback P2P	Proctor monitor	Learning analytics
AS - AT	Deliverable		O	O	OO	OO	-	OO	O	-	-	O
	Exposition		O	O	-	-	-	O	O	-	-	O
	Debate		-	-	-	-	-	-	O	OO	-	O
	Groupwork		-	-	-	-	-	-	O	O	-	O
AS - ST	Deliverable		O	O	OO	OO	OO	OO	O	-	OO	O
	Exposition		O	O	-	-	-	O	O	-	-	O
	Interview		-	-	-	-	OO	OO	O	-	OO	-
SS - ST	Deliverable		-	-	-	-	-	-	-	-	OO	-
	Interview		-	-	-	-	-	-	-	-	OO	-
	Internship		-	-	-	-	-	-	-	-	OO	-

O : Always active mechanism.
OO: Optional mechanism.
- : Not suitable mechanism.

FIGURE 2.4

Alignment of security mechanisms-activity types.

6 SIMULATION OF A TRUST-BASED ADAPTIVE ASSESSMENT SYSTEM

This section shows an experiment on how a general adaptive assessment is aligned with a non adaptive assessment system. The aim of the experiment is to show that the expected result of an adaptive assessment system is consistent. We have performed a simulation on the instructional process of the subject "Computer Fundamentals" of the Degree of Computer Science in the Open University of Catalunya. The experiment shows a correlation between the deployment of the final assessment activity based on different selective models that take into account different evidences (not only based on knowledge/competences acquisition) and the score of the FE of the course. Note that the system has not yet been implemented, the simulation was only intended to see how different selective models could impact in a hypothetical adaptive assessment system.

Currently the subject has three continuous assessment activities (CA), a final project (FP), and a FE. A web forum is used as a communication tool between learners and teachers. The subject also has an intelligent tutoring system called VerilUOC (Baneres et al., 2014) where learners solve exercises related to the design of digital systems. The intelligent tutoring system allows the collection of evidences from the learning and assessment process of each learner.

In this case, the objective of the adaptive assessment system would be to adapt the final assessment activity to a FE or a final validation (FV) activity based on the selective score computed by the proposed selective models. The summary of the experiment is shown in Fig. 2.5. For the sake of simplicity, the figure only shows the parameters that have been configured for the experiment.

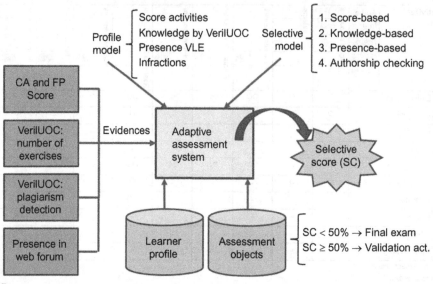

FIGURE 2.5

Parameterization of the system for the simulation.

The evidences collected in the subject are summarized below:

- *Learner's performance*: The scores of the continuous assessment activities (CA) and the final project (FP) are used to evaluate the knowledge acquisition and competence of each learner.
- *Number of exercises performed within the VerilUOC system*: This evidence is used to evaluate the learning progression of each learner.
- *Presence of the learner in the web forum*: This evidence evaluates the presence of the learner in the course and the knowledge he or she is demonstrating in the web forum.
- *Plagiarism detection*: VerilUOC tool also checks automatically for plagiarism among learners. This evidence validates authorship on submitted assessment activities.

Four different selective models have been used. For the sake of simplicity, each model generates a unique selective score that specifies the level of adaptation. The selective score has been normalized to values from 0% to 100% where 100% is the maximum score that could be generated by the model. A value larger than 50% in our hypothetical adaptive assessment system would deploy a FV activity instead of a FE.

- *Score-based model*: This model only takes into account the score of the continuous assessment. Therefore, the selective score is the score of the continuous assessment.[1]

---

[1]In case of the existence of a final project, the selective score is computed as the average between the CA and FP.

- *Knowledge-based model*: In addition to the score, this model takes into account the knowledge construction of the learner. The model defined in Maqsood and Durrani (2011) has been used:

$$\text{Selective}_{\text{score}} = \left(\frac{\text{TCE}}{\text{TAE}} \times \frac{1}{\text{TDE}}\right) \times \frac{\text{Score\_CA}}{\text{Max\_CA}}$$

  where TCE and TAE are the total correct and attempted exercises, TDE is the difficulty of all assessment activities, where we have assumed equal difficulty (set to 1), and Score_CA and Max_CA are the score and the maximum score that the learner can reach in the continuous assessment activity[2], respectively.
- *Presence-based model*: The presence shows the interaction of the learner within the course with other learners. Learners can show a certain level of trust based on the quality of his or her contributions in the web forum (submitted by means of messages). In this case, we added to the previous model a corrective factor using the trust-based model described in Basheer et al. (2015):

$$\text{Selective}_{\text{score}} = \frac{\alpha}{\alpha + \beta}$$

  where α represents good-quality messages, that is, messages with a meaningful impact in the instruction, for example messages that help other learners, proposal of solution to exercises, good questions, etc. In turn β represents the remaining messages submitted by the learner.
- *Authorship model*: In this case, plagiarism issues set the selective score to 0, otherwise, the current selective score is maintained. In case of plagiarism detection, the learner should perform the FE.

Note that, the combination of the four models can be defined as a trust-based model since different evidences from the instructional process are collected to compute a score. The model takes into account evidences from the Presence Evaluator (web forum activity), Cognitive Evaluator (Scores and Veri-lUOC activity), and Security Evaluator (plagiarism detection). Also note that, security issues related to authentication, integrity, and non repudiation are not taken into account in the model, since the checking process is done by the VLE system (the online campus provided by the Open University of Catalunya) and the intelligent tutoring system (the VerilUOC system).

Fig. 2.6 shows the correlation on the deployment of a FV activity. In case of the adaptive assessment system the FV activity is triggered when the selective score is larger than 50%. In case of a non adaptive system, we assume that a score in the FE larger than 50%, the FE would not be necessary and a FV activity would be enough. Two starting scores have been used: the continuous assessment (CA) and the final project (FP). The final project is a harder assessment activity that aims to assess in an integrated way all the concepts provided in the subject. Therefore, the correlation should be higher if the score of this activity is taken into account.

The table shows a high correlation in the score-based model. The activity selected using the score of the model in both starting scores (CA and FP) is highly correlated with the deployment based on the score of the FE of the learners. This result reflects that currently adaptive assessment systems based only on this indicator would infer that in many cases the FE is not needed and a simpler final assessment activity could be generated for learners with a good score.

---

[2]In case of the existence of a final project, the score and maximum score are computed as the average value between the CA and FP.

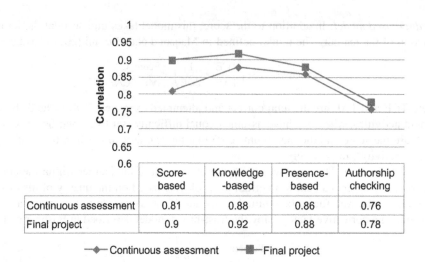

	Score-based	Knowledge-based	Presence-based	Authorship checking
Continuous assessment	0.81	0.88	0.86	0.76
Final project	0.9	0.92	0.88	0.78

—◆—Continuous assessment   —■—Final project

FIGURE 2.6

Correlation on the deployment of final validation activities between selective models and final performance.

However, the knowledge-based model increases the quality. Results extracted from VerilUOC utilization shows a more fine-tuned model to compute the selective score. Learners demonstrating a higher interaction with the tool prove more expertise related to the design of digital systems. Using this model, more learners should be able to avoid the FE, and perform a final assessment validation activity (FV).

The presence and authorship models also show interesting results. The presence model shows a reduction of the correlation. This is a consistent result and it is related to the fact that there are learners that do not interact in the web forum. They only access to the course to perform the assessment activities (CA and FP) and the exam (FE). If no presence is shown during the course, the selective score should decrease since the learner has not proved additional knowledge. Therefore, in a hypothetical adaptive assessment system, this learner should perform the FE instead of a FV activity.

The authorship model shows similar results. When security is analyzed, the detection of security issues will always impact negatively in the selective score. In this case, plagiarism detection automatically requires that learner does a FE.

7 DISCUSSION AND CHALLENGES

In this chapter an assessment model has been presented on the basis of an estimation of the trust level between a learner and his or her institution. The model does not affect the evaluation objectives of the activity (knowledge and competence to be acquired and/or evaluated), which are based on academic principles, but the model introduces security mechanisms that allow a move to a virtual assessment system while the guarantees of a fully face-to-face environment are maintained, and in some cases improved with authorship assurance.

The introduction of this new assessment model can help the educational institutions to spread their services to new markets and better fit the new reality of lifelong educational learning.

On the other hand, the presented model has many unresolved challenges. It is based on a trust score that is calculated using the activity of the learner in a program or even the information from previous programs in the same or other institutions. The techniques used for the score calculation are not perfect and confidence in each of them needs to be taken into account when obtaining the final score and when this score is used, even for decisions related to the violation of honor codes.

The combination of automatic and manual evidences is crucial in the definition of the model. In Section 6, we have shown the different models that have already been defined by other authors where only automatic evidences have been taken into account. In these models, all evidences had the same importance on the computation of the selective score, but it is important to note that the emphasis might be different on each model. In a fine-tuned model, the evidences should be assigned different levels of importance and these levels will be represented with different weights on the function that computes the selective score. Manual and automatic evidences will contribute distinctly to the trust score and these contributions will be defined with a large experimentation.

Another challenge is how the instructors will interact with the system. The instructors will manually add the evidences and the assessment objects will be added based on the different models that a subject and a program have defined. The selection of the assessment object should be transparent to the instructor based on a previous configuration of the system, but infractions will be checked manually since trust-based assessment systems have a level of uncertainty.

The large amount of information required for the trust score computation introduces new challenges to the information systems of the institutions. First of all, we need to incorporate information as the biometric models on the learner's profile, and to store all their contributions to the subjects and interactions with the VLE. Apart of the technological challenges related to the amount of data, how to store them, and how to maintain their availability to the learners, an important aspect to take into account is the legal one. The biometric information of learners can be considered sensitive information and requires to be stored and used in accordance with data protection regulations. The same considerations are also applicable to some activities like videos and audios containing the face/voice of the learner. The legal restrictions of each country will regulate the amount of time some information can be stored in the institution's information systems, and, therefore, if it will be available the entire time the learner is enrolled in a program or the institution itself.

Another important challenge is to communicate the adoption of such systems to the learners, to the teachers, and to the society in general. The novelty of some of the used mechanisms and the implications on the learning path of the learners can promote objections and mistrust, if things are not clearly explained. In the case of the learners, it can be difficult to explain why some indicators are not giving enough confidence, and in the case of society, the reduction of face-to-face evaluations can be seen as a lower guarantee of authorship and the exigency of the academic institutions to the discredit of the degree.

Finally, there are two collateral effects of the adoption of an adaptive trust-based e-assessment system. On the one hand, the diversity of information systematically collected by the system opens the door to the use of more intensive learning analytics techniques, which can facilitate the monitoring of the evaluation process and improve the educational model. On the other hand, adding additional guarantees to the authorship of assessment activities can allow the educational model to change in many aspects, one of the most direct being that the FEs that validate the authorship of the assessment activities delivered by the learners can be modified or even removed in some cases.

8 CONCLUSIONS AND FUTURE WORK

In this chapter, we have described a trust-based adaptive assessment system where activities can be adapted based on relevant evidences collected from the instructional process of a learner. The system has been derived from a general adaptive assessment system that is totally parameterizable with any profile model to build the learner profile and any selective model to adapt the assessment activities. Additionally, a simulation has been conducted to show how a trust-based assessment system can impact positively on the selection of an assessment activity.

The development of this system opens many challenges as we described in Section 7. The fine-tuning of the selective model, the definition of the learner profile, the need for the processing of a large amount of information, the definition of the best-suited evidences, the legal and ethical issues, the definition of a data-mart for the stored data, among others, summarize the most important areas for future work that need to be taken into account in order to deploy this system in a real setting.

ACKNOWLEDGMENTS

This research was funded by the Spanish Government through the project "ICT-FLAG" Enhancing ICT education through Formative assessment, Learning Analytics and Gamification (TIN2013-45303-P).

REFERENCES

Ala-Mutka, K.M., 2005. A survey of automated assessment approaches for programming assignments. Comput. Sci. Educ. 15 (2), 83–102.

Alzahrani, S., Salim, N., Abraham, A., 2012. Understanding plagiarism linguistic patterns, textual features, and detection methods. IEEE Trans. Syst. Man Cybern. Part C Appl. Rev. 42 (2), 133–149.

Armendariz, D., MacHardy, Z., Garcia, D.D., 2014. Octal: online course tool for adaptive learning. In: Proceedings of the First ACM Conference on Learning Scale Conference, LS '14. ACM, New York, NY, pp. 141–142.

Artz, D., Gil, Y., 2007. A survey of trust in computer science and the semantic web. Web Semant. 5 (2), 58–71.

Ashman, H., Brailsford, T., Brusilovsky, P., 2009. Personal services: debating the wisdom of personalisation. In: International Conference on Web-based Learning, pp. 1–11.

Baig, M.M., 2013. Learnonline: personal learning environment implementation in University of South Australia. Int. J. Knowl. Soc. Res. 4 (2), 19–26.

Baker, F., 2001. The basics of item response theory. In: Boston, C., Runder, L. (Eds.), second ed. ERIC Clearinghouse on Assessment and Evaluation, USA.

Baneres, D., Clariso, R., Jorba, J., Serra, M., 2014. Experiences in digital circuit design courses: a self-study platform for learning support. IEEE Trans. Learn. Technol. 7 (4), 360–374.

Basheer, G.S., Ahmad, M.S., Tang, A.Y., Graf, S., 2015. Certainty, trust and evidence: towards an integrative model of confidence in multi-agent systems. Comput. Hum. Behav. 45, 307–315.

Bella, G., Giustolisi, R., Lenzini, G., 2014. Secure exams despite malicious management. In: Twelfth Annual International Conference on Privacy, Security and Trust (PST), 2014, pp. 274–281.

Bra, P.D., Aroyo, L., Cristea, A., Bra, P.D., Aroyo, L., Cristea, A., 2004. Adaptive web-based educational hypermedia. In: Levene, M., Poulovassilis, A. (Eds.), Web Dynamics. Springer, Berlin, pp. 387–410.

Brusilovsky, P., 2001. Adaptive hypermedia. User Model. User-Adap. Inter. 11 (1-2), 87–110.

Brusilovsky, P., Maybury, M., 2002. From adaptive hypermedia to the adaptive web. Commun. ACM 45 (5), 30–33.

Champaign, J., Cohen, R., 2012. Modeling trustworthiness of peer advice in a framework for presenting web objects that supports peer commentary. In: UMAP Workshops.

Chen, S.Y., Magoulas, G.D., 2005. Adaptable and Adaptive Hypermedia Systems. IGI Global, Hershey.

Chika, I., Azzi, D., Hewitt, A., Stocker, J., 2009. A holistic approach to assessing students' laboratory performance using Bayesian networks. In: IEEE Workshop on Computational Intelligence in Virtual Environments, 2009. CIVE '09, pp. 26–32.

Chin, D.N., 2001. Empirical evaluation of user models and user-adapted systems. User Model. User-Adap. Inter. 11 (1-2), 181–194.

Choraś, M., Mroczkowski, P., 2007. Recognizing individual typing patterns. In: Pattern Recognition and Image Analysis. Lecture Notes in Computer Science, vol. 4478. Springer, Berlin, Heidelberg, pp. 323–330.

Cook, J., Jenkins, V., 2010. Getting Started with e-Assessment. University of Bath, Bath.

Crisp, G.T., 2007. The e-Assessment Handbook. Continuum, London.

Flior, E., Kowalski, K., 2010. Continuous biometric user authentication in online examinations. In: Seventh International Conference on Information Technology: New Generations (ITNG), IEEE, 2010, pp. 488–492.

Fluck, A., Pullen, D., Harper, C., 2009. Case study of a computer based examination system. Aust. J. Educ. Technol. 25 (4), 509–523.

Graven, O., MacKinnon, L., 2008. A consideration of the use of plagiarism tools for automated student assessment. IEEE Trans. Educ. 51 (2), 212–219.

Green, H., Facer, K., Rudd, T., Dillon, P., Humphreys, P., 2005. Futurelab: personalisation and digital technologies. Research report, https://telearn.archives-ouvertes.fr/hal-00190337.

Guerrero, A., Minguilln, J., 2007. Adaptive learning paths for improving lifelong learning experiences. In: Proceedings of the TENCompetence Workshop on Service Oriented Approaches and Lifelong Competence Development Infrastuctures. Manchester (UK), pp. 137–143.

Guerrero-Roldan, A.-E., Rodriguez, M.-E., 2014. A learner profile analysis based on competences to improve online teaching strategies. In: IEEE Frontiers in Education Conference (FIE), 2014, pp. 1–6.

Hammond, M., Shreeve, M., Davies, C., 2008. Developing personalisation for the information environment. Technical report, JISC. http://www.jisc.ac.uk/media/documents/programmes/amtransition/dpie2_personalisation_final_report.pdf.

He, S., Kinshuk, H., Patel, A., 2002. Granular approach to adaptivity in problem-based learning environment. In: Proceedings of IEEE International Conference on Advanced Learning Technologies (ICALT), Kazan, Rusia, pp. 3–7.

Herrera-Joancomarti, J., Prieto-Blazquez, J., Castella-Roca, J., 2004. A secure electronic examination protocol using wireless networks. In: Proceedings of the International Conference on Information Technology: Coding and Computing, ITCC 2004, vol. 2, pp. 263–267.

Ihantola, P., Ahoniemi, T., Karavirta, V., Seppälä, O., 2010. Review of recent systems for automatic assessment of programming assignments. In: Proceedings of the 10th Koli Calling International Conference on Computing Education Research, pp. 86–93.

Jøsang, A., Ismail, R., Boyd, C., 2007. A survey of trust and reputation systems for online service provision. Decis. Support Syst. 43 (2), 618–644.

Kambourakis, G., Damopoulos, D., 2013. A competent post-authentication and non-repudiation biometric-based scheme for m-learning. In: Proceedings of the 10th IASTED International Conference on Web-based Education (WBE 2013). ACTA Press, Innsbruck, Austria.

Kinnunen, T., Karpov, E., Franti, P., 2006. Real-time speaker identification and verification. IEEE Trans. Audio Speech Lang. Process. 14 (1), 277–288.

Koppel, M., Schler, J., 2003. Exploiting stylistic idiosyncrasies for authorship attribution. In: In IJCAI03 Workshop on Computational Approaches to Style Analysis and Synthesis, pp. 69–72.

Levy, Y., Ramim, M., 2007. A theoretical approach for biometrics authentication of e-exams. In: Chais Conference on Instructional Technologies Research. The Open University of Israel, Raanana, Israel, pp. 93–101.

Liu, Y., Chen, D., Sun, J., 2011. A trustworthy e-learning based on trust and quality evaluation. In: International Conference on E-Business and E-Government (ICEE), 2011, pp. 1–4.

Lu, Y.-C., Yang, Y.-S., Chang, P.-C., Yang, C.-S., 2013. The design and implementation of intelligent assessment management system. In: IEEE Global Engineering Education Conference (EDUCON), 2013, pp. 451–457.

Lukarov, V., Chatti, M.A., Ths, H., Kia, F.S., Muslim, A., Greven, C., Schroeder, U., 2014. Data models in learning analytics. In: Proceedings of DeLFI Workshops 2014, pp. 88–95.

Mampadi, F., Chen, S.Y., Ghinea, G., Chen, M.-P., 2011. Design of adaptive hypermedia learning systems: a cognitive style approach. Comput. Educ. 56 (4), 1003–1011.

Maqsood, R., Durrani, Q.S., 2011. Itsas: an approach towards adaptive student assessment. In: IEEE 3rd International Conference on Communication Software and Networks (ICCSN), IEEE, 2011, pp. 649–654.

Marinagi, C., Kaburlasos, V., Tsoukalas, V., 2007. An architecture for an adaptive assessment tool. In: Frontiers in Education Conference—Global Engineering: Knowledge Without Borders, Opportunities Without Passports, 2007. FIE '07. 37th Annual, pp. T3D-11–T3D-16.

Modiri, N., Farahi, A., Ketabi, S., 2011. Providing security framework for holding electronic examinations in virtual universities. In: Seventh International Conference on Networked Computing and Advanced Information Management (NCM), 2011, pp. 73–79.

Monaco, J., Bakelman, N., Cha, S.-H., Tappert, C., 2013. Recent advances in the development of a long-text-input keystroke biometric authentication system for arbitrary text input. In: European Intelligence and Security Informatics Conference (EISIC), 2013, pp. 60–66.

Nacheva-Skopalik, L., Green, S., 2012. Adaptable personal e-assessment. Int. J. Web-Based Learn. Teach. Technol. 29–39.

Nebot, A., Mugica, F., Castro, F., 2010. Fuzzy predictive models to help teachers in e-learning courses. In: The 2010 International Joint Conference on Neural Networks (IJCNN), pp. 1–7.

Neila, R., Rabai, L.B.A., 2014. Deploying suitable countermeasures to solve the security problems within an e-learning environment. In: Proceedings of the 7th International Conference on Security of Information and Networks, SIN '14, pp. 33:33–33:38.

Quarati, A., 2003. Designing shareable and personalisable e-learning paths. In: Proceedings of the International Conference on Information Technology: Computers and Communications (ITCC'03). IEEE Computer Society, pp. 454–460.

Rajamani, K., Kathiravan, V., 2013. An adaptive assessment system to compose serial test sheets using item response theory. In: International Conference on Pattern Recognition, Informatics and Mobile Engineering (PRIME), 2013, pp. 120–124.

Ramandalahy, T., Vidal, P., Broisin, J., 2009. Opening learner profiles across heterogeneous applications. In: Ninth IEEE International Conference on Advanced Learning Technologies, ICALT 2009, pp. 504–508.

Riecken, D., 2000. Introduction: personalized views of personalization. Commun. ACM 43 (8), 26–28.

Simon, C.B., Sheard, J., Carbone, A., Johnson, C., 2013. Academic integrity: differences between computing assessments and essays. In: Proceedings of the Koli Calling Int. Conf. on Computing Education Research, pp. 23–32.

Smith, N., Ferguson, N., SebSchomoller, 2006. Personalization in presentation services—a follow-up report for the JISC. Technical report, JISC. http://www.therightplace.net/jp/.

Stamatatos, E., 2009. A survey of modern authorship attribution methods. J. Am. Soc. Inf. Sci. Technol. 60 (3), 538–556.

Stathacopoulou, R., Magoulas, G., Grigoriadou, M., 1999. Neural network-based fuzzy modeling of the student in intelligent tutoring systems. In: International Joint Conference on Neural Networks, 1999. IJCNN '99, vol. 5pp. 3517–3521.

Sumithra, M., Devika, A., 2012. A study on feature extraction techniques for text independent speaker identification. In: International Conference on Computer Communication and Informatics (ICCCI), pp. 1–5.

Tsolis, D., Christia, P., Kampana, S., Polychronopoulos, E., Liopa, A., Tsakalidis, A., 2012. Owlearn: an open source e-learning platform supporting adaptivity and personalization. Int. Dec. Tech. 6 (2), 97–104.

Ueno, M., 2001. Student models construction by using information criteria. In: Proceedings IEEE International Conference on Advanced Learning Technologies, 2001, pp. 331–334.

Uz, T., Bebis, G., Erol, A., Prabhakar, S., 2009. Minutiae-based template synthesis and matching for fingerprint authentication. Comput. Vis. Image Underst. 113 (9), 979–992.

Vega, Y.L.P., Nieto, G.M.F., Bolanos, J.C.G., Baldiris, S.M., 2012. Application of item response theory (IRT) for the generation of adaptive assessments in an introductory course on object-oriented programming. In: Proceedings of the 2012 IEEE Frontiers in Education Conference (FIE), FIE '12. IEEE Computer Society, Washington, DC, pp. 1–4.

Wagner, A., Wright, J., Ganesh, A., Zhou, Z., Mobahi, H., Ma, Y., 2012. Toward a practical face recognition system: Robust alignment and illumination by sparse representation. IEEE Trans. Pattern Anal. Mach. Intell. 34 (2), 372–386.

Wang, F.-H., 2004. A fuzzy neural network for item sequencing in personalized cognitive scaffolding with adaptive formative assessment. Expert Syst. Appl. 27 (1), 11–25.

Wechsler, H., Phillips, J.P., Bruce, V., Soulie, F.F., Huang, T.S., 2012. Face Recognition: From Theory to Applications, vol. 163. Springer Science & Business Media, Berlin.

Weippl, E., 2005. Security in e-Learning. Advances in Information Security, vol. 16. Springer, Berlin.

Yaghmaie, M., Bahreininejad, A., 2011. A context-aware adaptive learning system using agents. Expert Syst. Appl. 38 (4), 3280–3286.

Zhao, W., Chellappa, R., Phillips, P.J., Rosenfeld, A., 2003. Face recognition: a literature survey. ACM Comput. Surv. 35 (4), 399–458.

e-ASSESSMENT FOR SKILL ACQUISITION IN ONLINE ENGINEERING EDUCATION: CHALLENGES AND OPPORTUNITIES

E. Hettiarachchi*, I. Balasooriya[†], E. Mor[†], M.A. Huertas[†]

University of Colombo School of Computing, Colombo, Sri Lanka[*] Universitat Oberta de Catalunya, Barcelona, Spain[†]

1 INTRODUCTION

E-learning is at the nexus point of the convergence of pedagogical and technological innovations. It is aimed at creating a community of inquiry independent of time and location through the use of information and communication technologies (Garrison, 2011). Courses where at least 80% of the content is delivered online is defined as an online course (Allen and Seaman, 2013) and with the rapid increase of online courses, the advancement of technology can offer a significant contribution to the assessment process through the introduction of e-assessment. Improving the quality of the student's learning experience and practical problem-solving skills are key issues in online higher education in engineering, and this is an area where it has been widely recognized that e-assessment can contribute (Dermo, 2009).

Assessment is defined as the measurement of the learner's achievement and progress in the learning process (Keeves, 1994; Reeves and Hedberg, 2009). It is perhaps the best way of identifying the support needed by learners (Gikandi et al., 2011). According to Bransford et al. (2000), assessment is a core component for effective learning and, therefore, the teaching and learning process needs to be assessment-centered to provide learners with opportunities to demonstrate their developing abilities and receive support to enhance their learning.

Crisp (2009) divides assessment into two broad areas: skill assessment and knowledge assessment. According to Gibbs and Simpson (2004), a skill can be classified as a practiced ability, expertise, or technique. The assessments for higher-order cognitive skills are time consuming to set and mark; skill assessment provides an easy and authentic approach (McAlpine, 2002). Higher-order cognitive skills are typically required to solve the exercises encountered in natural sciences, including engineering, computer science, and mathematics. These exercises rely on students being able to think in a structured way and to acquire skills in modeling (eg, of information flows, business processes, mathematical proofs, and medical diagnosis). Therefore, skill acquisition is a major part of engineering education in general. Research indicates that practice is the key to acquiring the skills that will lead to expertise in engineering education (Litzinger et al., 2011; Ambrose et al., 2010). This practice is also twofold:

Formative Assessment, Learning Data Analytics and Gamification. http://dx.doi.org/10.1016/B978-0-12-803637-2.00003-8

practice that develops "component skills" (personal skills) and practice that develops skills to address complex, realistic, and challenging tasks (Ambrose et al., 2010).

On the other hand, knowledge is defined as the remembering of previously learned material (Bloom, 1956). Majchrzak and Usener (2011, 2012) state that knowledge represents the lowest level of learning outcomes in the cognitive domain and, therefore, exercises that require knowledge to be memorized only account for a fraction of the overall examinations, particularly in computer science education. Knowledge assessment mostly uses simple forms of questions such as multiple choice questions (MCQ), multiple responses, short answers, filling in the blanks, matching, and crossword puzzles. They are generally easier to grade both by automatic and human means. This type of assessment can be delivered quickly, has a better chance at specific and directed feedback for students and can provide greater coverage in the curriculum (McAlpine, 2002). Atman et al. (2010) characterize the significant learning experience of the engineering student as integrating diverse knowledge and applying that knowledge and skills to real-world problems.

With the rising trend of e-learning, Allen and Seaman (2013) report that the number of students taking at least one online course increased by over 570,000 to a total of 6.7 million in the United States. They also report that 77% of academic leaders responded that online education is "as good as or better" than traditional face-to-face instruction. With significant increases of such statistics on online learning, online engineering education also takes a place of high importance. Therefore, in the online environment for engineering education, the principles of practice need to be modeled with an awareness of this importance. It is the course designer's or the instructor's responsibility to be mindful of this (Litzinger et al., 2011).

This chapter intends to capture the applicability of skill acquisition in online engineering education and discuss the existing challenges to address and opportunities to make the most of. For this purpose the main themes related to the topic, e-assessment and formative assessment, a state-of-the-art review of the literature and current different e-learning models, systems and tools that facilitate online engineering education and skill acquisition are outlined and then the challenges and opportunities are discussed.

2 e-ASSESSMENT

e-assessment, which is also known as online assessment, is the continuous electronic assessment process where information and communication technology is used for the presentation of assessment activity, and the recording of responses. This includes the end-to-end assessment process from the perspective of learners, tutors, learning institutions; awarding bodies and regulators; and the general public (Cook and Jenkins, 2010; Daly et al., 2010; JISC, 2007).

Crisp (2007) categorizes e-assessment as diagnostic, summative, and formative based on the learning stage at which the assessment is carried out. Diagnostic assessment is used as a test to evaluate the current level of knowledge of a student prior to taking a course, so that the learning activities match the student requirements. Formative assessments are continuous assessments where the student is tested for the purpose of keeping track of the learning curve and improvement of understanding of the course. Summative assessment is the final assessment after a course has been completed, which serves as a summing up assessment to grade the students, judge student skill development, and award certification (Crisp, 2007; Hettiarachchi and Huertas, 2012).

Ridgway et al. (2004) further distinguish between formative and summative assessment on multiple levels where the consequences of summative assessment are comparatively higher for the student and its value extends outside the classroom because of the certification value. Meanwhile the student may be an unwilling participant in the summative assessment process, the formative is used as a betterment process. They state that "formative assessment simply isn't formative assessment unless the student does something with it to improve performance." They also observe that formative assessment uses a variety of tools to achieve its purposes. The growing amount of research indicates that well designed and well deployed diagnostic and formative assessments can foster more effective learning to diverse learners (Nicol, 2006; Sharpe et al., 2006). Cook and Jenkins (2010) list the advantages of e-assessment in their study, where instant feedback, objectivity in marking, and a wide array of tasks and activities are highlighted among others.

Aside from the advantages, Whitelock and Brasher (2006) raise the questions of plagiarism detection, invigilation issues, accessibility issues, user identity, and reliability and validity of critical and high stakes assessments with regard to e-assessments. However, they mention that the principal barriers for the development of institution-wide e-assessment in any subject are the academic staff's time and training. There are also problems associated with the e-assessment software such as, interoperability with existing systems, scalability, performance, security and the limitations faced in upgrades, support and maintenance (Bull and Mckenna, 2004). e-assessment strongly depends on technological systems and tools. Many of these tools are mainly based on MCQ, true/false, short answer, and fill in the blanks questions. This is a common problem associated with e-assessment (Marriott, 2009; Pachler et al., 2010) because these types of tools and questions are used to test knowledge at the lower levels of Bloom's taxonomy (Bloom, 1956), addressing knowledge, comprehension and application. There is a need to introduce questions and tools which can be used to measure the skill level of the students (Gruttmann et al., 2008).

3 FORMATIVE e-ASSESSMENT

Formative e-assessment is essentially about improving student learning. A wide set of perspectives on the nature, structure, and value of formative e-assessment can be found in the literature. Formative e-assessment activities and tasks should be offered with timely and appropriate feedback; these tasks are primarily intended to have an impact on the current learning of students and most often use feedback to connect the formative task to potential improvements in student performance in subsequent summative tasks (Crisp, 2011). At the end, formative e-assessment can be considered as a means of promoting self-reflection and students taking control of their own learning (Whitelock, 2007).

Formative assessment is an essential aspect of classroom work and its development can raise standards of achievement (Black, 2002). However, its development should take into account significant aspects. Maughan et al. (2001) question the perception of formative assessment as a series of summative assessments, and argue for an emphasis on feedback in the learning process. With formative assessment in place, students learn more and become self-aware, self-regulated learners. They become capable of drawing evidence from their own learning and taking strategies to success. It makes the students more autonomous, confident and capable (Moss and Brookhart, 2009).

Black and Wiliam (2009) outline five key strategies of the formative assessment process that involve the three agents: teacher, learner, and peer. Although perceived from those three ends, they all add up to the progression of the learner and the learning process. The five key strategies can be noted as:

- engineering effective classroom discussion, questions, and learning tasks that elicit evidence of learning;
- providing feedback that moves learners forward;
- clarifying and sharing learning intentions and criteria for success;
- activating students as owners of their own learning; and
- activating students as instructional resources for one another.

While formative assessment may have significant effects on all students, Black (2002) identifies that it may have a much better outcome for the low-achievers and raise the overall level of a group. Continuous formative assessments, therefore, will be an important practice, since the low-achievers get an opportunity to act on the feedback (Sadler, 2013). Various authors (de Bruyn et al., 2011; Bull and Mckenna, 2004) emphasize the importance of timely and constructive feedback that will motivate students to learn more effectively.

The five strategies put forth by Black and Wiliam (2009) above resonates with other authors who state that the feedback received from the assessment is an opportunity for student reflection. The increased frequency of assessment would, therefore, improve student motivation (Oliver, 1988; Gibbs and Simpson, 2004). Kuh (2003) and Sadler (1989) also concur that the more students receive feedback, the more they tend to learn and be engaged.

4 e-ASSESSMENT MODELS, SYSTEMS, AND TOOLS

In this section, the most significant e-assessment models, systems, and tools currently used in higher education are discussed. In reference to e-assessment models, it is important to determine whether particular forms of assessment have a common framework or structure. Accordingly, it is essential to find the common underlying features of assessment types and the relationship between assessment components, scoring, and feedback mechanisms (Crisp, 2009). Considering this, models such as four-process architecture for assessment (Almond et al., 2002), Framework Reference Model for Assessment (FREMA) (Wills et al., 2007), Abstract Framework for Assessment (AFA) (AL-Smadi et al., 2009), Joint Information Systems Committee (2007), and an integrated model for designing computer-based assessments (Kuo and Wu, 2013) are analyzed.

Almond et al. (2002) proposes a four-process architecture model that should apply to any assessment, which includes activity selection, presentation, response processing, and summary scoring. In this model, both task level feedback and summary feedback are emphasized as they are important for improving students' learning processes. The model takes on the challenge of taking any form of assessment and breaking it down as a modular process, simplifying complex tasks with a clear view of the relationships between design framework and operational processes.

FREMA is a visual framework proposed by the University of Southampton for categorizing and organizing the entities and activities associated with assessment in e-learning. It represents an intensive guide for resources, standards, projects, people, organizations, software, services, and use cases in the assessment domain. The FREMA structure is based on concept maps describing the ontology that has been used to model the assessment domain (Wills et al., 2007).

AFA, proposed by AL-Smadi et al. (2009), takes a service-oriented approach with the ability to support standards and specifications. Service-oriented architectures allow the design and development of modular and flexible systems, where components can be added, replaced, or removed. Even new systems can be composed of a collection of suitable services. The service-oriented approach helps e-assessment systems to easily share and exchange content. Tests, items, marks, and student information can be implemented as services to be used by other services or systems.

Joint Information Systems Committee (2007) has also proposed a model with respect to e-assessment and effective learning. To provide effective progress for the learner, learning and e-assessment has to be integrated. According to this model, learning modules are provided either as e-learning or blended-learning through a learning management system. After completion of the learning module, students are provided with assessments either as formative or summative depending on the course. After completion of the assessment, if they have successfully completed it, they will be provided with feedback or the final qualification. If they are not successful in the assessment, they will also be given a constructive feedback and a revision module, which they can practice, and take the assessment at a later stage.

By considering computer-based assessments as integrated systems consisting of interrelated components, Bennett and Bejar (1998) introduce an integrated model for designing them. This model considers the interrelatedness of components such as assessment purpose, construct of interest, test and task design, examinee interface, and scoring procedure, taking into account the potential advantages offered by technology applications. In this model, assessment purpose and construct of interest are two central components. They serve as the driving forces affecting other linked parts through the test and task design component. According to Kuo and Wu (2013), the main four categories in the test and task design component are item presentations, response formats, adaptively individualized test activities, and curriculum-embedded assessments, because technology applications have been assumed to bring benefits in these categories. In this model, five more components such as Test Development Tool, Examinee Interface, Tutorial, Scoring, and Reporting Module are closely related to the central components. However, according to Kuo and Wu (2013), the information on the components of Test Development Tool, Tutorial, and Reporting Method was usually not available in the studies of computer-based assessments and was difficult to obtain, therefore it was not possible to derive any conclusions about the interplay between these components and others.

4.1 e-ASSESSMENT SYSTEMS

In e-assessment, as in e-learning, sharing and reutilization of learning resources as well as communicating with other systems has become a challenge. Several standards and specifications have been defined in order to build appropriate systems, components, and tools. With regard to building high-quality e-assessment systems, a set of elements and requirements have been identified. The central requirement is conforming to accepted standards while designing and implementing systems. Standards help to ensure the qualities such as interoperability, reusability, manageability, accessibility, and durability in e-learning and e-assessment systems (AL-Smadi et al., 2009). Considering this, standards and specification such as LOM (Learning Object Metadata), SCORM (Sharable Content Object Reference Model), IMS QTI (Question and Test Interoperability), IEEE PAPI (Public and Private Information),

IMS LIP (Learner Information Package), IMS LTI (Learning Tools Interoperability), and O.K.I (Open Knowledge Initiative) are recommended for e-assessment systems.

The IEEE standard LOM is a collection of XML data elements that describe a learning object. The goal is to simplify the discovery, management, and exchange of learning objects (Mohan and Brooks, 2003). A major feature of IEEE-LOM is its flexibility; to add new data elements and extend as required. This has encouraged developers to use the IEEE-LOM as a base standard (Al-Khalifa and Davis, 2006).

SCORM is a collection of standards and specifications designed by ADL (Advanced Distributed Learning initiative, http://www.adlnet.org). SCORM defines how content may be packaged into a transferable ZIP file called "Package Interchange Format." Easy portability of learning content between learning management systems and the reusability of learning objects are among the fundamental objectives of the SCORM (Bohl et al., 2002).

IMS QTI is a standard of sharing test and assessment data (Bacon, 2003), and it describes the data structures that are used to provide interoperability between question and test systems (Smythe and Roberts, 2000). It is intended for users who wish to import or export test questions, both simple and complex. The last available version (IMS QTI 2.0) implements a variety of item types: multiple choice, ordering, association (1:1), union (1: N), fill in the blanks, essays, hotspots, object positioning, and painting (Sanz-Santamaría et al., 2006). The usage of XML for coding the items and tests allows the visualization of items or tests on different devices like desktops, laptops, and mobile devices, which could be very useful in expanding the functionality of an e-learning system (IMS GLC, 2013).

IEEE PAPI was introduced by IEEE for the task of learner modeling. It is a specification devoted to supporting the exchange of learner data between different systems. It specifies both the syntax and semantics of a "Learner Model," which characterize a learner and his or her knowledge or abilities during studies with performance, portfolio, and certificate as its main indicators (Devedžić et al., 2007). According to Vassileva et al. (2003), the PAPI standard ranges from intelligent tutoring systems (ITS), where performance information is considered vital and the importance of interpersonal relationships is also emphasized.

IMS LIP is a specification defined by IMS GLC. "Learner Information" is a collection of pieces of information about a learner (individual or group learners) or a producer of learning content (creators, providers, or vendors). The IMS LIP specification enables the recording and managing of the learner's characteristics (Devedžić et al., 2007) and the interoperability of internet-based learner information systems with other systems that support the virtual learning environment (IMS GLC, 2013). It includes several rich structures for representing data about a user, such as identification, demographics, and goals, which are not necessarily learning related (Abel et al., 2009).

IMS LTI is a specification defined by the IMS GLC (2013) to establish a standard way of integrating rich learning applications, which are often remotely hosted and provided through third-party services, with learning management systems, portals, or other educational environments. IMS LTI provides simple and standardized links between tools and systems, which allows a seamless learning experience for students (IMS GLC, 2013).

OKI is an open and extensible architecture that provides detailed specifications on component interfaces and how they communicate with each other in a learning management environment (Da Bormida et al., 2004). It heavily considers interoperability, which allows the components to be developed and updated independently of each other (MIT, 2003). At the core of OKI are Java-based

Application Programming Interfaces (API) for use in Java-based systems and also as models for other object-oriented and service-based implementations.

These standards help achieve the seamless communication between different systems, security, and interoperability. The above-detailed standards are especially used to integrate different systems, such as LMS and e-assessment systems.

EASy (The e-Assessment System) is a tool developed by University of Münster, Germany for assessing higher-order cognitive skills in an online environment for general mathematical proofs (Gruttmann et al., 2008; Majchrzak and Usener, 2011, 2012). This tool was developed specifically for skill assessment rather than knowledge assessment and it does not support e-tutoring with feedback facility. The code of the *EASy* tool was not available and, therefore, it was not possible to customize and adapt it to other contexts. The developers of the tool were not able to check whether the tool could be replicated at other universities and whether it could be applied to other courses as well.

ACME is another web-based e-learning tool developed by the University of Girona targeted towards formative assessment, improving the teaching and learning of mathematics studies in Industrial Engineering and Engineering (Soler et al., 2002; Prados et al., 2011). According to Soler et al. (2002), the system can be adapted to subjects other than mathematics, but is not an open-source tool.

TRAKLA2, developed using Java by the Department of Computer Science and Engineering in Helsinki University of Technology, is an environment for learning data structures and algorithms using simulations. These simulation exercises can be automatically graded (Amelung et al., 2011; Trakla2 Software Project, 2009).

Amelung et al. (2011) also survey multiple tools available in online assessment for engineering and computer science areas. Among them, *Scheme-robo* provides automatic grading for programming assignments in Scheme (Saikkonen et al., 2001), *AutoGrader* designed by Miami University automatically identifies errors in Java program code and recommends corrections (Helmick, 2007), and *JACK* automatically grades and generates feedback for Java exercises (Goedicke et al., 2008). Other systems like *TuringsCraft CodeLab3* (for Java, C/C++, and Python programs) and Addison Wesley's *MyCodeMate* (Java and C/C++) support multiple programming languages. Project *Praktomat* from the University Passau (Zeller, 2000) allows submission, auto testing, and peer reviews of programming assignments.

WeBWorK is a free open-source web-based formative assessment system to generate, deliver, and automatically grade mathematics problems. Gotel and Scharff (2007) discuss adapting *WeBWorK* to grade fundamental programming problems as it is capable of assessing free-form program segments written in Java. The *DUESIE* system checks the coding style and functionality of students' program code (Usener et al., 2012). The *Autotool* system (Rahn and Waldmann, 2002) from the University of Leipzig takes on assignments in theoretical computer science and supports the assessment of grammar, regular expressions, automata, or graph properties.

Triantafillou et al. (2008) presents a mobile-device-based testing system for high school physics students in Greece, and their findings reveal that it is an effective and efficient assessment tool and that it can be scaled to other laboratory-based subjects such as chemistry. However, they also note that the timeliness of feedback could be improved as well as its accessibility.

Adesina et al. (2014) designed a gesture-based arithmetic problem-solving tool for elementary mathematics in their study. While they found no significant performance scores compared to traditional paper-pencil methods, they found that using the computer-aided tool they can more accurately assess students' understanding of mathematical concepts, and provide rich feedback while motivating students with interactive tasks.

There are more tools available for e-assessment in online education. Among some of the well-known are:

- SCHOLAR (Heriot-Watt University, 2014)
- ExamOnline (Intelligent Assessment Technologies Limited, 2014)
- Moodle Quizzes (Moodle, 2015)
- Moodle Assignments (Moodle, 2015)
- Turnitin (IParadigms, LLC, 2015)
- Hot Potatoes (Hot Potatoes, 2013)
- Maple T.A. (www.maplesoft.com/products/mapleta)
- Interact (www.tryinteract.com)
- Learningpod (www.learningpod.com)
- ExamTime (www.examtime.com/quiz-maker)
- Socrative (www.socrative.com)
- ProProfs (www.proprofs.com)
- QuestionPro (www.questionpro.com/tour/sample-questions.html).

Although there is a large sample of tools used for online engineering education, they are often not e-assessment tools. While many of them can be categorized as tools for learning or an ITS, only a few can be categorized as e-assessment systems. There are important differences between learning tools and e-assessment systems. In this regard, the aim of a learning tool or ITS is to provide customized support and feedback to students, usually simulating the presence of an e-tutor or learning-assistant (Huertas, 2011) and monitoring each step of a learning activity executed by students, while providing information about errors and advice. However, the primary objective of an e-assessment system is monitoring student progress through the learning process and, thus, it has to allow the performing of assessments using different kind of questions, immediate feedback, automatic marking, weighted-average grade calculation, personalization of quizzes, and statistical analysis among its characteristics, while promoting adaptive learning, and reducing the risk for cheating by randomizing questions along with the use of timers (Bull and Mckenna, 2004; Sitthiworachart et al., 2008; Tselonis and Sargeant, 2007).

5 CHALLENGES AND OPPORTUNITIES IN ONLINE ENGINEERING EDUCATION

As already mentioned, e-assessment offers a number of benefits to aid in the improvement of the learning process of students on the one hand, and to reduce the workload of teachers and administrators on the other. Among the main benefits, e-assessment activities can be delivered without the time or space restrictions of the paper-based and face-to-face examinations, immediate feedback makes a real formative assessment possible and plays a fundamental role in skill e-assessment, and the time saved for instructors by removing marking can be used in more productive ways, for example in a personalized monitoring of students.

5.1 SKILL ACQUISITION

Engineering is a field of study that encompasses the fundamental principles, methods, and modern tools for the design and implementation of systems. For example, computer engineering builds upon fundamental courses in mathematics, science, and the engineering disciplines to achieve a sound knowledge foundation and to develop breadth. Knowledge assessment in students of engineering and computer science too plays an important role in the learning process (Mihajlović and Čupić, 2012). Furthermore, according to Mihajlović and Čupić (2012), the teachers' goals are to enrich students' knowledge, improve students' ability to reason and nurture students' creativity. Therefore, not only knowledge, but also skill assessment is important for subjects in computer engineering and engineering in general.

Online learning environments should provide authentic problem-solving tasks and such tasks should foster the transfer of skills into real-world problems, application of knowledge and practical skill demonstration (Litzinger et al., 2011; McLoughlin and Luca, 2002). This can be seen as a direct application for engineering knowledge and skills, where students will have to apply their knowledge in practical terms. Many educators defend the idea that the goal of formal education is to teach self-regulatory skills to students (Boekaerts, 1997). Some of the programming and mathematics assessment tools presented in the earlier section have the capabilities of repeated submissions, self-assessment by trial and error which help nurture this idea. Schunk and Ertmer (1999) state that in learning computer-related skills, self-evaluations are beneficial. However, not all of the systems offer the functionality or the design for skill acquisition primarily. It can be seen that in many cases knowledge assessment has influenced e-assessment rather than skill acquisition.

The subject of Logic can be taken as a representative of many subjects in computer engineering because it requires a higher-level of skill acquisition. e-Assessment tools that can be used for a subject like Logic are usually assessment tools for mathematics that go beyond the MCQ paradigm, but are not specific for Logic; for example, *EASy* (Kuchen et al., 2009), *AiM* (Strickland, 2002), *OpenMark* (The Open University, 2013), or *ACME* (Prados et al., 2011). The problem is that they do not offer real skill assessment questions for all the different logic concepts, but for very general ones and in a simple way (mainly MCQs). On the other hand, when using specific learning tools or ITS for Logic, such as, for example, Pandora (Imperial College London, 2013), Organon (Dostalova and Lang, 2007), and AELL (Huertas, 2011), the problem is that they do not offer proper e-assessment activities. Thus, it was not possible to find a general e-assessment tool for skill acquisition in the Logic subject. In response, Hettiarachchi (2013) employed a first year Logic course of a computer science degree in the fully online university, Universitat Oberta de Catalunya (UOC) in Barcelona, Spain, to develop a technology enhanced assessment system (TEA) that integrated the practice-based skill acquisition as well as the skill assessment. Apart from Logic practices, it was equipped with a progress bar, competencies module, and gradebook with outcomes facilities and statistics, and it allowed improvements on students' learning process based on skills as well as to increase student engagement in the Logic subject.

5.2 FEEDBACK

Most of the previously presented systems and tools offer only simple types of questions, such as MCQ, true/false, short answer, and fill in the blanks questions (Marriott, 2009; Pachler et al., 2010) and this is common among the available e-assessment systems. But cognitive skills cannot be assessed via MCQ tests and equivalent forms of basic assessment items (Gruttmann et al., 2008). In order to provide rich feedback they need to go beyond simple types of questions (Millard et al., 2005) and provide more complex kinds of assessment activities, especially when it comes to providing formative e-assessment in engineering education. Practice through adequate feedback that helps students to improve their learning process is also very important (Sadler, 2013), and technology can add value to this aspect, while representing a major opportunity. There is a considerable potential for multimedia technologies to offer richer and more personal feedback. Also, the development of intelligent online tools that can support formative assessment may provide a qualitative leap in the use.

5.3 FORMATIVE SKILL ASSESSMENT

As a summary, e-assessment practices provide opportunities such as: more authenticity in assessment activities; improvement of student engagement through interactive formative assessments with adaptive feedback; choice in the timing and location of assessments; capture of wider skills and attributes not easily assessed by other means (eg, through simulations and interactive games); efficient and consistent marking; automatic and on-time analytics for data; immediate feedback; innovative use of creative media and online peer and self-assessment; and accurate, timely and accessible evidence on the effectiveness of curriculum design and delivery (JISC, 2010; Pachler et al., 2010). Thus, technology offers the potential for enhancing assessment and feedback in online higher education.

A research project carried out at the University of Bradford focused on measuring the impact of topic-based feedback in formative assessments. They selected two subjects, such as engineering and clinical sciences and for both subjects they had posed the questions in the style of MCQ, yes/no, short answers, and fill in the blanks (Dermo and Carpenter, 2011). For this project the main question was "Can MCQs/EMQs deliver quality feedback to enhance learning?" The impact of formative assessment was investigated by: measuring the total number of attempts per students, quantitative analysis of student progress in summative assessment, comparing with data from previous studies, analysis of student access patterns, evaluating student attitudes, and obtaining data on student use of the formative over the course of the semester through questionnaires and by comparing with tutor-delivered feedback. This can be taken as an example of where the "usual type" of questions, such as MCQ, yes/no, short answers, and fill in the blanks, were used for knowledge assessment. From the questionnaires, they had understood that students mainly used formative assessments as part of the learning process, as mock examinations and as for evaluating revisions. As a result they found that students valued feedback-rich formative e-assessments. Students had also indicated that their learning was benefited through engagement with online feedback and it was important not to carry-out over-assessment (Dermo and Carpenter, 2011).

Another example where students had used Moodle quizzes for formative e-assessment is a project subsidized by the Institute of Education Sciences at the Universitat Politecnica de Catalunya (Blanco Abellan and Ginovart Gisbert, 2012). The main aim of this project was to design and implement a number of Moodle quizzes for the formative e-assessment of students enrolled in mathematics courses for engineering bachelor's degrees. Subsequently, the reliability of the quizzes as assessment tools was analyzed to ensure the quality of the e-assessment system proposed. First of all, their fundamental idea was to evaluate the consistency of the e-assessment system used to align with that of the traditional assessment tools used. The correlation between scores in the quizzes and the final mark of each subject over 2 years showed that Moodle quizzes could be regarded as a suitable tool to inform students of their performance throughout the learning process. In addition, the particular use of the quizzes as low-stakes assessment activities for checking a particular chapter had contributed to the promotion of student self-regulation and regular work throughout the year. Therefore, through this research it was possible to obtain evidence that Moodle quizzes represented a consistent alternative to open-ended tests in terms of continuous and formative assessment. In order to meet the requirements of formative assessment, the e-assessment system had to supply tools for the lecturers to adapt an activity to the learners' needs, thus improving its reliability from the feedback obtained. The item analysis provided by Moodle's quiz module had turned out to be an interesting psychometric tool to estimate, refine, and improve the reliability of quiz questions. The fact that the students' ratings of the Moodle quizzes were very positive reinforced the idea that activities of this kind were suitable for mathematics teaching and learning, and that this Moodle system could be extrapolated naturally to other courses as well. According to this research, it can be stated that Moodle quizzes are a consistent and reliable tool for formative knowledge e-assessment.

Dopper and Sjoer (2004) reveal in their study how using self-test quizzes as a strategy for self-assessment for engineering students provided opportunities for self-monitoring, revision, and scaffolding learning. However, based on an experiment with the instructors, Niles (2007) stated that the faculty members may need extensive professional development training to successfully conduct online and blended formative assessment. This corresponds to Litzinger et al.'s (2011) observation of the instructors' responsibility towards creating the effective learning practice for engineering students.

In computer science and engineering courses it can be seen that ITS types of tools can offer opportunities for skill acquisition, but unfortunately these tools do not support most of the required e-assessment characteristics. This is a typical situation when looking for e-assessment systems aimed at higher-level cognitive subjects in engineering: general e-assessment systems have no appropriate questions for the specific subject, and ITS tools usually developed for a specific subject and not according to e-assessment standards and specifications, underperform as an e-assessment system. Since cognitive skills and application of methods cannot be best assessed via forms of basic assessment, the majority of existing e-assessment systems are inappropriate for use in mathematics and similar subjects in engineering education.

6 CONCLUSIONS

This chapter presented a literature review of the research on e-assessment of skill acquisition with a focus on engineering education. Aligned with this, skill and knowledge assessment, e-assessment, tools, standards, specifications, models, and approaches, challenges and opportunities for skill acquisition and assessment were discussed. According to the literature reviewed, most of the systems and tools fall under the knowledge assessment category rather than skill assessment. Even in situations where they are aimed at skill assessment, the questions are simple in structure, such as MCQs, multiple responses, short answers, fill in the blanks, matching, and crossword puzzles, etc. Cognitive skills and application of methods cannot be assessed using such basic assessment techniques. Skill acquisition in particular is heavily reliant on self-assessment and trial and error. Furthermore, assessment using authentic problem solving is required for fostering real-world problem-solving skills. From the findings of the survey, the best candidates of skill acquisition and assessment fall into the category of ITS, whereas other e-assessment tools were not fully equipped for the purpose of skill assessment. Although there are some general-purpose frameworks for e-assessment, there are no obvious general systems and tools, which support both skill and knowledge assessment. At the same time, these tools depend on a particular subject, therefore, it is not easy to apply or adapt them to another context.

REFERENCES

Abel, F., Heckmann, D., Herder, E., Hidders, J., Houben, G. J., Leonardi, E., van der Sluijs, K., 2009. Definition of an Appropriate User Profile Format. Technical report, Grapple Project, EU FP7, Reference 215434.

Adesina, A., Stone, R., Batmaz, F., Jones, I., 2014. Touch arithmetic: a process-based computer-aided assessment approach for capture of problem solving steps in the context of elementary mathematics. Comput. Educ. 78, 333–343.

Al-Khalifa, H.S., Davis, H.C., 2006. The evolution of metadata from standards to semantics in E-learning applications. In: Proceedings of the seventeenth conference on Hypertext and hypermedia. ACM, New York, pp. 69–72.

Allen, I.E., Seaman, J., 2013. Changing Course: Ten Years of Tracking Online Education in the United States. Sloan Consortium, Newburyport, MA.

Almond, R.G., Steinberg, L.S., Mislevy, R.J., 2002. Enhancing the design and delivery of assessment systems: a four-process architecture. J. Technol. Learn. Assess. (JTLA) 1 (5), 4–64.

AL-Smadi, M., Gütl, C., Helic, D., 2009. Towards a standardized e-assessment system: motivations, challenges and first findings. Int. J. Emerg. Technol. Learn. 4 (2), 6–12.

Ambrose, S.A., Bridges, M.W., DiPietro, M., Lovett, M.C., Norman, M.K., 2010. How Learning Works: Seven Research-Based Principles for Smart Teaching. John Wiley and Sons, Hoboken, NJ.

Amelung, M., Krieger, K., Rosner, D., 2011. E-assessment as a service. IEEE Trans. Learn. Technol. 4 (2), 162–174.

Atman, C. J., Sheppard, S. D., Turns, J., Adams, R. S., Fleming, L. N., Stevens, R., Lund, D., 2010. Enabling Engineering Student Success. The final report for the Center for the Advancement of Engineering Education. Morgan & Claypool Publishers, San Rafael, CA.

Bacon, D., 2003. IMS question and test interoperability. MSOR Connections 3 (3), 44–45.

Bennett, R.E., Bejar, I.I., 1998. Validity and automated scoring: it's not only the scoring. Educ. Meas., Issues Pract. 17 (4), 9–17.

Black, P., 2002. Working Inside the Black Box: Assessment for Learning in the Classroom. Granada Learning, London.

Black, P., Wiliam, D., 2009. Developing the theory of formative assessment. Educ. Assess. Eval. Account. 21 (1), 5–31.

Blanco Abellan, M., Ginovart Gisbert, M., 2012. On how moodle quizzes can contribute to the formative e-assessment of first-year engineering students in mathematics courses. RUSC 9 (1), 354–370. In: "Mathematicale-learning" [online dossier].

Bloom, B.S., 1956. Taxonomy of Educational Objectives, Handbook I: The Cognitive Domain. David McKay Co Inc., New York

Boekaerts, M., 1997. Self-regulated learning: a new concept embraced by researchers, policy makers, educators, teachers, and students. Learn. Instr. 7 (2), 161–186.

Bohl, O., Scheuhase, J., Sengler, R., Winand, U., 2002. The sharable content object reference model (SCORM) – a critical review. In: Proceedings of the International Conference on Computers in Education (ICCE'02), Auckland, New Zealand. IEEE, Auckland, pp. 950–951.

Bransford, J.D., Brown, A.L., Cocking, R.R., 2000. How People Learn: Brain, Mind, Experience, and School, expanded ed. National Academy Press, Washington, DC.

Bull, J., McKenna, C., 2004. Blueprint for Computer-Assisted AssessmentVol. 2. Routledge Falmer, London.

Cook, J., Jenkins, V., 2010. Getting Started with E-Assessment. Project Report. University of Bath, Bath.

Crisp, G., 2007. The e-Assessment Handbook. Continuum International Publishing Group, London.

Crisp, G., 2009. Interactive e-Assessment: moving beyond multiple-choice questions. In: Centre for Learning and Professional Development. University of Adelaide, Adelaide, pp. 12–31. 3.

Crisp, G., 2011. Teacher's Handbook on e-Assessment. Transforming Assessment – An ALTC Fellowship Activity.

Da Bormida, G., Di Girolamo, M., Dahn, I., Murelli, E., 2004. An open abstract framework for modeling inter-operability of mobile learning services. In: EduTech Computer-Aided Design Meets Computer-Aided Learning. Springer, USA, pp. 113–120.

Daly, C., Pachler, N., Mor, Y., Mellar, H., 2010. Exploring formative e-assessment: using case stories and design patterns. Assess. Eval. High. Educ. 35 (5), 619–636.

de Bruyn, E., Mostert, E., Schoor, A., 2011. Computer-based testing - the ideal tool to assess on the different levels of bloom's taxonomy. In: 14th International Conference on Interactive Collaborative Learning (ICL2011), September 2011. IEEE, Piešťany, Slovakia, pp. 444–449.

Dermo, J., 2009. e-assessment and the student learning experience: a survey of student perceptions of e-assessment. Br. J. Educ. Technol. 40 (2), 203–214.

Dermo, J., Carpenter, L., 2011. E-assessment for learning: Can online selected response questions really provide useful formative feedback? In: Whitelock, D., Warburton, W., Wills, G., Gilbert, L. (Eds.), 14th CAA International Computer Assisted Assessment Conference. University of Southampton, Southampton, UK.

Devedžić, V., Jovanović, J., Gašević, D., 2007. The pragmatics of current e-learning standards. IEEE Internet Comput. 11 (3), 19–27.

Dopper, S.M., Sjoer, E., 2004. Implementing formative assessment in engineering education: the use of the online assessment system Etude. Eur. J. Eng. Educ. 29 (2), 259–266.

Dostalova, L., Lang, J., 2007. ORGANON the web tutor for basic logic courses. Log. J. IGPL 15 (4), 305–311.

ExamTime (Online). Available from: www.examtime.com/quiz-maker (accessed 20 July 2015).

Garrison, D.R., 2011. E-Learning in the 21st Century: A Framework for Research and Practice. Taylor and Francis, London.

Gibbs, G., Simpson, C., 2004. Conditions under which assessment supports students' learning. Learn. Teach. High. Educ. 1 (1), 3–31.

Gikandi, J.W., Morrow, D., Davis, N.E., 2011. Online formative assessment in higher education: a review of the literature. Comput. Educ. 57 (4), 2333–2351.

Goedicke, M., Striewe, M., Balz, M., 2008. Computer Aided Assessments and Programming Exercises with JACK (No. 28). ICB-research report.

Gotel, O., Scharff, C., 2007. Adapting an open-source web-based assessment system for the automated assessment of programming problems. In: IASTED Web-Based Education Conference, Chamonix, France.

Gruttmann, S., Böhm, D., Kuchen, H., 2008. E-assessment of mathematical proofs: chances and challenges for students and tutors. In: 2008 International Conference on Computer Science and Software Engineering (CSSE 2008), December 2008, IEEE, Wuhan, China, pp. 612–615.

Helmick, M.T., 2007. Interface-based programming assignments and automatic grading of java programs. ACM SIGCSE Bull. 39 (3), 63–67.

Heriot-Watt University, 2014. SCHOLAR: A Programme of Heriot-Watt University. (Online). Available from: http://scholar.hw.ac.uk/ (accessed 27 June 2015).

Hettiarachchi, K.H., 2013. Technology-enhanced assessment for skill and knowledge acquisition in online education. PhD Thesis, Universitat Oberta de Catalunya (Online). Available from: http://hdl.handle.net/10803/130931 (accessed 4 December 2015).

Hettiarachchi, E., Huertas, M., 2012. Temporal aspects of mathematical e-assessment systems. eLC Res. Paper Ser. 4, 37–42.

Hot Potatoes, 2013. Hot Potatoes Home Page (Online). Available from: http://hotpot.uvic.ca/ (accessed 11 July 2015).

Huertas, A., 2011. Ten years of computer-based tutors for teaching mathematical logic 2000–2010: lessons learned. In: Blackburn, P., et al., (Eds.), Third International Congress on Tools for Teaching Mathematical logic (TICTTL 2011), LNAI 6680. Springer, Heidelberg, pp. 131–140.

Imperial College London, 2013. Pandora IV (Online). Available from: http://www.doc.ic.ac.uk/pandora/newpandora/index.html (accessed 11 July 2015).

IMS GLC, 2013. IMS Learner Information Package Specification (Online). Available from: http://www.imsglobal.org/profiles (accessed 5 July 2015).

Intelligent Assessment Technologies Limited, 2014. Intelligent Assessment Technologies. (Online) Available from:http://www.intelligentassessment.com/index3.htm (accessed 11 July 2015).

Interact (Online). Available from: www.tryinteract.com/ (accessed 20 July 2015).

IParadigms, LLC, 2015. Turnitin – Home (Online). Available from: http://turnitin.com/ (accessed 20 July 2015).

Joint Information Systems Committee, 2007. Effective Practice With e-Assessment: An Overview of Technologies, Policies and Practice in Further and Higher Education. JISC, Bristol.

Joint Information Systems Committee, 2010. Effective Assessment in a Digital Age, A guide to technology-enhanced assessment and feedback. JISC, Bristol.

Keeves, J.P., 1994. Assessment in Schools, Methods of Assessment, second ed. In: Husen, T., Neville Postlethwaite, T. (Eds.), The International Encyclopedia of Education, vol. 1. Pergamon Press, Oxford, pp. 362–370.

Kuchen, H., Gruttmann, S., Majchrzak, T., Usener, C., 2009. Introduction to EASy – A System for Formative e-Assessment in Higher Education. European Research Center for Information Systems, E-Learning Competence Center, Münster, Germany.

Kuh, G.D., 2003. What we're learning about student engagement from NSSE. Change 35 (2), 24–32.

Kuo, C.Y., Wu, H.K., 2013. Toward an integrated model for designing assessment systems: an analysis of the current status of computer-based assessments in science. Comput. Educ. 68, 388–403.

Learningpod (Online). Available from: http://www.learningpod.com/ (accessed 20 July 2015).

Litzinger, T., Lattuca, L.R., Hadgraft, R., Newstetter, W., 2011. Engineering education and the development of expertise. J. Eng. Educ. 100 (1), 123. Washington.

Majchrzak, T.A., Usener, C.A., 2011. Evaluating the synergies of integrating e-assessment and software testing. In: Proceedings of Information Systems Development Conference (ISD2011), 2011. Springer, Heidelberg.

Majchrzak, T.A., Usener, C.A., 2012. Evaluating e-assessment for exercises that require higher-order cognitive skills. In: 45th Hawaii International Conference on System Sciences, 2012. IEEE, Hawaii, pp. 48–57.

Maple, T.A. (Online). Available from: http://www.maplesoft.com/products/mapleta/ (accessed 20 July 2015).

Marriott, P., 2009. Students' evaluation of the use of online summative assessment on an undergraduate financial accounting module. Br. J. Educ. Technol. 40 (2), 237–254.

Maughan, S., Peet, D., Willmott, A., 2001. On-line formative assessment item banking and learning support. In: Proceedings of the 5th International Computer Assisted Assessment Conference. Loughborough University, Loughborough, UK.

McAlpine, M., 2002. Principles of Assessment. CAA Centre, University of Luton, Luton.

McLoughlin, C., Luca, J., 2002. A learner-centred approach to developing team skills through web-based learning and assessment. Br. J. Educ. Technol. 33 (5), 571–582.

Mihajlović, Ž., Čupić, M., 2012. Software environment for learning and knowledge assessment based on graphical gadget. Int. J. Eng. Educ. 28 (5), 1127–1140.

Millard, D., Howard, Y., Bailey, C., Davis, H., Gilbert, L., Jeyes, S., Price, J., Sclater, N., Sherratt, R., Tulloch, I., Wills, G., Young, R., 2005. Mapping the e-learning assessment domain: concept maps for orientation and navigation. In: Richards, G. (Ed.), Proceedings of World Conference on E-Learning in Corporate, Government, Healthcare, and Higher Education 2005, pp. 2770–2775.

MIT, 2003. Open Knowledge Initiative (Online). Available from: http://web.mit.edu/oki/learn/papers.html (accessed 20 July 2015).

Mohan, P., Brooks, C., 2003. Learning objects on the semantic web. In: Proceedings of the 3rd IEEE International Conference on Advanced Learning Technologies, July 2003, Athens, Greece, pp. 195–199.

Moodle, 2015. Moodle.org: Open-Source Community-based Tools for Learning. (Online) Available from: http://moodle.org/ (accessed 20 July 2015).

Moss, C.M., Brookhart, S.M., 2009. Advancing Formative Assessment in Every Classroom: A Guide for Instructional Leaders. Association for Supervision and Curriculum Development, Alexandria, VA.

Nicol, D., 2006. Increasing success in first year courses: assessment re-design, self-regulation and learning technologies. In: Proceedings of the 23rd Annual Ascilite Conference. University of Sydney, Sydney, Australia, pp. 589–598.

Niles, L.H.T., 2007. Engineering Faculty Members' Beliefs and Practices in a Technologically Equipped Classroom. ProQuest, Ann Arbor, MI.

Oliver, R., 1988. Experiences of assessing programming assignments by computer. In: Charman, D., Elmes, A. (Eds.), Computer Based Assessment, vol. 2. pp. 45–50.

Pachler, N., Daly, C., Mor, Y., Mellar, H., 2010. Formative e-assessment: practitioner cases. Comput. Educ. 54 (3), 715–721.

Prados, F., Soler, J., Boada, I., Poch, J., 2011. An automatic correction tool that can learn. In: Proceedings of Frontiers in Education Conference (FIE), 2011, Rapid City, USA. IEEE computer Society, Washington, DC. pp. F1D-1-1-F1D-5.

ProProfs (Online). Available from: www.proprofs.com (accessed 20 July 2015).

QuestionPro (Online). Available from: www.questionpro.com/tour/sample-questions.html (accessed 20 July 2015).

Rahn, M., Waldmann, J., 2002. The leipzig autotool system for grading student homework. In: Hanus, M., Krishnamurthi, S., Thompson, S. (Eds.), Functional and Declarative Programming in Education (FDPE).

Reeves, T.C., Hedberg, J.G., 2009. Evaluation strategies for open and distributed learning environments. In: Spratt, C., Lajbcygier, P. (Eds.), E-Learning technologies and evidence based assessment approaches. Information Science Reference, New York, pp. 234–253.

Ridgway, J., McCusker, S., Pead, D., 2004. Literature Review of e-Assessment. Nesta Future Lab, Bristol, UK.

Sadler, D.R., 1989. Formative assessment and the design of instructional systems. Instr. Sci. 18 (2), 119–144.

Sadler, D.R., 2013. Opening up feedback. In: Merry, S., Price, M., Carless, D., et al., (Eds.), Reconceptualising Feedback in Higher Education: Developing Dialogue with Students. Routledge, London, pp. 54–63.

Saikkonen, R., Malmi, L., Korhonen, A., 2001. Fully automatic assessment of programming exercises. In: Proceedings of the 6th Annual Conference on Innovation and Technology in Computer Science Education, 2001. ACM Press, New York, NY, pp. 133–136.

Sanz-Santamaría, S., Zorita, J.Á.V., Serrano, J.G., 2006. Mixing standards, IRT and pedagogy for quality e-assessment. In: Current Developments in Technology-Assisted Education. FORMATEX, Badajoz, Spain, pp. 926–929.

Schunk, D.H., Ertmer, P.A., 1999. Self-regulatory processes during computer skill acquisition: goal and self-evaluative influences. J. Educ. Psychol. 91 (2), 251.

Sharpe, R., Benfield, G., Roberts, G., 2006. The Undergraduate Experience of Blended e-Learning: A Review of UK Literature and Practice What is Blended Learning? Higher Education Academy, York.

Sitthiworachart, J., Joy, M., Sutinen, E., 2008. Success factors for e-assessment in computer science education. In: Bonk, C., et al., (Ed.), Proceedings of World Conference on E-Learning in Corporate, Government, Healthcare, and Higher Education.pp. 2287–2293.

Smythe, C., Roberts, P., 2000. An overview of the IMS question and test interoperability specification. In: Proceedings of the Conference on Computer Aided Assessment (CAA'2000), Leicestershire, UK.

Socrative (Online). Available from: www.socrative.com (accessed 20 July 2015).

Soler, J., Poch, J., Barrabés, E., Juher, D., Ripoll, J., 2002. A tool for the continuous assessment and improvement of the student's skills in a mathematics course. In: Proceedings of the Technologies de l'information et de la Communication dans les Enseignements d'Ingéieurs et dans l'Industrie (TICE 2002) Symposium, Lyon, pp. 105–110.

Strickland, N., 2002. Alice interactive mathematics AIM is based on Maple. MSOR Connections 2, 27–30.

The Open University, 2013. OpenMark Examples: Overview (Online). Available from: http://www.open.ac.uk/openmarkexamples/ (accessed 20 July 2015).

Trakla2 Software Project, 2009 (Online). Available from: http://www.cse.hut.fi/en/research/SVG/TRAKLA2/index.shtml (accessed 20 November 2015).

Triantafillou, E., Georgiadou, E., Economides, A.A., 2008. The design and evaluation of a computerized adaptive test on mobile devices. Comput. Educ. 50 (4), 1319–1330.

Tselonis, C., Sargeant, J., 2007. Domain-specific formative feedback through domain-independent diagram matching. In: Khandia, F. (Ed.), 11th CAA International Computer Assisted Assessment Conference. Loughborough University, Loughborough, UK, pp. 403–420.

Usener, C.A., Majchrzak, T.A., Kuchen, H., 2012. E-assessment and software testing. Interactive Technol. Smart Educ. 9 (1), 46–56.

Vassileva, J., McCalla, G., Greer, J., 2003. Multi-agent multi-user modeling in I-Help. User Model. User-Adap. Inter. 13 (1–2), 179–210.

Whitelock, D., 2007. Computer assisted formative assessment: supporting students to become more reflective learners. In: 8th International Conference on Computer Based Learning in Science, CBLIS, pp. 492–503.

Whitelock, D., Brasher, A., 2006. Developing a Roadmap for E-Assessment: Which Way Now? In: 10th International Computer Assisted Assessment Conference, 2006. Loughborough University, Loughborough, UK, pp. 487–501.

Wills, G., Bailey, C.P., Davis, H.C., Gilbert, L., Howard, Y., Jeyes, S., … Young, R., 2007. An e-learning framework for assessment (FREMA). In: International CAA Conference.

Zeller, A., 2000. Making students read and review code. In: Proceedings of the 5th Annual SIGCSE/SIGCUE ITiCSE Conference on Innovation and Technology in Computer Science Education, 2000. ACM Press, New York, pp. 89–92.

EVALUATION MODEL FOR e-ASSESSMENT

4

U. Tudevdagva

Mongolian University of Science and Technology, Ulaanbaatar, Mongolia

1 INTRODUCTION

Nowadays we need to learn many new things as a request of the rapidly developing technologies around us. Accordingly educators have to use various new teaching methodologies in teaching and learning. e-Learning is being used widely in conventional and continuing adult education and in corporate training because of its flexibility, richness, resource-sharing, and cost-effectiveness. In each education process we need to manage and control the quality of teaching and learning. Educational evaluation has a long tradition historically, but evaluation for e-learning is still being developed as a new branch of educational evaluation. The rapid development of computer and mobile technology has become the main motivation to change the teaching and learning methodology in e-learning. Therefore, in relation to teaching and learning methodologies, evaluation models and methods also require to be updated.

Many researchers and scientists developed different approaches and models for educational evaluation. Tyler (1949), Kirkpatrick (1959), Alkin (1969), Scriven (1967), Stufflebeam (1972) are pioneers in educational evaluation theory. Other researchers such as, Patton (1980), Ehlers and Pawlowski (2006), Khan (2005), Lam and Mcnaught (2006) and Ruhe and Zumbo (2009) extended and continued this research.

Educators can use different evaluation models or methods. The main condition is that the evaluation process should be transparent and traceable for groups involved in the e-learning process.

The quantitative models for evaluation of e-learning usually consider additive evaluation models. That means, depending on the considered evaluation goals, which are measured based on a defined scale, a linear function containing corresponding weight factors is used like, for example,

$$Q = \sum_{i=1}^{r} \alpha_i x_i.$$

Here denote α_i, $\alpha_i > 0$, given weight factors for the obtained evaluation values x_i, $i = 1, \ldots, r$, for the considered evaluation goals. The advantage of additive evaluation models is that they are easy to use. A side effect of these models is, that the choice of proper weight factors is subjective. It is difficult to define which element should be more highlighted and should have the highest weight factor.

According to our observations there is a gap here. The existing evaluation models usually have no clear data processing part. The planning of evaluation, creation of a survey or checklist, and the report of the evaluation results are, all parts of the evaluation process, which are extensively discussed in literature. But it is not easy to find materials which explain in detail how the collected data should be processed. In our view collected data have to be processed as objectively as possible without any subjective influence.

Formative Assessment, Learning Data Analytics and Gamification. http://dx.doi.org/10.1016/B978-0-12-803637-2.00004-X

The structure-oriented evaluation model (SURE) considered here consists of eight steps and includes theoretically substantiated calculation rules for data processing.

2 THE SURE MODEL

The idea of this model is based on practical aspects of e-learning processes. In early stages of e-learning, the superiors were the initiators of the evaluation process. The reason was that the word "evaluation" was understood as the process of measurement and ranking into orders of quality. Evaluation later began being used as a tool or instrument for the improvement of e-learning. The universities and educational institutions who develop and deliver e-courses can perform self evaluation. They can obtain dependable and trustworthy results from this SURE model. When the evaluation model is complete and transparent, people welcome the findings of an evaluation process.

This is assured through this evaluation model. The SURE consists of eight steps. All steps of the SURE model have a specific meaning. Output of the previous step will become the input of next step (Tudevdagva and Hardt, 2011).

That are the eight steps of the SURE model:

- Definition of key goals;
- Definition of sub goals;
- Confirmation of evaluation goals;
- Creation of checklist;
- Acceptance of checklist;
- Data collection;
- Data processing;
- The evaluation report.

Step 1. Definition of key goals

In the first step of the SURE model, the evaluation team has to define the key goals of evaluation. These goals are essential for the main mission of evaluation.

Example 1 We consider an e-learning process that consists of the following partial processes: registration process, course material support, and tutoring. The better these partial processes achieve their goals, the better the whole process is running. Hence we can consider the goals of these partial processes as the key goals of whole process. The achievement of these key goals is necessary for the achievement of the overall goal.

Without registration, the learners have no access to the e-learning framework. After registration the learners can access to learning materials. For that we need corresponding learning materials. If the learners studying the e-materials have no tutoring, they may loose their interest in learning and become inactive. The learners need tutor support and feedback during learning. These facts underline the choice of key goals.

Between the key goals and the overall goal is the following logical relation. Denote $B_1, B_2, B_3,$ and C as the fact that through the partial processes the assigned key goals are reached and subsequently the overall goal. This can be expressed formal with logical AND operator by $C = B_1 \cap B_2 \cap B_3$ such that C and $B_1, B_2,$ and B_3 are interconnected in the sense of a logical series structure as it is emphasized in Fig. 4.1A. If only one of the key goals fails then the overall process has failed its goal.

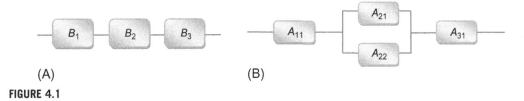

FIGURE 4.1

Logical structure of Examples 1 and 2. (A) key goal structure, (B) sub goal structure.

Step 2. Definition of sub goals

During this step the key goals defined in the previous step should be described, if possible, in a more detailed manner. For that we assume that a partial process with a corresponding key goal, say B_i, can be divided into sub processes which pursue the same goal as the partial process. Additionally we suppose that the learners are offered the possibility of parallel use of associated sub processes. The key goal B_i is reached then if at least one the sub processes achieves its goal. The goals of sub processes are denoted as sub goals of given key goal.

Formally this can be described as follows. We denote by B_i the fact that ith key goal is reached and we suppose that the considered partial process consists of two sub processes. Denote by A_{i1} is the fact that by the first sub process the key goal B_i is reached. Accordingly let A_{i2} be the fact, that the second sub process achieves the key goal B_i. Then, the key goal B_i can be written be means of logical OR as $B_i = A_{i1} \cup A_{i2}$. This relation can be emphasized by a logical parallel structure, see Fig. 4.1B, key goal B_2.

Example 2 Continuation of Example 1, definition of sub goals.

We start with key goal B_2, which refers to efficiency of the course material. We assume there are two ways by which the course content can be communicated: reading material as well audio and video material. Both materials can be used by learners in parallel.

Hence key goal B_2—the course content is provided by the course material—can be described by the means of two sub goals—A_{21} course content is provided by the written material and A_{22} course content is provided by the audio and video material—and it holds $B_2 = A_{21} \cup A_{22}$.

Let us consider key goals B_1 and B_2. Here we assume that the corresponding partial processes cannot be partitioned into sub processes that can be used in parallel by the students. Then key goals B_1 and B_3 cannot be decomposed into sub goals. In a more general interpretation, key goals B_1 and B_3 consist both of only one single sub goal A_{11} and A_{31} where $B_1 = A_{11}$ and $B_3 = A_{31}$ holds, respectively, see Fig. 4.2B.

Step 3. Confirmation of evaluation goals

This step is a very important step. The evaluation team has to confirm the final version of evaluation goals which have been defined during the previous two steps. Furthermore, the checklist for the survey has to be adapted to the accepted logical structure. When all members of the evaluation team agree as to the logical structure of the evaluation goals that should be fixed by a protocol. This is helpful in avoiding later conflicts between the evaluation team and stakeholders.

If necessary, the evaluation team can define the embedded or leveled logical structures until the evaluation goals are fully accepted by all members of the evaluation team.

Table 4.1 Checklist Design Proposal

Key Goal	Sub Goal	Question
B_1	A_{11}	Registration process was well organized
B_2	A_{21}	Reading material was sufficient for achieving the course goal
	A_{22}	Video material was sufficient for achieving the course goal
B_3	A_{31}	Support by tutors was useful for understanding of course content

Step 4. Creation of checklist

The checklist is the most often used data collection method. This method is well developed and there exist many commercial and open source software solutions to create an online survey or checklist. For example: *Monkey, LimeSurvey, fluidsurveys, iPerceptions, free online survey, kwik survey, easy polls, survey planet, Sogo survey, eSurveypro, esurvey creator, Stellarsurvey, Questionpro, esurv, questionform, panel place, survey crest,* and *addpoll.*

Moreover, there are several discussions on online survey and assessment for evaluation processes. We refer to Betsy (2005) and Blayney and Freeman (2004).

The evaluation criteria of the SURE model are specified based on the sub goals of logical structure. Table 4.1 shows a proposal for checklist design. The checklist can be supported by a corresponding software.

To create a checklist one can use different online software. The weakness of existing software solutions is that they cannot make reference to the logical structure of the evaluation goal of the SURE model. Moreover they do not include score calculation modules as is required by the SURE model. To use the SURE model in complete version we need specific application tools. This application should include functions like: create checklist, collect data, and data processing.

The formulation of questions is only one part of checklist. When the questions are ready the evaluation team has to decide which type of a survey can be used for the checklist. We listed above some sources for different designs of checklist. Depending on the target for evaluation, the checklist design may differ. The evaluation team has to focus its attention on this.

Step 5. Acceptance of checklist

When the criteria are fixed, the evaluation team has to confirm the situation formally. The evaluation team has to check whether the checklist is adapted according to the logical structure of the evaluation goal; whether the questions are easy to read, understandable, and unambiguous; and whether the questions are clearly formulated; whether there are any grammatical and semantic errors in sentences. Only the accepted checklist can be used for data collection.

The formulation of questions is only one aspect of checklist creation. A further important aspect is the design of checklist. Each member of the evaluation team has to check this aspect before confirmation and if necessary appearance and design of checklist should be improved.

Step 6. Data collection

Data can be collected in different ways. It can be paper based or web based. If it is possible the online version should be given preferrence because the paper-based method is prone to errors because of the high workload involved. If it is a web-based online version, it can be more objective. There are several techniques for data collection: surveys and questionnaires, tests and assessments, interviews, focus groups, action plans, case studies, and performance records (Phillips, 2010). The evaluation team can use any technique from above list. However, the SURE model should use the online survey. Online data collection is an efficient way to collect objective data from participants. Online survey data can be processed automatically; this avoids the human errors that usually occur during transferring the collected data to the data sheet and saves a lot of time of evaluation process. Collected data are directly input to the data processing step.

Step 7. Data processing

These are the main steps of data processing: let us consider an evaluation structure C which consists of r key goals B_i, $i = 1, \ldots, r$, where each key goal consists of s_i sub goals A_{ij}, $j = 1, \ldots, s_i$, $i = 1, \ldots, r$. Then we have

$$C = \bigcap_{i=1}^{r} B_i = \bigcap_{i=1}^{r} \bigcup_{j=1}^{s_i} A_{ij}.$$

We suppose that we have n checklist results obtained by a checklist adapted to goal structure C. The evaluation interval for sub goal A_{ij} be the interval $[x'_{ij}, x''_{ij}]$, $x'_{ij} < x''_{ij}$. Let

$$x_{11}^{(1)}, \ldots, x_{1s_1}^{(1)}, x_{21}^{(1)}, \ldots, x_{2s_2}^{(1)}, \quad \ldots \quad, x_{r1}^{(1)}, \ldots, x_{rs_r}^{(1)},$$
$$\cdots$$
$$x_{11}^{(n)}, \ldots, x_{1s_1}^{(n)}, x_{21}^{(n)}, \ldots, x_{2s_2}^{(n)}, \quad \ldots \quad, x_{r1}^{(n)}, \ldots, x_{rs_r}^{(n)},$$

be the corresponding sampling results of a sample of size n. Here denotes $x_{ij}^{(k)}$ for $k = 1, \ldots, n$ the obtained answer of kth student to the checklist question as to how the sub goal A_{ij} has been achieved. Then the empirical score (computed score based on sampling results) demonstrating that the aim of goal structure C has been reached is calculated by

$$Q^*(C) = \frac{1}{n} \sum_{k=1}^{n} Q^{*(k)}(C) = \frac{1}{n} \sum_{k=1}^{n} \prod_{i=1}^{r} \left(1 - \prod_{j=1}^{s_i} \left(1 - q_{ij}^{*(k)} \right) \right). \tag{1}$$

Here denotes $q_{ij}^{*(k)}$ as the empirical score for sub goal A_{ij} according to the kth checklist result $x_{ij}^{(k)}$, $k = 1, \ldots, n$. It is obtained by normalization of the checklist value $x_{ij}^{(k)}$. It holds that

$$q_{ij}^{*(k)} = \frac{x_{ij}^{(k)} - x'_{ij}}{x''_{ij} - x'_{ij}}. \tag{2}$$

Then it holds that $0 \le Q^*(C) \le 1$. $Q^*(C) = 0$ which means that referring to the survey the aim of goal structure C has failed, $Q^*(C) = 1$ and so the aim has been reached.

Beside the empirical score $Q^*(C)$ we can get estimation values for the key goal scores $Q(B_1), \ldots, Q(B_r)$ as well as for the sub goal scores $Q(A_{11}), \ldots, Q(A_{rs_r})$. These are special cases in terms formula (1). We get

$$Q^*(B_i) = \frac{1}{n} \sum_{k=1}^{n} \left(1 - \prod_{j=1}^{s_i} \left(1 - q_{ij}^{*(k)} \right) \right)$$

and

$$Q^*(A_{ij}) = \frac{1}{n} \sum_{k=1}^{n} q_{ij}^{*(k)}.$$

The precision of obtained estimation values can be described by confidence intervals, we refer to Tudevdagva (2014).

The score values $Q^*(C)$ and $Q^*(B_i)$ can be transformed by calibration into the empirical evaluation scores $Q_e^*(C)$ and $Q_e^*(B_i)$. They are defined by

$$Q_e^*(C) = \frac{1}{n}\sum_{k=1}^{n} \sqrt[r]{\prod_{i=1}^{r}\left(1 - \sqrt[s_i]{\prod_{j=1}^{s_i}\left(1 - q_{ij}^{*(k)}\right)}\right)} \tag{3}$$

and

$$Q_e^*(B_i) = \frac{1}{n}\sum_{k=1}^{n}\left(1 - \sqrt[s_i]{\prod_{j=1}^{s_i}\left(1 - q_{ij}^{*(k)}\right)}\right) \tag{4}$$

as well as

$$Q_e^*(A_{ij}) = Q^*(A_{ij}). \tag{5}$$

These evaluation scores allow a comparison of score values between the different goal structures. The empirical evaluation score can be interpreted as an index of the satisfaction of learners with an e-learning. This result holds further on $0 \leq Q_e^*(C) \leq 1$. A value $Q_e^*(C) = 0.5$ reflects an average level of satisfaction. Values over 0.5 are above average, and values less than 0.5 a below-average satisfaction.

Step 8. The evaluation report

Evaluations are expected to contribute value to sustainable development. Understanding what works, what does not and what should be improved promotes informed decision-making about programming choices, approaches, and practices. Good evaluation reports serve this process by accurately distilling and clearly articulating what is learned from evaluations (How to Perform Evaluations, 2002).

Using the SURE model the evaluation process includes quantitative and qualitative aspects. The first five steps, outcomes insure the qualitative part of the evaluation. Step 6 and 7 insure the quantitative part of evaluation. The evaluation report has to reflect both parts of the evaluation process. The evaluation report makes visible outcomes and findings of the evaluation process.

The type of report is different depending on the audience to whom that report is addressed. Using the SURE model we can calculate several evaluation scores. Which evaluation score can be used for what can be decided by the evaluation team. Corresponding graphics and charts can be generated by the SURE model application automatically, and these graphical representations can be used for the report.

The evaluation report has to be delivered to stakeholders or audiences at appropriate times. As a rule all interested groups expect a quick report after data collection.

3 THEORETICAL FOUNDATION FOR DATA PROCESSING

e-Learning is a complex process which consists of several environments. To evaluate the efficiency of a given e-learning process we have to define what we want to understand formally by an e-learning process as "process."

Each process consists of several process components. They are partial processes involved in the achievement of an overall process goal. This leads to the following definition.

Definition Let $G = \{A_1, ..., A_m\}$ be a given set of process components where to each component a functional goal is associated. A sub set $\mathcal{B} = \{A_1, ..., A_r\} \subseteq G$ of process components which interact in sense of the achievement of a defined overall goal is said to be a *process*.

Hence a simple random selection of process components forms as a rule not yet a process. The process components have to work together with respect to a defined overall goal. That means, beside the process components a process is characterized by structural properties. These structural properties describe how the involved process components contribute to the achievement of the total goal.

The functional structure of a process can be characterized formally by logical operations like AND and OR. In a set-theoretical interpretation these are intersection and union. The components of a process can interact together in different manners. Depending on how the components of the process contribute to the achievement of the total goal we distinguish two basic process structures.

Definition A process $\mathcal{B} = \{A_1, ..., A_r\} \subseteq G$ is a *series process* if the goal of the process is achieved and only if each process component $A_1, ..., A_r$ achieves its goal.

This property of a process can be described formally as follows. Let $\mathcal{B} = \{A_1, ..., A_r\} \subseteq G$ be a series process consisting of r process components $A_1, ..., A_r$. Denoted by B and $A_1, ..., A_r$ is the fact that the process $\mathcal{B}$ and the process components $A_1, ..., A_r$ achieve their goals, respectively. Then for a serial process the relation between B and $A_1, ..., A_r$ can be formally represented by

$$B = A_1 \cap \cdots \cap A_r = \cap_{i=1}^r A_i.$$

That means, a series process $\mathcal{B}$ achieves its total goal if all included process components achieve their goal. This can be emphasized graphically by a series scheme as is shown in Fig. 4.6. The order of process components in a series scheme is without of significance.

Beside series processes the following process type is of particular relevance.

Definition A process $\mathcal{B} = \{A_1, \cdots, A_s\} \subseteq G$ is a *parallel process* if the goal of process $\mathcal{B}$ is reached if at least one of the process components $A_1, ..., A_s$ achieves its goal.

Formally then holds

$$B = A_1 \cup A_2 \cup ... \cup A_r = \cup_{i=1}^s A_i.$$

This can be emphasized graphically by a parallel scheme, see Fig. 4.1. The total goal of a parallel process is already reached if one of the process components has reached its goal.

By the combination of series and parallel processes very complex process structures can be obtained.

Now we will describe how we can evaluate a process depending on its logical goal structure. For that we consider a process which consists of k, $k \geq 1$, process components $A_1, ..., A_k$, which cooperate together with the view of achieving of a defined process goal. Our aim is to evaluate in which quality the process has reached its process goal.

For that we use the general measure theory. Our aim is an evaluation approach whose score calculation rules are compatible with the corresponding rules as they are used in an established manner in the geometrical context for the measurement of length, areas or volumes, or in stochastics for the calculation of probabilities or reliabilities, for instance. By means of measure theory it becomes possible to evaluate the performance of e-learning on the same theoretical base as the fields mentioned above. Subjective influences at evaluation like one has that for instance at the use of weight factors are excluded then.

For the theoretical description of the evaluation of the process quality we have to proceed in two steps: first we have to describe the evaluation of the process components $A_1, ..., A_k$ in the theoretical sense by adapted measure spaces. After that we can join together these spaces to a common product space by which the evaluation of process performance with respect to a given process goal structure becomes possible.

I. *Measure spaces for the process components.* For the evaluation of how a process component $A_i \in \{A_1, ..., A_k\}$ has reached its process goal we consider a measure space $(\Omega_i, \mathcal{A}_i, Q_i)$. A measure space consists of three objects $\Omega_i, \mathcal{A}_i$, and Q_i which can be defined here as follows:

   (1) Let $\Omega_i = \{\omega_{i1}, \omega_{i2}\}$ be a two-element set. We denote the elements of this set as *elementary goals*. In this sense the element ω_{i1} is standing for: the process goal of process component A_i has been reached (is reached), the element ω_{i2} stands for: the process goal of process component A_i, which has not been reached (is not reached).

   The set Ω_i is denoted as *goal space* of process component A_i.

   (2) Let $\mathcal{A}_i$ be the set of all subsets of goal space Ω_i. Then we have

$$\mathcal{A}_i = \{\phi, A_{i1}, A_{i2}, \Omega_i\},$$

   The sub sets A_{i1} and A_{i2} are defined by $A_{i1} = \{\omega_{i1}\}$ and $A_{i2} = \{\omega_{i2}\} = \bar{A}_{i1}$, for instance. The elements of set system $\mathcal{A}_i$ can be interpreted as *goal structures* as follows:

   A_{i1}—process goal of process component A_i has been reached,
   $\bar{A}_{i1}$ —process goal of process component A_i has not been reached,
   Ω_i —any goal of process component A_i has been reached,
   ϕ —nothing has been reached.

   The set $\mathcal{A}_i$ is in terms of measure theory as an σ-algebra. An σ-algebra is an algebraic structure which is closed against set-theoretical operations with its elements like union, intersection, and complement. This means, set-theoretical or logical operations with the elements of an σ-algebra will not cause any confusions.

   We denote the elements of $\mathcal{A}_i$ as *goal structures* and the set $\mathcal{A}_i$ itself as *goal algebra* of the process component A_i. In this context we will say: the goal in terms of a goal structure $A \in \mathcal{A}_i$ has been reached (is reached) if an $\omega \in A$ has been observed (is observed). The structure of a goal algebra $\mathcal{A}_i$ is very simple and possesses a more formal meaning here. The goal algebras are needed if we are to go over to the corresponding product space for a common description of process components $A_1, ..., A_k$.

   (3) Let $Q_i : \mathcal{A}_i \rightarrow [0, 1]$ be an additive function from our goal algebra into the interval $[0, 1]$ where to any given real number q_i, $0 \le q_i \le 1$,

$$Q_i(A_{i1}) = q_i, \quad Q_i(\bar{A}_{i1}) = 1 - q_i \quad \text{and} \quad Q_i(\Omega_i) = 1$$

   holds. The values of numbers q_i and $1 - q_i$ are or can be interpreted as evaluation values for the goal structures A_{i1} and $\bar{A}_{i1}$. In this sense the values q_i and $1 - q_i$ are an evaluation distribution over the goal algebra A_i. The function Q_i is a normalized measure on (Ω_i, A_i). We denote $Q_i(A_{i1})$ as *score* demonstrating that the goal of process component A_i has been reached (is reached), analogously $Q_i(\bar{A}_{i1})$ is the corresponding score that the goal in terms of process A_i has not been reached (is not reached).

II. *Product measure space for entire process.* For evaluation of goal structures as they have been considered in Fig. 4.1 we need a multi-dimensional evaluation method by which a common consideration of different process components becomes possible. For that we consider the product space of measure spaces (Ω_i, A_i, Q_i), $i = 1, ..., k$, considered above. The product space consists again of three objects Ω, A, and Q which are defined as follows.

(1) Let $\Omega = \times_{i=1}^{k} \Omega_i$ be the cross product over goal spaces $\Omega_1, ..., \Omega_k$. The elements $\omega = (\omega_1, ..., \omega_k) \in \Omega$ are the k-dimensional elementary goals.

(2) Let A be the system of all sub sets of k-dimensional goal space Ω. This set system again forms an σ-algebra and contains all k-dimensional goal structures. These are goal structures that can be generated from the goals of the k involved partial processes by logical operations. Especially, the goal algebra A contains now the serial and parallel goal structures which have been discussed above. A sub goal A_i, which refers to ith of k involved in the partial processes, is then defined by

$$A_i = \Omega_1 \times \cdots \times \Omega_{i-1} \times A_i' \times \Omega_{i+1} \times \cdots \times \Omega_k \quad \text{with} \quad A_i' = \{\omega_{i1}\} \in A_i. \tag{6}$$

(3) For evaluation of goal structures we need finally a common measure Q on (Ω, A). For that we consider the product measure $Q = \otimes_{i=1}^{k} Q_i$ over (Ω, A). This measure is defined as follows: let $B \in A$ be a goal structure with

$$B = A_1' \times \cdots \times A_k' \quad \text{and} \quad A_i' \in A_i \quad \text{for} \quad i = 1, ..., k.$$

Then it holds

$$Q(B) = \prod_{i=1}^{k} Q_i(A_i').$$

For a sub goal A_i in sense of relation (6) this implies

$$Q(A_i) = Q_i(A_i').$$

The product measure Q is a uniquely defined measure on (Ω, A). For any goal structure $B \in A$ the value $Q(B)$ can be interpreted as a score value that describes the quality by which goal structure B achieves its goal. It holds $0 \leq Q(B) \leq 1$. $Q(B) = 1$ means goal B is completely achieved and $Q(B) = 0$—goal B is failed.

The product measure Q satisfies the same calculation rules as any normalized measure. For a goal structure

$$C = \bigcap_{i=1}^{r} B_i = \bigcap_{i=1}^{r} \bigcup_{j=1}^{s_i} A_{ij},$$

where $A_{ij} \in$ and A denote different sub goals with $Q(A_{ij}) = q_{ij}$, the score $Q(C)$ is calculated by

$$Q(C) = \prod_{i=1}^{r}\left(1 - \prod_{j=1}^{s_i}(1-q_{ij})\right), \tag{7}$$

see Tudevdagva (2014). This is the basic formula for calculation of scores for goal structure.

III. *Empirical scores.* For calculation of a score value $Q(C)$ by formula (7) we need the scores $Q(A_{ij}) = q_{ij}$ for $i=1,\ldots,r$ and $j=1,\ldots,s_i$. These scores are unknown as a rule and must be estimated based on checklist results, see formula (1).

In this way we obtain for each sampling record (check list data record) an estimation value for $Q(C)$ by

$$Q^{*(k)}(C) = \prod_{i=1}^{r}\left(1 - \prod_{j=1}^{s_i}\left(1-q_{ij}^{*(k)}\right)\right), \quad k=1,\ldots,n.$$

The arithmetic mean $Q^*(C)$ over these values, see formula (1), is an estimation value for $Q(C)$ based on a checklist sample of size n. We denote this value as an *empirical score* (sampling score) showing that the aim of goal structure C has been achieved.

For more details we refer again to Tudevdagva (2014). Additionally, how we can get confidence intervals for $Q(C)$ and how an empirical score value $Q^*(C)$ is transformed into a so-called empirical evaluation score $Q_e^*(C)$ is described, see formula (3). Empirical evaluation scores allow a comparison of empirical score values between different goal structures.

4 EXAMPLES FOR THE SURE MODEL

In this section we consider some simulation examples describing the behavior of the SURE model under several evaluation conditions. We assume that we have a goal structure

$$C = \bigcap_{i=1}^{r} B_i = \bigcap_{i=1}^{r} \bigcup_{j=1}^{s_i} A_{ij}$$

consisting of $r=6$ key goals $B_1,\ldots,B_6$ with

$$B_1 = A_{11}, \quad B_2 = A_{21} \cap A_{22}, \quad B_3 = A_{31} \cap A_{32} \cap A_{33}$$

and

$$B_4 = A_{41}, \quad B_5 = A_{51}, \quad B_6 = A_{61} \cap A_{62}.$$

The key goal structures B_1, B_4, and B_5 are simple goal structures, the key goal structures B_2, B_3, and B_6 are parallel structures. The logical scheme of this goal structure is shown in Fig. 4.2.

We assume that based on an adapted checklist a sample of size $n=25$ has been obtained. The evaluation scales are for all questions equal and include the numbers $0,1,\ldots,10$. Zero means the goal has failed, the maximum value 10 means that the goal has been reached.

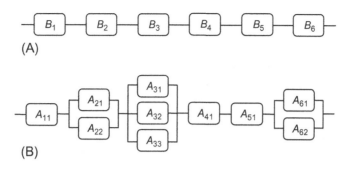

FIGURE 4.2

Goal structure of Examples 3, 4 and 5. (A) key goal structure, (B) sub goal structure.

Example 3. The satisfied students

We assume that students are satisfied with the course in the sense that all questions of checklist have been answered with scores between 4 and 10. Table 4.2 contains corresponding checklist results. The scores are realizations of a uniformly distributed random variable with values in the set $\{4, 5, ..., 10\}$. In the center of table we see the sample scores. They are highlighted according to a grey scale which is ranging from darkgrey over middle grey to white. White means goal has been achieved, middle grey corresponds an average evaluation, dark grey means goal was not achieved. Each row from 1 until 25 contains a checklist data record. The dominating grey values are white until middle grey, a first signal that the course is running well.

The third row from below contains the empirical scores $Q^*(A_{ij})$ of simple goals A_{ij}. These scores are identical with the empirical evaluation scores $Q_e^*(A_{ij})$. The next line shows the empirical key goal evaluation scores $Q_e^*(B_i)$. These values are comparatively high. This confirms the satisfaction of students in terms of the achievement of a single key goal. The last row contains the empirical standard scores for key goals $Q^*(B_i)$.

In the second last and last column of the table the empirical evaluation scores $Q_e^{*(k)}(C)$ and empirical standard scores $Q^*(k)(C)$ of checklist records for $k = 1, ..., 25$ are displayed. The arithmetic means of these scores provide the empirical evaluation score $Q_e^*(C)$ and the empirical standard score $Q^*(C)$. The bold gray scaled value in the right lower corner is the empirical evaluation score $Q_e^*(C)$, on the right hand of that we have the empirical standard score $Q^*(C)$.

We get $Q_e^*(C) = 0.73$. This value is greater than 0.5. Hence the course is evaluated above average. The value $Q_e^*(C) = 0.73$ stands for quite a high level of satisfaction for students of the course. It corresponds to an average satisfaction level of 73%. The empirical score $Q^*(C) = 0.31$ is comparatively small in comparison with empirical evaluation score $Q_e^*(C)$. This is a peculiar characteristic of product measure.

The lower table of Table 4.2 presents the confidence intervals for the evaluation score at confidence levels of 0.90, 0.95, and 0.99. The confidence intervals are quite wide. That is a consequence of the relatively small sample size of $n = 25$ here. No confidence interval contains the value 0.5. This is an indication that the deviation of obtained empirical evaluation score from value 0.5 can be considered as significant.

Table 4.2 Checklist Results, Scores, and Confidence Intervals for Example 3

k	B_1 A_{11}	B_2 A_{21}	A_{22}	B_3 A_{31}	A_{32}	A_{33}	B_4 A_{41}	B_5 A_{51}	B_6 A_{61}	A_{62}	$Q_e^{*}(k)$	$Q^{*}(k)$
1	10	4	7	4	9	5	4	9	10	9	0.72	0.29
2	7	6	7	4	7	5	8	6	6	4	0.63	0.20
3	8	5	9	5	10	8	10	8	6	6	0.82	0.51
4	8	9	6	6	10	5	4	6	9	7	0.71	0.18
5	10	5	5	6	9	9	10	5	4	10	0.77	0.37
6	5	9	10	7	10	7	9	6	4	6	0.72	0.21
7	8	5	7	6	9	4	6	8	6	8	0.70	0.29
8	6	7	8	4	8	8	10	8	5	7	0.74	0.37
9	6	9	4	10	4	4	10	5	7	6	0.73	0.25
10	4	6	8	6	5	7	10	5	7	7	0.63	0.16
11	6	7	9	9	6	5	4	6	10	4	0.67	0.14
12	6	5	7	4	8	7	5	10	9	6	0.68	0.24
13	5	8	10	8	8	10	9	9	4	8	0.80	0.36
14	7	8	6	7	4	8	10	9	6	6	0.75	0.47
15	10	9	6	6	8	9	5	6	4	5	0.67	0.20
16	7	9	8	6	8	6	7	9	5	8	0.75	0.38
17	4	7	7	6	5	4	5	9	6	8	0.60	0.13
18	7	9	8	10	5	9	7	9	7	8	0.81	0.41
19	9	10	4	7	4	7	5	7	6	4	0.68	0.23
20	7	9	10	8	6	5	10	10	5	5	0.78	0.50
21	9	10	7	8	6	6	4	8	6	5	0.69	0.22
22	9	5	7	4	8	9	6	4	8	10	0.68	0.18
23	10	9	9	6	8	5	10	8	7	5	0.81	0.65
24	5	4	10	8	7	9	10	5	8	9	0.75	0.24
25	10	10	10	5	10	7	10	6	7	10	0.92	0.60
$Q^{*}(A_{ij})$	0.73	0.74	0.76	0.64	0.73	0.67	0.75	0.72	0.65	0.68	0.73	0.31
$Q_e^{*}(B_i)$	0.73	0.80		0.78			0.75	0.72	0.71			
$Q^{*}(B_i)$	0.73	0.94		0.97			0.75	0.72	0.89			

Scale

0	1	2	3	4	5	6	7	8	9	10
0.00	0.10	0.20	0.30	0.40	0.50	0.60	0.70	0.80	0.90	1.00

Confidence intervals

Level	$Q_e^{*}(C)$	$q_{e,0}^{*}$	$q_{e,1}^{*}$	σ_e
0.90		0.70	0.75	
0.95	0.73	0.70	0.76	0.07
0.99		0.69	0.77	

In summary, the sample result indicates significant above-average satisfaction levels for students of the course at an average rate of approximately 73%. The empirical evaluation scores for key goals have values near the empirical evaluation score for the total goal. That means, the achievement of key goals is evaluated in the same direction like the achievement of the total course goal. There is no evidence for particular weak points in view of the key goals to be reached.

Example 4. The unsatisfied students

This is the counter example to Example 3. The students are unsatisfied overall with course. The score set is again the set $\{0, 1, ..., 10\}$. The students evaluate the success of single goals between 0 and 6. Table 4.3 shows the checklist results. The scores are now realizations of a uniformly distributed random variable with values in the set $\{0, 1, ..., 6\}$. The dominating grey values are dark grey until middle grey.

Table 4.3 Checklist Results, Scores, and Confidence Intervals for Example 4

k	B_1 A_{11}	B_2 A_{21}	A_{22}	B_3 A_{31}	A_{32}	A_{33}	B_4 A_{41}	B_5 A_{51}	B_6 A_{61}	A_{62}	$Q_e^{*}(k)$	$Q^{*}(k)$
1	10	4	7	4	9	5	4	9	10	9	0.72	0.29
2	7	6	7	4	7	5	8	6	6	4	0.63	0.20
3	8	5	9	5	10	8	10	8	6	6	0.82	0.51
4	8	9	6	6	10	5	4	6	9	7	0.71	0.18
5	10	5	5	6	9	9	10	5	4	10	0.77	0.37
6	5	9	10	7	10	7	9	6	4	6	0.72	0.21
7	8	5	7	6	9	4	6	8	6	8	0.70	0.29
8	6	7	8	4	8	8	10	8	5	7	0.74	0.37
9	6	9	4	10	4	4	10	5	7	6	0.73	0.25
10	4	6	8	6	5	7	10	5	7	7	0.63	0.16
11	6	7	9	9	6	5	4	6	10	4	0.67	0.14
12	6	5	7	4	8	7	5	10	9	6	0.68	0.24
13	5	8	10	8	8	10	9	9	4	8	0.80	0.36
14	7	8	6	7	4	8	10	9	6	6	0.75	0.47
15	10	9	6	6	8	9	5	6	4	5	0.67	0.20
16	7	9	8	6	8	6	7	9	5	8	0.75	0.38
17	4	7	7	6	5	4	5	9	6	8	0.60	0.13
18	7	9	8	10	5	9	7	9	7	8	0.81	0.41
19	9	10	4	7	4	7	5	7	6	4	0.68	0.23
20	7	9	10	8	6	5	10	10	5	5	0.78	0.50
21	9	10	7	8	6	6	4	8	6	5	0.69	0.22
22	9	5	7	4	8	9	6	4	8	10	0.68	0.18
23	10	9	9	6	8	5	10	8	7	5	0.81	0.65
24	5	4	10	8	7	9	10	5	8	9	0.75	0.24
25	10	10	10	5	10	7	10	6	7	10	0.92	0.60
$Q^{*}(A_{ij})$	0.73	0.74	0.76	0.64	0.73	0.67	0.75	0.72	0.65	0.68	0.73	0.31
$Q_e^{*}(B_i)$	0.73	0.80		0.78			0.75	0.72	0.71			
$Q^{*}(B_i)$	0.73	0.94		0.97			0.75	0.72	0.89			

Scale										
0	1	2	3	4	5	6	7	8	9	10
0.00	0.10	0.20	0.30	0.40	0.50	0.60	0.70	0.80	0.90	1.00

Confidence intervals				
Level	$Q_e^{*}(C)$	$q_{e,0}^{*}$	$q_{e,1}^{*}$	σ_e
0.90		0.70	0.75	
0.95	0.73	0.70	0.76	0.07
0.99		0.69	0.77	

This is first hint that something went wrong with that course. The empirical evaluation scores for key goals $B_1,...,B_6$ are, however, quite high. They range from 0.28 until 0.35, but the empirical total evaluation score $Q_e^*(C)$ is only 0.17. This is comparatively small and seems to be a contradiction to the values of the empirical scores for the key goals. In fact this value shows that the SURE model is working correct. The SURE model includes the whole logical structure of the total goal in the evaluation. This goal is failed, even if only one of key goals has failed. The second column from right shows that the total goal has failed in this sense in 11 out of 25 cases. This is the aspect reason for an empirical evaluation score $Q_e^*(C)$ of only 0.17.

This aspect of the SURE model is an important advantage over the linear evaluation model. Linear models react in such cases quite insensibly. They are not able to recognize such situations as a rule.

Example 5. The gambling students

This is a fictive situation where we assume that students do not answer to questions of checklist but randomly select a score value from $\{0,1,...,10\}$ as answer. The scores are realizations of a uniformly distributed random variable with values in the set $\{0,1,...,10\}$.

Table 4.4 contains a corresponding sampling result. Grey value is dominating now, all values between dark grey and white are represented. The empirical evaluation scores of simple goal range between 0.38 and 0.57 and reflect at first glance a tendency towards an average satisfaction level. The same applies to the key goals. These scores range between 0.38 and 0.67. Nevertheless, the total empirical evaluation score $Q_e^*(C)$ amounts only 0.31, which is quite far away from an average satisfaction at a rate of 50%. Again this is an indication of things going in the right direction. If we consider the scores $Q_e^{*(k)}(C)$ of checklist data records, then it appears that the total goal has failed eight times.

Hence, the example also underlines the advantages and necessity of result in structure-oriented evaluation. Nonobservance of logical goal structure may result in misjudgment.

The wide confidence intervals as well as the comparatively high value of the empirical standard deviation $\sigma_e = 0.24$ an indication as to a particularly pronounced random background during interrogation.

5 A TOOL FOR e-ASSESSMENT WITH THE SURE MODEL

The logical SURE needs a corresponding tool for implementation. As part of the frame of our research, we developed the beta version of an online tool for the SURE model (Tudevdagva et al., 2014).

The main architecture consists of five units.

1. The logical structure of the evaluation goals. This unit includes functions to create the key and sub goal sets. This logical structure is used in the fourth unit of the architecture for data processing.
2. The checklist for logical structure. Here the user can enter checklist questions using the checklist tool. The result of this unit will be an online survey questionnaire for the SURE model.
3. Online data collection. The function of this unit is to support users during an online survey. Administration of the tool can control and check data collection process via this unit.
4. Automatic processing of collected data. The SURE model's adapted calculation rules for data processing are advantageous. All collected data will be tabulated and processed by the SURE model calculation rules automatically.

Table 4.4 Checklist Results, Scores, and Confidence Intervals for Example 5

k	B_1 A_{11}	B_2 A_{21}	A_{22}	B_3 A_{31}	A_{32}	A_{33}	B_4 A_{41}	B_5 A_{51}	B_6 A_{61}	A_{62}	$Q_e^{*}(k)$	$Q^{*}(k)$
1	6	1	1	5	1	4	1	6	1	1	0.22	0.00
2	2	5	6	4	3	5	5	5	6	4	0.42	0.02
3	5	2	1	5	2	2	4	0	3	4	0.00	0.00
4	6	5	4	6	2	5	5	0	3	3	0.00	0.00
5	2	0	4	4	2	4	4	4	2	5	0.31	0.01
6	3	2	1	6	0	0	2	3	3	4	0.25	0.00
7	6	5	3	2	0	0	2	1	0	6	0.22	0.00
8	5	2	2	2	6	6	5	0	3	6	0.00	0.00
9	5	0	6	2	3	6	4	4	2	6	0.41	0.03
10	0	3	1	2	6	2	3	4	1	6	0.00	0.00
11	2	0	6	5	1	0	0	3	0	5	0.00	0.00
12	2	4	1	5	1	6	5	2	1	4	0.29	0.00
13	1	4	4	5	2	2	0	4	5	3	0.00	0.00
14	6	0	3	4	5	2	0	6	6	3	0.00	0.00
15	0	0	0	4	2	6	2	4	5	0	0.00	0.00
16	4	0	5	6	0	3	2	5	1	2	0.29	0.00
17	6	5	4	4	4	4	4	3	4	2	0.40	0.02
18	5	5	0	3	4	0	3	2	3	6	0.32	0.01
19	5	1	6	5	2	3	2	3	2	3	0.32	0.01
20	2	3	0	3	0	3	3	6	3	6	0.29	0.00
21	1	0	3	4	6	3	0	5	3	1	0.00	0.00
22	2	3	4	5	0	6	5	2	3	6	0.33	0.01
23	0	4	1	6	6	3	3	5	1	4	0.00	0.00
24	0	5	3	1	0	4	5	5	3	6	0.00	0.00
25	2	2	1	3	2	4	1	2	1	4	0.19	0.00
$Q^{*}(A_{ij})$	0.31	0.24	0.28	0.40	0.24	0.33	0.28	0.34	0.26	0.40	0.17	0.00
$Q_e^{*}(B_i)$	0.31	0.28		0.35			0.28	0.34	0.35			
$Q^{*}(B_i)$	0.31	0.46		0.70			0.28	0.34	0.56			

Scale										
0	1	2	3	4	5	6	7	8	9	10
0.00	0.10	0.20	0.30	0.40	0.50	0.60	0.70	0.80	0.90	1.00

Confidence intervals				
Level	$Q_e^{*}(C)$	$q_{e,0}^{*}$	$q_{e,1}^{*}$	σ_e
0.90		0.12	0.22	
0.95	0.17	0.11	0.24	0.16
0.99		0.09	0.26	

5. Graphical tools for the evaluation report. This beta tool for the SURE model includes simple functions to support the evaluation report of the evaluation scores. The tool can generate different types of charts and graphics with this unit.

Fig. 4.3 shows the software architecture of the SURE model tool. Its architecture corresponds to the waterfall diagram. Input of the tool is the logical structure of the evaluation goal. The SURE model can store several surveys in a survey library. All data are collected in a database. The database consists of collected original data. The data processing part computes evaluation scores using the calculation rules. The output unit can generate graphics and statistics for empirical evaluation scores.

Access to the tool distinguishes between two types of users: "Admin" and "User." Admin is a user who has access to all five units of tool. Admin has following rights:

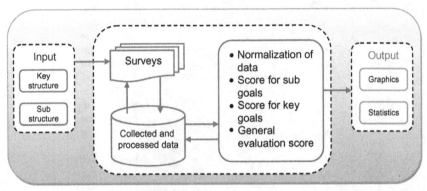

FIGURE 4.3

The architecture of tool for the SURE model.

- Create new surveys
- Edit existing surveys (Hide, Delete, Change order)
- Manage comment fields
- Generate accounts for users
- Check survey process
- Create sheets for accounts
- Tabulate collected data
- Process collected data
- Tabulate computed scores
- Create graphics.

A user is a person who receives a unique access code from the administrator or from the evaluation team. The user can use the access code until he/she submits his/her answers and has an overview of answer progress. The user can submit answers only if he/she has answered all the questions.

Accordingly users have the following possibilities:

- Access to open survey using own code
- Interrupt answer and continue later
- See statistic about own answer progress

- Change answer before submit
- Give additional comments to questions
- Fully answered survey can submit.

Fig. 4.4 shows data flow diagram of the SURE tool.

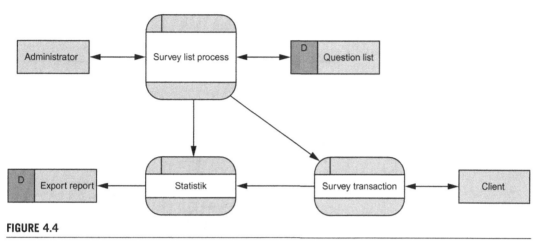

FIGURE 4.4

Data flow diagram of the SURE tool.

Admin creates an online survey based on the goal structures of evaluation. The tool can process several surveys parallel. The online survey can be active and visible or passive and invisible. The question list has different access. Admin has complete access rights here and the user works only with in his/her own created surveys. Users get a randomly generated unique access code and have access only to survey questions. The collected data are processed by calculation rules of the SURE model. The tool can generate different graphics and tables with evaluation results.

Fig. 4.5 shows the relation of objects and Fig. 4.6 shows an activity diagram of tool for the SURE model.

The main target of the tool design was to establish basic architecture that could be adapted to concepts of further applications for the tool. The screen design has to change depending on the browser and digital devices that are used by end users and admin.

6 CONCLUSION

e-Learning is a complex process that involves many different groups with specific tasks and roles. Evaluating such a process it should be possible to include in the evaluation the expectations and interests of all involved groups. Moreover, the evaluation method has to be able to make reference to the logical

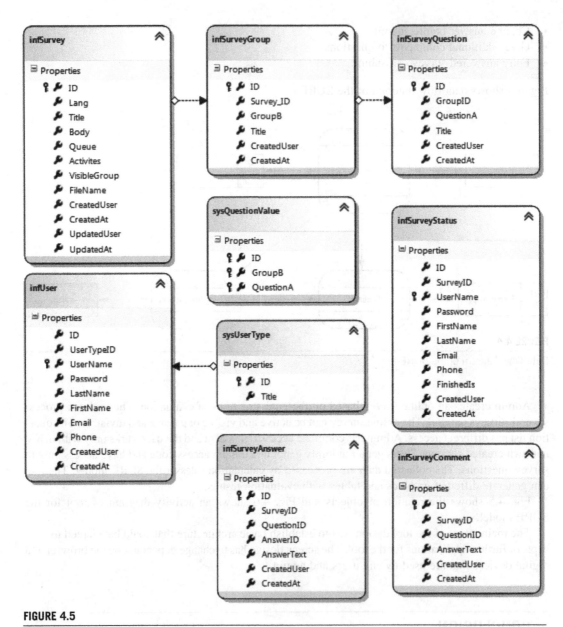

FIGURE 4.5

Relation of objects.

structure of the total goal of e-learning. Finally, the corresponding evaluation principles and their score calculation rules should be consistent with the calculation rules of general measure theory, which forms the proven scientific basis for measurements in the geometrical context or the evaluation of probabilities in probability and statistics, for instance. This is realized by the SURE model. The model consists

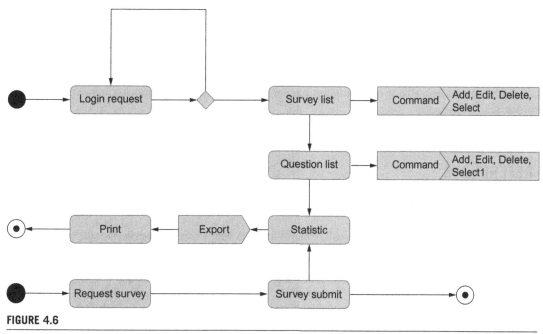

FIGURE 4.6

Activity diagram.

of eight steps that form the methodical concept for a structure-oriented evaluation. An essential advantage of SURE model is that this model works without weight factors, which are needed in the linear evaluation models. Hence, the SURE model is more objective than the linear models.

For the evaluation of a logical goal structure we distinguish between key and sub goals which are linked by logical AND and OR relations. Key goals are goals that have to be achieved so that the main goal can be achieved. Sub goals describe different goal alternatives to achieve a key goal or the main goal. By means of measure spaces in terms of general measure theory for the sub goals and embedding of the relevant sub goals into a product measure space a multidimensional evaluation of complex goal structures becomes possible. The obtained product space allows the calculation of scores for the evaluation of the logical structured goals of e-learning. The product measure satisfies the same calculation rules like any normalized measure of general measure theory. Depending on the contribution of sub goals to the achievement of an e-learning goal, logical series and parallel structures play an important part. For these goal structures corresponding score calculation rules are derived. Through a combination of these rules a consistent evaluation of complex goal structures becomes possible.

Based on the calculation rules an estimation method for scores is developed. By this method empirical scores can be calculated for sampling results obtained by adapted checklists. For a comparison of scores for the evaluation of different e-learning processes, a score calibration is recommended. This calibration transforms a SURE model score value into an evaluation score value. This value enables a further interpretation of score values and is helpful at final analysis of the sampling data for the evaluation report. An estimation for the evaluation score based on checklist results can be obtained at empirical score. The precision of empirical scores or empirical evaluation scores can be estimated by confidence intervals.

Two essential advantages of the SURE model compared to other evaluation approaches, like, for example, linear evaluation models, are the measure theoretical background and the corresponding transparent calculation rules used for data processing, which are derived from this. In this way the model becomes applicable in an analogous manner to the evaluation of administration or organization processes, for instance.

REFERENCES

Alkin, M.C., 1969. Evaluation theory development. Eval. Comment 2, 2–7.

Betsy, M.A., 2005. WeBal: a web-based assessment library to enhance teaching and learning in engineering. IEEE Trans. Educ. 48 (4), 764–771.

Blayney, P., Freeman, M., 2004. Automated formative feedback and summative assessment using individualised spreadsheet assignments. Australas. J. Educ. Tech. 20 (2), 209–231. Australasian Society for Computers in Learning in Tertiary Education.

Ehlers, U.D., Pawlowski, J.M. (Eds.), 2006. Handbook of Quality and Standardisation in E-Learning. Springer, Heidelberg.

How to Perform Evaluations, 2002. How to perform evaluations—evaluation reports, Canadian International Development Agency, report 7, January 2002, Available from: http://www.oecd.org/derec/canada/35138852.pdf.

Khan, B.K., 2005. Managing E-learning: Design, Delivery, Implementation and Evaluation. Information Science Publishing, London.

Kirkpatrick, D.L., 1959. Techniques of evaluating training programs. J. Am. Soc. Train. Dev. 13, 3–9.

Lam, P., Mcnaught, C., 2006. A three-layered cyclic model of elearning development and evaluation. In: Pearson, E., Bohman, P. (Eds.), Proceedings of EdMedia: World Conference on Educational Media and Technology 2006. Association for the Advancement of Computing in Education (AACE), Waynesville, pp. 1897–1904.

Patton, M.Q., 1980. Qualitative Evaluation and Research Methods, second ed. Sage Publications, Thousand Oaks, CA.

Phillips, P.P., 2010. ASTD Handbook of Measuring and Evaluating. ASDT Press, Alexandria, Virginia.

Ruhe, V., Zumbo, B.D., 2009. Evaluation in Distance Education and E-learning: The Unfolding Model. The Guilford press, New York.

Scriven, M., 1967. The methodology of evaluation. In: Stake, R.E. (Ed.), AERA Monograph Series on Curriculum Evaluation. In: vol. 1. Rand McNally, Chicago.

Stufflebeam, D.L., 1972. The relevance of the CIPP evaluation model for educational accountability. SRIS Q. 5, 3–6.

Tudevdagva, U., 2014. Structure Oriented Evaluation Model for E-Learning, Wissenschaftliche Schriftenreihe Eingebettete Selbstorganisierende Systeme. Chemnitz University of Technology, Chemnitz, Germany.

Tudevdagva, U., Hardt, W., 2011. A new evaluation model for eLearning programs. In: Technical Report CSR-11-03. Chemnitz University of Technology, Chemnitz, Germany.

Tudevdagva, U., Tomorchodor, L., Hardt, W., 2014. The beta version of implementation tool for SURE model. J. Commun. Comput. Inform. Sci. 466, 243–251.

Tyler, R.W., 1949. Basic Principles of Curriculum and Instruction. University of Chicago Press, Chicago.

FURTHER READING

Survey Monkey, n.d.a. Survey Monkey, Available from: https://de.surveymonkey.com.

Limesurvey, n.d.b. Limesurvey, Available from: https://www.limesurvey.org/en/.

Fluid Surveys, n.d.c. Fluid Surveys, Available from: http://fluidsurveys.com/.

Iperceptions, n.d.d. Iperceptions, Available from: http://signup.iperceptions.com/online-survey.html?gclid=CPqAg63g-LgCFYKS3god1GAAUg.

Free online surveys, n.d.e. Free online surveys, Available from: http://freeonlinesurveys.com/.

Kwik Survey, n.d.f. Kwik Survey, Available from: http://kwiksurveys.com/.

Easy polls, n.d.g. Easy polls, Available from: http://www.easypolls.net/.

Survey planet, n.d.h. Survey planet, Available from: https://www.surveyplanet.com/.

Sogo survey, n.d.i. Sogo survey, Available from: http://www.sogosurvey.com/.

Esurveyspro, n.d.j. Esurveyspro, Available from: http://www.esurveyspro.com/free-online-survey.aspx.

Esurvey creator, n.d.k. Esurvey creator, Available from: https://www.esurveycreator.com.

Stellar survey, n.d.l. Stellar survey, Available from: http://stellarsurvey.com/.

Questionpro, n.d.m. Questionpro, Available from: http://www.questionpro.com/.

Esurv, n.d.n. Esurv, Available from: http://esurv.org/.

Questionform, n.d.o. Questionform, Available from: http://questionform.com/.

Panelplace, n.d.p. Panelplace, Available from: http://www.panelplace.com/.

Surveycrest, n.d.q. Surveycrest, Available from: http://www.surveycrest.com/.

Addpoll, n.d.r. Addpoll, Available from: http://www.addpoll.com/.

Quick Surveys, n.d.s. Quick Surveys, Available from: https://www.quicksurveys.com/.

CONFIDENCE AND LEARNING: AFFECTIVE AND COGNITIVE ASPECTS IN ONLINE MATHEMATICS WITH AUTOMATIC FEEDBACK

5

N. Escudero-Viladoms*, T. Sancho-Vinuesa[†]

Autonomous University of Barcelona, Barcelona, Spain* Open University of Catalonia, Barcelona, Spain[†]

1 INTRODUCTION

The percentage of students who do not complete specific subjects in their degree courses is one of the key aspects of online higher education, especially in subjects such as mathematics and physics, where dropout rates are at their highest (Smith and Ferguson, 2005; Mensch, 2010).

In light of various studies on the subject, Castles (2004) categorizes the positive and negative factors that lead adult students (especially online students) to finish the course or to drop out. These factors are classified into three groups: social and environmental (in the student's life), traumatic (during the term) and intrinsic (including attitudes and motivation). Specific factors are mentioned in mathematics and physics studies. First, Smith and Ferguson (2005) point out that higher dropout rates are linked to specific problems related to mathematical notation and the use of graphic representation within asynchronous communication. Second, Sancho-Vinuesa and Gras-Martí (2010) maintain that these high dropout rates in mathematical courses are due to the profile of online students and the isolation of distance learning students. Indeed, this profile in online engineering studies is very specific. On the one hand there are external factors, such as they are adults with work and family responsibilities, with a lack of time to devote to the course; on the other hand they are accustomed to a more traditional form of education, based on learning with paper and pencil, and not based on learning through TIC resources (Steegmann et al., 2008). After more than 15 years of experience in online mathematics, our current approach is based on an understanding of online students' learning processes, taking into account the affective perspective.

The main aim of this research is to explain confidence in terms of the mathematical ability of a group of selected students and their performance in the online learning process, as well as to explore the relationship between confidence and learning in a course of basic mathematics. Following a

Formative Assessment, Learning Data Analytics and Gamification. http://dx.doi.org/10.1016/B978-0-12-803637-2.00005-1

qualitative analysis, we will identify student profiles in terms of confidence and mathematical performance and we will study the possible relationships between them.

1.1 SCENARIO UNDER STUDY

Specifically, the research was carried out in the context of *Introduction to Engineering Mathematics* at the Universitat Oberta de Catalunya (UOC), an online course in basic mathematics for future engineering students, where an innovative teaching methodology is applied. This is based on a learning model using a weekly activity plan with an e-assessment tool providing immediate and automatic feedback. One of the findings of a study on this teaching and learning experience is that a tool like this leads to a significant decrease in the dropout rate in this subject (Sancho-Vinuesa and Escudero, 2012).

1.1.1 Teaching methodology

The teaching plan of this subject consists of a set of activities and the resources to aid in the teaching process, as well as an assessment system to certify the objectives' achievement.

The web-based study material includes a series of interactive applications, text material in PDF format and supplementary material with links to online resources. The communication tools are a forum in the virtual classroom and e-mail.

Practice activities and weekly assessment tests with automatic feedback are carried out for continuous monitoring of the students' learning. Every week, the students are given a practice test and an assessment test on the contents of each unit. Students complete the practice tests whenever they want and as often as they wish. The automatic feedback provided after completion (score as well as comments) is for training purposes and is not included in the final mark. An assessment test must be completed weekly, and the final mark for each section is the average of the scores of the assessment tests for that section. The final mark of the subject is the average of the final marks for each section.

The questions contained in the tests (multiple choice, matching, short answer, true/false and essay) were produced using the WIRIS Quizzes tool.[1] The teaching strategy was developed as part of a teaching innovation project that involved specifying the course design, drafting the tests, and monitoring performance in a pilot test (Sancho-Vinuesa and Escudero, 2012).

1.1.2 Students

The population under study consisted of students on the *Introduction to Engineering Mathematics* course at the UOC during the second term of 2010–11. The number of students in the virtual classroom was 37, of which only nine were women (24.3%). Twenty-seven responded to a survey, which provided us with an initial profile of the students (Figs. 5.1–5.3).

---

[1]http://www.wiris.com/hosting.

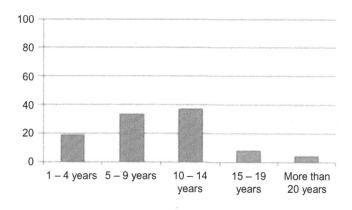

FIGURE 5.1

Number of years since last mathematics course taken.

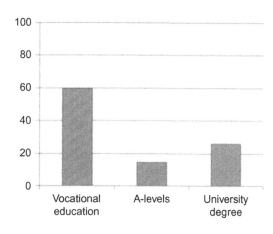

FIGURE 5.2

Previous academic qualifications.

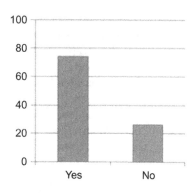

FIGURE 5.3

Previous experience at UOC.

1.1.3 The teacher

The main role of the teacher was to answer students' questions within 24 h. In general, the teacher did not send personal messages of encouragement unless the student asked for them. He/she thus remained neutral when answering questions and clarifying doubts.

2 THEORETICAL FRAMEWORK

2.1 MATHEMATICAL CONFIDENCE

Affective issues play a key role in mathematics learning (McLeod, 1992). This role is widely accepted by researchers in mathematics education in face-to-face learning. In fact, since the late 1980s most of the research on learning processes in mathematics education has begun to focus on affective issues (Gómez-Chacón, 2008). Nevertheless, there has been no theoretical approach to these issues in online education research. This study aims to contribute to the understanding and definition of affective issues in online mathematics, and particularly to that of mathematical confidence.

Mathematical confidence is defined by means of the *affective dimension* established by McLeod (1992) regarding the beliefs, attitudes, and emotions used to describe the wide range of emotional responses to mathematics. These terms represent increasing levels of emotional involvement, decreasing levels of cognitive involvement, intensity levels of increasing response and stability levels of decreasing response. For example, beliefs are strongly stable whereas emotions may appear and disappear quickly. McLeod (1992) considers confidence to be the student's belief in his or her competence in mathematics. However, in subsequent studies, confidence is considered an attitude (Fogarty et al., 2001; Pierce et al., 2007; Cretchley, 2007). In our research, we assume mathematical confidence to be a student's attitude, as we consider it is an "inclination to value (positively or negatively) that determines intentions and influences behaviour" (Gómez-Chacón, 2008). Furthermore, mathematical confidence is the result of emotional reactions that have been assumed and automated to generate feelings of moderate intensity and reasonable stability. However, as stated by Pehkonen and i Pietilä (2003), statements in an attitude questionnaire could be considered as both beliefs and attitudes. For example, in the attitudes questionnaire used in this research, the statement "I know I can overcome difficulties in learning Maths" may be considered a student's belief about him/herself based on experience and the result of a long period of time, but also as an attitude because it establishes a student's intention that influences the student's behavior during the mathematical learning process.

Most of the studies that consider mathematical confidence as an attitude towards mathematics often deal with it from an emotional perspective. For example, students who believe that their efforts will be rewarded are not concerned about learning difficult concepts; they expect to get good results and they feel comfortable with mathematics as a subject (Galbraith and Haines, 1998). Pierce et al. (2007) consider the perception of students in relation to their ability to obtain good results and self-confidence in overcoming difficulties in mathematics. In the context of this research, we understand mathematical confidence in its broader sense, considering the three components of attitude (cognitive, affective, and intentional) discussed by Hart (quoted in Gómez-Chacón, 2008). As an attitude, it is, therefore, evidenced and measured in three areas: mathematical competence, behavioral commitment and no need for interaction:

- *Mathematical competence* is the affective component in the same sense as the definition of mathematical confidence used by the authors mentioned in this section, and gives us information about the students' attitudes towards mathematics and learning.

- The cognitive component is incorporated through the *behavioral commitment*, evidenced by mathematical attitudes, which inform us about mathematical confidence based on how the students prefer to use their skills during the learning process.
- As online learning is the context of this research, the intentional component of the student's mathematical confidence is incorporated into the element that we call *no need for interaction*. We believe that in this context, mathematical confidence is also evidenced by students' expectations of independently making progress in their learning, without relying on interaction with other students and/or with their teacher (or another expert in the field).

2.2 MATHEMATICAL LEARNING

Mathematical learning concepts and processes have been extensively studied from several points of view for many years. In fact, as well as theoretical approaches, such as those of Dubinsky (1991), there are others linked to the educational experience. For example, Engelbrecht (2010) says that the process of understanding is a process of thin layers where greater understanding is gained with every layer. These layers are probably thinner the more advanced the student's level of knowledge. It is, therefore, an infinite process, the limit of which is a complete understanding of the specific content. The idea of this first-time exposure to a new idea or concept followed by a consolidation based on repeated exposure does not contradict an experimental constructivist approach, but, according to Engelbrecht (2010), it lays the foundations for a deeper understanding of mathematics. The teaching methodology of the course studied follows this idea. Henceforth, the difficulty lies in characterizing learning mathematics by measurable indicators.

In mathematical reasoning, contents do not completely characterize students' knowledge. According to Lithner (2008), the NCTM Principles and Standards (NCTM, 2000) complement the five standards of content (number and operations, algebra, geometry, measurement, and data analysis and probability) with five process standards (problem solving, reasoning and proof, connections, communication, and representation). Other authors (Niss, 2003) refer to mathematical skills. In this study, competences of reasoning and proof, and communication skills have been chosen to characterize online learning in addition to academic performance.

Like Brown (1994), Richards (1982) and Thurston (1995), Engelbrecht (2010) considers that the acquisition of advanced mathematics skills is a process of two phases: a first phase of understanding the content and a second of being able to communicate it in written format. In both phases, students need to know the scientific language and use it appropriately both orally and in writing. This facilitates the reading of textbooks, understanding class explanations and viewing videos and drafting problem-solving exercises. Moreover, according to Whitin and Whitin (2000), communicative competence enables the teacher to determine the student's progress in the learning process and the student to determine what they think, what connections they make, and even how they engage in the process. Based on Thurston (1995) and taking into account that communication in online learning is basically textual, communicative competence (in mathematics) is a key variable in the learning process.

2.3 THE RELATIONSHIP BETWEEN MATHEMATICAL CONFIDENCE AND MATHEMATICAL PERFORMANCE

A strong relationship between attitudes towards mathematics and student performance is frequently assumed. However, Ma and Kishor (1997) point out that existing studies have failed to provide consistent results that confirm this relationship and that the relationship between attitudes towards mathematics and performance is statistically significant but not strong enough. In addition, trying to establish a causal relationship from this meta-analysis, they say that the effect of attitudes on performance is not strong and has no important practical implications, and that the effect of these attitudes on mathematics achievement is not significant. It is important to note that these authors attribute these results to instruments for measuring attitudes, and, consequently, recommend refinement of these measures. Following this recommendation, we compared the subjective view of the students reflected in questionnaires with an analysis of the learning process by means of the evidence of the activity in the virtual classroom.

However, other studies have found a quite strong relationship between mathematical confidence and mathematical performance. Tartre and i Fennema (1995) conclude that confidence is positively correlated, and consistent with the performance. Barkatsas et al. (2009) obtained a significant correlation between levels of mathematics confidence, and behavioral commitment and performance in mathematics. Ercikan et al. (2005) also mention confidence in mathematics as a very important variable in predicting student performance in mathematics. These studies underlie the importance of the mathematical relationship between confidence and performance in mathematics through quantitative analysis. Our research is qualitative, and based on an analysis of the learning process of four students.

It is important to note that unlike the studies mentioned above, this work does not study the relationship between mathematical confidence and performance in terms of the grades obtained by the students on a course. The primary aim of this research is to look into the relationship between mathematical confidence and mathematical learning. We, therefore, consider not only a mark according to the level of the achievement of the objectives, but also the student's progress in two fundamental aspects: communication and mathematical reasoning.

3 RESEARCH METHODOLOGY

The nature of the research objectives presented here suggests a flexible methodology, of a predominantly qualitative nature in which the research questions and goals are not only linked to established theory, but also generated in the research process.

As an exploratory study, we select a few students and analyze the learning process in-depth tracking a set of indicators over 14 weeks. These indicators characterize the variables studied (mathematical confidence and mathematical learning) in each topic of the course, and in the construction of a multiple case study. The values for each indicator are obtained through various data sources. Each variable takes a numerical value on a scale of 1–5 that varies week to week according to the planning of the course. This will provide a graphical representation of the evolution of variables over the 14 weeks of the course. We qualitatively interpret the variation of these variables (and the relationship between them) by means of this evolution.

3.1 PARTICIPANTS

We selected four students—three men and one woman, taking into account the quality, variety and richness of information available. We present the information provided in the initial survey for the students selected in Table 5.1.

Table 5.1 Information About the Students Under Study

	Years Since Last Mathematics Course Taken	Previous Academic Qualifications	First Term at UOC	PC Use at Work	PC Use at Home
Student A	5–9 years	Vocational Education	Yes	Always	Always
Student B	5–9 years	Vocational Education (previously A-levels)	No	Always	Sometimes
Student C	5–9 years	Vocational Education	No	Always	Always
Student D	10–14 years	University Degree	No	Frequently	Frequently

3.2 DATA COLLECTION AND ANALYSIS

There are five main instruments for data collection: (a) a survey of attitudes towards mathematics in which students have to evaluate each statement on a 5-point Likert scale (Escudero, 2013); (b) a log activity for the Moodle classroom; (c) text documents to store messages sent by students; (d) quizzes and practice tests submitted by students for evaluation; and (e) an interview.

3.2.1 Mathematical confidence

The level of the students' mathematical confidence is based on the students' responses to a survey on attitudes towards mathematics. This survey was collected twice, at the beginning and in the middle of the term. We then compared the students' self-perception with unbiased data on their progress on the course (Escudero, 2013). A comparison of the two perspectives was needed as in most studies related to attitudes, there is a significant discrepancy between the attitudes expressed in a student survey and real attitudes (Hannula, 2002).

Summing up, the main data for establishing the level of mathematical confidence are as follows:

- Results of the survey on mathematical attitudes and towards mathematics.
- A time-related monitoring of the course, including the date, the time spent and the results of practice and assessment tests as well as the amount, date and type of messages sent by students to the forum as well as to the teacher's mailbox.

After assigning a value to each item that defines mathematical confidence, (a) mathematical competence, (b) behavioral commitment, and (c) no need for interaction, the arithmetic mean was calculated.

3.2.2 Mathematical learning

In order to establish the level of mathematical learning of each student the main data come from:

- The open assessment question in the assessment test which is analyzed qualitatively.
- Practice and assessment tests.

To measure mathematical learning, we established three items: (a) the degree of achievement of a specific content; (b) the level of mathematical communication, and (c) mathematical reasoning.

To measure communication and mathematical reasoning, we qualitatively analyzed the open question in the assessment test, as well as messages sent by students with mathematical content. For communication, we analyzed the use of mathematical terms and mathematical notation as well as the structure and clarity of communication. In mathematical reasoning, we considered the level of logical-deductive reasoning and explanation, justification and application procedures. After this analysis, a value was assigned to each item. In order to measure the achievement of specific content, we analyzed the procedures and concepts evaluated in each assessment test to establish the extent to which each student attained the contents evaluated. The items and grading established can be viewed in detail in Escudero (2013). Finally, the level of the student's mathematical learning was obtained by calculating the mean of the values assigned to each of the items above.

Furthermore, an online interview in which the student evaluates the usefulness of practice tests and discusses his/her perception of the teaching methodology is analyzed.

To store and manage data from different resources, spreadsheets were used. The information registered automatically from Moodle environment, a time sequence for each student was created in another spreadsheet.

Analysis plan
After data were collected they were represented graphically. For each student, the graphical representation of mathematical confidence and mathematical learning was created through the specified items which define them. As soon as analysis for each variable was done, we explored the combination of both defining several student's profiles.

4 MAIN FINDINGS AND DISCUSSION
In this section, the main findings about confidence, learning and the relationship between them will be shown.

4.1 MATHEMATICAL CONFIDENCE
The items described in the methodology section have been represented with the data collected through the survey moderated by students' interventions in the forum or the teacher's mailbox (Figs. 5.4–5.7).

Accordingly, main findings are presented and discussed.

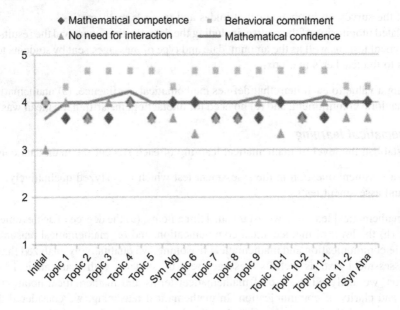

FIGURE 5.4

Mathematical confidence: student A.

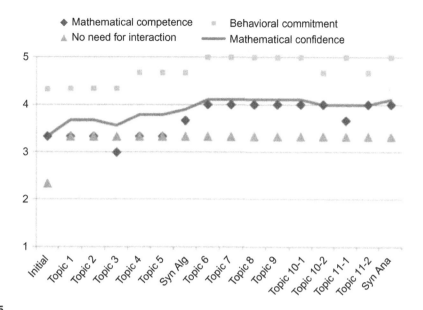

FIGURE 5.5

Mathematical confidence: student B.

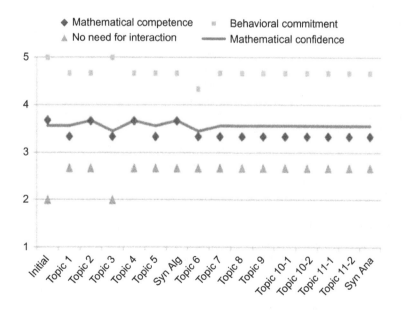

FIGURE 5.6

Mathematical confidence: student C.

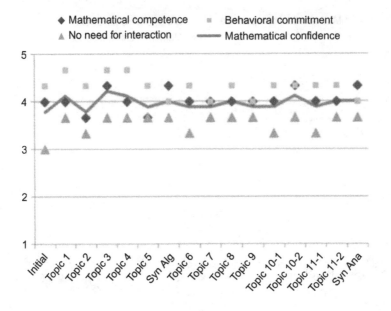

FIGURE 5.7

Mathematical confidence: student D.

R1. Medium-high level of confidence

The mathematical confidence level of the students studied is similar.

The fact that the mathematical confidence level of the four students is medium-high (Figs. 5.4–5.7) contradicts our initial hypothesis of the characteristics of the students having a significant and negative confidence level in mathematics. The students studied spent a considerable length of time disengaged from mathematics (at least 5 years) and decided to take an introductory course to refresh their mathematical knowledge. Given these characteristics, we expected a medium-low level or, at best, a medium level of mathematical confidence. Despite this contradiction, the medium-high mathematical confidence level for the four students is consistent with the results obtained by Galbraith and Haines (1998) in a study of first-year students on face-to-face scientific degree courses. We agree with these authors that the choice of studies in the field of engineering, with a high mathematical component, plays a significant role in the students' mathematical confidence level. According to these results, the student's choice of studies carries more weight than the adverse features initially considered.

R2. Stability of mathematical confidence level

The mathematical confidence level remained stable throughout the term for our four students (Figs. 5.4–5.7). Only a slight increase was seen in student B's results (Fig. 5.5).

McLeod (1992) notes that the stability of beliefs, attitudes, and emotions differ in terms of the affective responses they represent, and states that beliefs and attitudes are generally stable. As a result, the stability obtained in the mathematical confidence level analyzed, with only slight variations during the term, is consistent with the characteristics of confidence as an attitude. However, the stability obtained can be influenced by the fact that the student's perception is only directly obtained twice—at the beginning and in the middle of the term—and mathematical confidence in each topic is obtained by contrasting this perception with the student's analysis of the learning process. The objection could be raised that the values obtained do not faithfully reflect the student's perception in each topic. However, the study conducted by Rovira and Sancho-Vinuesa (2012), in the same context as our research and where mathematical confidence directly assesses each topic, confirms these results.

Moreover, the observed variability in the level of confidence and the slight increase observed in student B's mathematical confidence is consistent with the cyclical relationship established between the emotions, attitudes, and beliefs (Gómez-Chacón, 2008).

R3. High behavioral commitment

We found that of the three items that allow us to measure mathematical confidence, behavioral commitment is in almost all subjects the highest-scoring item for the four students analyzed (Figs. 5.4–5.7).

The high level of behavioral commitment is due to a high level in the three sub-items involved. These sub-items indicate that students:

- persist in the correction of mathematical errors,
- test the contents by solving questions and problems, and
- try to connect the knowledge learned with their previous knowledge.

Other studies (Galbraith and Haines, 1998; Rovira and Sancho-Vinuesa, 2012) with a similar definition of behavioral commitment also obtained high levels for the corresponding variables. As we also noted in our research, Galbraith and Haines (1998) found that students significantly valued their commitment to the subject as reinforcing their learning experiences. From our point of view, although this high level of commitment is generally reasonable, it is even more striking in our context, in which despite the students' work and family commitments, they decided to start engineering studies after years away from academia.

R4. No need for interaction with "the expert"

We found that, of the three items that enable us to measure mathematical confidence, the item with the lowest level is *no need for interaction* (Figs. 5.4–5.7), although in students A, B, and D (Figs. 5.4, 5.5, and 5.7, respectively) this level rates as medium and medium-high.

Students say they need interaction with peers and teachers (or another expert in the field) to progress in their learning of mathematics. In particular, the medium or medium-low level obtained in our study is mainly due to the item which assesses whether the student can progress in learning mathematics without constant monitoring and a support staff teacher, or any other expert in the field. This means that students believe they cannot move forward without the help of a teacher or another expert. This need is consistent with the results of the research conducted by Mupinga et al. (2006), which shows that one of the three major expectations for online students is good communication with the teacher. According to Mupinga et al. (2006), online students require frequent communication with the teacher to avoid a sense of isolation, and for reassurance that they are not missing anything in the learning process.

4.2 MATHEMATICAL LEARNING

In this section, we present the results for the mathematical learning level of the students (Figs. 5.8–5.11) defined based on mathematical communication level, mathematical reasoning, and the achievement of specific content. We have no information about Integration 11-1 for student B (Fig. 5.9), as the submission was missed for personal reasons, and we have no information on the trigonometric function topics for student C (Fig. 5.10) due to technical problems when accessing the test.

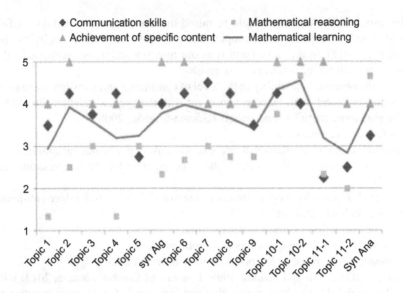

FIGURE 5.8

Mathematical learning level: student A.

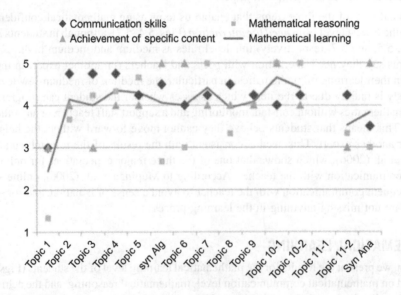

FIGURE 5.9

Mathematical learning level: student B.

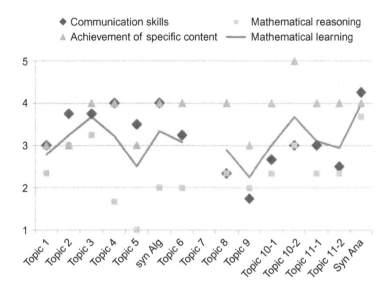

FIGURE 5.10

Mathematical learning level: student C.

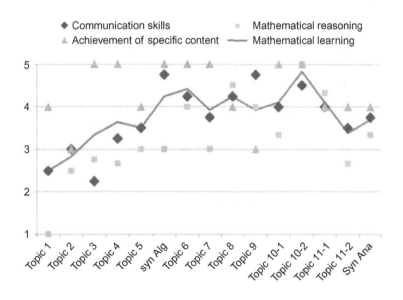

FIGURE 5.11

Mathematical learning level: student D.

In general, we found that mathematical learning, considered as a combination of communication skills, mathematical reasoning and the achievement of content (grades in the assessment tests), varies depending on the student and the topic. However, except in some specific topics, the variability moves between two points and in all cases except one, the grades obtained are higher than the levels of mathematical communication and mathematical reasoning.

R5. Variability of mathematical learning depending on content

The students' levels of mathematical learning vary depending on the content, and some students' variation is more pronounced than others (Figs. 5.8–5.11). There are no similarities among the four students in terms of either the topic with the highest level of mathematical learning, nor the lowest. However, for all the students there is an increase in one of the derivation topics (10-1 or 10-2) and a decrease in the level of learning in integration topics (11-1 and 11-2). This is a traditionally difficult topic for students.

The factors that may affect the acquisition of mathematical content have been widely studied in primary and secondary educational level and published in journals about research in mathematics education. Although it is beyond the scope of this paper to consider the multiple causes of a certain level of online mathematical learning (eg, external factors, insufficient previous knowledge or specific difficulties in applying procedures), we have confirmed that there is a variation in the level of mathematical learning and there are differences in the variation of this level for each student throughout the term, consistent with the idea of a progressive learning layer (Engelbrecht, 2010).

R6. Difficulties in mathematical reasoning

In our four students under study, we observed that of the three items that allow us to measure mathematical learning in the majority of topics mathematical reasoning had the lowest level (Figs. 5.8–5.11).

Escudero (2013) established possible causes for this low level of mathematical reasoning based on an analysis of each student's learning process. At the beginning of the course, this low level of mathematical reasoning may be partly due to an inexpert use of the evaluation tool. However, incomplete explanations and justifications and incomplete applications of procedures are later due to, firstly, gaps in the understanding of concepts and, secondly, the belief that reasoning is not needed in certain procedures. While the ability to explain, verbalize and communicate the reasoning undertaken is essential in any educational setting (Engelbrecht, 2010), it is not seen as necessary for online engineering students in a mathematics subject.

4.3 EXPLORING THE RELATIONSHIP BETWEEN CONFIDENCE AND MATHEMATICAL LEARNING: STUDENT'S PROFILE

When the results of the variables "mathematical confidence" and "mathematical learning" are combined for each student over the term (Figs. 5.12–5.15) we are able to identify three profiles that are consistent with the profiles observed in our teaching experience over more than 15 years:

- A profile in which the level of mathematical learning is lower than the mathematical confidence level (Figs. 5.12 and 5.14);
- A profile in which the level of mathematical learning is higher than the mathematical confidence level (Fig. 5.13); and

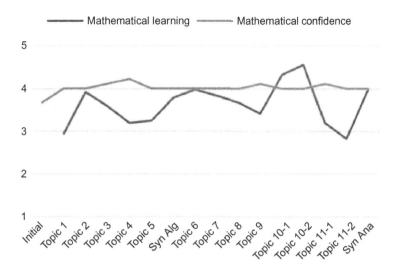

FIGURE 5.12

Mathematical confidence and mathematical learning of student A.

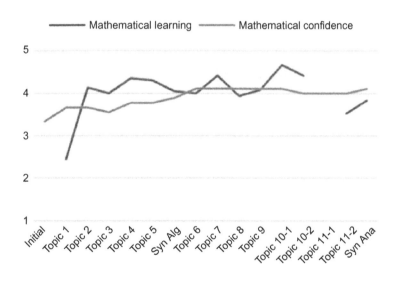

FIGURE 5.13

Mathematical confidence and mathematical learning of student B.

- A profile in which the level of mathematical learning is initially lower than the level of mathematical confidence, but increases over time until it is finally higher (Fig. 5.15).

However, these profiles are not absolutely stable, that is, in most of the topics, the relationship between confidence and learning we have described for each profile is stable, but this relationship is occasionally reversed.

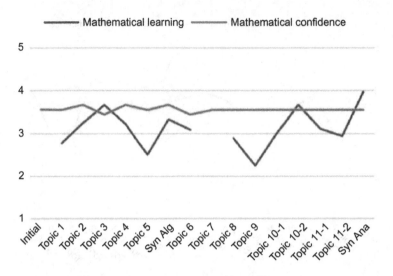

FIGURE 5.14

Mathematical confidence and mathematical learning of student C.

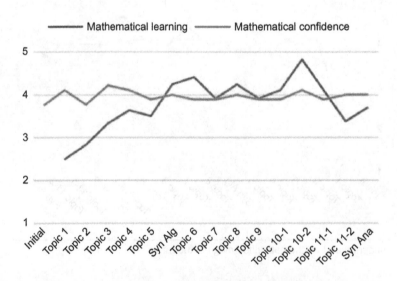

FIGURE 5.15

Mathematical confidence and mathematical learning of student D.

5 CONCLUSIONS AND FUTURE LINES

The main aim of the research was to study the relationship between mathematical confidence and mathematical e-learning. To achieve this aim, we characterized and analyzed two main variables, mathematical confidence and mathematical learning, in an online course at the Universitat Oberta de Catalunya.

The first variable was measured by means of a qualitative analysis of responses to a survey of attitudes toward learning mathematics and mathematical attitudes, monitoring the activity in the virtual classroom and messages sent by the student. The second variable was measured by a qualitative analysis of mathematical communication (in the assessment tests and emails) and the results of the evaluation tests.

We collected data from four students selected according to the richness of the information provided from their voluntary participation in research. Although it is not a representative sample of the classroom, it provides a sufficient range for achieving the exploratory aim of this research.

We present the conclusions of this research below.

First, the mathematical confidence level is similar for the students under study and is quite high. The similarity of the levels of confidence obtained is important if we consider that no specific selection of the students analyzed took place. In addition, this quite high level is significant considering that it is a result that we did not initially anticipate in light of the students' profile. Furthermore, these students had decided to take an introductory course before tackling mathematics-related subjects in an engineering degree. This shows that they needed to revise mathematical content and were determined to do so. Nevertheless, this quite high confidence level is consistent with the results of Galbraith and Haines (1998) in a study which was also carried out in the context of higher education. According to these authors, choosing an engineering degree is among the most significant factors determining an online students' level of confidence. This choice is, therefore, more relevant than other factors that are characteristic of online learners (age, long period without studying mathematics and insufficient prior knowledge).

Second, the level of learning through mathematical reasoning, communication and math skills tests varies depending on the topics and depends on the student. This result is consistent with the idea of a learning layer enabling the gradual acquisition of mathematical content that prevents the acquisition of new content without a sufficient prior approximation (Engelbrecht, 2010). In our context, in a pre-university mathematics course, the level of prior knowledge is essential for understanding each student at all times. Another point is that, according to the results, the main difficulties lie in students' mathematical reasoning. Indeed, this is a year of transition to advanced mathematics, and students must apply deductive reasoning to solve the issues raised. To understand students' difficulties with thinking mathematically, we must analyze their profile carefully: the students are adults who disengaged from learning mathematics a long time ago. Most of them use general thinking based on empirical induction to do the exercises. This difficulty is not just a problem in mathematics-related subjects, it is a proven difficulty in various subjects within engineering degrees that require work with definitions and theorems.

Finally, one of the important results of this work is the establishment of three profiles for mathematical learning and mathematical confidence, and the fact that they remained stable over the entire term. The establishment of these profiles, linked to a fairly high level of mathematical confidence, opens up the possibility of study of the existence of more profiles linked to other levels of mathematical confidence. Furthermore, the incorporation of other affective elements in the analysis of the learning process, such as attitudes or beliefs toward mathematics, could enhance this initial approach. In a mathematical context, the studies focused on emotional aspects are scarce (Gómez-Chacón, 2008). In an online context, the research regarding affective dimension in mathematics learning is an open field. Then we consider that this is an interesting research line, specially oriented to students who are starting higher education.

Another aspect that may become significant in an online learning process is the feedback provided to the student. If we define a measure of feedback effect in the student performance, we will be able to explore the relationship between feedback and the level of mathematical confidence as well as the level of mathematical achievements. In addition, we could explore the relationship between feedback effect and the student's profile based on the level of confidence and mathematical performance.

Despite this being a four-case study, the results obtained provide specific knowledge in the field of online mathematics learning that can be projected to other contexts and situations. One way to move beyond the confirmation of these results would be to use the data collected automatically in the virtual classroom for all students and define behavior patterns with data mining techniques. Furthermore, all the knowledge generated from this information could be used with a real time intervention in order to improve the learning process.

ACKNOWLEDGMENTS

This research was funded by the Spanish Government through the project "ICT-FLAG" Enhancing ICT education through Formative assessment, Learning Analytics and Gamification (TIN2013-45303-P).

REFERENCES

Barkatsas, A., Kasimatis, K., i Gialamas, V., 2009. Learning secondary mathematics with technology: exploring the complex interrelationship between students' attitudes, engagement, gender and achievement. Comput. Educ. 52, 562–570. Elsevier Ltd.

Brown, T., 1994. Towards a hermeneutical understanding of mathematics and mathematical learning. In: Ernest, P. (Ed.), Studies in Mathematics Education. Falmer Press, London.

Castles, J., 2004. Persistence and the adult learner: factors affecting persistence in Open University students. Act. Learn. High. Educ. 5 (2), 166–179.

Cretchley, P., 2007. Does computer confidence relate to levels of achievement in ICT-enriched learning models? Educ. Inf. Technol. 2, 29–39.

Dubinsky, E., 1991. Reflective abstraction in advanced mathematical thinking. In: Tall, D.O. (Ed.), Advanced Mathematical Thinking. Kluwer, Dordrecht.

Engelbrecht, J., 2010. Adding structure to the transition process to advanced mathematical activity. Int. J. Math. Educ. Sci. Technol. 41 (2), 143–154. http://dx.doi.org/10.1080/00207390903391890.

Ercikan, K., McCreith, T., Lapointe, V., 2005. Factors associated with mathematics achievement and participations in advanced mathematics courses: an examination of gender differences from an international perspective. Sch. Sci. Math. 105 (1), 5–14.

Escudero, N., 2013. Feedback, confiança matemàtica i aprenentatge matemàtic en un entorn d'aprenentatge en línia (Doctoral Thesis). Universitat Autònoma de Barcelona, Spain. Available from, http://www.tdx.cat/handle/10803/117440.

Fogarty, G.J., Cretchley, P., Harman, C., Ellerton, N., Konki, N., 2001. Validation of a questionnaire to measure mathematics confidence, computer confidence, and attitudes to the use of technology for learning mathematics. Math. Educ. Res. J. 13 (2), 154–160.

Galbraith, P., Haines, C., 1998. Disentangling the nexus: attitudes to mathematics and technology in a computer learning environment. Educ. Stud. Math. 36, 275–290.

Gómez-Chacón, I.M., 2008. Matemática emocional. Los afectos en el aprendizaje matemático. Editorial Narcea.

Hannula, M.S., 2002. Attitude towards mathematics emotions, expectations and values. Educ. Stud. Math. 49 (1), 25–46.

Lithner, J., 2008. A research framework for creative and imitative reasoning. Educ. Stud. Math. 67 (3), 255–276.

Ma, X., Kishor, N., 1997. Attitude towards self, social factors, and achievement in mathematics: a meta-analytic review. Educ. Psychol. Rev. 9 (2), 89–120.

McLeod, D.B., 1992. Research on affect in mathematics education: a reconceptualization. In: Douglas Grouws, A. (Ed.), Handbook of Research on Mathematics Teaching and Learning. MacMillan Publishing Company, New York.

Mensch, S., 2010. Issues in offering numeric based courses in an online environment. J. Instr. Pedagog. 3. Available from: http://www.aabri.com/manuscripts/09405.pdf.

Mupinga, D.M., Nora, R.T., Yaw, D.C., 2006. The learning styles, expectations, and needs of online students. Coll. Teach. 54 (1), 185–189.

National Council of Teachers of Mathematics, 2000. Principles and Standards for School Mathematics. The Council, Reston, VA.

Niss, M., 2003. Mathematical competencies and the learning of mathematics: the Danish KOM project. In: Proceedings of Third Mediterranean Conference on Mathematics Education, pp. 115–124.

Pehkonen, E., i Pietilä, A., 2003. On relationships between beliefs and knowledge in mathematics education. In: Mariotti, M.A. (Ed.), Proceedings of CERME 3.

Pierce, R., Stacey, K., Barkatsas, A., 2007. A scale for monitoring students' attitudes to learning mathematics with technology. Comput. Educ. 48, 285–300. Elsevier.

Richards, P., 1982. Difficulties in learning mathematics. In: Cornelius, M. (Ed.), Teaching Mathematics. Nichols Publishing Company, London.

Rovira, E., Sancho-Vinuesa, T., 2012. The relationship between cognition and affect on online mathematics and their interaction over time. eLC Res. Pap. Ser. 4, 43–55.

Sancho-Vinuesa, T., Escudero, N., 2012. A proposal for formative assessment with automatic feedback on an online mathematics subject. RUSC Rev. Univ. Soc. Conoc. 9 (2), 240–260.

Sancho-Vinuesa, T., Gras-Martí, A., 2010. Teaching and learning undergraduate mathematics in an online University. In: Kinuthia, W., Marshall, S. (Eds.), Educational Technology in Practice: Research and Practical Case Studies from the Field. Information Age Publishing Inc., Charlotte, NC. ISBN 978-1-60752-452-6. LD: LB 1028.3.E3335 2010.

Smith, G.G., Ferguson, D., 2005. Student attrition in mathematics e-learning. Australas. J. Educ. Technol. 21 (3), 323–334.

Steegmann, C., Huertas, M.A., Juan, A.A., i Prat, M., 2008. E-learning de las asignaturas del ámbito matemático-estadístico en las universidades españolas: oportunidades, retos, estado actual y tendencias. Revista de Universidad y Sociedad del Conocimiento 5 (2), 97. http://rusc.uoc.edu.

Tartre, L.A., i Fennema, E., 1995. Mathematics achievement and gender: a longitudinal study of selected cognitive and affective variables (grades 6-12). Educ. Stud. Math. 28, 199–217. Kluwer Academic Publishers.

Thurston, W.P., 1995. On proof and progress in mathematics. Learn. Math. 15, 29–37.

Whitin, P., Whitin, D.J., 2000. Maths is language too: talking and writing. The Mathematics Classroom. NCTE, Urbana.

TEACHING AND LEARNING METHODS AT THE OPEN UNIVERSITY OF JAPAN: TRANSITION FROM THE BROADCASTING MODEL TO A MORE PERSONALIZED LEARNING MODEL

6

K. Aoki

The Open University of Japan, Chiba, Japan

In traditional methods of teaching and learning, especially those conducted at a distance, formative assessment has not been a main focus, but teaching, in terms of content delivery, has. However, the importance of formative assessment as a core component of effective teaching and learning has now been realized and the paradigm nowadays seems to be slowly shifting from content delivery towards providing students with engaging activities and assessing those activities to support and stimulate learning. Gikandi et al. (2011), in their extensive review of literature on online formative assessment, state that embedding formative assessment within online courses fosters a sense of an interactive and collaborative online learning community.

This is easier said than done as the shift requires a drastic change in the perceptions of teachers as well as students, not to mention the administrative and organizational structure of formal educational institutions. This chapter illustrates the case study of a distance education university in Japan in terms of its struggle to get on the tidal wave of the formative assessment and learner-centered learning.

1 THE OPEN UNIVERSITY OF JAPAN

The Open University of Japan (OUJ) was established in 1983. Modeled after the UK Open University it combined broadcast lectures with correspondence texts and visits to local centers; OUJ began its instruction via television and radio broadcasts in Apr. 1985. In Japan, the idea of establishing a university that utilized broadcasting as its instructional medium was first conceived in 1967 by the Minister of Education. However, it took more than 10 years for the idea to be actually implemented due to an assortment of political issues.

Formative Assessment, Learning Data Analytics and Gamification. http://dx.doi.org/10.1016/B978-0-12-803637-2.00006-3

What is particularly unique about OUJ is that since its inception the university has owned and operated an over-the-air broadcast television and radio station to deliver its instructional programs. Such instructional broadcasting services mean that not only registered students, but anybody who can receive the broadcasting signals can watch or listen to its instructional programs. It was determined by the government that OUJ would broadcast instructional programs over the air at that time to fulfill the mission of providing a second chance to people who had missed the opportunity to receive higher education due to economical and personal reasons during the World War II and the economic downturn afterwards.

With the financial support of the Japanese Ministry of Education, Culture, Sports, Science and Technology (MEXT) for the provision of university and continuing education services and the help of the Japanese Ministry of Internal Affairs and Communications (MIC) in the running and operating of broadcasting stations, OUJ has operated its broadcast-based education system for the past 30 years.

Over 300 subject courses are being broadcast each semester through terrestrial digital broadcasting, as well as satellite broadcasting, which covers the entire country as its footprint. Each of the broadcast courses accompanies a textbook that has been written solely for the broadcast course. The standard model for a student to take a broadcast course is to watch or listen to a 45-minute broadcast program each week for 15 weeks, and take the final exam at the end of the semester, which is conducted at one of the 50 study centers around the country.

In addition to those broadcast courses, face-to-face classes are offered at each of the 50 study centers. In total over 3000 classes per semester are offered at the 50 study centers throughout the country, though all the classes are independently planned and offered at each of the study centers without much relation to the broadcast courses. These face-to-face classes are usually offered at the weekend using the full days of Saturday and Sunday and adjunct instructors who teach at local universities. There are usually no exams and student assessment is usually done on site either solely by attendance/participation or by some in-class exercises or reports. It is very rare that the assessment is conducted after the weekend classes are over as the swift submission of the students' grades is required as an implicit policy of the classes. The classes are planned and organized independently of the broadcast courses by the director of each study center. The focus of the central curriculum committee's attention is usually only on the broadcast courses despite the fact that undergraduate students have to take a minimum of 20 credits within the face-to-face classes in order to graduate.

If students have questions with regards to the content of the broadcast instructional programs or the accompanying textbooks, they can send the questions either via postal mail or via the university portal site, which are first sent to the administrative office and then relayed to the instructor(s) if necessary. In other words, there are few channels for direct communication between students and the teacher(s) of the broadcast programs. It has been carefully designed this way even on the new course portal, which was just introduced in Apr. 2014, because some of faculty members strongly object to the direct interaction with students. The culture of "sage on the stage" still prevails in many of higher education institutions in Japan, especially at OUJ, mainly because most faculty members at OUJ are established academics who have been hired to create broadcast instructional programs as authorities in the given fields.

There are so-called mid-term correspondence assignments for each broadcast course, which occur during the set period in the middle of a semester. Most courses offer multiple-choice quizzes for the mid-term assignments, which can be answered either online or on the computer-readable sheets sent through postal mail. Some courses offer essay assignments that are sent via postal mail, except one course that uses online essay assignments. For these essay assignments, teachers read and grade them and the feedback is sent back to the students, while for all the multiple-choice quizzes the grading is done automatically. This mid-term correspondence assignment does not count for part of the each student's course grade, but gives students the eligibility to take the final credit-earning exam for the course.

As stated above, the final exams are conducted at the study centers all over the country. For each course the exam schedule is centrally determined and the exam is conducted at the same time at all the 50 study centers. Hence, it requires a thorough logistical coordination and students have to take the exam on the scheduled date and at a scheduled time. In fact, many students determine which course to take at the beginning of the semester according to the exam schedule because if they cannot take the exam, they cannot earn credits for the course they are registered for.

2 FIRST ONLINE COURSES AT OUJ

As discussed, OUJ has been offering the teaching and learning system for the last 30 years based on its broadcasting programs, print materials, and study centers located nation-wide. However, the recent decline in its student enrollment and the potentials of online learning realized and recognized widely in the forms of MOOCs (Massive Open Online Courses) are now pressing OUJ to reconsider its systems of teaching and learning, and to try something new for the first time in its history. In fact, the first online courses started in Apr. 2015, which is a revolutionary phenomenon for OUJ, but the first online courses are far from those which take full advantage of online learning as explained below.

The first two online courses at OUJ were offered out of necessity as the institution was asked by MEXT to offer certification courses for those who want to upgrade their licenses from nursing school teachers to kindergarten teachers. As the courses had to be made relatively quickly (in 1 year) and also all the time slots for television broadcasting courses had been already filled, the university decided to offer two courses of one credit online.

The courses had to be started in Apr. 2015 and the teams for creating the courses were assembled in Apr. 2014. However, usually at OUJ course development takes 3 years from its inception to the actual delivery, these online courses were tasked to be developed from inception to delivery within a year. As for the instructors for the courses, faculty members in a traditional university were selected as they are experts in the topic field of the courses. However, none of them had any experience of teaching in a distance learning environment or online.

As for the platform of the online courses, Moodle was selected as it is the most widely used open source learning management system (LMS) worldwide and it has been already utilized at OUJ, though with very limited scope. However, as OUJ possessed little in the way of human resources to develop and maintain the system in-house, all the technical work for implementing the online courses was outsourced, which severely limited the flexibility of the course design as any extra work that was not specified in the beginning would require additional cost, which would need to go through a cumbersome budget approval process.

Soon after the first assembly of the teams, it was realized that in order to develop the online courses within such a limited timeframe and with such limited resources, the courses had to be made to resemble the traditional broadcasting courses as closely as possible in order to utilize the existing resources and minimize confusion among people involved. Hence, although they were online courses, the utilization of online formative assessment in those courses ended up being minimal, with only the self-test tools that were placed in each section. These self-test tools give immediate automatic feedback to students as to whether their understanding is correct or not and why their original responses were incorrect. According to Oellermann and van der Merwe (2015), these self-test tools are considered an important and meaningful strategy that engages students in valuable learning experiences.

As for assessment for the course grade, these courses utilize the same system of mid-term assignments that comprise multiple-choice questions to be automatically graded by computers, and in-person final exams to be conducted at the study centers. The questions in mid-term assignments and those in the final exams are taken from the self-test quiz questions so that the courses are designed in such a way that those who studied well online using the self-test tools will perform better in the assessment for the course.

Discussion boards are also placed. However, discussion activities are not assessed as part of the course grade and, hence, students participation in discussion boards have been nonexistent.

It has been suggested that improving learner engagement through active learning and formative assessment is critical and developing a learning community is important (Yoder and Hochevar, 2005; Gikandi et al, 2011; Vonderwell and Boboc, 2013; Oellermann and van der Merwe, 2015). However, many factors prevent these learning ideals from being implemented. These factors are classified into teacher-oriented, student-oriented, and institutional/administrative, and explained in the following.

2.1 TEACHER-ORIENTED FACTORS

Effective integration of formative assessment in online courses requires well-structured strategies that are very different from summative assessment. In summative assessment teachers only need to come up with the final assessment strategy for giving a course grade, while in formative assessment teachers have to provide ongoing monitoring of student learning and adequate feedback. Various researchers suggest that such feedback should be timely, ongoing, formatively useful and easy to understand (Gaytan and McEwen, 2007; Koh, 2008; Wang et al, 2008; Wolsey, 2008; Gikandi et al., 2011), especially in asynchronous learning environments to sustain students' engagement (Tallent-Runnels et al., 2006). Effective feedback also enables meaningful interactions in order to share learning goals and expected outcomes (Gaytan and McEwen, 2007).

Giving appropriate individual feedback in facilitating students' learning is an onus task not to be taken lightly either by the teacher him/herself or by the institution. Often the teachers are not fully aware of this, although it is a core process of teaching and learning.

At OUJ, it has been commonly understood that the main responsibility of faculty members is to create course materials in terms of writing a textbook for each course and creating broadcasting programs for the course. It usually takes a 1 full year to write and complete a textbook and another full year to produce 15 45-minute broadcasting programs. In creating these broadcasting programs, faculty members are responsible for all the content in terms of developing ideas for visuals to be presented on television, writing scripts for the programs, and also appearing and performing lectures in front of camera. It is a very time-consuming task to produce content for every course. The content creation task consumes most of the faculty members' energy and time, and on average a full-time faculty member has to create a new course every other year and renew existing courses every 4 years. Due to the fact that content creation takes up most of the faculty members' time and energy, it becomes very difficult to spare time and energy for interaction with the students and it is considered as "unnecessary extra burden."

2.2 STUDENT-ORIENTED FACTORS

OUJ students have been accustomed to the study style in which students watch video lectures and read print materials on their own and prepare for in-person exams at the end of a semester. Most OUJ students are mature students and they are highly motivated to study, as shown in the average dropout rate being less than 10%. However, the students are used to the passive mode of learning where few opportunities to interact with peers and ask the instructors questions directly are provided.

In addition, as is often seen in Eastern culture, students tend to be hesitant to ask questions or discuss matters openly. As became evident, when the development team was designing the platform for online courses there were frequent requests to make class discussions anonymous, as many students are afraid of embarrassment and losing face even online.

Another student-oriented factor is that OUJ students are accustomed to the academic schedule in which their only time-bound requirements are to submit a mid-term assignment, which usually requires answering machine-gradable multiple-choice questions and the final exam, which students take in person at study centers. Thus, many students tend to study in a hurry just before the assignment due date and the final exam without the habit of a regular weekly schedule of study.

There is also a concern regarding the digital literacy of students. The majority of OUJ students are nontraditional students, as 62% of its student population is over 40 years old and 21% is over 60 years old. As the university touts itself as a broadcasting university, students are not usually expected to have a high level of digital literacy. In order to overcome this situation, face-to-face classes on digital literacy have been implemented in many study centers, but still these are not enough to raise the level of digital literacy of all the students.

2.3 INSTITUTIONAL/ADMINISTRATIVE FACTORS

OUJ is a large distance education university in which approximately 90,000 students are enrolled and there are many courses in which more than 1000 students are enrolled. It is almost impossible for an instructor to give feedback to individual students and most grading is done automatically using multiple-choice questions.

Such universities where a large number of students are expected to enroll in one course tend to have the system of tutors who oversee the day-to-day activities of students besides instructors who are responsible for overall content of the course. At OUJ, there is a system in which instructors can hire assistants for grading the mid-term assignments as well as the final exams. However, there is no system or budget allocated to provide formative assessment to a large number of students.

Another institutional/administrative factor that prevents formative assessment from being implemented in courses is the rigidity of teaching and learning systems at the university. OUJ has been operated as a nation-wide university in which students learn by watching or listening to broadcast programs using textbooks. Due to the massive nature of teaching and learning, the assessment methods are rigidly defined as being carried out only using in-person exams at study centers. Because the exam for the same course has to be done at the same time across different study centers, these exams are centrally organized and their schedule is set well in advance. All the exam questions are rigorously reviewed by peers and the printed exam usually goes through three iterations of checking by the instructor who has written the exam questions.

3 POSSIBLE SOLUTIONS TO THE OBSTACLES

As discussed above, the obstacles to implementing formative assessment at the university level mainly come from the rigidity of the teaching and learning system. It may be of utmost importance that the university has to become nimble and flexible in order to adapt to the changing needs of the students as well as the society in general. However, owning the broadcasting station itself is now somewhat crippling the innovation of the university, as a certain amount of the budget and human resources has to be set aside to operate and maintain the broadcasting station, but there are some measures that can be taken to overcome the discussed obstacles. The following discusses the measures that may be taken for the betterment in teaching and learning system and for more personalizing learning experiences for students.

3.1 COMPUTER-BASED FORMATIVE ASSESSMENT

Formative assessment does not necessarily have to be done by human. The online learning platform can be programmed to give feedback based on the student's response or behavior. Computer-based formative assessment (CBFA) is defined as a purposefully designed instrument embedded within a learning process (Bennett, 2011). The most easily understandable example of CBFA would be the feedback given right after answering a self-test quiz question. It is known that feedback providing students with additional information about the question besides correct answers would be more effective than the feedback informing students whether their answer is correct or not (Van der Kleij et al., 2013).

Another kind of feedback possible in CBFA is feedback aimed at self-regulation, which focuses on a learner's self-evaluation or confidence in order to engage further. Such CBFAs can influence the self-regulatory processes of a learner by generating feedback on his/her performance and providing him/her with the opportunity to monitor or evaluate his/her own performance by comparing his/her actual level of performance with the intended level of performance (Timmers et al., 2015).

CBFAs are effective for learning at cognitive and affective levels and also are cost effective once the number of students reaches a certain point. They don't usually require a change in the institution of teaching and learning systems and are more readily implementable than peer assessment.

3.2 TUTOR SYSTEM

Another way to take the responsibility away from the instructors for implementing formative assessment in teaching and learning is to utilize tutors. The tutor system has been common in many distance education programs around the world, although the system is still uncommon in distance education programs in Japan.

The Open University in UK (OU) has been utilizing tutor system employing so-called "Associate Lecturers" who are in charge of directly interacting students while so-called "central academics" are mostly in charge of designing and developing the curriculum and the course content. Actually, the strength of OU's teaching and learning lies in this tutor system as they centrally train, manage, supervise, and evaluate these tutors in a very systematic and professional way.

It is said that in order to have meaningful interactions and feedbacks, a tutor is needed for every 20–30 students, which means from 30 to 50 tutors are needed for a class of 1000, a typical class size at OUJ. Without a well-designed system, it is impossible to manage such a large number of tutors and maintain a similar quality across the different tutors for a course. It also requires a significant budget allocation.

3.3 PEER ASSESSMENT

Peer assessment may also lighten the instructor/tutor burden of implementing formative assessment, although there has been a prevailing distrust of peer assessment and it is not commonly used for grading and certification purposes yet. However, there have been studies carried out recently that have shown a high correlation between staff assessment scores and peer assessment scores based on the data obtained from MOOCs (Kulkarni et al., 2013). Peer assessment is also found to be useful for learning as students become more aware of the criteria for good scores by assessing others' work and see the work from an assessor's perspective.

Implementing peer assessment, however, is not an easy task as a detailed rubric with detailed instructions needs to be developed to make peer assessment possible and useful for students as well as teachers. Developing a detailed rubric for peer assessment itself may be a very meaningful exercise for teachers in order to realize the objective of the assignment in relation to the objective of the course.

4 CONCLUSIONS

Formative assessments have been recognized as being very useful in supporting the students' learning processes and facilitating their learning, as well as assessing students' performance in a more authentic way. In addition, formative assessments give feedback to instructors and institutions in terms of pedagogical strategies and course design. With the use of online platforms, such as LMSs, theoretically the more data that can be gathered regarding student learning and student progress the better it can be tracked. However, in order for an institution and an instructor to take full advantage of this process, the implementation of formative assessments needs to be carefully designed and planned.

In a traditional distance education institution like OUJ, it is not an individual instructor's decision or strategy to implement formative assessments, but the implementation of formative assessments needs to be decided first at an institutional level. With the massive numbers involved in online courses at a distance education university, some advanced strategies, such as CBFAs or peer assessments, may be used as alternative means to formative assessments by instructors.

The first online courses offered by OUJ have shown some promise for CBFA. Among the 72 students who answered the evaluation questionnaire online, all of them replied positively to the question asking if the quizzes were useful in studying the materials. In open-ended responses, several students specifically emphasized the usefulness of the quizzes at the end of each unit. The focus group of five students who took the above online courses also revealed that the quizzes, in combination with the feedback comments for the incorrect choices, were very useful in studying a practical subject in which correct answers do exist.

It is important for instructors as well as administrators to realize the importance of formative assessments, especially in distance education, to provide students with more personalized learning environments. Just a small step forward from the existing one-way broadcasting courses in providing formative assessment has shown great promise with regards to student satisfaction at OUJ. Strategic planning in implementing formative assessment further in regular teaching and learning systems in distance education programs is called upon to improve the quality of distance education.

REFERENCES

Bennett, R.E., 2011. Formative assessment: a critical review. Assess. Educ. Princ. Policy Pract. 18 (1), 5–25.

Gaytan, J., McEwen, B.C., 2007. Effective online instructional and assessment strategies. Am. J. Dist. Educ. 21 (3), 117–132.

Gikandi, J.W., Morrow, D., Davis, N.E., 2011. Online formative assessment in higher education: a review of literature. Comput. Educ. 57, 2333–2351.

Koh, L.C., 2008. Refocusing formative feedback to enhance learning in pre-registration nurse education. Nurse Educ. Pract. 8 (4), 223–230.

Kulkarni, C., Wei, K.P., Le, H., Chia, D., Papadopoulos, K., Cheng, J., Koller, D., Klemmer, S.R., 2013. Peer and self assessment in massive online classes. ACM Trans. Comput. Hum. Interact. 9 (4). Article 39.

Oellermann, S.W., van der Merwe, A., 2015. Can using online formative assessment boost the academic performance of business students? An empirical study. Int. J. Educ. Sci. 8 (3), 535–546.

Tallent-Runnels, M.K., Thomas, J.A., Lan, W.Y., Cooper, S., Thern, T.C., Shaw, S.M., et al., 2006. Teaching courses online: a review of the research. Rev. Educ. Res. 76 (1), 93–135.

Timmers, C.F., Walraven, A., Veldkamp, B.P., 2015. The effect of regulation feedback in a computer-based formative assessment on information problem solving. Comput. Educ. 87, 1–9.

Van der Kleij, F.M., Feskens, R., Eggen, T.J.H.M., 2013. Effects of feedback in computer-based learning environment on students' learning outcomes: a meta-analysis. In: Paper Presented at the NCME, San Francisco.

Vonderwell, S., Boboc, M., 2013. Promoting formative assessment in online teaching and learning. TechTrends 57 (4), 22–27.

Wang, T.-H., Wang, K.-H., Huang, S.-C., 2008. Designing a web-based assessment environment for improving pre-service teacher assessment literacy. Comput. Educ. 51 (1), 448–462.

Wolsey, T., 2008. Efficacy of instructor feedback on written work in an online program. Int. J. E-Learn. 7 (2), 311–329.

Yoder, J.D., Hochevar, C.M., 2005. Encouraging active learning can improve students' performance on examinations. Teach. Psychol. 32 (2), 91–95.

LEARNING ANALYTICS

PART

2

LEARNING ANALYTICS

AN ASSESSMENT ANALYTICS FRAMEWORK (AAF) FOR ENHANCING STUDENTS' PROGRESS

Z. Papamitsiou, A.A. Economides

University of Macedonia, Thessaloniki, Greece

1 INTRODUCTION

Students' learning and progress are inferred from the systematic process of assessment (Erwin, 1991; Swan et al., 2006). Performance assessments, "do not offer a direct pipeline into a student's mind. [...] assessment is a tool designed to observe students' behavior and produce data that can be used to draw reasonable inferences about what students know" (Pellegrino, 2013, p. 261). Current theoretical, cultural and technological developments influence teaching and learning practices, resulting in an increasingly accepted need for rethinking assessment. The motivation for automating the assessment process originates from the need to alleviate the practical problems introduced by large classes and to harness potential pedagogical benefits.

e-Assessment (or computer-based assessment, CBA; computer assisted assessment, CAA; technology-enhanced assessment, TEA) is the use of information technologies (IT) (eg, desktop computers, mobiles, web-based, etc.) to automate and facilitate assessment and feedback processes (Chatzopoulou and Economides, 2010; Sancho-Vinuesa and Escudero-Viladoms, 2012; Triantafillou et al., 2008), and is usually categorized into formative and summative. While formative assessment provides developmental and prescriptive feedback to learners on their current understanding and skills to assist them in reaching their goals, summative assessment is about establishing whether students have attained the goals set for them, and usually lead to a formal qualification or certification of a skill (Birenbaum, 1996; Economides, 2006, 2009a). Examples of e-assessment methods include portfolio assessment, rubrics, self-assessment, peer assessment (eg, Peat and Franklin, 2002), and, more recently, collaborative and social assessment (Caballé et al., 2011).

The introduction of digital technologies into education opens up new possibilities for tailored, immediate and engaging assessment experiences. Drivers for the adoption of e-assessment include perceived increases in student retention, enhanced quality of feedback, flexibility for distance learning, strategies to cope with large student/candidate numbers, objectivity in marking and more effective use

Formative Assessment, Learning Data Analytics and Gamification. http://dx.doi.org/10.1016/B978-0-12-803637-2.00007-5

of virtual learning environments (Whitelock and Brasher, 2006). Recent studies highlight the importance of continuous e-assessment for learning (Whitelock, 2011).

From a more generalized viewpoint, the use of digital technologies for assessment purposes allows for remote progress tracking and evaluation and is strongly correlated to increased student and teacher (self-)awareness regarding students' learning achievements (Leony et al., 2013; Carnoy et al., 2012). This is one of the reasons why improvement of e-assessment services has been under the microscope of learning analytics research and constitutes one of its main objectives (Chatti et al., 2012; Papamitsiou and Economides, 2014; Tempelaar et al., 2013).

Assessment analytics (AA) is not a new field of enquiry. In fact, it is a subset of the wider area of learning analytics, and by itself it is an emerging research field. Like any other context-aware system, an AA procedure monitors, tracks and records data related to the context, interprets and maps the real current state of these data, organizes them (eg, filter, classify, prioritize), uses them (eg, decide adaptations, recommend, provide feedback, guide the learner) and predicts the future state of these data (Economides, 2009b).

In a sense, AA is about applying analytic methods to multiple types of data in an effort to reveal the intelligence held in e-assessment systems. More specifically, AA attempts to shed light to how students will improve their performance by (a) making practical use of detailed assessment psychometrics data held in e-assessment systems and (b) providing feedback accordingly (MacNeill and Ellis, 2013). It is important to get appropriate adaptive and personalized feedback to both students and teachers (instructors), based on data on the user's (behavioral) model and the learning context (Chatti et al., 2012).

In other words, the main objective of AA is to efficiently and effectively support the improvement of the assessment process. This means that AA's goals target (directly) assisting students, teachers and learning administrators (and indirectly at supporting/informing other stakeholders, like parents or even the Ministry of Education). For students, AA could passively support self-awareness, self-reflection, or self-regulation or actively trigger emotional change, challenge their participation, and motivate further engagement in assessment (and/or learning) activities. In order to explicitly set out the relationship between assessment systems and the sorts of epistemic challenges students might encounter, Knight et al. (2013) discuss the relationships between learning analytics, epistemology, pedagogy and assessment. The authors associated their approach to learning analytics with that of assessment for learning (AfL), which uses continuous assessment with formative feedback to facilitate learning, in contrast to a focus on summative assessment, often through examinations.

As far as it concerns the efficiency of AA for teachers (or similarly for learning administrators), these processes could be used to facilitate the estimation of students' performances, improve the detection and target prevention for students at-risk, enhance the detection of misconceptions and gaps in students' understandings, allow for the identification of students' guessing or cheating behavior, and many more.

The landscape in the domain of AA so far is quite diverse. Indicative research examples in this domain include the selection of the most appropriate next task during adaptive testing (Barla et al., 2010), the recognition of affects and mood during self-assessment (Moridis and Economides, 2009), the determination of students' satisfaction level during mobile formative assessment (Chen and Chen, 2009), the assessment of participatory behavior, knowledge building and performance during discussion processes (Caballé et al., 2011), as well as the construction of sophisticated measures of assessment (Wilson et al., 2011; Worsley and Blikstein, 2013) and many more, which we will discuss in the next sections.

The purpose of this chapter is to provide an AA framework as a reference point suitable to address complex problems in AA systems for which no clear guidelines are available as yet.

The remainder of this chapter is organized as follows: after elaborating on the motivation to develop the proposed AA framework and explicitly setting out the research questions that need to be addressed (see Section 2), we present the methodology we adopted in this study (see Section 3). Next, we describe the framework in general terms and the central concepts it involves (see Sections 4.1 and 4.2). Then, we analyze each dimension of the framework and discuss on the research questions initially posed (see Section 4.3). Finally, we elaborate on other important issues raised during the development of the framework, concerning mostly the security/privacy and ethics during data gathering, authorization and sharing (see Section 5).

2 MOTIVATION

As stated in the introduction, along with the promise and potential embodied in e-assessment systems come many challenges, which are due to the opening up of new possibilities for more personalized, immediate and engaging assessment experiences. Some challenges are foundational and faced by all assessment designers, such as establishing the validity, reliability, precision of measurement, and fairness of the new measures. Other challenges are less trivial and target to the AA experts, such as responsiveness to real-world contexts in real-time, evaluation of complex assignments in large courses (eg, massive open online courses, MOOCs), detection of gaps and misconceptions during assessment and more. Even the broader inclusion of students in developing accurate assessment measures seems to be a challenge for AA designers. This is because previous studies on e-assessment have shown that students find the use of e-assessment more promising, credible, objective, fair, interesting, fun, fast and less difficult or stressful (Conole and Warburton, 2005; Dermo, 2009; McCann, 2010).

A deeper observation of these findings through the microscope of AA partially reveals the intrinsic capabilities of these processes to support self-reflection and self-regulation during assessment procedures. Accordingly, AA should certainly be considered as part of any teaching and learning strategy, due to their potential benefits to better understand the reasons for students' progress or failure during assessment. However, both students and teachers must be well supported in their use. Simply providing the data (in the form of a dashboard, for example) is unlikely to be effective unless students and teachers are offered training in its interpretation and accessible strategies to act upon it.

In all cases, assessment and AA designers require the appropriate tools to conceptualize and tackle design challenges. A thorough search of the literature resulted in various examples of research works examining related issues and evidencing the adoption of AA. The search did not yield any theoretical/conceptual framework for AA. Even the approach suggested by Knight et al. (2013) does not provide a framework for understanding, building and interpreting AA, since it focuses on beliefs about the nature of knowledge, for which analytics grounded in pragmatic, sociocultural theory might be well placed to explore.

In general, a theoretical framework is a visual or written representation that "explains either graphically or in narrative form the main things to be studied—the key factors, concepts or variables—and the presumed relationships among them" (Miles and Huberman, 1994, p. 18). The role of a framework is to provide a theory that will be used to interpret existing AA data and to code them for future use. In that way, a framework would explicitly validate AA results and could be used to move beyond descriptions of "what" to explanations of "why" and "how." Articulating the theoretical framework would permit the transition from simply observing and describing AA to generalizing its various aspects (Jabareen, 2009).

Taking into consideration the diversity of approaches for AA (stated in the introduction) and the need for a framework that explicitly shapes, interprets and validates AA results, in this chapter we propose a theoretical framework. The goal is to develop a conceptual representation to act as a reference point/structure for the discussion of the literature, the methodologies followed and the results from former research studies concerning AA. The framework will also act as a useful guide to understand more deeply, evaluate and design analytics for assessment. In this chapter, we associate related literature to the main concepts of AA and justify the choice of the components of the suggested framework. We identify the key points that need to be closely examined and highlight the critical dimension of AA.

3 METHODOLOGY

After reviewing the existing frameworks for learning analytics (Greller and Drachsler, 2012; Fernández-Gallego et al., 2013; Shum and Crick, 2012), learning and assessment (Economides, 2009b; Haertel et al., 2012), our chosen approach leading to the proposed framework consisted of a sequence of gathering and analysis processes. In particular, we followed an inductive and deductive inquiry methodology for conceptual mapping for sensemaking. This methodology is considered appropriate since the use of inductive analysis is recommended when there are no previous studies dealing with the phenomenon or when knowledge is fragmented. Furthermore, a deductive approach is useful if the aim is to test an earlier theory or to compare categories.

In an inductive approach, once a substantial amount of data has been collected, the next step is the identification of patterns in the data in order to develop a theory that could explain those patterns. This process includes free coding, creating categories and abstraction. The purpose of creating categories is to provide a means of describing the phenomenon, to increase understanding and to generate knowledge. Formulating categories by inductive analysis, leads to a decision, through interpretation, as to which things to put in the same category (Dey, 1993). An inductive approach starts with a set of observations and then moves from data to theory or from the specific to the general.

Moreover, deductive analysis is in general based on earlier work such as theories, models, mind maps and literature reviews and is often used in cases aiming at retesting existing data in a new context (Marshall and Rossman, 1995).

In our approach, we applied a methodology consisting of three discrete steps. More specifically:

1. We initially searched the literature for studies that report results, best practices, central issues, variable construction, measurement techniques, etc., or sparse theoretical approaches regarding AA. Then, we categorized the objectives, methods, measures and results reported in the studies we had collected, into upper classes-concepts of concern. This classification led to an early introduction of the basic general concepts (induction).
2. Creating categories is both an empirical and a conceptual challenge, as categories must be conceptually and empirically grounded (Dey, 1993). Thus, we sought to identify the relationships between these clusters and which more general questions they address, in order to shape the conceptual map. A concept map (Novak, 1981) is a formal, structured diagram showing relationships among a number of unique concepts (concept mapping).
3. Finally, in our study, we designed the framework and tested whether the collected papers fit in that schema (deduction).

4 RESULTS

4.1 INDUCTION PHASE: LITERATURE REVIEW OF ASSESSMENT ANALYTICS APPROACHES

As stated in the introduction, the landscape in the domain of AA so far is often quite dispersed. The main objectives of research examples in this domain include the provision of adaptive feedback during summative assessment, the selection of the most appropriate next task during adaptive testing (Barla et al., 2010; Papamitsiou et al., 2014), student-oriented formative assessment support in real-time (Whitelock et al., 2015) and performance assessment of real-world skills (Knight and Littleton, 2015; Sao Pedro et al., 2013). Other major issues include the recognition of affects and mood during self-assessment, the determination of students' satisfaction level during mobile formative assessment, the assessment of participatory behavior, knowledge building and performance during discussion processes, as well as the construction of sophisticated measures of assessment (eg, Caballé et al., 2011; Chen and Chen, 2009; Moridis and Economides, 2009; Wilson et al., 2011; Worsley and Blikstein, 2013).

More specifically, research on providing appropriate and adaptive feedback during summative assessment targets at adapting the next quiz item to students' abilities during computer-based testing. The combination of different classification methods for selection of the most appropriate next task based on the topic selection using course structure, on item response theory (IRT)—selection of the k-best questions with most appropriate difficulty for the particular user—and on history-based prioritization of questions (eg, not recently asked questions) (Barla et al., 2010) and classification of students' response times according to the correctness of the submitted answers and the amount of time the students remained idle (not submitting an answer) (Papamitsiou et al., 2014) have presented interesting results. Based on students' temporal engagement in summative assessment activities, the different student temporal models of behavior during testing were used aiming at adapting the next quiz item to the students' abilities, as opposed to the more complicated algorithms that make use of psychometrics. The authors also proposed different visualizations of the temporal dimension of students' behavior for increasing awareness during assessment (Papamitsiou and Economides, 2015).

However, the multiple choice questions (MCQs) traditionally used in summative assessment are in general limited in their ability to provide the necessary analyses for guiding real-time scaffolding and remediation for students. Accordingly, student-oriented formative assessment support in real-time has been a major research topic for many authors. To address this issue, approaches to real-time formative assessment have included analyses of student action logs and real-time processing of free-text in open-ended learning environments (OELEs) inside and outside of classroom (Monroy et al., 2013; Sao Pedro et al., 2013; Tempelaar et al., 2013). Furthermore, Worsley and Blikstein (2013) aimed to detect factors and define metrics that could be used primarily as formative assessment tools for sophisticated learning skills acquisition in process-oriented assessment. A combination of speech recognition with knowledge tracing was proposed by the authors as the method for multimodal assessment.

However, interpreting and assessing students' learning behavior is inherently complex; at any point in time, there may be a dozen or more "correct next steps" from which students may choose. The space of possible learning paths—mostly in OELEs—quickly becomes intractable. An AA approach to this issue has been the Model-Driven Assessments, which consist of a model of the cognitive and metacognitive processes important for completing the learning task (Segedy et al., 2013). This approach leverages the cognitive and metacognitive model in interpreting students' actions and behavior patterns (ie, sequences of actions) in terms of the cognitive and metacognitive processes defined by the model. From a different point of view, tracking and examining how students go about solving a problem step-by-step makes transaction-level assessment possible by focusing on diagnosing persistent misconceptions and knowledge gaps using transaction-level data (Davies et al., 2015).

Performance assessments are also central to AA research. Providing performance assessment of real-world skills through real-world behaviors was suggested either as an evidence-centered approach to designing a performance assessment for epistemic cognition (Knight and Littleton, 2015) or as a learner-centered approach to formatively assess the situation of a real-world learner at a given time (Okada and Tada, 2014). In the first case, the study took place in the context of complex multiple document-processing tasks in which students read and synthesize information from multiple documents. In the second study, the objective was to evaluate the performance of individual learners participating in collaboration activities in the real world, through the systematic integration of the spatiotemporal occurrence information of real-world behavior. Finding a way to combine heterogeneous factors—learners' internal situations, their external situations, and their real-world learning field—was identified as a central issue for their research.

Another approach for performance assessment led to the development of a tool that uses six computational intelligence theories according to the web-based learning portfolios of an individual learner, in order to discover useful fuzzy association rules relating to the learning performance assessment and measure students' satisfaction during mobile formative assessment (Chen and Chen, 2009). Learning portfolios provide rich information for reflecting and assessing the performances and achievements of learners, and help learners to engage in meaningful learning accordingly.

In the context of gaining insight into formative assessment procedures from the scope of students' emotional states, recent studies attempted to estimate the students' emotions (eg, boredom, confusion, delight, or frustration) during formative assessment, using sensor data (eg, data from a fixed video camera, a pressure-sensitive mouse, and a pressure-sensitive chair) (D'Mello and Graesser, 2009; Kobayashi et al., 2011; Moridis and Economides, 2009).

Assessment of collaborative and/or teamwork is also considered as a central issue for assessment analytics research (Caballé et al., 2011; Perera et al., 2009). Indicative examples in this direction include a text mining approach to automate teamwork assessment in chat data (Shibani et al., 2015) as well as the use of activity theory (Nardi, 1995) applied to the assessment of computer supported collaborative learning (CSCL) (Xing et al., 2014). In the latter case, the goal was to assess student activities by using cluster analysis to evaluate strengths and weaknesses in individual students' participation in collaborative activities. Moreover, peer assessment in the evaluation of complex assignments in large courses, as in the context of MOOCs (Vozniuk et al., 2014) was also explored. Furthermore, other studies examined the improvement of the collaborative learning process in terms of participation behavior, knowledge building, and performance in the context of learning through discussion (Caballé et al., 2011).

4.2 CONCEPT MAPPING PHASE: CLASSIFICATION OF STUDIES AND MAIN CONCEPTS

The conducted literature review has revealed a number of commonalities and differences in the proposed and explored approaches. More precisely, all of these studies take under consideration the context of the assessment procedure and explore possible ways of providing fruitful and comprehensive feedback to the students being assessed. Moreover, in all studies, the measures adopted and the purpose/scope of the assessment process (either summative or formative) are clearly and explicitly stated. Furthermore, the data gathering and analysis methods/algorithms along with the pedagogical appropriation and benefits, as well as the potential limitations, are explicitly explained. Finally, the implications of the proposed methods and approaches for potential end users (either teachers, learners, institutions, or developers) are discussed.

From the above analysis it becomes apparent that the central concepts involved in an AA framework should include the following: the context, the objectives, the scope, the methods, the instruments, the resources, the people involved, and the limitations and boundaries. Having as reference points both the Model for Learning Analytics suggested by Chatti et al. (2012) and the generic framework for Learning Analytics suggested by Greller and Drachsler (2012), these initial upper-class concepts are mapped to the categories identified from the literature review as illustrated in Fig. 7.1.

Furthermore, these categories can be abstractly assigned to and organized into five more general classes: the who, the how, the why, the what, and the when/where, illustrated in Figs. 7.2 and 7.3.

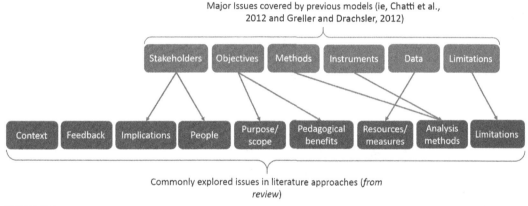

FIGURE 7.1

Mapping of the upper-class concepts to identified categories for assessment analytics.

4.3 THE ASSESSMENT ANALYTICS FRAMEWORK

As stated in the introduction, like any other context-aware system, an AA procedure monitors, tracks and records data related to the context, interprets and maps the real current state of these data, organizes these data (eg, filter, classify, prioritize), uses these data (eg, decide adaptations, recommend, provide feedback, guide the learner) and predicts the future state of these data (Economides, 2009b). Consequently, the suggested assessment analytics framework (AAF) is composed of four "blocks": *input*, *process*, *output* and *feedback* (Fig. 7.4).

The above literature review has revealed a number of commonalities and differences in the proposed and explored approaches. Based on the analysis of these studies, the input to the AA system is contextual information related to (a) *what* should be tracked and assessed (eg, measurements, assessment setting, and infrastructure), (b) *why* is the assessment necessary (eg, objectives, scope, and type of assessment), (c) *who* is the subject and receiver of the assessment (eg, learner-oriented, teacher-oriented) and (d) *when/where* the

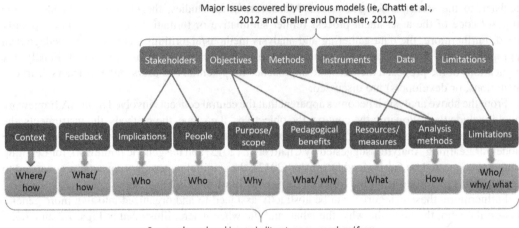

FIGURE 7.2

Abstract classification of identified categories for assessment analytics.

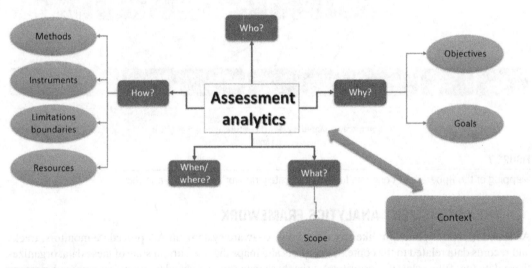

FIGURE 7.3

Upper-class concepts for assessment analytics.

assessment takes place (eg, environmental conditions, time, etc.). The AA *process* itself mostly concerns issues related to *how* it is applied and which parameters are being exploited during the procedure (eg, methods, resources, instruments, limitations and boundaries, pedagogy and instructional design, etc.). The *output* of the AA system is related to the process results and includes (a) *what* should be done next (eg, actions, pedagogical theories, algorithmic changes, educational policy, etc.), (b) *why* it should be done

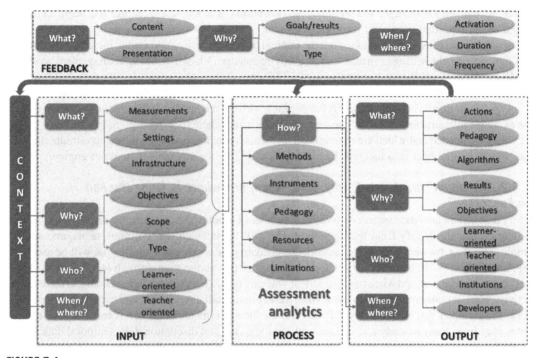

FIGURE 7.4

The proposed assessment analytics framework (AAF)—general schema.

(eg, based on the results and objectives achievement) and (c) *who* is the final receiver of the results (eg, parents, institutions, software developers—beyond students and teachers). Finally, the *feedback* is related to the delivery of the results to the recipient of the assessment result (eg, content, presentation, frequency, type, etc.) in order to change the initial state of the context (Economides, 2005).

The schema also presents the inherent connections and relationships between the major concepts. More specifically, the size and direction of the arrows represent the depth of the analysis from a more abstract to a more concrete concept.

We will discuss each of these blocks individually in the following section and exemplify their instantiations and impact on the AA process and the benefits and opportunities they may determine. We will also elaborate on apparent problem zones and limitations that may hinder any envisaged benefits.

4.3.1 The role of the context

Any information that can be used to characterize the situation of an entity (eg, person, place or object) would be considered as context (Dey and Abowd, 2000). In the field of learning sciences, the belief that context matters leads to the conclusion that research paradigms that simply explore the learning processes as isolated variables within laboratory settings will necessarily lead to an incomplete understanding of their relevance in real-life settings. Context estimation (eg, place of interest, learning topics, unattained knowledge, and tendency of viewpoint) of a real-world learner has been acknowledged as an important parameter during assessment.

In the domain of AA, all studies set out the context of the research experiments, including classroom settings, real-world settings, virtual learning environments (VLEs), learning management systems (LMSs), MOOCs, intelligent tutoring systems (ITS), etc.

The role of context in the AAF is to provide the necessary input information to the AA system (ie, the whole AA system, and not only the analytics engine): who are the learners, who are the teachers, what is the available infrastructure, what will be measured, when and where these measurements will take place, why they are needed and which are their objectives? This initial information will next constitute the "input" block, ie, the input data that will be under processing by the assessment analytics engine.

4.3.2 The "input" block: what, why, who, when, and where is being tracked and assessed?

Every assessment analytics system consists of a number of input parameters that describe it as an entity. It is important to identify from the beginning who will be assessed (eg, children, teenagers, adults, employees, etc.), by whom (eg, self-assessment, the instructor, a computer, etc.), what will be assessed (eg, knowledge, skills, behaviors, etc.), for what purpose (eg, summative, formative, predictive, diagnostic, etc.), and where and when the assessment will take place (eg, in classroom, at home, at an outdoor activity, etc.). It is also important to define from the beginning what will be tracked, which measures will act as the variables that will be analyzed and generate the assessment result. In AA research, these variables vary from study to study and include activity logs, chat and discussion data, temporal data, emotional data, free text, and many more. However, the selection of the most appropriate data type should be aligned with the overall assessment objective and research purpose (fit-for-purpose), and next analyzed with the most appropriate technique (not one-size-fit-all).

4.3.3 The "process" block: how the collected data are analyzed and interpreted?

The heart of every AA system is its processing engine, the mechanisms that are employed in analyzing the input data and producing the exploitable results. The literature review revealed the rich variety of different methods, algorithms and resources involved in the process of analysis. Examples of these components are linguistic analysis, text mining, speech recognition, classification techniques, association rule mining, process mining, machine learning techniques, affect recognition, and many more. Different instruments are adopted for the data processing, including algorithms and modeling methods. Table 7.1 summarizes the cases (application scenarios) according to the learning setting, the data-types and the analysis methods that have been employed.

In addition, the underlying pedagogical usefulness acts as a strong criterion that drives the whole analysis process in order to produce valid and useful results. However, most cases draw the attention to boundaries and limitations related mostly to ethics and security issues on the data manipulation.

4.3.4 The "output" block: what, why, who, when, and where is the outcome of the assessment process?

The result of the assessment procedure is also a central request during the designing of an AA system. According to the analysis of the literature, intelligent feedback, adaptation, personalization, and recommendations, are usually the outcome of the process, along with the diagnosis of misconceptions and knowledge gaps, participation rates, learning portfolios, achievements and summative results, like

Table 7.1 Summary of Application Scenarios With Learning Setting, Data-Types, Analysis Methods

Authors and Year	Learning Setting	Data-Type (Resources)	Data Analysis Method
Barla et al. (2010)	Web-based education—adaptive testing	Question repository—consider test questions as a part of educational material and improve adaptation by considering their difficulty and other attributes	Combination of item response theory with course structure annotations for recommendation purposes (classification)
Caballé et al. (2011)	Computer supported collaborative learning (CSCL) for assessing participation behavior, knowledge building and performance	Asynchronous discussion within virtual learning environment; post tagging, assent, and rating	Statistical analysis
Chen and Chen (2009)	Mobile learning and assessment (mobile devices used as the primary learning mediator)	Web-based learning portfolios—personalized e-learning system and PDA; attendance rate, accumulated score, concentration degree (reverse degree of distraction)	Data mining: statistic correlation analysis, fuzzy clustering analysis, gray relational analysis, K-means clustering, fuzzy association rule mining and fuzzy inference, classification; clustering
Davies et al. (2015)	Computer-based learning (spreadsheets) for detection of systematic student errors as knowledge gaps and misconceptions	Activity-trace logged data; processes students take to arrive at their final solution	Discovery with models; pattern recognition
Leeman-Munk et al. (2014)	Intelligent tutoring systems (ITS) for problem-solving and analyzing student-composed text	Digital science notebook; responses to constructed response questions; grades	Text analytics; text similarity technique; semantic analysis technique
Moridis and Economides (2009)	Online self-assessment tests	Multiple choice questions	Students' mood models—pattern recognition
Okada and Tada (2014)	Real-world learning for context-aware support	Wearable devices; sound devices; audio-visual records; field notes and activity maps; body postures; spatiotemporal behavior information	3D classification; probabilistic modeling; ubiquitous computing techniques
Papamitsiou et al. (2014)	Web-based education—computer-based testing	Question repository—temporal traces	Partial Least Squares—statistical methods
Perera et al. (2009)	CSCL to improve the teaching of the group work skills and facilitation of effective team work by small groups	Open source, professional software development tracking system that supports collaboration; traces of users' actions (create a wiki page or modify it; create a new ticket, or modify an existing, etc.)	Clustering; sequential patterns mining

Continued

Table 7.1 Summary of Application Scenarios With Learning Setting, Data-Types, Analysis Methods—cont'd

Authors and Year	Learning Setting	Data-Type (Resources)	Data Analysis Method
Sao Pedro et al. (2013)	ITS—for inquiry skill assessment	Fine-grained actions were timestamped; interactions with the inquiry, changing simulation variable values and running/pausing/resetting the simulation, and transitioning between inquiry tasks	Traditional data mining, iterative search, and domain expertise
Segedy et al. (2013)	Open-ended learning environments (OELEs) for problem-solving tasks and assess students' cognitive skill levels	Cognitive tutors; causal map edits; quizzes, question evaluations, and explanations; link annotations	Model-driven assessments; model of relevant cognitive and metacognitive processes; classification
Shibani et al. (2015)	Teamwork assessment for measuring teamwork competency	Custom-made chat program	Text mining; classification
Tempelaar et al. (2013)	Learning management systems (LMS) for formative assessment	Generic digital learning environment; LMS; demographics, cultural differences; learning styles; behaviors; emotions	Statistical analysis
Vozniuk et al. (2014)	MOOCS—peer assessment	Social media platform—consensus, agreement, correlations	Statistical analysis
Xing et al. (2014)	CSCL—virtual learning environments (VLE) for participatory learning assessment	Log files about actions, time, duration, space, tasks, objects, chat	Clustering enhanced with activity theory

grades and performance scores. The output of the AA system will become available to the learner, the instructor, the institution, or even the system developer. In all cases, the goal is for this output to be interpretable and comprehensive in order to increase the awareness of its receiver regarding the change that has occurred and been measured by the assessment itself. Of course, this output has to be aligned with (a) the initial objectives of the assessment procedure (eg, automate teamwork assessment, measure students' satisfaction, support in real-time students to successfully complete an assignment, etc.), and (b) the pedagogical goals set by the assessor. It also should provide results that will be accurate, accessible and useful to the end user of the system.

4.3.5 The "feedback" block: what, why, when, and where is delivered to close the loop effectively?

As mentioned before—in the "output" block—the outcome of the assessment process is usually some type of feedback. Accordingly, in an AA system, feedback acts in a twofold way: (a) it constitutes the feedback of the assessment process, ie, it informs the final user (eg, student, teacher, learning administrator, etc.) about the result of the assessment process, and (b) at the same time, it acts like the feedback loop of any iterative system, by keeping the loop continuing and feeding the shift of the former situation of the person under assessment back to the context. Economides (2006) provides a comprehensive description of feedback characteristics, which include the feedback activation reasons, the purposes of feedback and its expected effect, the type (eg, affective, cognitive, positive, negative, etc.), presentation issues of feedback, as well as issues related to the frequency, timing and duration of feedback.

4.4 DEDUCTION PHASE: VALIDATION OF THE AAF

In order to test and validate the proposed AAF, we followed a deduction approach: we aimed at retesting existing data (ie, already published studies) in the new context (ie, the AAF). Thus, we randomly chose two studies from the domain of AA research—not previously used during the induction phase of our methodology—and explored whether they fit in the suggested schema. Table 7.2 illustrates the results of this process, and provides a brief proof-of-concept regarding our proposed theory.

Table 7.2 Validation of the Assessment Analytics Framework—Analysis of Two Studies

Study	Context	Input	Process	Output	Feedback
Leeman-Munk et al. (2014)	Open-ended learning environments—STEM education (science education)	**What:** knowledge—short-text answers to science questions	**How:** text similarity combined with semantic analysis—classification of submitted answers	**Who:** teacher-oriented	**What:** correctness of submitted answer
		Why: real-time formative assessment		**Why:** early warning indicators to teachers to strategize as to how to allocate instructional interventions	**Why:** "train" the system to predict the student's performance
		When/Where: classroom		**What:** grades	**Where/ When:** after every submitted answer
Whitelock et al. (2015)	Academic course assignment – online assessment	**What:** students' essays during writing	**How:** linguistic analysis	**What:** graphical representation related to key linguistic characteristics of the document under development +grades	**What:** multiple types of feedback

Continued

Table 7.2 Validation of the Assessment Analytics Framework—Analysis of Two Studies—cont'd

Study	Context	Input	Process	Output	Feedback
		Why: summative assessment of free-text answers—provide meaningful advice for action		**Why:** self-reflection and support	**Why:** increase students' self-awareness
		Who: the students during writing the essay		**Who:** student-oriented	**Where/When:** during the development of the document—on demand
		Where/When: real-time online during the assignment		**Where/When:** online—during the assignment	

5 DISCUSSION AND CONCLUSIONS

As stated in the motivation section, a deeper observation of the e-assessment research findings through the microscope of AA partially reveals the intrinsic capabilities of these processes to support self-reflection and self-regulation during assessment procedures.

In this chapter we suggested a framework for analyzing and better understanding current research on AA. In order to design and evaluate the framework we followed a deductive and inductive inquiry methodology for concept mapping for sense making. The procedure ended up with a conceptual map consisting of four major clusters, each of which is further analyzed in more specific dimensions. For the validation of the framework we used a number of studies on AA in order to provide a proof-of-concept regarding the theory. In that way, the suggested framework explicitly validates AA results and can be used to move beyond descriptions of "what" to explanations of "why" and "how." By employing a general schema, the proposed framework for AA covers all dimensions of the assessment process and considers them as part of any teaching and learning strategy. The target is to explain the potential benefits of AA to better understand the reasons for students' progress or failure.

However, what is still missing from the existing literature and, consequently, not yet included in details in the proposed framework, are issues related to the security and privacy of tracked and analyzed information during the assessment procedure. For example, students should be able to access their personal data, as well as authorize when and with whom their data are shared. Moreover, students should be able to refuse to make their data available for sharing and to determine who else could have access or exercise control over how their personal data are shared. Further research is required in that direction.

To conclude, we believe that the suggested approach, which is the first of its kind (to the best of our knowledge), has covered central issues for AA. Improvements and extensions are necessary in order to add value and strength to the theory so that it may gain acceptance.

REFERENCES

Barla, M., Bieliková, M., Ezzeddinne, A.B., Kramár, T., Šimko, M., Vozár, O., 2010. On the impact of adaptive test question selection for learning efficiency. Comput. Educ. 55 (2), 846–857.

Birenbaum, M., 1996. Assessment 2000: towards a pluralistic approach to assessment. In: Birenbaum, M., Dochy, F.J.R.C. (Eds.), Alternatives in Assessment of Achievements, Learning Processes and Prior Knowledge. Springer, Netherlands, pp. 3–29.

Caballé, S., Daradoumis, T., Xhafa, F., Juan, A., 2011. Providing effective feedback, monitoring and evaluation to on-line collaborative learning discussions. Comput. Hum. Behav. 27 (4), 1372–1381.

Carnoy, M., Jarillo Rabling, B., Castano-Munoz, J., Duart Montoliu, J.M., Sancho-Vinuesa, T., 2012. Who attends and completes virtual universities: the case of the Open University of Catalonia (UOC). High. Educ. 63, 53–82.

Chatti, M.A., Dyckhoff, A.L., Schroeder, U., Thüs, H., 2012. A reference model for learning analytics. Int. J. Technol. Enhanc. Learn. 4 (5/6), 318–331.

Chatzopoulou, D.I., Economides, A.A., 2010. Adaptive assessment of student's knowledge in programming courses. J. Comput. Assist. Learn. 26 (4), 258–269.

Chen, C.-M., Chen, M.-C., 2009. Mobile formative assessment tool based on data mining techniques for supporting web-based learning. Comput. Educ. 52 (1), 256–273.

Conole, G., Warburton, B., 2005. A review of computer assisted assessment. Altern. J. 13 (1), 17–31.

D'Mello, S.K., Graesser, A.C., 2009. Automatic detection of learners' emotions from gross body language. Appl. Artif. Intell. 23 (2), 123–150.

Davies, R., Nyland, R., Chapman, J., Allen, G., 2015. Using transaction-level data to diagnose knowledge gaps and misconceptions. In: Proceedings of the 5th International Conference on Learning Analytics and Knowledge (LAK '15). ACM, New York, pp. 113–117.

Dermo, J., 2009. E-Assessment and the student learning experience: a survey of student perceptions of e-assessment. Br. J. Educ. Technol. 40 (2), 203–214.

Dey, I., 1993. Qualitative Data Analysis. A User-Friendly Guide for Social Scientists. Routledge, London.

Dey, A.K., Abowd, G., 2000. Towards a better understanding of context and context-awareness. In: Proceedings of Conference on Human Factors in Computing Systems. The Hague, The Netherlands.

Economides, A.A., 2005. Personalized feedback in CAT. WSEAS Trans. Adv. Eng. Educ. 3 (2), 174–181.

Economides, A.A., 2006. Adaptive feedback characteristics in CAT. Int. J. Instruct. Technol. Dist. Learn. 3(8).

Economides, A.A., 2009a. Conative feedback in computer-based assessment. Comput. Sch. 26 (3), 207–223.

Economides, A.A., 2009b. Adaptive context-aware pervasive and ubiquitous learning. Int. J. Technol. Enhanc. Learn. 1 (3), 169–192.

Erwin, T.D., 1991. Assessing Student Learning and Development: A Guide to the Principles, Goals, and Methods of Determining College Outcomes. Jossey-Bass Inc., San Francisco, CA.

Fernández-Gallego, B., Lama, M., Vidal, J.C., Mucientes, M., 2013. Learning Analytics framework for educational virtual worlds. Procedia Comput. Sci. 25, 443–447.

Greller, W., Drachsler, H., 2012. Translating learning into numbers: a generic framework for learning analytics. Educ. Technol. Soc. 15 (3), 42–57.

Haertel, E., et al., 2012. NAEP: looking ahead—leading assessment into the future. In: A Whitepaper Commissioned by the National Center for Education Statistics. US Department of Education, Washington, DC.

Jabareen, Y., 2009. Building a conceptual framework: philosophy, definitions, and procedure. Int. J. Qual. Methods 8 (4), 49–62.

Knight, S., Littleton, K., 2015. Developing a multiple-document-processing performance assessment for epistemic literacy. In: Proceedings of the 5th International Conference on Learning Analytics and Knowledge (LAK '15). ACM, New York, pp. 241–245.

Knight, S., Shum, S.B., Littleton, K., 2013. Epistemology, pedagogy, assessment and learning analytics. In: Suthers, D., Verbert, K., Duval, E., Ochoa, X. (Eds.), Proceedings of the 3rd International Conference on Learning Analytics and Knowledge (LAK '13). ACM, New York, pp. 75–84.

Kobayashi, A., Muramatsu, S., Kamisaka, D., Watanabe, T., Minamikawa, A., Iwamoto, T., Yokoyama, H., 2011. User movement estimation considering reliability, power saving, and latency using mobile pone. IEICE Trans. Inf. Syst. E94-D (6), 1153–1163.

Leeman-Munk, S.P., Wiebe, E.N., Lester, J.C., 2014. Assessing elementary students' science competency with text analytics. In: Proceedings of the 4th International Conference on Learning Analytics And Knowledge (LAK '14). ACM, New York, pp. 143–147.

Leony, D., Muñoz Merino, P.J., Pardo, A., Kloos, C.D., 2013. Provision of awareness of learners' emotions through visualizations in a computer interaction-based environment. Expert Syst. Appl. 40 (13), 5093–5100.

MacNeill, S., Ellis, C., 2013. Acting on assessment analytics. JISC CETIS Anal. Ser. 2(2).

Marshall, C., Rossman, G.B., 1995. Designing Qualitative Research. Sage Publications, London.

McCann, A.L., 2010. Factors affecting the adoption of an e-assessment system. Assess. Eval. High. Educ. 35 (7), 799–818.

Miles, M.B., Huberman, A.M., 1994. Qualitative Data Analysis: An Expanded Source Book, second ed. Sage, Newbury Park, CA.

Monroy, C., Rangel, V.S., Whitaker, R., 2013. STEMscopes: contextualizing learning analytics in a K-12 science curriculum. In: Proceedings of the 3rd International Conference on Learning Analytics and Knowledge (LAK '13). ACM, New York, pp. 210–219.

Moridis, C.N., Economides, A.A., 2009. Mood recognition during online self-assessment test. IEEE Trans. Learn. Technol. 2 (1), 50–61.

Nardi, B., 1995. Context and Consciousness: Activity Theory and Human-Computer Interaction. MIT Press, Cambridge, ISBN 0-262-14058-6.

Novak, J.D., 1981. The Use of Concept Mapping and Gowin's "V" Mapping Instructional Strategies in Junior High School Science. Report of the Cornell University 'Learning How to Learn' project, Ithaca, New York.

Okada, M., Tada, M., 2014. Formative assessment method of real-world learning by integrating heterogeneous elements of behavior, knowledge, and the environment. In: Proceedings of the 4th International Conference on Learning Analytics and Knowledge (LAK '14). ACM, New York, pp. 1–10.

Papamitsiou, Z., Economides, A.A., 2014. Learning analytics and educational data mining in practice: a systematic literature review of empirical evidence. Educ. Technol. Soc. 17 (4), 49–64.

Papamitsiou, Z., Economides, A.A., 2015. Temporal learning analytics visualizations for increasing awareness during assessment. Int. J. Educ. Technol. Higher Educ. 12 (3), 129–147.

Papamitsiou, Z., Terzis, V., Economides, A.A., 2014. Temporal learning analytics for computer based testing. In: Proceedings of the 4th International Conference on Learning Analytics and Knowledge (LAK '14). ACM, New York, pp. 31–35.

Peat, M., Franklin, S., 2002. Supporting student learning: the use of computer based formative assessment modules. Br. J. Educ. Technol. 33 (5), 515–523.

Pellegrino, J.W., 2013. Measuring what matters in a digital age: technology and the design of assessments for multisource comprehension. In: Sampson, D.G., et al., (Ed.), Ubiquitous and Mobile Learning in the Digital Age. Springer Science & Business Media, New York, pp. 259–286.

Perera, D., Kay, J., Koprinska, I., Yacef, K., Zaiane, O.R., 2009. Clustering and sequential pattern mining of online collaborative learning data. IEEE Trans. Knowl. Data Eng. 21 (6), 759–772.

Sancho-Vinuesa, T., Escudero-Viladoms, N., 2012. A proposal for formative assessment with automatic feedback on an online mathematics subject. Revista de Universidad y Sociedad del Conocimiento (RUSC) 9 (2), 240–260.

Sao Pedro, M.A., Baker, R.S.J.D., Gobert, J.D., 2013. What different kinds of stratification can reveal about the generalizability of data-mined skill assessment models. In: Suthers, D., Verbert, K., Duval, E., Ochoa, X.

(Eds), Proceedings of the 3rd International Conference on Learning Analytics and Knowledge (LAK '13). ACM, New York, pp. 190–194.

Segedy, J.R., Loretz, K.M., Biswas, G., 2013. Model-driven assessment of learners in open-ended learning environments. In: Suthers, D., Verbert, K., Duval, E., Ochoa, X. (Eds.), Proceedings of the 3rd International Conference on Learning Analytics and Knowledge (LAK '13). ACM, New York, pp. 200–204.

Shibani, A., Koh, E., Hong, H., 2015. Text mining approach to automate teamwork assessment in group chats. In: Proceedings of the 5th International Conference on Learning Analytics and Knowledge (LAK '15). ACM, New York, pp. 434–435.

Shum, S.B., Crick, R.D., 2012. Learning dispositions and transferable competencies: pedagogy, modelling and learning analytics. In: Buckingham Shum, S., Gasevic, D., Ferguson, R. (Eds.), Proceedings of the 2nd International Conference on Learning Analytics and Knowledge (LAK '12). ACM, New York, pp. 92–101.

Swan, K., Shen, J., Hiltz, S.R., 2006. Assessment and collaboration in online learning. J. Async. Learn. Network. 10, 45–62.

Tempelaar, D.T., Heck, A., Cuypers, H., van der Kooij,, H., van de Vrie, E., 2013. Formative assessment and learning analytics. In: Verbert, Katrien, Duval, Erik, Ochoa, Xavier (Eds.), Proceedings of the 3rd International Conference on Learning Analytics and Knowledge (LAK '13), Dan Suthers. ACM, New York, pp. 205–209.

Triantafillou, E., Georgiadou, E., Economides, A.A., 2008. The design and evaluation of a computerized adaptive test on mobile devices. Comput. Educ. 50 (4), 1319–1330.

Vozniuk, A., Holzer, A., Gillet, D., 2014. Peer assessment based on ratings in a social media course. In: Proceedings of the 4th International Conference on Learning Analytics and Knowledge (LAK '14). ACM, New York, pp. 133–137.

Whitelock, D., 2011. Activating assessment for learning: are we on the way with Web 2.0? In: Lee, M.J.W., McLoughlin, C. (Eds.), Web 2.0-Based-E-Learning: Applying Social Informatics for Tertiary Teaching. IGI Global, Hershey, Pennsylvania, pp. 319–342.

Whitelock, D.M., Brasher, A., 2006. Developing a roadmap for e-assessment: which way now? In: Danson, M. (Ed.), Proceedings of the 10th CAA International Computer Assisted Assessment Conference. Professional Development, Loughborough University, Loughborough, UK, pp. 487–501.

Whitelock, D., Twiner, A., Richardson, J.T.E., Field, D., Pulman, S., 2015. OpenEssayist: a supply and demand learning analytics tool for drafting academic essays. In: Proceedings of the 5th International Conference on Learning Analytics and Knowledge (LAK '15). ACM, New York, pp. 208–212.

Wilson, K., Boyd, C., Chen, L., Jamal, S., 2011. Improving student performance in a first-year geography course: examining the importance of computer-assisted formative assessment. Comput. Educ. 57 (2), 1493–1500.

Worsley, M., Blikstein, P., 2013. Towards the development of multimodal action based assessment. In: Suthers, D., Verbert, K., Duval, E., Ochoa, X. (Eds.), Proceedings of the 3rd International Conference on Learning Analytics and Knowledge (LAK '13). ACM, New York, pp. 94–101.

Xing, W., Wadholm, B., Goggins, S., 2014. Learning analytics in CSCL with a focus on assessment: an exploratory study of activity theory-informed cluster analysis. In: Proceedings of the 4th International Conference on Learning Analytics and Knowledge (LAK '14). ACM, New York, pp. 59–67.

AUTOMATING LEARNER FEEDBACK IN AN eTEXTBOOK FOR DATA STRUCTURES AND ALGORITHMS COURSES

E. Fouh, S. Hamouda, M.F. Farghally, C.A. Shaffer

Virginia Tech, Blacksburg, VA, United States

1 INTRODUCTION

Perhaps the greatest contribution of the computer to education is the ability to give immediate feedback to a learner about the state of their knowledge. This feedback often comes in the form of automated assessment for practice problems. Assessment systems with automated feedback provide more practice for students with less grading time for instructors. Self-assessment can increase learners motivation, promote students' ability to guide their own learning, and help them internalize factors used when judging performance (Andrade and Valtcheva, 2009; McMillan and Hearn, 2008). Other forms of feedback include "gamification" elements where students are informed about progress through the material, and they might be given "rewards" for progress in an effort to provide motivation. Instructors interested in experimenting with new pedagogical approaches (blended learning, "flipped" classroom, etc.) might find that the path to implementing these pedagogies is easier due to the affordances provided by new learning technology.

Online educational systems can also provide feedback to system developers and instructors about the performance of their students. The most obvious type of feedback to instructors is level and time of completion for individual students. Another type of feedback is student analytics data in the form of logs to record keystrokes, mouse clicks, and timestamps, as well as higher-order information such as performance on practice problems. Such information is sometimes referred to as learning analytics (Ferguson, 2012; Siemens and Baker, 2012). With such information, developers can hope to first deduce patterns of student behavior, then correlate the different behavior patterns to successful outcomes, and finally improve the system so as to enhance student performance in various ways.

In this chapter, we discuss all of these aspects of feedback given by online courseware to students, instructors, and system developers. We provide a number of case studies. The context for our case studies is the OpenDSA eTextbook system (Fouh et al., 2014b). OpenDSA is an open-source project with international collaboration that seeks to create an infrastructure and a body of materials appropriate for use in a range of computer science courses. The bulk of the content relates to data structures and algorithms (DSA). This particular topic area lends itself to an eTextbook treatment for two reasons.

First, a significant fraction of the content relates to understanding the dynamic process of computer algorithms. This means that visualizations of the behavior of the algorithms (referred to as algorithm visualizations or AVs) can be especially useful to learners. Second, as with many disciplines, students are traditionally unable to get sufficient practice exercises due to limitations on the part of instructors' abilities to give feedback through grading of the students' work. With OpenDSA, we are able to give students a rich collection of practice questions and exercises.

The basic instructional unit for OpenDSA materials is the module, which represents a single topic or part of a typical lecture, such as a single sorting algorithm. Each module is a complete unit of instruction and typically contains AVs, interactive assessment activities with automated feedback, and textbook quality text. Modules can be grouped together into chapters, such as might be found in traditional paper books. OpenDSA content is built using HTML5 and JavaScript, making it device and browser independent. AVs are built using the JavaScript algorithm visualization (JSAV) library (Karavirta and Shaffer, 2013). OpenDSA includes extensive support for collecting learning analytics data.

Many OpenDSA exercises are "algorithm simulations." These require that the student manipulate a data structure to show the changes that an algorithm would make to it, such as clicking to swap elements in an array or clicking on appropriate nodes in a tree or graph. The AVs and algorithm simulation exercises are specifically designed to be manipulated either through mouse and pointer interactions or touch interactions when using touchscreen devices. We generally refer to algorithm simulation exercises, as "proficiency exercises." This type of exercise was inspired by the TRAKLA2 system (Korhonen et al., 2003), and many of OpenDSA's proficiency exercises were created in collaboration with the team that created TRAKLA2. We make use of the Khan Academy framework (http://github.com/Khan/khan-exercises) to provide support for multiple choice, T/F, and custom interactive exercises that we call "mini-proficiency" exercises. We will refer to these collectively as KA exercises. All exercises are automatically graded and provide immediate feedback to the user. Students can repeat exercises as many times as they want until they get credit, or repeat them as a study aid for an exam.

Several experiments have shown the pedagogical effectiveness of TRAKLA2's proficiency exercises. Laakso et al. (2005, 2009) reported on the use of TRAKLA2 exercises in data structures and algorithms courses at two universities in Finland. TRAKLA2 exercises were incorporated as classroom (closed lab) exercises, and supplemented lecture hours and classroom sessions. TRAKLA2 exercises were also incorporated into the final exam (one out of five questions) and midterm (they replaced half of a question with a TRAKLA2 exercise in a total of five questions). A year after the introduction of TRAKLA2 in the curriculum, the activity of students increased in all aspects of the course, not only the part involving TRAKLA2 exercises. The average performance in classroom exercises rose from 54.5% to 60.3% (as percentage of exercises completed). A study (Karavirta et al., 2013) of several TRAKLA proficiency exercises translated to OpenDSA demonstrated that they remain equally effective. Student opinions of TRAKLA2 were collected through an online survey. Eighty percent of the students reported having a good opinion of TRAKLA2. After a year of using TRAKLA2, the opinion of students on its suitability for instruction rose significantly. Ninety-four percent of students agreed that TRAKLA2 exercises helped in their learning process. Their opinion did not change regarding their preference on the medium used to access and perform the exercises: they preferred a mixed (online and traditional classroom) experience.

2 MONITORING THE STUDENT LEARNING PROCESS: WHAT WE LEARN FROM SURVEYS AND LEARNING ANALYTICS

Online courseware systems provide the opportunity to automatically log massive amounts of user interaction data in fine detail, to the level of individual mouse events. This wealth of information might be used in a number of ways to improve the pedagogical value of online materials. Developers can hope to learn from interactive log data simple things like, which exercises are taking an unreasonable amount of time or which ones appear too easy because students never get them wrong. But careful analysis of log data can hope to deduce more complex behavior.

For example, by examining the times of various interactions, we should be able to determine whether students are reading the materials before attempting the associated exercises. We can hope to tell whether students are viewing all of the slides in a visualization, or are skipping through them. We should be able to tell whether students are going back to the materials to use them to study for a test by the fact that they look at them a day or two before the test, even if they had previously received credit for completing them.

Based on this feedback, we can then try to better engineer the courseware, for example, to make sure that students do not solve problems by guessing, or skip over key material. Intelligent tutoring systems (Corbett et al., 1997; Roll et al., 2011; Feng et al., 2014) can be built to react to the behavior of an individual student, attempting to identify and directly address the underlying misconception that leads to providing an incorrect answer to an exercise. Instructors can be given better feedback on student performance. For all of these reasons, learning analytics and techniques for analyzing the data are poised to become a major focus of CS education research (and, more generally, CS contribution to education research in all disciplines).

OpenDSA collects log data for all user interactions occurring on an OpenDSA web page. Since Spring 2013, we have been able to collect detailed interaction data for hundreds of students per year who are using the system, amounting to millions of individual interaction events. Interaction log data plays the central role in all of the feedback mechanisms that we discuss in this paper. The act of collecting the data itself typically does not directly impact students (though more sophisticated intelligent tutoring systems can use this information for better adaptive feedback (Roll et al., 2011)). But it is this log data that allows us to deduce most of the results presented in the following sections about how students are using the system. This allows us to understand the role that feedback to the students is actually having on student learning. This in turn can allow us to actively improve the system in ways that will lead to better learning outcomes.

In this section, we first present several use cases for using interaction log data to understand student behavior with the OpenDSA system. We then present data that we have collected related to student perceptions regarding the value of OpenDSA, and their preferences for how the system should be used in courses.

Throughout this paper, our case studies and our discussions of student surveys and log data will refer to various classes. The vast majority of classes that have used OpenDSA so far can be categorized as one of two types. We use the term "CS2" to refer to a second semester programming course in computer science. This course is typical for most CS departments, and includes some combination of basic software engineering and introductory data structures (linear structures, some simple sorting algorithms, and some introductory material on binary trees). We use the term "CS3" to mean a course that comes after the typical CS2 course, primarily focused on more advanced data structures. This typically includes algorithm analysis, advanced sorting algorithms, advanced tree structures, hashing, and perhaps an introduction to file structures.

2.1 MONITORING LEVELS OF STUDENT ENGAGEMENT

Instructors have always recognized that students have difficulty with certain topics. In at least some instances that we have studied, we find that one source of this difficulty relates to a consistent lack of engagement of students with the learning materials on that particular topic. In other cases, we find that difficulty arises from insufficient time spent by students engaging with the material due to lack of necessary practice activities. We illustrate both of these situations in our case studies. Further details can be found in Fouh et al. (2014a).

2.1.1 Case study: Recursion

Recursion is known to be a hard topic at both the CS2 and CS3 levels. Surveys from 15 instructors for CS2 courses indicate that these instructors believe students should spend an average of 10 h studying and practicing recursion outside of class. Surveys of 54 students in a CS2 course indicate that students were spending an average of only 4 h in out-of-class study and practice of recursion. The instructors unanimously felt that students were not spending enough time, even before having this confirmed by the survey data. Students come out of the typical instructional experience with a below-average feeling of confidence (2.6 out of 5 on a Likert scale for the students that we surveyed).

This information provides guidance for the design of a new tutorial on recursion. We see that goals for an online tutorial should include a significant body of practice exercises, and that reading tutorial content and working through the exercises should be calibrated to encourage students to spend about 10 h on the topic.

We created an online tutorial on recursion, presented as a chapter in OpenDSA. Students using this material during Spring 2015 reported spending an average of 7.3 h out of class, a marked increase over the prior semester's average of 4 h. From analyzing log data, we find that the median time spent on the recursion tutorial exercises is approximately 5 h. This does not include time spent reviewing the tutorial content (reading material and viewing the slideshows). Measuring reading times is much more difficult since our only logged interactions come when the page is opened and then when it is closed or passed on to another page. This means that actual measurements for "reading" material could include time spent away from the computer. However, it appears that our log data confirms the student estimates of 7 h or so. This is a significant finding in itself, since it supports a claim that we can trust data collected from either one of these sources (interaction log data or survey data where students estimate time spent on an activity).

2.1.2 Case study: Recursion exercises

The recursion tutorial discussed earlier includes a substantial number of programming exercises. A few of these exercises are relatively difficult for many of the students. As a result, many students are motivated to seek ways to get around doing the exercises.

The exercises are implemented based on the Khan Academy Exercise Framework. The fundamental approach is that a given programming "exercise" contains several specific programming problems. Of these individual problems, students are supposed to do a random subset, say two or three randomly selected out of five. Unfortunately, students can view the problem instance that comes up, then reload the page without penalty to get another problem at random. As a result many students will do one problem, then keep reloading the page until that problem repeats, then do it again. Through analysis of student responses to the programming exercises, we have found the following:

1. 52% of students who attempt the programming exercises do — on at least one instance — exhibit this behavior of reloading the page to get the same problem that they have just solved correctly, then resolve it to get a second credit instead of solving another one. We will name those students "Proficiency Seekers."
2. 93% of the "Proficiency Seekers" have exhibited this behavior in the exercises the students consider as hard. According to the student surveys, the students consider the exercises that ask them to write a full function or complete a nonsimple recursive function that has more than one recursive call or base case as hard. We have not found that students exhibit this behavior for simple code completion or the tracing exercises.
3. 42% of "Proficiency Seekers" have repeated this behavior for all three recursive function writing exercise sets.

This case study illustrates several points:

1. Log data allows us to deduce this behavior.
2. The details of exercise framework implementation have a huge impact on student behavior.

As a result of this study, we are reengineering first the tutorial and then the framework infrastructure to avoid the negative behavior.

2.1.3 Case study: Algorithm analysis

For a topic such as a particular sorting algorithm, an OpenDSA module (like a typical textbook presentation) contains both material on the dynamic behavior of the algorithm, and analytical material in the form of a runtime analysis (that is, the "algorithm analysis") of that algorithm. While dynamic behavior is well presented in OpenDSA by use of AVs, the analytical material relies mainly on textual discussion supported by static images. In other words, OpenDSA has historically presented algorithm analysis topics in a manner indistinguishable from a standard textbook. As a whole, the AV development community has a lot of experience with creating visualizations for the dynamic behavior of algorithms, but almost none with presenting analytical material (Shaffer et al., 2010). We also know from prior research into AVs in general that the level of student interaction with the material is a crucial factor in learning (Hundhausen et al., 2002; Naps et al., 2002). Unfortunately, algorithm analysis is also one of the most difficult topics in a typical CS2 course (Parker and Lewis, 2014). Thus we have the situation that our least engaging content is on one of our most difficult topics.

In order to see whether the typical "textbook" approach to presenting algorithm analysis content is effective for students, we analyzed student interaction logs from a CS3 course during Fall 2014. In particular, we focused on student engagement with OpenDSA's algorithm analysis material presented in the sorting chapter. This chapter contains more than 40% of all algorithm analysis material in that course. Unfortunately, OpenDSA's data collection tools (Breakiron, 2013) don't provide a direct method that we can use to estimate the time spent by students reading the analysis material in each module, because the main focus of these tools is to collect user interactions with the interactive content. Accordingly, the OpenDSA authoring system was extended to support wrapping arbitrary module sections behind a "show/hide" button as is done with other interactive content. When the student first sees the module that presents a given sorting algorithm, the algorithm analysis material is initially hidden, and a button is shown in its place. When the button is pressed, the analytical content is displayed. The time is recorded, and can be used as an estimate of the time when the student started reading the material. The time for finishing the material can be estimated from the time of the next user interaction, such as loading the next exercise or leaving the module which is recorded by the data collection tools.

We analyzed the interaction logs available for three OpenDSA book instances used at three different universities (Virginia Tech, University of Texas El Paso, and University of Florida). Fig. 8.1 presents the distribution of the estimated reading time for three sorting modules (Insertionsort, Mergesort, and Quicksort) for the Virginia Tech students. Similar results were found for students at the other universities. Results are summarized in Table 8.1. As we see from the results, more than 74% of the students spent <1 min on the analysis material for each of the three modules. Based on this result, we believe that most of the students are not reading the analysis material.

When the students were asked to provide suggestions for improving the presentation of the analysis material in OpenDSA, we found that most of them are expecting a more interactive presentation in the form of visualizations. Representative quotes from the survey include: "Visualizations definitely help," "I think making the click through pictures into actual animations would be nice," "more animation, the visualizations are great!," "more visualizations is always good," "Visualizations always help," "visualizations showing each step of analysis would help," "an animation will make a much bigger difference."

Based on this information, we determined to make new presentations for this content that would result in students spending more time using the material. This could happen in two ways. One is to motivate students to spend more time through the use of a more appealing presentation, perhaps visualization. The other is to force students to spend more time as a byproduct of completing specific tasks that are required to get credit for completing the tutorial. This might be engineered through a combination of requiring students to view slideshows (though these might be quickly skipped through), answering questions, and working exercises.

As an initial step, we have taken the approach of providing a visual presentation of the material. Inspired by the concept of visual proofs (Goodrich and Tamassia, 1998), a set of algorithm analysis visualizations were implemented for OpenDSA sorting modules (Insertionsort, Bubblesort, Selectionsort, Mergesort, Heapsort, Quicksort, Radixsort, and the lower bounds for sorting). Fig. 8.2 shows some examples of the new visualizations.

We have collected preliminary data with two small classes using the sorting analysis visualizations. Summary results for the two modules teaching Insertionsort and Quicksort appear in Table 8.2. We performed Kruskal Wallis tests to see if there is any significant difference between the time spent on text versus visualizations for these two modules. In each case, the difference in the means is significant ($p < 0.00002$), indicating that students spend more time on the material when presented as visualizations.

2.1.4 Case study: Student use of exercises for study

We sought to determine if students would only use OpenDSA when required for homework credit, or if they would use it voluntarily such as to review for exams. Participants included in this study were students enrolled in a CS2 course and a CS3 course at Virginia Tech during Spring 2015. We used

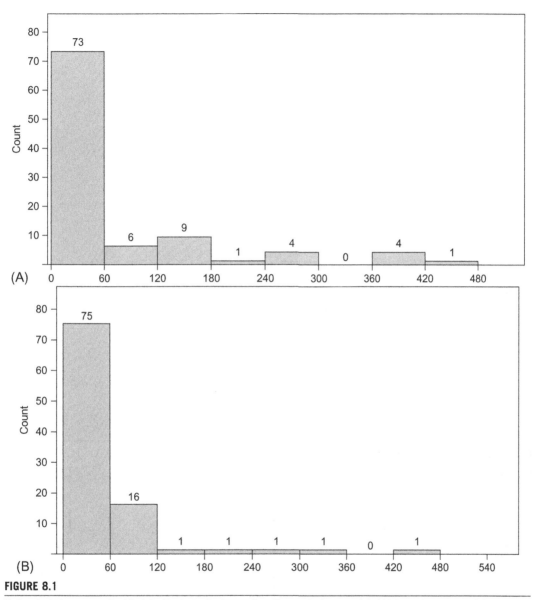

FIGURE 8.1

Estimated time spent by Virginia Tech students reading the analysis material. (A) Insertionsort module, (B) Mergesort module, and

Continued

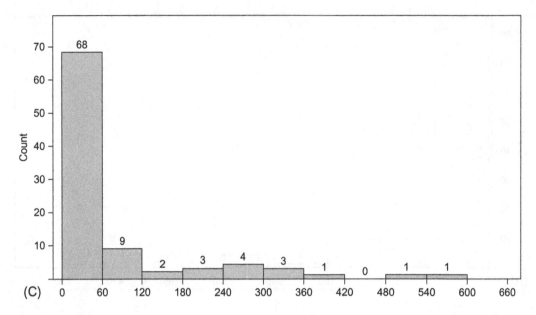

FIGURE 8.1, CONT'D

(C) Quicksort module.

Table 8.1 Results Summary

University	Module	N	Mean (S)	% <1 min
Virginia Tech	Insertionsort	98	63.57	74.48
	Mergesort	96	39.79	78.12
	Quicksort	92	64.71	73.91
UTEP	Insertionsort	26	49.84	80.76
	Mergesort	22	41.45	77.27
	Quicksort	16	16.18	93.75
Florida	Insertionsort	53	40.39	84.90
	Mergesort	44	18.63	95.45
	Quicksort	39	26.12	92.30
All	Insertionsort	177	54.6	78.52
	Quicksort	147	49.2	80.94

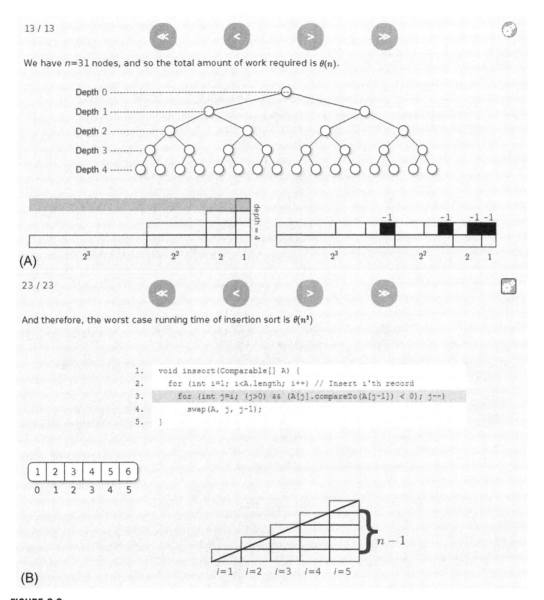

FIGURE 8.2

Visualizations illustrating the running time analysis of some sorting algorithms. (A) Build heap analysis, (B) Insertionsort worst case analysis,

Continued

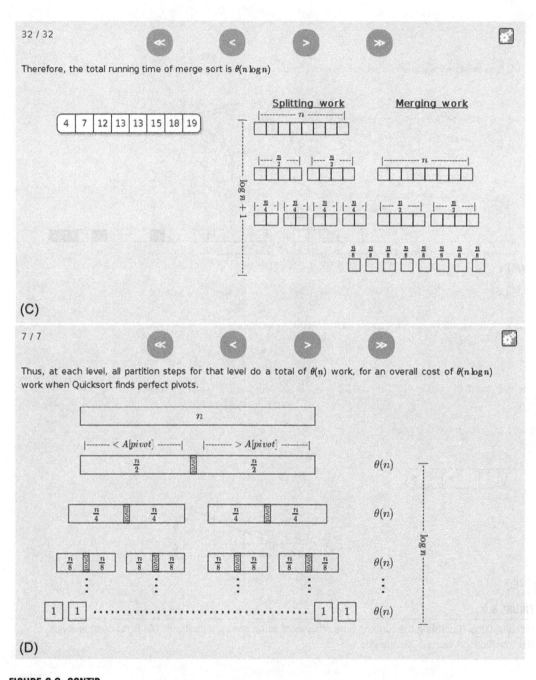

Therefore, the total running time of merge sort is $\theta(n \log n)$

Thus, at each level, all partition steps for that level do a total of $\theta(n)$ work, for an overall cost of $\theta(n \log n)$ work when Quicksort finds perfect pivots.

FIGURE 8.2, CONT'D

(C) Mergesort analysis, and (D) Quicksort best case analysis.

Table 8.2 Text vs. Visualization Times, Measured in Seconds

Module	Text			Slideshow		
	Median Time	Mean Time	Standard Deviation	Median Time	Mean Time	Standard Deviation
Insertionsort	10	54.6	99.4	46	67.7	69.0
Quicksort	6	49.2	102.7	40.5	70.3	73.9

interaction log data to analyze student use of OpenDSA. We plotted the timelines of interactions within OpenDSA and added class events (homework due date, exams date) to the graph.

Logs analysis showed that students used OpenDSA to review for exams, thus indicating the usefulness of OpenDSA as a study aid. Figs. 8.3–8.5 present timelines showing exercise completions. Clusters of interactions appear at homework due dates as expected. But there are also spikes in the number of interactions immediately prior to the exams.

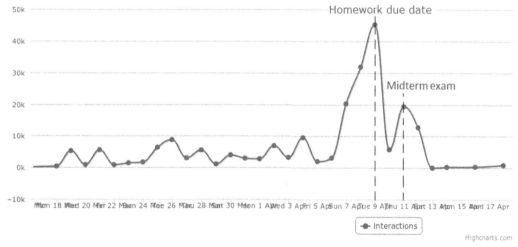

FIGURE 8.3

Timeline of interactions: CS3 at Virginia Tech, Spring 2013 (sorting and hashing chapters).

2.2 STUDENT PERCEPTIONS OF OpenDSA

Some of the case studies from the previous section are rather negative, in that they paint a picture of students avoiding reading content and skipping at least some exercise types whenever possible. However, students routinely offer positive feedback about the system and experience as a whole. Whenever surveyed, students always give a positive value to OpenDSA. In this section, we report on some specific survey feedback from students. We then provide one further case study of student behavior, related to voluntary use of OpenDSA as a study aid and its relationship to grades.

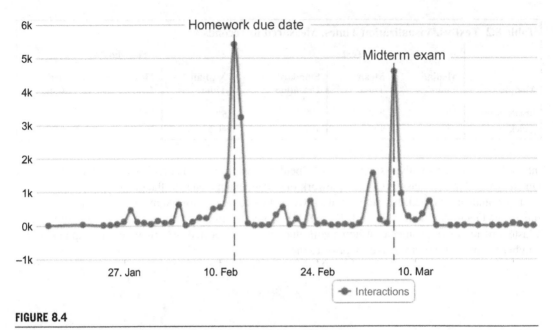

FIGURE 8.4

Timeline of interactions: CS2 at New York University, Spring 2014.

2.2.1 Student ranking of OpenDSA exercises

We investigated how students ranked OpenDSA exercises in terms of perceived learning benefits, specifically as related to other course elements. Participants comprised 54 students enrolled in a CS2 course at Virginia Tech. This is a programming-intensive class with 2 h of programming labs each week. OpenDSA exercises were used as weekly mandatory homework assignments. At the end of the semester, students answered survey questions to report about their experience using OpenDSA.

Students were asked: "This class included these elements: (1) lectures, (2) OpenDSA Exercises, (3) textbook (paper), (4) programming labs, (5) reading quizzes, and (6) interacting with instructor. Please rank these in order from the one that gave you the most learning gains to the one that gave you the least." Thus they ranked class items from 1 — most useful to 6 — least useful in regards to their learning gains in the course.

Students on average ranked OpenDSA exercises second, with an average score of 2.48. Note that OpenDSA materials were used for only part of the course. The main course textbook was a traditional paper textbook. Programming labs were ranked first with an average score of 1.42, the course (paper) textbook was ranked third (average score = 3.77). Lectures, interacting with instructor, and reading quizzes were ranked fourth, fifth, and sixth with average scores 4.13, 4.19, and 4.57, respectively.

A Friedman test was run to identify if the difference between perceived leaning benefits was statistically significant. Because the Friedman test is only applicable to complete block designs, we discarded incomplete blocks (ie, data from students who did not rank all six class elements). Thus 11 incomplete evaluations were discarded resulting in 43 evaluations used in our analysis. The Friedman test revealed a significant difference between the ranking of class items ($X^2(5) = 101.5$, $p < 0.01$). A post hoc Wilcoxon test with Bonferroni correction identified three clusters of items.

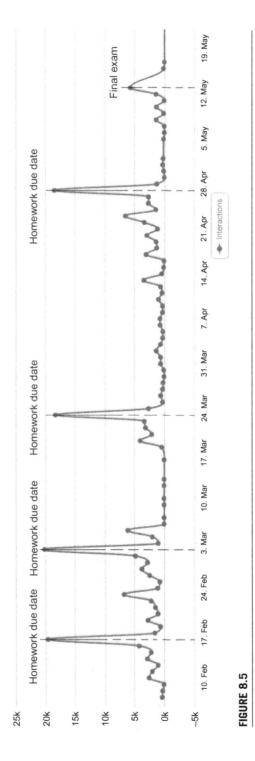

FIGURE 8.5

Timeline of interactions: CS2 at Virginia Tech, Spring 2014.

The highest-ranking cluster consisted of the programming labs. The second highest-ranking cluster consisted of the OpenDSA exercises. The remaining, lowest-ranking cluster included all other items: the paper textbook, lectures, instructor, and reading quizzes. Students attributed most of the learning gains in the course to programming labs first, then to OpenDSA exercises. The other class items were perceived to have a significantly lower impact in learning benefits.

2.2.2 Student self-efficacy regarding learning DSA material

OpenDSA's assessment activities provide the learner with many mastery-based experiences, thus improving students' abilities to learn course material. We asked students to rate their ability to succeed in the course under various scenarios of use for OpenDSA. This information came from a survey carried out on two courses, a CS2 course during Spring 2014 at Virginia Tech, and a CS3 course during Fall 2014 also at Virginia Tech. In both groups, OpenDSA exercises were used as mandatory assignments. OpenDSA was the sole class textbook in the CS3 course.

At the end of the semester, students answered survey questions asking them to rate their ability to learn course material under several (hypothetical) scenarios. We asked students in the CS2 course to use a Likert scale of 1 (low confidence) to 5 (high confidence) to rate their confidence in their ability to learn the course materials under the following conditions:

- Scenario 1: I could succeed in learning the course material if the class was only taught using a standard textbook with Moodle quizzes.
- Scenario 2: I could succeed in learning the course material using OpenDSA on my own if I was required to do the OpenDSA exercises for a grade.
- Scenario 3: I could succeed in learning the course material using OpenDSA on my own with no graded exercises.
- Scenario 4: I could succeed in learning the course material using OpenDSA if the instructor goes over OpenDSA's content during a lecture but I am NOT required to do the exercises for a grade.
- Scenario 5: I could succeed in learning the course material using OpenDSA if the instructor goes over OpenDSA's content during a lecture and I AM required to do the OpenDSA exercises for a grade.

Students enrolled in the CS3 course were asked to answer the same questions, but Scenario 1 was removed since OpenDSA was the textbook of the course and the course did not include Moodle quizzes.

Our analysis of student responses showed that students ranked scenarios involving using OpenDSA during lecture and for graded assignment higher. In CS2, out of the 49 responses that we collected, 38% gave Scenario 5 the highest score of 5, and 69% of the responders ranked their confidence in succeeding in the class under Scenario 5 with a score of 4 or 5. Scenarios involving mandatory OpenDSA exercises (for grading) received higher ability to learn course content scores, thus showing that students have a preference for that type of use of OpenDSA. The above results also corroborate our hypothesis that the mastery-based experience provided by OpenDSA exercises will help student ability to learn course materials. We found similar results from the CS3 responses.

A Kruskal Wallis test revealed for scenarios of use a significant effect on predicted ability to learn course materials for both CS2 ($X^2(4) = 51.9, p < 0.01$) and CS3 ($X^2(3) = 48.5, p < 0.01$). A post hoc test using Wilcoxon tests with Bonferroni correction identified two clusters for CS2 data: Scenario 5 versus the other four scenarios. In other words, Scenario 5 was significantly preferred over all other responses, among which the ordering was not significant.

A post hoc test using Wilcoxon tests with Bonferroni correction identified three clusters for CS3 data. Again, Scenario 5 was most preferred, and the difference was significant. Scenario 2 was the clear second choice. Scenarios 3 and 4 were the least preferred, but their relative order was not significant.

To summarize, the results show that students believe that a class format with lecture content on OpenDSA material, combined with mandatory assignments, will be most effective.

2.2.3 Effects of OpenDSA exercises on student performance

Given the holistic nature of many courses, it can be difficult to extract the effects of one aspect of a course on performance outcomes. Students get information about course content from many sources. We have searched for potential relationships between use of OpenDSA and student performance on exams. Some preliminary results do show a relationship between OpenDSA exercises worked and student performance. Unfortunately, so far we only have sufficient data to show correlation, not causation.

We categorized OpenDSA exercises into three types. Multiple choice, T/F, and fill-in-the-blank questions implemented using the Khan Academy framework are identified as "KA." Algorithm proficiency exercises implemented using the Khan Academy framework are generally short and scored as correct or incorrect; these are identified as "KAV." Full algorithm proficiency exercises with multiple steps are identified as "PE." For each exercise type (KA, KAV, PE), we computed the mean number of exercises completed by the subjects before Midterm 1 and before Midterm 2 in a CS3 course at Virginia Tech during Fall 2013.

The book instance used in our analysis had a total of 95 required exercises, of which 36 were KA simple questions sets (each with several multiple choice or T/F questions), 30 were KA "mini-proficiency" exercises (KAV), 26 were full proficiency exercises (PE), and 3 were other interactive activities. Before Midterm 1, students were required to solve a total of 15 KA simple question sets, 12 KAV exercises, and 6 PE exercises. Between Midterm 1 and 2, they had to complete 19 KA simple question sets, 18 KAV exercises, and 20 PE exercises.

We wanted to see if there would be a difference between the students who correctly completed many exercises "postproficiency" (that is, repeated exercises after receiving credit as a study aid) and those who did not. We found a low correlation between the number of correct exercises (regardless of the type) completed by the students and exam scores. A negative correlation observed between the total number of KA simple questions attempted might be an indication that some students were just using a trial-and-error strategy when solving those exercises, resulting in a lot of incorrect answer submissions (and thus driving up the total number of attempts).

We computed the average number of correct exercises performed by students grouped by score quartile as follows: $q0$ represents students who performed below the 25th percentile; $q1$ represents students with a score between the 25th and the 50th percentile; $q2$ represents students with a score between the 50th and the 75th percentile; and $q3$ represents students with a score above the 75th percentile. In order to compare OpenDSA use across quartiles, we computed the mean number of completed exercises for each quartile. Tables 8.3 and 8.4 show the statistics of the different groups. As shown in Fig. 8.6, *students with higher exam scores tend to complete more exercises correctly than those with lower exam scores*. Since nearly all students complete enough exercises correctly as needed to get full credit for the OpenDSA assignments, what this means is that there is a correlation between repeating more exercises (correctly) as a study aid, and getting a better score on the exam.

Table 8.3 Average Correct Exercises Completed, Grouped by Midterm 1 Score

Groups	Correct.KA	Correct.KAV	Correct.PE
$q0$ ($N=35$)	15.14 (SD=8.04)	9.17 (SD=4.85)	9.37 (SD=7.36)
$q1$ ($N=37$)	19.05 (SD=9.82)	11.43 (SD=4.11)	11.75 (SD=8.36)
$q2$ ($N=32$)	19.43 (SD=5.89)	11.53 (SD=3.91)	13.93 (SD=14.43)
$q3$ ($N=31$)	23.64 (SD=9.15)	12.70 (SD=5.71)	13.87 (SD=12.18)

Table 8.4 Average Correct Exercises Completed, Table Grouped by Midterm 2 Score

Groups	Correct.KA	Correct.KAV	Correct.PE
$q0$ ($N=38$)	15.42 (SD=5.91)	14.55 (SD=6)	26.89 (SD=12.76)
$q1$ ($N=31$)	16.83 (SD=10.11)	14.22 (SD=6.57)	26.45 (SD=13.08)
$q2$ ($N=33$)	18.09 (SD=7.27)	16.33 (SD=4.55)	31.24 (SD=14.93)
$q3$ ($N=33$)	24.60 (SD=12.09)	18.78 (SD=5.75)	34.03 (SD=11.85)

The difference in the average number of correct exercises between student groups was significant at the $p < 0.05$ level for KA simple questions and KAV exercises for Midterm 1 and 2. However, the difference was not statistically significant for PE exercises. The difference was still not significant when merging the number of correct KAV exercises with the number of correct PE exercises.

We can say that higher scores on written tests are correlated with a high number of correct exercises (beyond the minimum level required to receive full homework credit). These findings can be used to detect struggling students, since they are less likely to use an exercise for study purposes. In addition, students with the lowest grades have the lowest "number of correct exercises to number of exercises attempted" ratio. In other words, they appear to be using some suboptimal behavior such as guessing or viewing hints in an attempt to build a catalog of correct answers, rather than actively using their knowledge to correctly answer the question.

3 GAMIFICATION: HOW FEEDBACK MOTIVATES STUDENT BEHAVIOR
3.1 INTRODUCTION

There can be no doubt that many people are motivated by indications of progress and closure. For example, witness the feeling of satisfaction that many people get from the simple act of crossing a task off of a "to do" list. We have implemented several types of feedback to users regarding completion of an exercise, and progress toward completion of modules and chapters. This feedback can be considered a form of "gamification." Gamification is the use of game design elements in nongame contexts (Deterding et al., 2011).

Here we are interested in exploring how visual elements (indicators) and other techniques borrowed from game design influence student behavior when using OpenDSA. In this section, we first enumerate the gamification features within OpenDSA, and report on a survey of student opinions on these

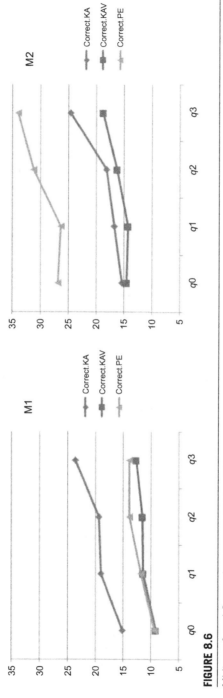

FIGURE 8.6

Midterm 1 and 2 exercises means per quartile.

features. We then report on indications from our log data about how the presence of visual indicators influences student interactions with OpenDSA. Further details on some aspects of this section can be found in Fouh (2015).

3.2 RELATED WORK

One element of gamification is the use of motivational affordances in order to encourage particular behaviors (Hamari et al., 2014). Zhang (2008) identified five main motivational sources and argued that games and learning system design should be influenced by cognitive (achievements and accomplishments) motivations and needs. Elements present in games that have been mainly used in educational systems design include scores, leaderboards, achievements/badges, and level (Hamari et al., 2014; Deterding et al., 2011). Some elements like scores have always been part of educational systems, and seem to be motivating. On the other hand, there is little evidence in the literature to conclude that there is a positive impact from badges on student engagement or effectiveness (Falkner and Falkner, 2014). Despite this, badges are increasingly being used in computer science education systems. Haaranen et al. (2014) awarded badges to students for completing exercises in a data structures course, where badges were displayed within the learning management system. They reported a mixed impact on student learning behavior. A leaderboard and badges were used in an introductory media computation course, and are credited with contributing to positive experiences for students and high overall engagement (Latulipe et al., 2015).

3.3 OpenDSA GAMIFICATION ELEMENTS

OpenDSA aims to provide students with visual indicators upon successful completion of an interactive activity. Such indicators are used in conjunction with a traditional points system for homework assignments. Points are earned when an exercise has been solved correctly. OpenDSA uses a mastery-based approach, meaning that students can attempt an exercise as many times as desired until completion credit has been given (and the exercise can continue to be used after that, perhaps as a study aid). While some "exercises" are merely static multiple choice or T/F questions, many generate a new problem instance each time, making them repeatable in a meaningful way for additional practice. OpenDSA exercises are fundamentally implemented in two ways. Most exercises use the Khan Academy exercises framework (KA exercises). Such exercises provide students with hints to help them answer a question. Fig. 8.7 shows an example of a Khan Academy exercise in which the student can click on the "I'd like a hint" button to get help. Once a hint is used, that problem instance is not graded.

Other exercises are referred to as "JSAV-Proficiency exercises" (PE exercises). These are always algorithm simulations, where the student will manipulate a data structure such as an array or tree through a series of steps to reproduce the behavior of some algorithm. The initial state of the data structure (such as the specific values in an array for a sorting algorithm, or the order of the inputs for insertion into a tree) specifies a new problem instance. For each such instance, a visualization for a model solution is automatically generated. Fig. 8.8 shows an example of a PE with the model solution visible. Students can chose to see the model answer without (or before) solving the exercise. Once a model answer has been displayed, that problem instance will not be graded. So to get credit for the exercise, the student will need to request a new problem instance to work on.

Now we describe the visual indicators displayed when an interactive activity is completed.

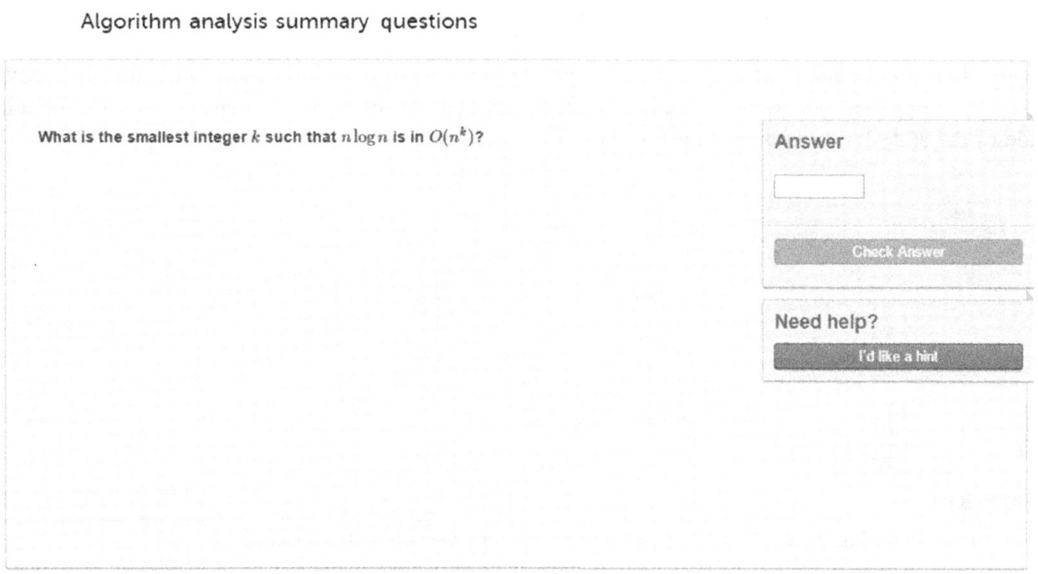

Algorithm analysis summary questions

What is the smallest integer k such that $n \log n$ is in $O(n^k)$?

Answer

[ ]

Check Answer

Need help?

I'd like a hint

FIGURE 8.7

Khan Academy exercise.

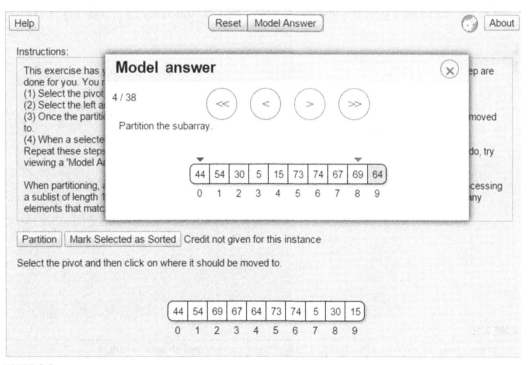

FIGURE 8.8

Proficiency exercise.

3.3.1 Proficiency for embedded slideshows

OpenDSA visualizations often come in the form of embedded slideshows, which generally are relatively short presentations of a specific example. Users are given an indication when the slideshow has been completed (all slides viewed), shown by the appearance of a green check mark on the left side of the slideshow container (see Fig. 8.9).

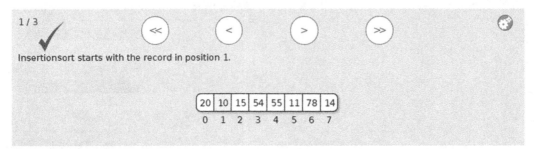

FIGURE 8.9

Insertionsort mini-slideshow with *green* (*dark gray* in the print versions) check mark.

3.3.2 Proficiency for embedded exercises

Completion of an exercise is indicated by the color of the button used to control whether the exercise is to be shown or hidden. A red button indicates that the user is not yet given credit for being proficient, as shown in Fig. 8.10. Green indicates that the user has received proficiency credit (see Fig. 8.11).

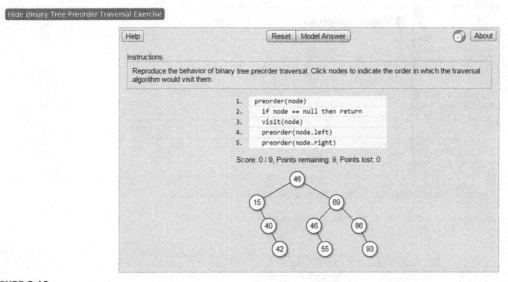

FIGURE 8.10

Tree preorder traversal exercise with *red* (*dark gray* in the print versions) show/hide button.

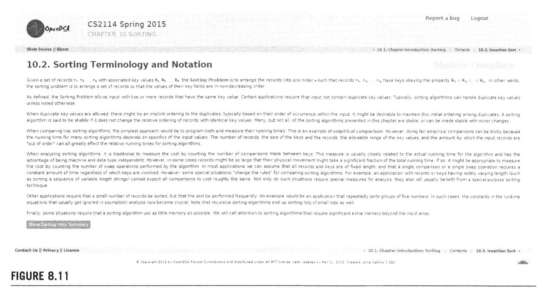

FIGURE 8.11

Module page with proficiency indicator for module and exercise.

3.3.3 Proficiency for modules

Modules in OpenDSA cover a specific topic or part of a topic. Operationally, a module corresponds to a single HTML page within a book instance. Each module typically includes one or more slideshows and one or more interactive exercises. Module proficiency occurs when a user obtains proficiency for all the required exercises and completes viewing all of the slideshows in a module. Proficiency is signaled to the user by the words "Module Complete" that appear in green at the top of the module page (see Fig. 8.11). A given book instance can optionally be configured to show "Module Complete" automatically when the module is viewed, for modules with no exercises or visualizations. At this point, we have not studied whether it is desirable or not to indicate "Module Complete" signals for such modules. But anecdotal evidence suggests that students prefer this.

3.3.4 Table of contents indicators

A small green check mark appears next to a module title in the Table of Contents when that the module has been completed (see Fig. 8.12).

3.3.5 OpenDSA gradebook

Perhaps the most important notification information that students receive comes through the *gradebook page*. This page shows score status for all exercises and modules. Those for which the user is proficient are highlighted in green. The gradebook is a hierarchical display that allows users to toggle between showing or hiding portions of the gradebook. Fig. 8.13 shows a gradebook page with two modules expanded, one down to the exercise level. Completed exercises within the expanded display for the module are highlighted in green.

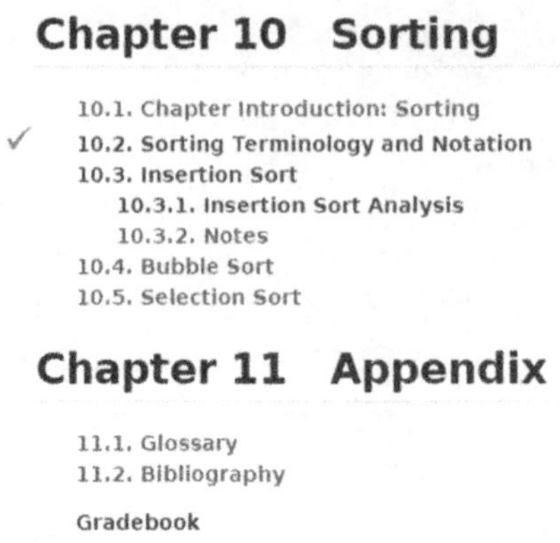

Chapter 10 Sorting

10.1. Chapter Introduction: Sorting
✓ 10.2. Sorting Terminology and Notation
10.3. Insertion Sort
10.3.1. Insertion Sort Analysis
10.3.2. Notes
10.4. Bubble Sort
10.5. Selection Sort

Chapter 11 Appendix

11.1. Glossary
11.2. Bibliography

Gradebook

FIGURE 8.12

Section of table of content with module proficiency indicator.

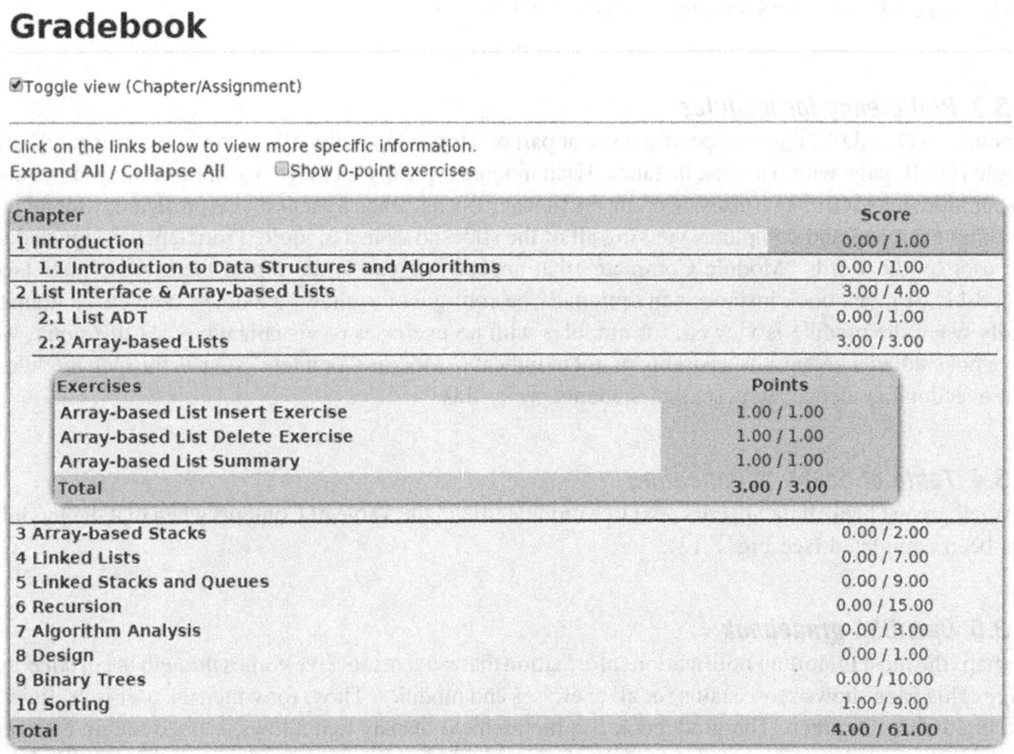

Gradebook

☑Toggle view (Chapter/Assignment)

Click on the links below to view more specific information.
Expand All / Collapse All ☐Show 0-point exercises

Chapter	Score
1 Introduction	0.00 / 1.00
1.1 Introduction to Data Structures and Algorithms	0.00 / 1.00
2 List Interface & Array-based Lists	3.00 / 4.00
2.1 List ADT	0.00 / 1.00
2.2 Array-based Lists	3.00 / 3.00

Exercises	Points
Array-based List Insert Exercise	1.00 / 1.00
Array-based List Delete Exercise	1.00 / 1.00
Array-based List Summary	1.00 / 1.00
Total	3.00 / 3.00

Chapter	Score
3 Array-based Stacks	0.00 / 2.00
4 Linked Lists	0.00 / 7.00
5 Linked Stacks and Queues	0.00 / 9.00
6 Recursion	0.00 / 15.00
7 Algorithm Analysis	0.00 / 3.00
8 Design	0.00 / 1.00
9 Binary Trees	0.00 / 10.00
10 Sorting	1.00 / 9.00
Total	4.00 / 61.00

FIGURE 8.13

Gradebook page.

3.4 STUDENT PERCEPTIONS OF OpenDSA GAMIFICATION ELEMENTS

We conducted a survey of OpenDSA users in order to understand what they think of the gamification elements. Participants were 143 students enrolled in a CS3 course at Virginia Tech during Fall 2014, from whom we collected 83 survey responses. OpenDSA was used as the main textbook, and students had until the end of the semester to complete all of the OpenDSA exercises. Completion of OpenDSA exercises accounted for 20% of the course final grade.

The survey asked the following questions:

1. OpenDSA includes a number of features to help you track which exercises and modules you have completed. These include green checkmarks by the slideshows, green text saying "Module Complete" at the top of the page, green marks in the table of contents, and green bars in the student gradebook. On a scale of 1–5, with 1 meaning not important and 5 meaning very important, how important are these signals for completing material to you?
2. Does the existence of the green checkmarks and other signals of completion of material affect your behavior in any way? If so, how?

We used a qualitative method of content analysis when examining student responses to Question 2. We used interaction log data to analyze and understand how visual indicators influenced student use of OpenDSA.

3.4.1 Student perceptions on visual feedback indicators

To the question "how important are these (OpenDSA visual) signals for completing material to you," respondents gave an average score of 4.01 on a five-point Likert scale. Fig. 8.14 shows the response distribution. A majority of students (75%) indicated that visual indicators were important when using OpenDSA to study course content.

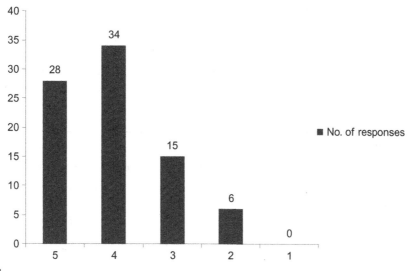

FIGURE 8.14

Responses distribution for each rank.

3.4.2 Effects of visual feedback indicators on student behavior

We used codes to label ideas expressed in each response to the question "Does the existence of the green checkmarks and other signals of completion of material affect your behavior in any way? If so, how?" The codes attempt to capture how the visual indicators affected students' learning behavior. We derived the codes from students' responses, and grouped responses with the same code together. Table 8.5 summarizes the results. In this table, we show the average score from the first question for the students in each code group.

Out of 80 responses collected, 65% reported that visual elements had an effect on their behavior while 35% reported no impact. Thirty-one percent reported using visual indicators to keep track their progress. Similarly, 15% indicated using the visual elements to track work remaining (labeled as "Goal tracking"). Students can easily track their progress (or work that remains) by looking at the greened items in the gradebook or by the presence of green checkmarks in front of sections in the table of contents. Three students acknowledged actively seeking the green checkmarks while working. One student wrote "Yes (completion signals affected my behavior), I try to get checkmarks on everything."

Among the students who reported using visual indicators to keep track of the goal (amount of work left), 10 indicated that the visual indicators *motivated them to do more work*. A student wrote "Yeah it's fun to see it all get completed makes me want to do it more," while another one wrote "yes, made me more willing to complete everything."

Nine students reported that *visual indicators reinforced their learning*. They indicated liking them and being happy to see them. Examples of comments in that category include "Yes, I think it's rewarding and make me feel better," "They make me feel accomplished so I work harder," and "I can be sure I have completed the graded material." Students in this category on average gave the highest importance score to visual indicators (mean $= 4.77$).

Among the students who reported using visual indicators to track their accomplishments, eight indicated that *they stopped working on items as soon as they are marked as completed, until they needed to study for a test*. A student noted that "Usually after it's checked I don't go back unless I have a test or need it for a project." Another wrote "(I) don't continue practicing them (checked items) until test review time." This trend needs to be taken into consideration when deciding a proficiency threshold for an exercise. A low proficiency threshold might not provide the students with enough practice. Some students reported that visual indicators are a better way to track progress than a points system. For example, a student wrote "Kind of gave concrete evidence on completion as opposed to 'What is my grade now'."

Table 8.5 Student Response Summary

Code	Value	Frequency	Percentage	Avg. Score	Agg. Score
1	Accomplishment tracking	25	31	4.12	4.33
2	Goal tracking	12	15	4.08	
3	Accomplishment/goal tracking	2	3	4.5	
4	Verification grade saved on server	2	3	4	
5	Reinforcement	9	11	4.77	
6	Reinforcement/goal tracking	2	3	4.5	
7	No impact	28	35	3.57	3.52
	Total	80	100		

A Wilcoxon rank sum test revealed they ranked visual indicators as more important when they reported that these indicators affected their behavior ($W(79) = 995, p < 0.01$). This is to be expected, but it also rules out a situation where people feel compelled to get all of the marks since they are there, but would have preferred that they not be visible.

3.5 IMPACT OF PROFICIENCY INDICATORS ON STUDENT TIME SPENT ON SLIDESHOWS

Visual proficiency indicators appear upon correct completion of an interactive element and remain visible thereafter. Therefore, it is unlikely that visual indicators will motivate students to complete the same exercise or slideshow after they gain proficiency. Students receive points only for exercises. However, the "Module Complete" message and the green checkmarks in the table of contents only appear if they have gone through all the visualizations (on top of the exercises).

Previous studies (Breakiron, 2013; Fouh et al., 2014a) have shown that many students go straight to the exercises upon loading a module and they rush through slideshows (during their first viewing). We investigated the time spent by students on slideshows before proficiency (first viewing) and post proficiency (second viewing) to see if students behavior changed once they got the green checkmark for completing a slideshow.

The majority of students viewed most slideshows at least twice. Ninety-eight percent of the students completed more than 50% of the slideshows at least twice, with 20 (out of 135) students completing all the slideshows at least two times. Fig. 8.15 shows the distribution of students' subsequent slideshow completion (reattempt ratio). The mean fraction of slideshows that were viewed multiple times was 80%.

Student's behavior during their second viewing should not be influenced by the check mark (since the visual status cannot change at this point). In Fig. 8.16, for each slideshow we have plotted the mean time

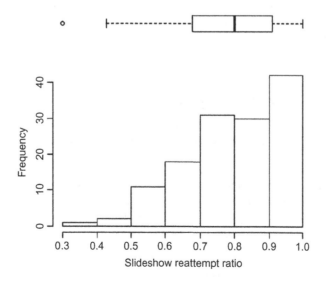

FIGURE 8.15

Multiple viewings of slideshows. Each bar in the histogram shows the fraction of students who revisited that fraction of slideshows.

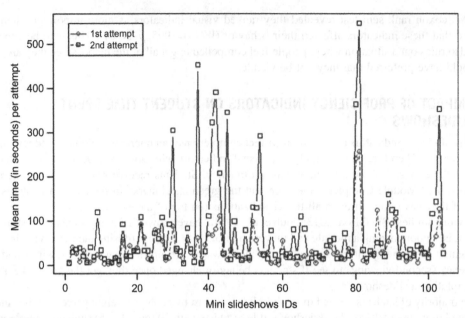

FIGURE 8.16

Mean time per slideshow per viewing.

spent by students during the first and second viewings. (There were not enough third viewings to analyze.) Students spent a mean of 36 s and a median of 24 s on each slideshow during their first viewing. They spent a mean of 73 s and a median of 31 s on each slideshow on their second viewing. A Wilcoxon rank sum test showed that the increase in time spent on each slideshow between the first and the second viewings was statistically significant ($W(1125) = 995$, $p < 0.01$). Since rushing through slideshows is more pronounced on the first viewing, it seems that preproficiency work is influenced by the green checkmark, and postproficiency work is more influenced by learning, especially to review for exams.

3.6 STUDENTS USE OF THE GRADEBOOK

There were 171 HTML pages in the book instance used by students enrolled in the CS3 course offering at Virginia Tech in Fall 2014. We examined which pages were most visited. The top four pages, in order, were as follows:

1. The book's Table of Contents page was the most visited (with 31,496 hits).
2. The second most visited page presented examples of hashing functions (with 12,838 hits).
3. The gradebook page was the third most visited page (with 9905 hits).
4. The page covering Quicksort was the fourth most visited page (with 6155 hits).

As shown in Fig. 8.18, students enrolled in the course visited the gradebook page on average 61 times during the course of the semester (117 days). The median number of gradebook visits was 25. Eight percent (11 out of 135) of the students enrolled in the course never looked at the gradebook. The average OpenDSA exercise completion rate for student who never visited the gradebook was 91% while the average completion rate for the rest of the class was 92%.

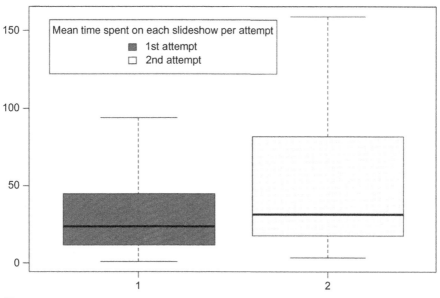

FIGURE 8.17

Distribution of time per slideshow, by viewing. In each case, we see a boxplot with median line.

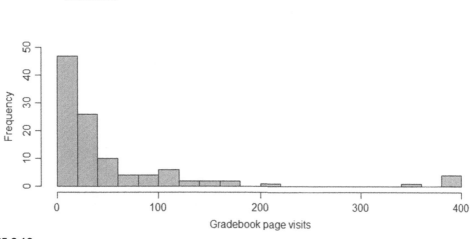

FIGURE 8.18

Distribution for number of times a given student visited the gradebook during the semester. The right-most bin includes all students who viewed the gradebook 400 times or more.

There was a strong correlation ($r=0.9$) between the overall daily total number of exercises attempted and daily total gradebook page hits as shown in Fig. 8.19. This indicates that students used the gradebook to check their progress while working on exercises. On any given day, only a mean of 40% (SD$=23\%$, median$=35\%$) of the students who attempted an exercise viewed the gradebook that same day.

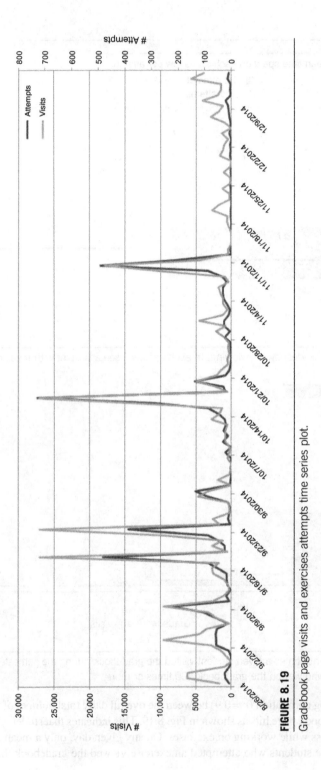

FIGURE 8.19

Gradebook page visits and exercises attempts time series plot.

We sought to investigate if there was a difference in the number of exercises attempted between students who visited the gradebook a lot and students who did not. We ranked students by the number of gradebook visits and grouped them into quartiles. There was no statistically significant difference in the mean number of exercises attempted among quartiles for gradebook use. We concluded that the presence of the gradebook has no impact on the amount of student interaction with OpenDSA exercises.

3.7 DISCUSSION

Our investigation of the impact of proficiency visual indicators revealed the following:

- Student responses indicated that the display of the green checkmarks (and other visual elements) is a motivating factor. Visual indicators are used in this case for reinforcement. Students like them and many students try to get closure from completion everywhere possible.
- Despite the fact that students like the gamification elements, we have so far found no evidence of positive impact on students' learning behavior due to them. Analysis of log data revealed that students often do not engage in a meaningful way with slideshows on their first attempt. They rush through slideshows, we assume to get the green checkmarks. However, they do spend more time on the slideshows during subsequent attempts. OpenDSA slideshows aim to present course material in a way that will encourage students to engage more deeply with the content. The fact that students do not spend enough time on slideshows despite the presence of reinforcements indicates that we should include other mechanisms that will better encourage students to engage with them.
- Students regularly refer to the gradebook to check their progress (though there is no evidence that this affects or is even correlated to their performance). Further study using data from courses in which students are assigned frequent assignments needs to be done in order to have a complete picture of student use of the gradebook. We found no relationship between gradebook page visits and the amount of exercises attempted by students.

Given these findings, the next step is to use this information in order to improve student outcomes. This can most likely be accomplished by modifications to the way that materials are presented. Such modifications might include further use of gamification elements. In order for students to learn the material better, it seems that the key goal needs to be to get them to engage more with the types of content that they tend to avoid now. Here are a number of ideas that might be promising avenues for future study:

- Increase the use of visualizations (slideshows) and interactive elements as much as possible, as this is a proven technique to increase student attention.
- Create "progression" mechanisms that lock access to certain aspects of the content until minimum requirements have been met. For examples, access to an exercise might be blocked until students have viewed the corresponding visualization. Access to proficiency exercises might require completion of simpler screening questions.
- Visualizations might themselves incorporate simple questions that must be passed in order to continue. This might discourage skipping through the slideshows for completion checkmarks.
- Add (optional) challenges for students who want to do more work.

- Add public "leaderboards" (perhaps using aliases) to let students see their performance in comparison to others in the class.

These ideas need careful consideration and experimentation before deployment. Some of them carry the risk of failing in various ways, in that they lead to unintended behavior. Or they might simply lead to increased frustration on the part of the users.

4 CONCLUSION AND FUTURE WORK

Visual interactive content, rich interactive exercises, automated assessment, detailed student analytics, and adaptive tutoring techniques can be combined in many ways to give students rich courseware that goes well beyond the capabilities previously available. However, we find that with any new courseware techniques, it is important to carefully monitor how it affects student learning. Often the results are not entirely as expected. Prior research, such as the rich body of work around cognitive theory of multimedia presentations (Mayer, 2008), provides us with a practical basis for developing multimedia content. However, the research community has only scratched the surface with respect to understanding the effects of student analytics, gamification, and interactive exercises with automated assessment. We are hopeful that the education research community can over time develop best practice principles to guide future course content and online educational systems.

ACKNOWLEDGMENTS

This material is based upon work supported by the National Science Foundation under Grant Numbers DUE-1139861, IIS-1258571, and DUE-1432008.

REFERENCES

Andrade, H., Valtcheva, A., 2009. Promoting learning and achievement through self-assessment. Theory Pract. 48 (1), 12–19. http://www.tandfonline.com/doi/abs/10.1080/00405840802577544.

Breakiron, D.A., 2013. Evaluating the integration of online, interactive tutorials into a data structures and algorithms course. Master's thesis, Virginia Tech.

Corbett, A.T., Koedinger, K.R., Anderson, J.R., 1997. Intelligent tutoring systems. In: Helander, M.G., Landauer, T.K., Prabhu, P.V. (Eds.), Handbook of Human-Computer Interaction. Elsevier, pp. 849–874.

Deterding, S., Dixon, D., Khaled, R., Nacke, L., 2011. From game design elements to gamefulness: defining "gamification", In: Proceedings of the 15th International Academic MindTrek Conference: Envisioning Future Media Environments (MindTrek 2011). ACM, New York, NY, USA, pp. 9–15.

Falkner, N.J.G., Falkner, K.E., 2014. "Whither, badges?" or "Wither, badges!": a metastudy of badges in computer science education to clarify effects, significance and influence. In: Proceedings of the 14th Koli Calling International Conference on Computing Education Research. ACM, New York, NY, USA, pp. 127–135.

Feng, M., Roschelle, J., Heffernan, N., Fairman, J., Murphy, R., 2014. Implementation of an intelligent tutoring system for online homework support in an efficacy trial. In: Intelligent Tutoring Systems. Springer, pp. 561–566.

Ferguson, R., 2012. Learning analytics: drivers, developments and challenges. Int. J. Technol. Enhanc. Learn. 4 (5–6), 304–317.

Fouh, E., 2015. Building and evaluating a learning environment for data structures and algorithms courses. Ph.D. thesis, Virginia Tech, May.

Fouh, E., Breakiron, D.A., Hamouda, S., Farghally, M.F., Shaffer, C.A., 2014a. Exploring students learning behavior with an interactive etextbook in computer science courses. Comput. Hum. Behav. 41, 478–485.

Fouh, E., Karavirta, V., Breakiron, D.A., Hamouda, S., Hall, S., Naps, T.L., Shaffer, C.A., 2014b. Design and architecture of an interactive etextbook — the OpenDSA system. Sci. Comput. Program. 88, 22–40.

Goodrich, M.T., Tamassia, R., 1998. Teaching the analysis of algorithms with visual proofs. ACM SIGCSE Bull. 30, 207–211.

Haaranen, L., Ihantola, P., Hakulinen, L., Korhonen, A., 2014. How (not) to introduce badges to online exercises. In: Proceedings of the 45th ACM Technical Symposium on Computer Science Education (SIGCSE 2014). ACM, New York, NY, USA, pp. 33–38.

Hamari, J., Koivisto, J., Sarsa, H., 2014. Does gamification work? A literature review of empirical studies on gamification. In: 47th Hawaii International Conference on System Sciences (HICSS). IEEE Computer Society Press, Los Alamitos, CA, USA, pp. 3025–3034.

Hundhausen, C.D., Douglas, S.A., Stasko, J.T., 2002. A meta-study of algorithm visualization effectiveness. J. Vis. Lang. Comput. 13 (3), 259–290.

Karavirta, V., Shaffer, C.A., 2013. JSAV: the JavaScript algorithm visualization library. In: Proceedings of the 18th ACM Conference on Innovation and Technology in Computer Science Education (ITiCSE 2013). ACM, New York, NY, USA, pp. 159–164.

Karavirta, V., Korhonen, A., Seppälä, O., 2013. Misconceptions in visual algorithm simulation revisited: on UI's effect on student performance, attitudes, and misconceptions. In: Proceedings of Learning and Teaching in Computing and Engineering, Macau.

Korhonen, A., Malmi, L., Silvasti, P., Nikander, J., Tenhunen, P., Mård, P., Salonen, H., Karavirta, V., 2003. TRAKLA2 website. http://www.cse.hut.fi/en/research/SVG/TRAKLA2/.

Laakso, M.-J., Salakoski, T., Grandell, L., Qiu, X., Korhonen, A., Malmi, L., 2005. Multi-perspective study of novice learners adopting the visual algorithm simulation exercise system TRAKLA2. Inform. Educ. 4 (1), 49–68.

Laakso, M.-J., Myller, N., Korhonen, A., 2009. Comparing learning performance of students using algorithm visualizations collaboratively on different engagement levels. Educ. Technol. Soc. 12 (2), 267–282. URL http://www.ifets.info/abstract.php?art_id=945.

Latulipe, C., Long, N.B., Seminario, C.E., 2015. Structuring flipped classes with lightweight teams and gamification. In: Proceedings of the 46th ACM Technical Symposium on Computer Science Education. ACM, New York, NY, USA, pp. 392–397.

Mayer, R., 2008. Applying the science of learning: evidence-based principles for the design of multimedia instruction. Am. Psychol. 63 (8), 760–769.

McMillan, J.H., Hearn, J., 2008. Student self-assessment: the key to stronger student motivation and higher achievement. Educ. Horiz. 87 (1), 40–49. URL http://www.eric.ed.gov/ERICDocs/data/ericdocs2sql/content_storage_01/0000019b/80/41/9e/80.pdf.

Naps, T.L., Rößling, G., Almstrum, V., Dann, W., Fleischer, R., Hundhausen, C., Korhonen, A., Malmi, L., McNally, M., Rodger, S., et al., 2002. Exploring the role of visualization and engagement in computer science education. ACM SIGCSE Bull. 35, 131–152.

Parker, M., Lewis, C., 2014. What makes big-O analysis difficult: understanding how students understand runtime analysis. J. Comput. Sci. Coll. 29 (4), 164–174.

Roll, I., Aleven, V., McLaren, B.M., Koedinger, K.R., 2011. Improving students help-seeking skills using metacognitive feedback in an intelligent tutoring system. Learn. Instr. 21 (2), 267–280.

Shaffer, C.A., Cooper, M.L., Alon, A.J.D., Akbar, M., Stewart, M., Ponce, S., Edwards, S.H., 2010. Algorithm visualization: the state of the field. ACM Trans. Comput. Educ. 10 (3), 1–22.

Siemens, G., Baker, R.S.d., 2012. Learning analytics and educational data mining: towards communication and collaboration. In: Proceedings of the 2nd International Conference on Learning Analytics and Knowledge. ACM, New York, NY, USA, pp. 252–254.

Zhang, P., 2008. Technical opinion: motivational affordances: reasons for ICT design and use. Commun. ACM, 51 (11), 145–147.

CREATING UNIVERSITY ANALYTICAL INFORMATION SYSTEMS: A GRAND CHALLENGE FOR INFORMATION SYSTEMS RESEARCH

I. Guitart, J. Conesa

Open University of Catalonia, Barcelona, Spain

1 INTRODUCTION

Data are the most valuable assets of organizations. The analysis of data from organizations, and from other relevant sources, with the objective of getting more information about the organization context, the improvement of opportunities and detection of potential problems is what is called analytics (or business analytics in the context of for-profit organizations). Over recent decades the implementation of analytical systems has been a priority for companies when investing in information technology and communications. The use of analytical systems have several benefits (Sieber et al., 2006) mainly focused on improving the organization management and gain competitive advantage. Additionally, having analytical systems provides management tools to guide the organization towards strategic goals and encourage the decision-making process based on data and evidences (Sieber et al., 2006; Guitart and Conesa, 2014).

Out of all the different kinds of organizations, there is one type that has applied analytics successfully with a higher degree of performance: the for-profit organization. This type of organization creates analytical information systems, called business intelligence (BI) Information Systems, to gather relevant data and integrate and analyze such data in order to find out relevant information that helps in the improvement of the business. The benefits of adopting or implementing BI systems are independent of the business sector.

In universities, and in higher education in general, BI systems have been applied as well, though less successfully. The reason is that these systems usually deal with management data of universities: enrolment, accountability, finance, etc. However, they do not deal with the data that can be extracted from the teaching-learning process or the research process, which are the focus of universities. As a result, the existing analytical systems only partially cover the organization, being unable to deal with the real activity of universities (teaching and research), resulting in systems that cannot address the main problems a given university may have and the potential improvements that can raise its position in relation to competence.

Why analytical systems in universities remain so immature is not clear. In our humble point of view it is not because of a single reason, but some several interlinked ones. What is clear is that complexity in the creation of BI systems is not the reason. Their creation may be very hard, time and resource consuming, involving a great deal of people with different roles and skills, however, more complex systems have been created in the business sector. One of the main reasons may be the lack of both academic and research data gathered during last decades by universities. Other reasons may be the lack of maturity in data recovering and management within the academic field, such as the lack of standards, software tools or the perseverance with the use of classical lectures, and the lack of vision of the university managers to see that their analytic systems do not only have to support decision-taking in accountancy and finances, but also in teaching and research. However, over the last decade, the adoption of virtual learning environments (VLEs) for most universities, including traditional face-to-face universities, has opened the minds of academics to the huge amount of academic data that can be gathered from VLE and the benefits that an efficient analysis of such data can provide to teaching. The result of this new perception has brought about new disciplines, such as action, academic and learning analytics, and new standards/specifications in e-learning, such as Whyte (2015) and the adoption of old ones such as IEEE-Learning Object Metamodel IEEE-LOM (2011), Dublin Core (2001), xAPI (2012), or IMS-Caliper (2015).

Due to the momentum, the increasing interest in the topic, the size of the learning analytic community and the availability of the huge quantities of data in most universities, this is a good time to thoroughly analyze the BI systems and how these systems can be applied to universities. Unfortunately, to our knowledge, there is not a single piece of research that has analyzed in detail the analytical necessities of universities, why current BI systems do not satisfy such necessities and what adaptations should be done to BI systems so that they can be successfully applied to deal with university needs. In addition, BI techniques are hardly ever applied in projects where analytics are performed on academic data. The proposed study would provide several guidelines to help users to adapt BI pieces to deal with small learning analytic projects, making its design and implementation easier and improving its performance in this arena.

For all these reasons we believe that adapting BI systems to higher education is not only an interesting goal to pursue but a grand challenge for the new era. The paper will answer the question "Creating Business Intelligence (or analytic) Systems in Universities is a grand challenge?"; using the grand challenge definition of Tony Hoare (2003). According to Hoare, a grand challenge:

> represents a commitment by a significant section of the research community to work together towards a common goal, agreed to be valuable and achievable by a team effort within a predicted timescale. The challenge is formulated by the researchers themselves as a focus for the research that they wish to pursue in any case.

In the next section, we briefly review the notion of business analytical IS, the benefits they provide, the issues they pose and the evolution these systems have had over the last decades. Later, Section **3** describes what analytical information systems are used in universities, what their scope is, how they are evolving and the unsolved problems people face when creating analytical IS in universities. Section **4**, presents what we believe should be a fully integrated analytical IS in a university. Our proposal is generic and describes the proposed scope of the system, the components it may have, the kind of information it should deal with, the critical factors that should be taken into account in its creation and a comparison of the proposed system with the actual analytical systems within universities, in order to see the difference between the ideal and the current.

In order to create an analytical system for universities as proposed, several research problems should be solved. In order to be qualified as a grand challenge, a research goal has to meet several criteria. In Section **5** we assess the proposed goal according to these criteria. Finally, Section **6** concludes the paper.

2 BUSINESS ANALYTICAL IS

There exist different definitions in the literature about enterprise information systems (EIS). They depend on how EIS are regarded, such as management, strategy or technology. In this paper we see EIS as *an information system for integrating and extending business processes across the boundaries of business functions at both intra-organizational and inter-organizational levels* (Da Xu, 2011). EIS provide organizational effectiveness, reduce costs, increase profits, create greater differential value, increase the organization's ability to respond quickly to consumer demands, and help to improve services, the quality of products, competitiveness and the decision-making process. In summary, these systems allow the enterprises not just to survive, but to prosper in the global economy (Arnold, 2010). EIS tend to be generic, but can be customized to the specific requirements and features of each organization, up to certain limits.

EIS have their origins in material requirements planning (MRP) and manufacturing resource planning (MRP-II) systems, which were two of the earliest business applications. They were not integrated into finance and accounting processes (Olson and Kesharwani, 2010). ERP systems evolved from MRP-II and integrated into one system a set of functionalities from different areas of the organization, such as sales and distribution, planning, purchasing, production, accounting, and finance. ERP-II extends ERP functionalities by providing a broad set of modules that support the back-office and front-office functionalities (including CRM and SCM systems as additional modules), as well as integrating processes across diverse enterprises, supporting the management of business networks (McGaughey and Gunasekaran, 2009). IERP systems include the features of ERP-II systems, adding modules such as KMS and BI. They are also adapted to deal with government institutions.

Nowadays, when we think about an EIS, we imagine an information system that is composed of the following kinds of information systems:

- Enterprise resource planning (ERP), designed to integrate and optimize the business processes and to support information flows within the organization in order to enhance efficiency and maintain a competitive position (Addo-Tenkorang and Helo, 2011).
- Customer relationship management (CRM) system, aims to organize and handle the business actions connected to customer relationships through the entire life cycle of the partnership with the customers. CRM requires a customer-centered business philosophy (Cheng, 2009).
- Supply chain management (SCM) system, which provides the systemic, strategic coordination of the traditional business functions and the tactics across these business functions within a particular company and across businesses within the supply chain, for the purpose of improving the long-term performance of the individual companies and the supply chain as a whole (Mentzer et al., 2001).

- Business intelligence (BI) system, which transforms raw data into information and useful knowledge for the company.
- Knowledge management system (KMS), which supports and enhances the organizational processes of knowledge creation, storage, retrieval, transfer, and application. KMS is also an integrated, user-machine system for providing information or knowledge to support operations, management, analysis, and decision-making (Wu and Wang, 2006).

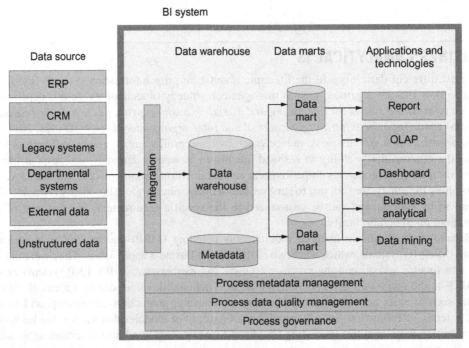

FIGURE 9.1

Components of a BI system.

Roldán, J.L., Carrión, G.A.C., González, J.L.G., 2012. Los sistemas de inteligencia de negocio como soporte a los procesos de toma de decisiones en las organizaciones. Papeles de economía española 132, 239–260.

Therefore, a *BI system represents a broad category of applications, technologies and processes that are designed to collect, store, access and analyze data to help users make better decisions* (Roldán et al., 2012). From the definition we can infer that the BI systems are composed of three main steps: the collection of data from different sources (ERP, CRM, departmental information systems, external data, etc.), the storage of data in a way that facilitates analysis (data warehouse or data mart), the access and analysis of data through technologies and BI applications to achieve the objective of the business (Curto and Conesa, 2010).

BI systems are not a new trend; they began as "decision support systems" in the 1960s and redefined later in the 1990s, when the term BI was introduced, as a set of technologies and processes that use data to understand and analyze business performance, and became popular in business and TIC communities. Later, in twenty-first century the focus has shifted slightly to business analytics, which is seen as the key component in a BI. Business analytics is defined as the extensive use of data, statistical and quantitative analysis, explanatory and predictive models, and fact-based management to drive decisions and actions.

Fig. 9.1 presents some of the main components of a BI system:

- Data warehouse (DW) is a data repository that provides a global, common and integrated vision to the organization.
- Data mart (DM) contains subsets of the DW that focus to a particular department, a set of users or are necessary to perform a certain analysis.
- Processes that extract, transform and integrate data (also known as ETL processes) into the data warehouse or the data marts.
- Metadata that provide information about the data and the processes within BI system. They describe the contents of the data, their semantics and how the data are transformed.
- Business analytics comprise a set of software tools designed for reporting, querying and analyzing data, such as queries, data mining, text mining, web mining, and advanced statistical and mathematical tools.
- Dashboards and visualization tools. They use graphics and interactive elements to enhance the in-depth analysis and understanding of information.

A BI system can be composed of only one component (such as a DW) or may be constructed of a set of components that range from the extraction of data to the visualization of analyzed information on a dashboard. Companies that adopt a BI system can pass through different stages of maturity.

The main advantages for companies of the implementation of BI systems are Laudon and Laudon (2004) and Sieber et al. (2006): the reduction of both expenses and resource consumption, an increasing competitive advantage, improving the organization productivity, increasing satisfaction and customer loyalty, the capture of new customers and, ultimately, an increase in economic benefits. The benefits of adopting or implementing BI systems are independent of the business sector. Success has been obtained for major industries in very different sectors, from the health sector to information technology to telecommunications industries (Laudon and Laudon, 2004; Sieber et al., 2006; Roldán et al., 2012).

The potential benefits of implementing a BI system are great, but the risks are also great, since a high percentage or implementations fail. In order to work proactively to avoid failure in BI implementation, several critical success factors (CSF) should be taken into account (Watson and Wixom, 2007; Kimball, 2008; Yeoh and Koronios, 2010):

- Senior management should believe in and should promote the use of BI.
- The use of information and analytics is part of the organization's culture.
- There should be an alignment between the business and the BI strategies.
- There should be an effective BI governance.
- There should be a strong decision support data infrastructure.
- Users should have the necessary tools, skills, knowledge, and support to be successful.

BI systems have greatly improved in relevance and functionalities in the last years. The reason is the great quantity of available data, the possibilities of analyzing such data for organizations and the apparition of several Big Data techniques and technologies that make it possible to deal with very large data stores. Big Data and Big Data analytics are concepts that emerged to describe a set of data and analysis techniques for dealing with large volumes of data (from terabytes to exabytes), with very heterogeneous data (coming from sensors, social media, geolocalization, images, video, etc.) and that require high velocity in their processing (Chen et al., 2012).

Companies developing software packages know the relevance of analytics in all processes of the organization. Hence, they have identified an opportunity for integrating analytics into the management information systems in order to push the analytics directly to the user and to support the operative decisions (the daily decisions) with knowledge extracted from an accurate analysis of data. For example, CRM system nowadays incorporate an analytic module, called CRM analytic, that uses data mining to get to know the needs of clients better; this, therefore, allows them to make decisions that increase client' satisfaction (Xu and Walton, 2005).

When using internal data, BI systems can explain things about the company, but in a global and competitive world like the current one, is the availability of external information that makes a BI system so useful for improving the position of a company against its competitors (Sawka, 1996). External data is used mainly in strategic decision-making, but in the case of social networks they can also be useful for supporting short- and mid-term decisions. The use of external data improves knowledge about clients, suppliers, partners, stakeholders and others companies competence and allows a company to see its position in relation to competence.

3 UNIVERSITIES ANALYTICAL IS

An organization is a stable, formal social structure that takes resources from the environment and processes them to produce outputs (Laudon and Laudon, 2004). Organizations can be classified as profit or non-profit. An enterprise is an organization, especially a business and especially one that will earn money: (taken from the *Cambridge British dictionary*). A university is a non-profit organization that provides a public service and whose main purpose is to serve the progress of society.

Enterprises are characterized by their lucrative purpose. Therefore, an enterprise implements analytical systems to increase the enterprise's profits, as well as to improve its competitive advantage (because this is also an effective method of improving benefits/ensuring continuity). A university's goal is to contribute to universal knowledge (Lukman and Glavic, 2007), making individuals who are educated, prepared and self-sufficient regarding professional knowledge within economic sustainability. Since the mission of university is social (Sterling, 2004), the purpose of their analytical systems should not be mainly economic. They will have to deal with economical aspects, but only to guarantee sustainability.

Some, but not the only, objectives that can be pursued by universities in the creation of analytical systems are:

- Make informed decisions in the short term;
- Plan for the long term;
- Continue to provide educational opportunities that are relevant for students;
- Meet compliance reporting requirements;
- Continue to attract and retain students;
- Manage employees and human resources;
- Mange economic-financial institutions; and
- Increase scientific publications and research projects.

Actually, most universities have already implemented BI systems. However, the institutional initiatives in these systems are usually concerned with improving organizational processes, such as personnel management or resource allocation, improving efficiency within the university management. These systems are also focused on measuring and monitoring indicators defined by third-party evaluators (government or external quality agencies) and internal indicators, which are related to the strategic objectives of the university (Dell'Aquila et al., 2008; Muntean et al., 2011; Sakys and Butleris, 2011). However, there is a lack of integral BI systems that also deal with educational and research data in order to help the decision-making in teaching and research activities (Guitart and Conesa, 2015).

The more advanced BI systems in universities (Dell'Aquila et al., 2008; Di Tria et al., 2012) also allow didactic data and research data to be dealt with. The reader may think that these systems deal with the whole university at once, however the data about the real activity of university (teaching, learning and researching) are not taken into account. The reason is that these systems analyze neither data about the teaching-learning process nor research, but their outputs. As "didactic," they deal with educative data (about enrollment and student's performance) and research (they only deal with data of researchers and granted projects). A lot of data about learning (and research) processes are not taken into account and, therefore, these systems cannot deal with the relevant educational and research data, as required.

However, there are also initiatives where BI systems are used to improve the academic aspects of universities. Some of the more relevant are:

- Student tracking: the navigation of students within the VLE is analyzed to establish a set of indicators related to the activities' performance and students' patterns of behavior in VLE (Chatti et al., 2012; Duval, 2011).
- Survey management of student satisfaction: the strategic planning of university is modified based on student satisfaction (Dongsheng and Wenjing, 2009). It implements a DW that integrates data from the satisfaction surveys, the assessments and personal data of students.
- Enrolment prediction: it provides reports to the upper positions of the university (rector, dean) that forecast the future enrolments according to the students interest (Baranovic et al., 2003). Its DW includes student performance data, subject content data and data representing the order in which content are sequenced.
- Management of at-risk students: it identifies how students at risk of dropping-out behave. The system gives support at institutional level and defines a set of indicators to monitor the academic activity of students (Piedade and Santos, 2010).
- Research management: it defines a set of indicators to give support to monitor the research activity, such as the number of scientific publications grouped by authors and departments (Di Tria et al., 2012).
- Learning management: it uses VLE data to provide reports about the teaching and learning processes to teachers (Falakmasir et al., 2010).

In addition, international research centers such as EDUCAUSE, have defined concepts such as learning analytics (Siemens and Long, 2011) and academic analytics (Campbell et al., 2007) to define analytical systems in the context of education.

3.1 OTHER ANALYTICAL PROJECTS IN THE CONTEXT OF HIGHER EDUCATION

Academic analytics is the application of BI in education and emphasizes analytics at institutional, regional, and international levels (Campbell et al., 2007; Goldstein and Katz, 2005). Action analytics is a new generation of tools, solutions, and behaviors that are giving rise to more powerful and effective utilities through which colleges and universities can measure performance and provoke pervasive actions to improve it (Norris et al., 2008). Academic and action analytics are regarded as BI systems at university and are focused at an institutional level (Goldstein and Katz, 2005; van Barneveld et al., 2012). These systems do not fulfill the analytical goals for universities since they only work at institutional level (council, deans' department and management), but lack decision support systems for students, teachers and researchers. They use BI techniques to deal with different aspects of education, such as to identify the students at risk of dropping out, to retain students and to coach them to complete their study goals.

Learning analytics (LA) is the measurement, collection, analysis and reporting of data about learners and their contexts, for purposes of understanding and of improving learning and the environments where it occurs (Siemens and Long, 2011). LA is more specific and focuses on the learning process, including the relation between students, learning resources, subject content, teachers and the institution (Siemens and Long, 2011). Management data are, in general, of no interest for LA systems.

There are fewer projects belonging to academic and action analytics, eg, Signals (Arnold, 2010) and Lectopia system (Phillips et al., 2010). Most of analytic projects developed within universities are LA, such as eLAT (Dyckhoff et al., 2012) or GLASS (Leony et al., 2012). A variety of examples of LA projects performed in universities and their full description can be found in Verbert et al. (2013) and Park and Jo (2015).

In general, the academic and action analytics projects share the same characteristics (Campbell et al., 2007; Norris et al., 2008; Siemens et al., 2013) (see Table 9.1): they are strategic projects for the university that usually work top-down; the project evolution is monitored and controlled through key performance indicators; the project team should comprise several roles, which requires a very diverse and transversal set of competences; the university provides the needed resources and infrastructure; the complexity necessitates a great deal of technology, methodology and organizational structure and should be managed carefully; they do not depend on a single person but on a project team; and the created tools are integrated into the university IS.

LA projects are different to academic and action analytic projects in that they are smaller, usually focusing on a subject or a classroom (Siemens and Long, 2011; van Barneveld et al., 2012). They tend to be directly proposed, designed and implemented by the person who experiences the problem that needs to be solved (the teacher) and follow a bottom-up deployment. Since the initiation does not

Table 9.1 Main Characteristics of Learning Analytics, Action Analytics, and Academic Analytics		
	Level of	Main Objective
Learning analytics	Classroom, subject, teacher, subject coordinator	Improving performance and reducing dropping out
Action academic and academic analytics	Faculty, campus, university, national, and international	Effective management and strategic decision-making

usually originate from the institution, sponsorship from a higher level is rare, access to data becomes difficult and final integration of the created tools into the university IS is infrequent. These projects tend to be more focused on technology and implementation, giving less importance to methodology or project management aspects.

3.2 WEAKNESSES OF ANALYTICAL IS IN UNIVERSITIES

Analytical projects (and tools) in universities suffer from restrictions and weakness. The main restrictions that affect all kinds of analytical systems are the management of data privacy and what ethical aspects should be enforced (Kay et al., 2012; Slade and Prinsloo, 2013).

According to BI tools the limitations remain in the partial coverage they provide to universities. As previously mentioned, these systems focus on the use of management data, the results being ineffective in the improvement of the main university activities. They also share the same weaknesses of action and academic analytics (Goldstein and Katz, 2005; Norris et al., 2008; Siemens et al., 2013), the current immaturity in the development of academic analytic IS, their high economic costs, the required involvement of almost all university staff in the process, the lack of commercial software components that satisfy the academic needs of universities, the lack of external experts with experience in the educative environment, culture barriers and the change management.

Since LA experiences are more numerous, their weaknesses can be easily stated. Their main areas of weakness are presented and classified by whether they are focused on the analytical tool or the project required to create it (Ferguson, 2012; Clow, 2013; Siemens et al., 2013).

- Weaknesses related to LA tools:
  - They exist on a small scale and are difficult to generalize: they are usually very specific tools, specified to solve the particular problems of a given teacher, making it difficult to widen their application to other contexts (subjects for example).
  - They experience barriers to data access or reusability: since they are not institutionally sponsored projects, the access of data is difficult. In addition, under a thorough study of LA projects, we found that most do not provide ways to reuse the analyzed data for others, ie, they do not provide a DW/DM accessible to teachers and researchers.
  - Their development requires a great diversity and deep level of skill and knowledge, such as database, statistics, programming and business knowledge, that few people may possess.
  - Commercial vendors are growing in the LA field, but their tools are still immature. Therefore, university leaders often face vendor-provided solutions, whose functionalities do not respond the questions or requirements the university has.
- Weaknesses related to LA projects:
  - They are not sponsored or lead by institution.
  - They do not originate from the strategic planning of universities.
  - They are not integrated into the global information systems of universities: they begin as local projects (usually focused on a given subject or classroom) related to a particular teacher's initiatives.
  - They remain centered on a perspective of analytics as a technology, as a tool, and as a means to measure and not as a service.

- They usually originate from a pilot test but are not designed to be deployed at institutional level. Therefore, they lack a management plan on the cultural change, an implementation methodology, a formation plan for users and do not consider critical success factors (CSF), among others.
- A high level coordination does not exist to define and develop the strategy and processes to create LA projects and their necessary infrastructure.

4 TOWARDS A GLOBAL UNIVERSITY ANALYTICAL IS

From our point of view, the goal of an analytical IS at university should be to create a global system (at university level) that is used by all the university staff and is integrated within the university IS. We propose that the system be named University Analytical Information System (UAIS).

An UAIS *is a set of processes and tools that collect and analyze the internal and external data of the university, converting them into meaningful and useful information that can be used to enable more effective and timely strategic decision-making about the activities of university*. The analytical system comprises the full range of activities in universities, affecting administration, teaching and research. Thereby, the main objectives a university IS must satisfy are:

- Improve administrative decision-making and organizational resource allocation.
- Reinforce the quality of the decision-making of teachers and researchers.
- Provide tools to students to make their learning more effective and personalized
- Create a shared understanding of the institution's successes and challenges.
- Increase organizational productivity and effectiveness.
- Identify the value generated by the university, as well as each of their activities.
- Identify opportunities and threats in the internal and external environment of university.

An UAIS should be composed of different pieces. We propose adapting the BI structure in order to facilitate the creation of UAIS. Under this assumption the system will be composed, at least, of the following components (see Fig. 9.2):

- A DW that stores the data needed for decision-making at a high level for management, teachers, and researchers. The source data that will be used to populate the DW come from different enterprise information systems such as ERP or CRM, departmental information systems, student information systems, VLE, digital library and external data sources, such as the Internet. According to the necessities of each university other complementary analytical databases may be needed, such as different DMs to deal with particular problems, an operational data store to reduce the temporal gap between analyzed and real data or a staging area to facilitate the population of the different analytical databases.
- A set of data sources: they are the origin of the data that will be used to perform analytics. Therefore, it is key to have data sources of different kinds to answer the relevant analytical questions for the university at a global level. The minimum data needed for the analytical system are: management data (includes information about accountability, finance, human resources, enrolment and alumni), educational data (includes information about students, teachers, academic programs, subjects), performance data (includes information about enrolment, student assessment,

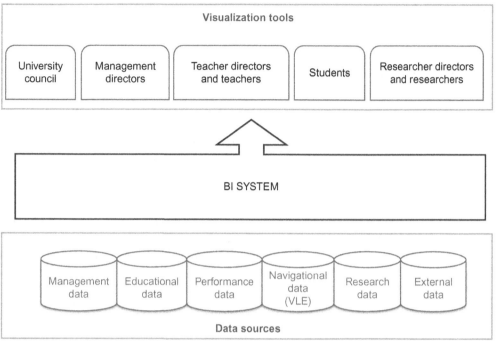

FIGURE 9.2

University analytical IS.

subject performance), navigational data (includes information about the contributions—and accesses—of students to communication forums, learning resources consumption, and VLE accesses), research data (includes information about research projects, grants, collaborations, research production, congresses attendance), and external data (data about other universities—performance, enrolment, academic offer, and labour market).

- A set of processes, namely ETL processes, that populate the DW (and the other analytical databases) from the source data. ETL processes extract and transform data from different sources. Then they improve and integrate the data into a unique database.
- A set of analytical techniques that process the information of DW and DM to create a useful knowledge base: these techniques include OLAP, data mining (and their variants such as opinion mining, text mining, or educational data mining), and simulation techniques. The goal of these techniques is to respond the asked questions and identify relations between different data.
- A set of visualization techniques: their goal is to show the result of analysis and allow further analysis. These tools include reports, alerts, dashboards, recommender systems and visualization analytics in real-time. The more popular visualizations are reports and dashboards. Dashboard displays a set of indicators. Every dashboard will provide graphics and interactive elements to facilitate understanding of the requested information and to provide such information at different levels of detail.

The proposed analytic system can be seen as a conceptual framework that subsumes current analytic information systems (action analytics, academic analytics, and learning analytics), adds new functionalities not available in such systems and uses the lessons learnt in the BI field in order to both improve the success of analytical development projects and evaluate thoroughly the usefulness of analytical tools.

The new functionalities UAIS provide are:

- The availability of all the data the university deals with facilitates the creation of 360 degree services that give complete information about any aspect from different viewpoints and abstraction levels.
- The use of external data and the possibility of comparing such data with any aspect of the organization can provide accurate information about what is the position of the university according to the environment: competence, labor market, potential collaborations, strengths, fields in which their academics excel, etc.
- Advanced analytical techniques, such as opinion mining, natural language processing and visualization analytics, can be applied more comprehensively to educational and research environments. Current systems usually take into account the educational and research data related to their outcomes (student performance, number of published journal papers per researcher, etc.), but not to their processes. Having access and analyzing the processes would allow, potentially, more knowledge and more value to be obtained. Examples of such process could be performing an analysis about social interactions of students, teachers and researchers within the VLE and in Internet social networks. That analysis could provide information about the notoriety of each person and their influence, aspects that can be used to improve teaching, create networks to research projects or chose what students should be invited to participate in certain activities.
- The analytic tools are integrated and provide a unique access to each users that allows any analytical question related to the university to be answered from the same place.
- The evaluation of the usefulness of analytical tools can be thoroughly analyzed, adapting some of the models proposed within the BI field.

Universities can use the lessons learnt in the BI field in the specification, implementation and evaluation of BI systems by adapting their CSF, which are a set of features to be taken into account in order to avoid problems in BI implementation. Some of the main CSFs that universities may reuse to reduce the risk of failure in UAIS implementations include the following:

- The analytical strategy must be aligned with the institution vision, mission and aims. All the institution members must be committed (teachers, students, management, and researchers).
- Council university should sponsor the project.
- The use of information and analytics should be seen as part of the university's culture.
- There should be an effective BI governance proposal.
- A flexible technology platform that allows the collecting, mining, and analysis of data should be available.
- Tools and training should be proposed to management, teaching, researching, and student users.

Current analytic systems can be seen as particular examples of the presented UAIS. For instance, an LA tool for teachers that monitors the student performance can be seen as a subset of the proposed analytical system depicted in Fig. 9.3. A subset that has two different data sources—data about the performance of students (Performance data source) and about where the student enrolled (Educational data source)—and is focused on teachers (to support the daily activities and try to recover students at risk of failing) and teacher directors (to see whether the directed subject is going as expected or whether some urgent action is required).

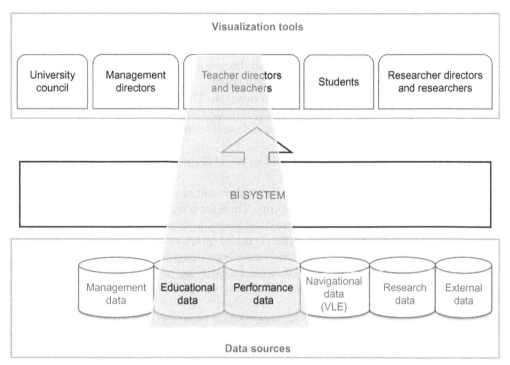

FIGURE 9.3

Learning analytics in University analytical IS.

5 IS THIS A GRAND CHALLENGE?

As it can be extracted from previous sections, creating UAIS is a research goal. Even if aspects of this research goal are already present in some of the actual research proposals, mainly in Academic Analytics, there is a long way to go until analytical IS of universities provide information that takes into account management data, educational data, performance data, navigational data and external data.

In this section we assess the creation of analytical IS for universities by adapting BI knowledge. To do so, we use two sets of criteria:

1. The key properties of a long-range research goal, proposed by Jim Gray (2003).
2. The desirable properties of a quality research goal as a grand challenge, proposed by Tony Hoare (2003).

5.1 A GOOD LONG-RANGE RESEARCH GOAL?

We evaluate first the research goal with respect to the five key properties of a good long-range research goal, described in Gray (2003).

Understandable. The proposed goal is simple not only for people working in the information systems field to understand, but also the university staff and even the general public. Most people are aware of what analytics is and what benefits it can provide due to the common, usage of BI systems in companies. In addition the term analytics is well known within today's universities. Most universities have already performed some LA projects and are aware of the problems this kind of system may have. Therefore, we believe that the research goal, and its justification, is easily understood by the research and university communities.

Challenging. It is not obvious how to achieve this goal. The ideas of adapting BI systems in universities and performing analytics with academic data have been in existence for more than a decade, but the results obtained so far are not sufficient for the universities' needs and the current high competence that exists.

Useful. If the goal is achieved, the results will be useful to most universities, teachers, researchers, students, and administrative staff.

Testable. The goal will be achieved when the deployment of an analytical IS in a university produces improvement at its analytical maturity. There are some models (Popovič et al. 2012; Hou, 2012) that allow the calculation of the analytical maturity of an institution and others that allow the evaluation of whether a BI system is useful (gives solution to the analytical questions of the institution). Even though these models have been designed for use in the context of lucrative organizations, we believe that they can be easily adapted to universities. Therefore, the adaptation of such models in the case of universities would allow the testing of whether the research goal has been achieved.

Incremental. The goal can be divided into intermediate incremental milestones at different levels (Kimball, 2008): (1) improving UAIS implementation projects: what set of CSFs are relevant to each project, what metrics should be used to assess the evolution of a project, what is the required integration of the proposed UAIS system with the existent IS, what is the required team to address projects with minimum guaranties, what implantation and formation plan should be defined and what is the required sponsorship; (2) improving UAIS functionalities: how can one integrate different kinds of data within the same analytical data store, how can one adapt BI and Big Data techniques to deal with data efficiently, how can one adapt BI methodologies to discover the requirements and indicators in each case, who are the expected users and what are their analytical needs and what is the most efficient way to analyze and visualize data; and (3) evaluating UAIS usefulness: what is the usefulness of UAIS, what properties should a UAIS satisfy to be useful and how can one create models to evaluate a UAIS' usefulness?

5.2 A GRAND CHALLENGE?

Tony Hoare (2003) suggested seventeen criteria that must be satisfied by a research goal in order for it to qualify as a grand challenge. These criteria include the five key properties dealt with in the previous section. Twelve additional criteria relate mainly to the maturity of the discipline and the feasibility of the goal. This section assesses the proposed research goals with respect to the additional criteria.

Fundamental. Creating analytic systems that deal with educational data in universities is a fundamental concern in the information systems and the e-learning fields.

Astonishing. The results of a system like the proposed one would bring analytics to another level, allowing the creation of decision support systems useful for teachers, teacher managers, students and researchers. These decision support systems would allow teachers to improve their teaching activities (the perceived quality of learning resources, the main doubts of students, students' perceptions of the subject by analyzing the messages they have written in the communication messages, a 360 degree view of students to easily detect the strengths and weaknesses for each of them, etc.). Managers learn to update the subjects or academic programs they manage according to the job market needs; students experience a more personalized learning experience, where the resources, activities and feedback will depend on their performance and expectations; and researchers have more information about their related research and are able to better deal with the infoxication they experience due to the huge amount of papers that are published. In our past experience (Guitart and Conesa, 2014; Guitart et al., 2013; Guitart et al., 2015; Guitart and Conesa, 2015), these agents are not aware of the possibilities of analytics for learning processes and in some cases even some resistance was found at the beginning of the project because people believed that the analytical questions the project needed to solve where irresoluble.

Revolutionary. If the goal is achieved, it will lead to a radical change in universities. In particular, an analytical system as proposed, would change the way in which teaching and learning are performed.

Research-directed. Significant parts of the goal can be achieved only through research. Among these are the gathering and integration of diverse data in the context of universities, the management of very large volumes of data, heterogeneity, defining methodologies to address UAIS projects more effectively, defining metrics and evaluation models to state the relevance and usefulness of UAIS systems in a given environment, and efficiently adapting the lessons learnt from BI in enterprises to the higher education context.

Inspiring. The goal (using analytics in education) has the support of almost the entire e-learning research community and the university community.

International. The goal has an international scope. Researchers from all around the world are already participating in it by working in LA and related areas.

Historical. The goal of creating analytic information systems in the context of universities has already been proposed in the past (Merriam, 1998; Rothschild and White, 1995). Since then the use of analytics in universities has continued to be a very prolific research area, which has led to different approaches. Some of these have focused on reformulating analytics for use in universities, eg, learning analytics (Ferguson, 2012), academics analytics (Campbell et al., 2007) and action analytics (Norris et al., 2008). Others focused on advancing in small steps to take full advantage of analytics in the context of universities, such as educational data mining (Romero and Ventura, 2010), or the definition of standards and specifications in universities (IEEE-LOM, 2011; Dublin Core, 2001).

Feasible. The goal is now more feasible than ever. Over the last few years the crisis has worsened the panorama for universities, creating new constraints: less public funds, more competition and more exigent students with more expectations and higher economical restrictions. In this new panorama universities have to be managed efficiently and gain competitively in order to guarantee their sustainability. In this context, the university staff has focused on working on analytical approaches in order to improve their internal management, understand better their context and stakeholders, and improve their main activities (teaching and research). The new analytical approaches, mostly under the umbrella of learning analytics, have improved the awareness of university staff about the relevancy of analytics. Then, UAIS are more feasible than ever, because there is a critical mass of researchers working in this direction, a lot of novel and relevant approaches are being created and universities have the culture to adopt and use UAIS efficiently. In addition, the advancement of other research areas that may help in the attainment of the goal of UAIS, such as Big Data or Visual Analytics, potentially support its feasibility as well.

Cooperative. The work required to achieve the proposed goal can be parceled out to teams working independently. For example, some groups may focus on the definition of the skeleton of an analytical IS for universities, other on the definition of relevant indicators that should be taken into account in universities, and others on the data management techniques necessary to deal with the huge quantity of data gathered from the VLE and in the definition of models to evaluate analytic IS in university context. Different groups can perform these different research activities concurrently and their outcomes can be adapted by other groups to create an integrated analytical system cooperatively.

Competitive. The proposed goal encourages and benefits from competition among teams. Cultural aspects of different universities and the high levels of autonomy teachers enjoy make each university a particular scenario with its own actors, processes and politics. The inclusion of analytics cannot limit the autonomy of teachers and researchers, but promotes their creativity and productivity. Otherwise, the academic field would be standardized and the academic community as we know would disappear. This heterogeneity that universities promote means that most of the problems related to the research agenda have different solutions with different ranges of application and different levels of efficiency for each university.

Effective. The promulgation of the necessity of creating analytical IS for universities is intended to cause a shift in the attitudes and activities of the relevant research, student, academic and professional communities. Academics should be aware of the amount of data that is generated during teaching activities and the amount of data that can be extracted from their learning resources. Accordingly they should begin to participate in the definition of the key indicators that may help in their work and to document thoroughly the learning resources used in order to facilitate data extraction. VLE developers should begin to gather data from all the implementations they perform. The success of analytics depends greatly on the amount of data gathered, so each process implemented in a VLE should gather and store the data related to the process and the involved actors. Researchers in the field of LA, educational data mining and action analytics should take into account the lessons learnt in the BI field, profiting from their methodologies, knowledge, technologies and tools to create analytical systems that are simpler, more powerful, more generalizable and more testable. Students should be aware that all their data (personal, enrollment, performance, navigational, etc.) can be used in order to create services that improve teaching, learning and university sustainability. These new services will surely improve the learning experience of students but at the cost of their privacy. Therefore, students should be aware of this fact and play an active role in stating what privacy they agree to forgo in order to gain a better learning experience.

Risk-managed. The main critical risks to the project arise from the impossibility of gathering relevant information from some learning resources, privacy aspects and adoption of the analytical IS for the leadership of universities. Text learning resources (such as PDF files, ePub books, etc.) can be parsed to get information from their content in order to nourish the analytical systems. However, the parse of some kinds of resources cannot generate relevant information, such as videos or audio files. In this case, information can be extracted from its use (how students consume the resources) but not from its content. This mismatch between different learning resources may pose difficulties to the creation of some analytical services related to the content of courses. This problem can be minimized if universities develop a governance of what kind of formats should be used for each learning resource. Another potential problem would be to convince the university leaders of the necessity of creating analytical ISs for teachers, researchers and students. There exists the risk of implementing systems considering only the technical perspective and not as a management project that uses a right methodology to solve a given problem. That may result in the failure of the project and generate incomplete results that do not reach the expected objectives and are not generalizable. The development of this kind of system is very expensive. If they are seen as systems that benefit academics in a task they are supposed to do with or without the system, the temptation may be to not invest in such analytical systems. In order to avoid this problem, validation models should be created to evaluate the usefulness of analytical ISs and measures such as Return of Investment or Payback should be rewritten in the case of universities to show clearly how the improvement of teaching and research can impact in university sustainability. The privacy problem is ongoing and is out with the scope of this research community. However, some measures can be taken in order to avoid collecting personal information of students and using anonymization systems in order to make sure that particular students cannot be singled out from the analysis of data.

6 CONCLUSIONS

This paper states that adapting BI systems to universities is a great challenge. It describes what BI is, how BI systems are used in enterprises and the benefits they provide; what the analytical systems adopted by universities are, what their flaws are and the different research fields that appear to address such limitations; and how BI can be integrated into universities to create information systems that give full support to all analytical necessities and to all university staff, as well as the benefits of applying lessons learnt in BI in enterprises. To be able to formally conclude that "Creating University Analytical IS" is a grand challenge, several properties defined by Gray (2003) and Hoare (2003) have been analyzed. The fulfillment of these properties demonstrates that the proposed research problem is a long-range research goal and a grand challenge.

ACKNOWLEDGMENTS

This research was partly funded by the eLearn Center from the UOC and the Spanish Government, through the project TIN2013-45303-P "ICT-FLAG" (Enhancing ICT education through Formative assessment, Learning Analytics, and Gamification).

REFERENCES

Addo-Tenkorang, R., Helo, P., 2011. Enterprise resource planning (ERP): a review literature report. In: Proceedings of the World Congress on Engineering and Computer Science, Vol. 2, pp. 19–21.

Arnold, K.E., 2010. Signals: applying academic analytics. Educ. Q. 33 (1), n1.

Baranovic, M., Madunic, M., Mekterovic, I., 2003. Data warehouse as a part of the higher education information system in croatia. In: Proceedings of the 25th International Conference on Information Technology Interfaces, ITI 2003. IEEE, Cavtat, pp. 121–126.

Campbell, J.P., DeBlois, P.B., Oblinger, D.G., 2007. Academic analytics: a new tool for a new era. EDUCAUSE Rev. 42 (4), 40.

Chatti, M.A., Dyckhoff, A.L., Schroeder, U., Thüs, H., 2012. A reference model for learning analytics. Int. J. Technol. Enhanc. Learn. 4 (5–6), 318–331.

Chen, H., Chiang, R.H., Storey, V.C., 2012. Business intelligence and analytics: from big data to big impact. MIS Q. 36 (4), 1165–1188.

Cheng, H., 2009. An integration framework of ERM, SCM, CRM. In: International Conference on Management and Service Science. MASS'09. IEEE, Wuhan, China, pp. 1–4.

Clow, D., 2013. An overview of learning analytics. Teach. High. Educ. 18 (6), 683–695.

Curto, J., Conesa, J., 2010. Introduccional Business Intelligence. Editorial UOC, Barcelona (España).

Da Xu, L., 2011. Enterprise systems: state-of-the-art and future trends. IEEE Trans. Ind. Inf. 7 (4), 630–640.

Dell'Aquila, C., Di Tria, F., Lefons, E., Tangorra, F., 2008. Business intelligence solution for university management. In: Proceedings of the 10th WSEAS International Conference on Mathematical Methods and Computational Techniques in Electrical Engineering. World Scientific and Engineering Academy and Society (WSEAS), Sofia, Bulgaria, pp. 318–324.

Di Tria, F., Lefons, E., Tangorra, F., 2012. Research data mart in an academic system. In: 2012 Spring Congress on Engineering and Technology (S-CET). IEEE, Xi'an, China, pp. 1–5.

Dongsheng, Z., Wenjing, J., 2009. Design and implementation of university educational decision support system on the students satisfaction survey. In: International Forum on Computer Science-Technology and Applications, 2009. IFCSTA'09, Vol. 3. IEEE, Chongqing, China, pp. 428–430.

Dublin Core Specifications, 2001. http://dublincore.org/specifications/ (last visited March 2016).

Duval, E., 2011. Attention please!: learning analytics for visualization and recommendation. In: Proceedings of the 1st International Conference on Learning Analytics and Knowledge. ACM, Banff, Alberta, Canada, pp. 9–17.

Dyckhoff, A.L., Zielke, D., Bültmann, M., Chatti, M.A., Schroeder, U., 2012. Design and implementation of a learning analytics toolkit for teachers. J. Educ. Technol. Soc. 15 (3), 58–76.

Falakmasir, M.H., Habibi, J., Moaven, S., Abolhassani, H., 2010. Business intelligence in e-learning: (case study on the Iran University of Science and Technology Data Set). In: 2nd International Conference on Software Engineering and Data Mining (SEDM), 2010. IEEE, Chengdu, China, pp. 473–477.

Ferguson, R., 2012. Learning analytics: drivers, developments and challenges. Int. J. Technol. Enhanc. Learn. 4 (5), 304–317.

Goldstein, P.J., Katz, R.N., 2005. Academic analytics: the uses of management information and technology in higher education. In: 8th Research Study of the EDUCAUSE Center for Applied Research. (https://library.educause.edu/resources/2005/12/academic-analytics-the-uses-of-management-information-and-technology-in-higher-education).

Gray, J., 2003. What next?: a dozen information-technology research goals. J. ACM 50 (1), 41–57.

Guitart, I., Conesa, J., 2014. Uso de analítica para dar soporte a la toma de decisiones docentes. Jornadas de Enseñanza Universitaria de la Informática, Oviedo.

Guitart, I., Conesa, J., 2015. Analytic information systems in the context of higher education: expectations, reality and trends. In: Complex, Intelligent, and Software Intensive Systems (CISIS) International Conference. IEEE, Taipei, pp. 294–300.

Guitart, I., Conesa, J., Villarejo, L., Lapedriza, À., Masip, D., Perez, A., Planas, E., 2013. Opinion mining on educational resources at the Open University of Catalonia. In: Seventh International Conference on Complex, Intelligent, and Software Intensive Systems (CISIS), 2013. IEEE, Taichung, pp. 385–390.

Guitart, I., Moré, J., Duran, J., Conesa, J., Baneres, D., Gañan, D., 2015. A semi-automatic system to detect relevant learning content for each subject. In: Complex, Intelligent, and Software Intensive Systems (CISIS) International Conference. IEEE, Taipei, pp. 301–307.

Hoare, T., 2003. The verifying compiler: a grand challenge for computing research. In: Modular Programming Languages. Springer, Berlin Heidelberg, pp. 25–35.

Hou, C.K., 2012. Examining the effect of user satisfaction on system usage and individual performance with business intelligence systems: an empirical study of Taiwan's electronics industry. Int. J. Inf. Manag. 32 (6), 560–573.

IEEE-Learning Object Metadata Standard, 2002. https://standards.ieee.org/findstds/standard/1484.12.1-2002.html (last visited March, 2016).

IMS Caliper Analytics Interoperability Standards. https://www.imsglobal.org/pressreleases/pr150506.html (last visited March 2016).

Kay, D., Korn, N., Oppenheim, C., 2012. Legal, risk and ethical aspects of analytics in higher education. CETIS Anal. Ser. 1 (6), 1–30.

Kimball, R., 2008. The Data Warehouse Lifecycle Toolkit. Wiley Publishing, Inc., Indianapolis, Indiana.

Laudon, K.C., Laudon, J.P., 2004. Management Information Systems: Managing the Digital Firm. Prentice Hall, New Jersey. 8.

Leony, D., Pardo, A., de la Fuente Valentín, L., de Castro, D.S., Kloos, C.D., 2012. GLASS: a learning analytics visualization tool. In: Proceedings of the 2nd International Conference on Learning Analytics and Knowledge. ACM, New York, Vancouver, British Columbia, pp. 162–163.

Lukman, R., Glavic, P., 2007. What are the key elements of a sustainable university? Clean Techn. Environ. Policy 9 (2), 103–114.

McGaughey, R.E., Gunasekaran, A., 2009. Enterprise resource planning (ERP): past, present and future. In: Selected Readings on Strategic Information Systems. IGI Global, Hershey, PA, pp. 359–371.

Mentzer, J.T., DeWitt, W., Keebler, J.S., Min, S., Nix, N.W., Smith, C.D., Zacharia, Z.G., 2001. Defining supply chain management. J. Bus. Logist. 22 (2), 1–25.

Merriam, S.B., 1998. Qualitative Research and Case Study Applications in Education. Revised and Expanded from "Case Study Research in Education", Jossey-Bass Publishers, San Francisco, CA.

Muntean, M., Bologa, A., Bologa, R., Florea, A., 2011. Business intelligence systems in support of university strategy. In: Recent Researches in Educational Technologies.pp. 118–123.

Norris, D., Baer, L., Leonard, J., Pugliese, L., Lefrere, P., 2008. Action analytics: measuring and improving performance that matters in higher education. EDUCAUSE Rev. 43 (1), 42.

Olson, D.L., Kesharwani, S., 2010. Enterprise Information Systems: Contemporary Trends and Issues. World Scientific Publishing Co. Pte. Ltd., Singapore.

Park, Y., Jo, I.-H., 2015. Development of the learning analytics dashboard to support students' learning performance. J. Univers. Comput. Sci. 21 (1), 110–133.

Phillips, R., Preston, G., Roberts, P., Cumming-Potvin, W., Herrington, J., Maor, D., Gosper, M., 2010. Using academic analytic tools to investigate studying behaviours in technology-supported learning environments. In: ASCILITE-Australian Society for Computers in Learning in Tertiary Education Annual Conference, Vol. 2010, No. 1pp. 761–771.

Piedade, M.B., Santos, M.Y., 2010. Business intelligence in higher education: enhancing the teaching-learning process with a SRM system. In: 5th Iberian Conference on Information Systems and Technologies (CISTI), 2010. IEEE, Santiago de Compostela, Spain, pp. 1–5.

Popovič, A., Hackney, R., Coelho, P.S., Jaklič, J., 2012. Towards business intelligence systems success: effects of maturity and culture on analytical decision making. Decis. Support. Syst. 54 (1), 729–739.

Roldán, J.L., Carrión, G.A.C., González, J.L.G., 2012. Los sistemas de inteligencia de negocio como soporte a los procesos de toma de decisiones en las organizaciones. Pap. de Econom. Esp. 132, 239–260.

Romero, C., Ventura, S., 2010. Educational data mining: a review of the state of the art. IEEE Trans. Syst. Man Cybern. Part C Appl. Rev. 40 (6), 601–618.

Rothschild, M., White, L.J., 1995. The analytics of the pricing of higher education and other services in which the customers are inputs. J. Polit. Econ. 573–586.

Sakys, V., Butleris, R., 2011. Business intelligence tools and technologies for the analysis of university studies management. Transform. Bus. Econ. 10 (2), 125–136.

Sawka, K.A., 1996. Demystifying business intelligence. Manage. Rev. 85 (10), 47–52.

Sieber, S., Valor, J., Porta, V., 2006. Los sistemas de información en la empresa actual. McGrawHill, Madrid.

Siemens, G., Long, P., 2011. Penetrating the fog: analytics in learning and education. EDUCAUSE Rev. 46 (5), 30.

Siemens, G., Dawson, S., Lynch, G., 2013. Improving the Quality and Productivity of the Higher Education Sector: Policy and Strategy for Systems-Level Deployment of Learning Analytics. Office for Learning and Teaching, Canberra. (https://solaresearch.org).

Slade, S., Prinsloo, P., 2013. Learning analytics ethical issues and dilemmas. Am. Behav. Sci. 57 (10), 1510–1529.

Sterling, S., 2004. Higher education, sustainability, and the role of systemic learning. In: Higher Education and the Challenge of Sustainability. Springer, Netherlands, pp. 49–70.

van Barneveld, A., Arnold, K.E., Campbell, J.P., 2012. Analytics in higher education: establishing a common language. EDUCAUSE Learn. Initiat. 1, 1–11.

Verbert, K., Duval, E., Klerkx, J., Govaerts, S., Santos, J.L., 2013. Learning analytics dashboard applications. Am. Behav. Sci. 57, 1500–1509.

Watson, H.J., Wixom, B.H., 2007. The current state of business intelligence. Computer 40 (9), 96–99.

Whyte, A., 2015. IMS Caliper: a learning analytics specification for higher education. In: At Open Apereo 2015 Conference.

Wu, J.H., Wang, Y.M., 2006. Measuring KMS success: a respecification of the DeLone and McLean's model. Inf. Manag. 43 (6), 728–739.

Experience API, xAPI 2012, https://github.com/adlnet/xAPI-Spec/blob/master/xAPI.md (last visited November 2015).

Xu, M., Walton, J., 2005. Gaining customer knowledge through analytical CRM. Ind. Manage. Data Syst. 105 (7), 955–971.

Yeoh, W., Koronios, A., 2010. Critical success factors for business intelligence systems. J. Comput. Inf. Syst. 50 (3), 23–32.

METHODOLOGY OF PREDICTIVE MODELING OF STUDENTS' BEHAVIOR IN VIRTUAL LEARNING ENVIRONMENT

10

M. Munk, M. Drlík

Constantine the Philosopher University in Nitra, Nitra, Slovakia

1 INTRODUCTION

Over the last few years many researchers have begun to apply data mining methods to help all stakeholders of the virtual learning environment (VLE) to improve their teaching and learning competencies or to design, create and develop more efficient and attractive e-learning courses.

If we talk about the application of data mining methods to data from the VLEs, as a modern approach to the analysis of data stored in the VLEs, we have to mention two closely connected contemporary research areas—Educational Data Mining (EDM) (Romero and Ventura, 2010) and learning analytics (LA) (Baker and Siemens, 2014). Their application domains overlap partially.

However, EDM and LA are technically and methodologically different. The EDM is an emerging interdisciplinary research area that deals with the application of data mining techniques to educational data (Romero and Ventura, 2010). A typical EDM process converts raw data coming from VLEs into useful information that could potentially have a great impact on educational research and practice (Romero et al., 2014). EDM deals with the development of new techniques and methods for discovering students' behavioral patterns from unstructured, semi-structured or structured data, which comes from the interaction of stakeholders within the VLEs, adaptive or intelligent tutoring systems, or other educational software. The EDM tries to solve the problems that arise during different phases of the learning process. For that reason, the main application areas of the EDM are the data analysis and visualization, decision support for teachers and administrators based on students' feedback, automatized recommendation, forecast of students' performances and achievements, user model creations, students' social networks identification and many others (Romero et al., 2010; Peña-Ayala, 2014a).

On the other hand, the LA deals with an institutional level of impact of analyzed data obtained from the learning process and stored in the VLEs. The main objective of the LA is a decision-making process support of educational institutions. LA deals with measurement and analysis of available data about learners for the purposes of understanding and optimization of the learning process and the whole environment where the learning process is realized (Baker and Siemens, 2014).

Formative Assessment, Learning Data Analytics and Gamification. http://dx.doi.org/10.1016/B978-0-12-803637-2.00010-5

The aim of both disciplines is to design models, tasks, methods, and algorithms for data exploration in the educational settings, to analyze educational data, to find out patterns and to make predictions that characterize learners, to observe the progress of the students, to allow an identification of the critical points of study and to define actions of improvement (Peña-Ayala, 2014a; Drlik et al., 2014). Both are useful for user behavioral pattern modeling, user knowledge and experience modeling, user profiling or for VLE personalization and adaptation.

VLEs store the data in their persistent database layers, which we can also analyze by using conventional statistical methods or utilizing the advanced data mining methods. VLEs usually provide their own analytical tools for simple statistical evaluation and visualization of e-learning course visit rate, for different types of learning resources or activities counting and mostly for basic analysis of e-learning course using.

Considering obtained results and their combination with several other objectives and measurable outcomes, we can identify what is properly performed on the e-learning course and which learning resources are most frequently used. On the other hand, we can ascertain what is wrong, what kind of learning materials are unused, missing or what is not suitable for the students' requirements.

Tools integrated into the VLEs can identify the highest level of student activity during the working day or during the whole term. The correct interpretation of such findings or visualizations requires a relatively high portion of pedagogical intuition and tacit skills, the responsibility for which inevitable falls to teachers, managers or e-learning course creators, so that they may sensitively respond to the changing requirements and behavior of the observed group of students.

However, the deep consequences of e-learning course visitors' or VLE stakeholders' behavior, the identification of their learning styles or preferences, the description of their relationships or the intensity of different types of communication among them, remain hidden. Therefore, if we need to find or analyze such indices or parameters in detail using the available tools of VLE, we still will be entirely dependent on our own subjective evaluation.

Predictive methods, structure discovery, relation mining, a distillation of data for human judgment and discovery with models belong to the most frequent categories of the EDM and LA methods (Baker and Siemens, 2014; Rodríguez, 2011). However, none of the above-mentioned categories explicitly covers methods of modeling behavior of the VLE stakeholders depending on time.

For that reason, we adapted a multinomial logit model (MLM) for modeling the probability of accesses of VLE stakeholders with a reference to time. The MLM represents a special case of a generalized linear model. Its applications mostly can be found in econometrics, genetics and natural language processing, but its usage in the research area of EDM or LA is uncommon (Rodríguez, 2011; Baltagi, 2007).

Considering the background as described, the contribution of the proposed methodology to the EDM and LA research fields can be evaluated from the data preparation, data modeling and practical point of view. From the data preparation perspective, it comprises a methodology design and recommendations for acquiring reliable data from the log files of the VLE. In terms of data modeling, the chapter brings a detailed model description and methodology for modeling of students' and teachers' behaviors with reference to time. Moreover, the description of the possibilities for the use of obtained knowledge may also represent a valuable part of this chapter.

The rest of the chapter is structured as follows. The next section provides a short review of scientific resources, which are closely related to the topic of the chapter. We introduce a methodology and describe a MLM in detail in the third section. This section leads the reader through the typical phases of the CRISP-DM methodology (Chapman, 1999). Finally, we discuss the results and conclude that the multinomial regression model finds its application in various stages of the e-learning course's development life cycle, as well as in the personalization of the course content and learning management.

2 **RELATED WORK**

The multiple logistic regression model introduced in this chapter was described in detail by Hosmer and Lemeshow (2005). The MLM is a special type of generalized linear model (Anděl, 2007). The basis for this theory was gathered from the works of Rodríguez (2011) and Baltagi (2007).

There are several examples of logit model applications in the scientific literature. We can find its applications mostly in econometrics (Baltagi, 2007), genetics and natural language processing (Munk et al., 2011b). If the multiple logistic regression model is used, then it is used mainly for choice prediction (Macfadyen and Dawson, 2010).

MLM can also be used for behavior modeling of website visitors with anonymous accesses (Munk et al., 2011b) or modeling VLE stakeholders' behavior (Munk et al., 2011a).

The scientific progress in EDM research area can be followed in reviews (Romero and Ventura, 2007, 2010). The last comprehensive state-of-the-art reviews of EDM were by Romero et al. (2010) and Peña-Ayala (2014a,b). These EDM reviews provided many examples of the close relation between web data mining based on log files analysis and education (dos Santos Machado and Becker, 2003; Kleftodimos and Evangelidis, 2013).

VLEs provide communication, collaboration, administration and reporting tools extensively used in the distance and blended learning. Many of the available methods for application of data from VLE log files were used to perform: a segmentation of VLE visitors, an extraction of the behavior patterns of the visitors, or a search for associations among visited web areas, with the aim to personalize or optimize (restructure) web-based educational systems according to the way they were browsed (Wei et al., 2004; Mor and Minguillon, 2004; Talavera and Gaudioso, 2004).

The educational data used in this chapter comes from the log system of the VLE Moodle. The VLE Moodle has been one of the mostly extensively used VLEs for several years. Therefore, it is not surprising that many researchers focused their research on the implementation of data mining and especially web mining methods using educational data recorded in this system (Romero et al., 2008; Marquardt et al., 2004).

Dimopoulos et al. (2013) provided a summary of data mining tools, which interoperate with Moodle. However, these tools provide mainly analysis and visualization of the educational data and combine a didactical theory with VLE stakeholders' requirements (Mazza et al., 2014). They do not deal with modeling of the VLE Moodle stakeholders' behavior over time in detail.

Records of the VLE stakeholders' activity, which are stored in log files of the VLE Moodle, represent a source of time-oriented data. Several studies focused on the students' interaction with VLEs considering the times of accesses, showing time-sensitive patterns of student behavior (Hwang and Li, 2002; Tobarra et al., 2014; Fakir and Touya, 2014; Haig et al., 2013). Ceddia et al. (Ceddia et al., 2007; Ceddia and Sheard, 2005) developed a web-based educational system WIER and analyzed the students' behavior at the different levels of log file data abstraction with reference to time. However, these studies usually analyzed only the behavior of the students in a particular activity; eg, in the discussion forum. They did not research their behavior based on the modeling of probabilities of accesses.

In this chapter we will introduce a methodology for modeling the probabilities of stakeholders' accesses estimated through a MLM. None of the above-mentioned methods models the VLE stakeholders' behavior depending on the probability of the time of access to the different parts of the VLE.

3 METHODOLOGY OF PREDICTIVE MODELING

We used the CRISP-DM methodology (Fig. 10.1) (Chapman, 1999; Kurgan and Musilek, 2006) for managing a process of students' behavior and teachers' behavior modeling with reference to time.

As we mentioned earlier, the proposed methodology of predictive modeling described in this chapter closely relates to the EDM and LA because it focuses on modeling stakeholders' behavior in the VLE. The methodology put emphasis on data preparation, which often represents the most time-consuming part of the whole process. At the same time, it focuses on data modeling with reference to time, which is seldom addressed in both research disciplines.

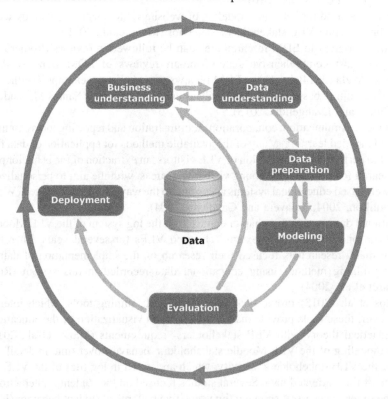

FIGURE 10.1

The process diagram shows the relationship between the different phases of CRISP-DM (Jensen, 2012).

The primary goals of the methodology result from these two aspects. The first goal focuses on simplification of data preparation in the process of modeling students' behavior in the VLE, and the second one focuses on the modeling of different groups of VLE stakeholders' behavior with reference to time.

The proposed methodology is usually structured into the following phases and steps:

1. Business understanding
   a. Task prediction,
2. Data understanding
   a. Data collection and selection,
3. Data preparation
   a. Data cleaning,
   b. Session identification and path completion,
   c. Definition of variables,
   d. Reduction of cases,
4. Modeling
   a. Model determination,
   b. Parameters estimation,
   c. Logits estimation,
   d. Probability estimation,
   e. Probability visualization,
5. Evaluation
   a. Empirical counts determination,
   b. Theoretical counts estimation,
   c. Visualization of differences in the empirical and theoretical counts of accesses,
   d. Extremes identification,
   e. Calculation of relative empirical counts of accesses,
   f. Comparison of the distribution of the relative empirical counts of accesses with the estimated probabilities of selecting the web part j in hour i,
   g. Calculation of empirical logits,
   h. Visualization of empirical and theoretical logits for individual web parts except the referential,
   i. Further evaluation methods of MLM.

We will closely describe the individual steps of the methodology in the next part of the chapter. We will not deal with the theoretical aspects of the methodology alone, we will also present an example of the probability modeling of access to the different parts (activities, courses, course categories) of the VLE with reference to time, which will familiarize the reader with the possible applications of this methodology.

3.1 BUSINESS UNDERSTANDING

The business understanding phase focuses on understanding the aims that define the problem from the initiator's point of view. This phase also focuses on a class of tasks identification in terms of knowledge discovery. In other words, we try to classify modeled problems into one of the widely accepted classes of data modeling (mining) (Munk, 2011):

- Data description and summarization,
- Segmentation,
- Concept description,

- Classification,
- Prediction,
- Analysis of dependence.

We intend to model the VLE stakeholders' behavior during several academic years. In other words, the stakeholders' behavior modeling with reference to time is the main objective of our experiment. Later, we will define several variables of the time-predictors. For that reason, we solve the problem, which belongs to the prediction class of data modeling.

3.2 DATA UNDERSTANDING

The data understanding phase can be divided into data collection and selection parts.

Many VLEs store information about their users not in server log files but mainly in relational database systems. VLEs usually have the same three-tier software architecture like other web-based systems or applications. For that reason, VLEs store data in the database systems. We can find there not only the data creating the content, defining the structure or the state of the systems, but also metadata and a huge amount of data about the VLE stakeholders' activities.

Compared to other data mining applications, a relational database system provides an integrated and structured source of data saving on the pre-processing effort (Gaudioso and Talavera, 2005). The known structure of the tables simplifies the process of data collection by enabling the database system to be queried using SQL. Usually, we try to identify tables storing the records about the users' activity in the VLE and to prepare a set of SQL queries selecting the *userID*, *timestamp*, *IP* and other information about the given *activity*.

We have to pay special attention to the attribute *activity*. In further logs analysis, it is useful to take different abstractions of the data to enable an analysis that is more meaningful. Romero et al. define the abstractions as groupings of records that are related in some way (Romero et al., 2010). The examples of these abstractions are Page view, session, task or activity. The activity represents a sequence of semantically meaningful page accesses related to a particular activity or task that a stakeholder of the VLE performs. In other words, an activity is an abstraction of the discrete behavioral activity of the stakeholder (Sheard, 2011). It categorizes individual web parts (web pages) of the VLE into particular activities.

We will create other necessary variables from this set of attributes in the data preparation phase.

3.3 DATA PREPARATION

The information available on the web is heterogeneous and unstructured. The goal of data preparation is to transform the raw data stored in log files into a set of user sessions. Data preparation consists of several steps, such as data cleaning, user identification, session identification, and path completion (Liu, 2011; Cooley et al., 1999).

We used logs created from a database of the VLE Moodle, which was launched in 2007 as an e-learning portal at the university level. The teachers and students from all faculties of the university use the portal. The average number of daily unique student logins is more than 800.

To understand and contextualize the results of the methodology of predictive modeling it is necessary to note that the university management has not defined a strong e-learning implementation policy. However, the available e-learning courses have been created considering the outcomes of several educational projects focused on the e-learning courses' development, which have been realized at the university. The e-learning courses are mainly in the blended learning form.

For the purpose of this study we wrote an SQL query, which selected the attributes ID, userID, IP, course, time, module, action from the table mdl_log and mdl_logstore_stantard, representing the primary storage of logs in the VLE Moodle. Since the log system of the VLE Moodle has changed, the records about the users' activity in the e-learning course opened in the academic year 2015 had to be mapped into the structure of the previous academic years.

We extracted records related only to the e-learning courses focused on database systems fundamentals. These courses were opened in the academic years 2009–15. These sources were used predominantly in the blended learning form. The content of the course was slightly modified each year to reflect the changes in the curriculum and schedule of the academic year. During the mentioned period, 861 unique participants enrolled and actively participated in the courses. We selected only the accesses that belonged to the students and teachers who were enrolled in the observed e-learning courses.

3.3.1 Data Cleaning

In the VLE context, unlike other web-based domains, the user identification is a straightforward problem because the students have to log in using their unique ID in most cases (Ba-Omar et al., 2007). Therefore, not all preparation tasks were necessary in the presented experiment, because the VLE Moodle did not allow an anonymous login into e-learning courses. Each user had a unique user ID. For this reason, only the activities of e-learning course visitors were recorded in the log files.

The records were cleaned of irrelevant items. The original log file contained 338,667 entries. We removed entries about users other than the student or teacher. After performing this task, we defined a set WALS (Web Access Log Set) (Table 10.1) of accesses into the VLE stored in a log file and ordered by time

Table 10.1 Part of the Web Access Log Set Obtained From VLE Moodle Tables

ID	Time	UserID	IP	Course	Module	Action
106778	1192100731	60	194.160.213.155	124	Assignment	View
106781	1192210744	60	194.160.213.155	124	Data	View
120727	1192380691	60	213.215.123.228	124	Forum	View forum
120728	1192380698	60	213.215.123.228	124	Forum	View forum
120729	1192380700	60	213.215.123.228	124	Forum	View discussion
120732	1192380855	60	213.215.123.228	124	Course	View
120734	1192380873	60	213.215.123.228	124	Data	View
120738	1192380892	60	213.215.123.228	124	Forum	View forum
120742	1192380907	60	213.215.123.228	124	Resource	View
120754	1192381146	60	213.215.123.228	124	Assignment	View
120755	1192381155	60	213.215.123.228	124	Assignment	View
120758	1192381187	60	213.215.123.228	124	Data	View
120760	1192381231	60	213.215.123.228	124	Data	View
120762	1192381241	60	213.215.123.228	124	Assignment	View all
120824	1192381776	60	213.215.123.228	124	Assignment	View

$$WALS = \{\langle ID, time, userID, IP, module, action\rangle\}.$$

The part of final WALS is depicted in Table 10.1. Finally, 330,553 entries in the WALS were accepted for use in the next task.

3.3.2 Session Identification and Path Completion

A user session is defined as a sequence of requests made by a particular user over a certain navigation period. A user may have one or multiple session(s) during this period. The session identification is a process of segmenting the log data of each user into disjointed sequences of individual sessions (Romero and Ventura, 2007). We found a comprehensive review of session identification techniques in (Romero et al., 2014; Munk et al., 2013).

At the beginning of this process, we needed to identify a particular user. In the context of VLEs, unlike other web-based domains, the user identification is a straightforward problem because in most VLEs the learners must log in using their unique user ID (Ba-Omar et al., 2007).

We can identify user sessions in several ways. The reactive technique of user session identification assumes that we process records about accesses of the user to a particular web part of the VLE after they are handled. On the other hand, the proactive technique supposes that the same process occurs during the interactive browsing of web parts of the VLE by the user. We decided to use the reactive technique of user session identification.

Reactive session identification uses time or navigation-driven heuristics. Concerning the specific features of the VLE Moodle, the navigation driven heuristics was not applicable. We turned our attention to the time-driven heuristics (Cooley et al., 1999):

- Session duration based method,
- Timeout threshold based method.

The session duration based method assumes, if we can estimate the duration of the session θ then we can define the session as a sequence of visited web parts in the VLE where each part has its own timestamp, for which:

$$USS = \{\langle userID, IP, \langle ID_1, time_1\rangle, ..., \langle ID_k, time_k\rangle\rangle\}, time_k - time_1 \leq \theta,$$

where USS means User Session Set, $USS \subset WALS$, $time_k$ is the timestamp of the last record in a session, $1 \leq k \leq n$ and n is a count of records in $WALS$. Other records of the WALS, which have a timestamp greater than $time_1 + \theta$, belong to the next session.

On the other hand, timeout threshold based method assumes, if we can estimate the timeout threshold δ then we can define the session as a sequence of visited web parts in the VLE where each part has its own timestamp for which:

$$USS = \{\langle userID, IP, \langle ID_1, time_1\rangle, ..., \langle ID_k, time_k\rangle\rangle\}, time_i - time_{i-1} \leq \delta,$$

where $USS \subset WALS$, $time_k$ is a timestamp of the last record in a session and $1 \leq i \leq k$. If the inequality is not true for two consecutive records from the WALS, then the records belong to two different sessions (Munk et al., 2013; Kapusta et al., 2012).

Against this background, we decided to use a reactive time-oriented heuristic method based on time threshold for identifying the users' sessions.

Moreover, we adopted a 100-minutes timeout threshold to start a new session regarding the setting in the VLE despite the recommended 30-minute-long timeout threshold (Munk and Drlik, 2011). We mentioned earlier that the e-learning courses were used to support blended learning. The teachers and students also used them during face-to-face lessons. For that reason, we selected a 100-minutes timeout threshold, which represents a typical duration of a lesson at the university (90 min of lessons + 10 min to finish and upload assignment or another task).

The path reconstruction represents the next step of the data preparation phase. Path completion technique depends on the precision of identified sessions. It covers an analysis of the backward path completion or reconstruction of the visitor's activities in the VLE. The reconstruction of activities is focused on retrograde completion of records on the path followed by a user using the back button of a web browser, since the use of such button is not automatically recorded into log records.

We analyzed several approaches to the path completion issues mentioned in the literature (Spiliopoulou et al., 2003; Yan and Bo-qin, 2009).

Our previous research results indicated that the data preparation in the educational context could be reduced to the reconstruction of the activities of VLE users. Identification of transactions/sequences of visitors to the VLE did not have a significant impact on the quality and quantity of useful sequential rules in the realized experiment (Munk et al., 2013). We assumed that in the case of a system providing sophisticated navigation options and a rigid structure of the content (which is characteristic for not just VLEs), the path's completion is not an inevitable step in data preparation for the process of discovering patterns of web users' behavior (Munk et al., 2013).

3.3.3 Definition of Variables

The different web parts of the VLE can be represented by the variables. An independent variable was a time variable t with values from the interval 0–23 in our case study. We identified the type of dependence on time considering the results of calculation and visualization of empirical logits. It was proven that logits compose a quadratic function of time (Munk et al., 2011b). For that reason we defined a new variable, which represented the square of the variable time t^2.

We could also consider other independent variables based on time and use them in MLM. For example, we could distinguish different week days (Munk et al., 2011b), eventually working days and weekends (Munk et al., 2011a).

In some other cases, it is desirable to create several models for different groups of users or types of accesses to the defined web parts of the observed system (Munk et al., 2011b). For example, we could identify IP addresses of the ordinary visitors. Moreover, if we know the series of IP addresses of the university or other institution, we could easily identify accesses from inside and outside of the university (Munk et al., 2011a). This distribution of accesses can be useful, for example, in situations when the face-to-face students and students of the external form of education extensively use an e-learning course in the same period of study. The construction of some derived variables was the last step of the data preparation stage.

We suggested not modeling the probabilities of accesses to the individual web pages of a particular e-learning course, but to the different activities contained in this e-learning course (Munk and Drlík, 2014). We mentioned earlier the usefulness of this abstraction of web parts into semantically more meaningful activities, mainly in cases where the accesses to the web parts were low (Munk et al., 2011b). The original variables *action* and *module* took many values, which lead to the lower counts of accesses. Therefore, we derived a new variable—*activity*—which grouped the semantically related

Table 10.2 Pivotal Table TEACHER × ACTIVITY

Teacher	Action_type Navigation	Action_type Learn	Action_type Create	Action_type Manage	Totals
0	59,429	239,045	0	9804	308,278
Column %	90.40%	95.20%	0.00%	55.66%	
Row %	19.28%	77.54%	0.00%	3.18%	
Total %	17.55%	70.58%	0.00%	2.89%	91.03%
1	6312	12,063	4204	7809	30,388
Column %	9.60%	4.80%	100.00%	44.34%	
Row %	20.77%	39.70%	13.83%	25.70%	
Total %	1.86%	3.56%	1.24%	2.31%	8.97%
Totals	65,741	251,108	4204	17,613	338,666
Total %	19.41%	74.15%	1.24%	5.20%	100.00%

actions, mentioned in the VLE Moodle log files. As a result, the variable *activity* with categories: *learn*, *manage*, *create*, and *navigation* characterizes the type of activity performed by the teacher or student in the e-learning course. The category *learn*, represents all teaching activities of the teacher.

Considering the fact, that the students and teachers can differ in their activities during the hours of a day, we added a variable *teacher* (0, 1). The pivot table (Table 10.2) confirms the correctness of our decision. We can see that with reference to the role of teacher a new category was identified—*create*—which covered the actions joined with the e-learning course content modification. This variable caused the decision to separate MLM for students' and for teachers' accesses.

The original log file contained only the variable *datetime*. We calculated other variables t (hours in a day) and its square t^2 for the purpose of our case study (Table 10.3).

Furthermore, we added the variable *session* into the final log file based on the results of the session identification step.

3.3.4 Reduction of Cases

In relation to cases, we have already identified sessions we can exclude from further analysis as the least visited web parts in terms of the results of association rule analysis. In other words, we can reduce the count of categories of an observed variable. We assume that we used identified transactions, where transaction represents a set of web parts visited by a particular user during one session (Munk et al., 2011a,b).

3.4 MODELING

We used a MLM for probability modeling of accesses on web parts of the e-learning course with reference to time. We were able to predict the visit rate of individual web parts (web pages, content categories, activities, etc.) according to the particular hour of the day or other variables.

Table 10.3 Final Attributes of the WALS Used in the Experiment

ID	Time	UserID	Teacher	Session	IP	Course	Module	2014	2013	2012	2011	2010	2009	Action	Activity	Datetime	Day	t	t^2
164477	1.263E+09	2657	0	17054	195.91.86.31	356	Assignment	0	0	0	1	0	0	View	Learn	7.1.2010 17:25	4	17	289
164478	1.263E+09	2657	0	17054	195.91.86.31	356	Course	0	0	0	1	0	0	View	Navigation	7.1.2010 17:26	4	17	289
164479	1.263E+09	2657	0	17054	195.91.86.31	356	Assignment	0	0	0	1	0	0	View	Learn	7.1.2010 17:26	4	17	289
164480	1.263E+09	2657	0	17054	195.91.86.31	356	Assignment	0	0	0	1	0	0	View	Learn	7.1.2010 17:26	4	17	289
164481	1.263E+09	2657	0	17054	195.91.86.31	356	Assignment	0	0	0	1	0	0	View	Learn	7.1.2010 17:26	4	17	289
164482	1.263E+09	2657	0	17054	195.91.86.31	356	Assignment	0	0	0	1	0	0	View all	Learn	7.1.2010 17:30	4	17	289
164483	1.263E+09	2657	0	17054	195.91.86.31	356	Course	0	0	0	1	0	0	View	Navigation	7.1.2010 17:30	4	17	289

The data used in our example describes individual accesses of students and teachers to the activities of e-learning courses during the period of seven academic years. The e-learning courses were created in the VLE Moodle.

At the beginning of this phase, we describe the variables that needed to be included in the model. The investigated categorical dependent variable was a variable *activity* with categories: *learn, manage,* and *navigate* for the model Student and *learn, manage, create,* and *navigate* for the model Teacher. The category *learn* covers all teaching activities of the teacher.

The time t with values 0–23 represented a independent variable. We used variables *2009, 2010, 2011, 2012, 2013, 2014* as dummy variables. Moreover, we included the variable square of time t^2 in the model.

3.5 MODEL DETERMINATION

Probability distribution of accesses Y_{ij} in time i to category j with observations y_{ij}, if count of accesses is given $n_i = \sum_j y_{ij}$ in time i is multinomial

$$P[Y_{i1} = y_{i1}, Y_{i2} = y_{i2}, ..., Y_{iJ} = y_{iJ}] = \frac{n_i!}{y_{i1}!y_{i2}!...y_{iJ}!}\pi_{i1}^{y_{i1}}\pi_{i2}^{y_{i2}}...\pi_{iJ}^{y_{iJ}}.$$

Since $\sum_{j=1}^{J}\pi_{ij} = 1$, we need to estimate $J - 1$ unknown probabilities. The estimations of accesses are calculated using the Maximum Likelihood method. In the logarithmic function of likelihood (without constants)

$$\sum_i \sum_{j=1}^{J} y_{ij}\, \ln \pi_{ij}. \tag{1}$$

This uses logit transformation (the last category was selected as reference)

$$\eta_{ij} = \ln \frac{\pi_{ij}}{\pi_{iJ}}.$$

We suppose at the same time, that logits η_{ij} are linear functions of independent variables (covariates),

$$\eta_{ij} = \alpha_j + \mathbf{x}_i^T \boldsymbol{\beta}_j.$$

We apply an inverse transformation and get

$$\pi_{iJ} = \frac{1}{1 + \sum_{j=1}^{J-1} e^{\eta_{ij}}}, \pi_{ij} = e^{\eta_{ij}}\pi_{iJ}, j = 1, 2, ..., J-1,$$

respectively

$$\pi_{iJ} = \frac{1}{1 + \sum_{j=1}^{J-1} e^{\alpha_j + \mathbf{x}_i^T \boldsymbol{\beta}_j}}, \pi_{ij} = \frac{e^{\alpha_j + \mathbf{x}_i^T \boldsymbol{\beta}_j}}{1 + \sum_{j=1}^{J-1} e^{\alpha_j + \mathbf{x}_i^T \boldsymbol{\beta}_j}}, j = 1, 2, ..., J-1.$$

The logarithm function is a likelihood function with unknown parameters α_j a $\boldsymbol{\beta}_j$ $(j = 1, 2, ..., J-1)$ after substituting such expressed π_{ij} into Eq. (1).

3.6 PARAMETER ESTIMATION

We estimated the model's parameters α_j, β_j by maximizing the logarithm of multinomial likelihood function. We used *STATISTICA Generalized Linear/Nonlinear Models* for parameter estimation of individual values. The significance of parameters was tested using the Wald test (Table 10.4).

We modeled the probabilities of accesses of students and teachers to the individual activities of e-learning course depending on time and academic year. Time was represented by the variable t and by its square. Academic years were represented by dummy variables.

We could confirm that the parameters of models Student and Teacher were statistically significant considering the results of the test of all effects for both models (Table 10.4).

The academic years, which were implemented as dummy variables (2014, 2013, ...) in the models, represented statistically significant characteristics of the created logit models.

Similarly, hours of the day, which were represented by variables t and its square, were statistically significant.

We also used STATISTICA *Generalized Linear/Nonlinear Models* software for estimation of the model's parameters. The significance of the parameters was tested using the Wald test. Significant parameters are shaded in Tables 10.5 and 10.6.

We can see (Table 10.5) the significant dependence of logits of activities *navigation* and *learn* on hours of the day and its square. The values of these logits were also significantly influenced by the academic years in the case of the students. For instance, we can see an impact of academic years 2010–14 in the case of activity *navigation*.

Likewise, the logits of activities *navigation* and *learn* were significantly dependent on hours of the day and square of hours in a model of teachers' activity (Table 10.6). However, the logits of activity *create* were dependent only on the square of time.

We calculated estimations of logits using these estimated parameters. Consequently, we calculated the probabilities of selection of individual activities in a given hour of the day. These results were in line with the calculated probabilities (Fig. 10.2).

The estimation of the probabilities represents the outputs of the logit model. However, the knowledge of the model's parameters has the same importance. Their absolute value informs us about which

Table 10.4 Test of all Effects for a Model Student and a Model Teacher

Student	df	Wald Stat.	p	Teacher	df	Wald Stat.	p
Intercept	2	3,470,729	0.0000	*Intercept*	3	278,782	0.0000
t	2	10,135	0.0063	*t*	3	140,757	0.0000
t^2	2	242,571	0.0000	t^2	3	209,945	0.0000
2014	2	461,985	0.0000	*2014*	3	139,229	0.0000
2013	2	1,109,172	0.0000	*2013*	3	930,632	0.0000
2012	2	336,210	0.0000	*2012*	3	539,276	0.0000
2011	2	114,206	0.0000	*2011*	3	272,054	0.0000
2010	2	80,708	0.0000	*2010*	3	1,618,377	0.0000
2009	2	112,436	0.0000	*2009*	3	1,963,788	0.0000

Table 10.5 Model Student Parameter Estimation

Student	Level of Response	Estimate	Standard Error	Wald Stat.	p
Intercept 1	Navigation	1.805	0.094	369,142	0.0000
t	Navigation	0.039	0.013	9114	0.0025
t^2	Navigation	−0.003	0.000	55,604	0.0000
2014	Navigation	−0.478	0.041	135,431	0.0000
2013	Navigation	1.007	0.048	436,446	0.0000
2012	Navigation	0.799	0.071	126,780	0.0000
2011	Navigation	0.514	0.061	70,237	0.0000
2010	Navigation	0.313	0.040	61,017	0.0000
2009	Navigation	0.011	0.037	0.089	0.7649
Intercept 2	Learn	3.528	0.089	1,554,922	0.0000
t	Learn	0.039	0.012	10,061	0.0015
t^2	Learn	−0.005	0.000	155,001	0.0000
2014	Learn	−0.731	0.038	363,300	0.0000
2013	Learn	1.333	0.046	828,019	0.0000
2012	Learn	1.054	0.068	236,969	0.0000
2011	Learn	0.603	0.059	105,632	0.0000
2010	Learn	0.340	0.038	80,315	0.0000
2009	Learn	−0.156	0.035	20,148	0.0000

Table 10.6 Model Teacher Parameter Estimation

Teacher	Level of Response	Estimate	Standard Error	Wald Stat.	p
Intercept 1	Navigation	−1.359	0.116	138,345	0.0000
t	Navigation	0.188	0.016	134,680	0.0000
t^2	Navigation	−0.008	0.001	205,926	0.0000
2014	Navigation	−0.378	0.077	23,857	0.0000
2013	Navigation	0.278	0.053	27,767	0.0000
2012	Navigation	0.854	0.094	82,098	0.0000
2011	Navigation	0.346	0.075	21,270	0.0000
2010	Navigation	0.880	0.059	219,290	0.0000
2009	Navigation	0.428	0.051	69,399	0.0000
Intercept 2	Learn	−1.495	0.096	240,053	0.0000
t	Learn	0.052	0.012	17,736	0.0000
t^2	Learn	−0.003	0.000	51,782	0.0000
2014	Learn	0.707	0.082	73,441	0.0000
2013	Learn	1.833	0.061	892,207	0.0000
2012	Learn	2.177	0.096	511,839	0.0000
2011	Learn	1.356	0.083	266,891	0.0000
2010	Learn	2.641	0.066	1,600,472	0.0000
2009	Learn	2.570	0.059	1,880,126	0.0000
Intercept 3	Create	−0.969	0.111	76,639	0.0000
t	Create	0.026	0.015	2863	0.0907
t^2	Create	−0.002	0.001	13,439	0.0002
2014	Create	−0.150	0.087	2963	0.0852
2013	Create	0.548	0.060	82,303	0.0000
2012	Create	1.306	0.099	174,583	0.0000
2011	Create	0.395	0.088	19,955	0.0000
2010	Create	0.902	0.069	171,837	0.0000
2009	Create	0.509	0.060	72,097	0.0000

one of the predictors mostly influences the observed variable. The high absolute value of the parameter denotes high dependence. The positive (negative) value means proportional (inversely proportional) dependence.

3.7 LOGIT ESTIMATION

The estimation of logits η_{ij} for all values of independent variables is

$$\hat{\eta}_{ij} = a_j + \mathbf{x}_i^T \mathbf{b}_j, j = 1, 2, ..., J - 1.$$

We used the MLM for modeling the distribution of a categorical variable. In our case, the observed variable was *activity*. This variable has three categories (*navigation*, *learn*, and *manage*) in the case of students. In the case of model Teacher, we also observed a category *create*.

Finally, we created two models: model Teacher and model Student. We used academic year, which was represented by dummy variables, and time, represented by the hour of the day and its square, as predictive variables

$$\eta_{ij} = \alpha_j + \beta_{1j} t_i + \beta_{2j} t_i^2 + \gamma_{1j} 2014_i + \gamma_{2j} 2013_i + \gamma_{3j} 2012_i + \gamma_{4j} 2011_i + \gamma_{5j} 2010_i + \gamma_{6j} 2009_i.$$

3.8 PROBABILITY ESTIMATION

This step of modeling phase of the CRISP-DM methodology contains two tasks:

1. Probability estimation of accesses π_{iJ} in time i for reference activity J

$$\hat{\pi}_{iJ} = \frac{1}{1 + \sum_{j=1}^{J-1} e^{\hat{\eta}_{ij}}}.$$

2. Probability estimation of accesses π_{ij} in time i for activity j

$$\hat{\pi}_{ij} = e^{\hat{\eta}_{ij}} \hat{\pi}_{iJ}, j = 1, 2, ..., J - 1.$$

3.9 PROBABILITY VISUALIZATION

Finally, we could visualize the probability of activity j at time i, $j = 1, 2, ..., J, i \in \{0, 1, ..., 23\}$.

We prepared a set of charts (Figs. 10.2–10.11) that visualized the probability of selection of observed activities by students or teachers with reference to time in the observed academic years. We can see that the probabilities of accesses to the particular category with reference to time.

We show the most interesting visualization in the following section.

1. Visualization of teachers' behavior in the individual academic years.

Fig. 10.2 depicts the probability of teachers´ accesses to the individual activities in the academic year 2009. The probability of activity *learn* was very high, with the maximum at midnight (0.59) and with a minimum at night (0.51). The probability of other activities was very low, in the interval 0.1–0.2. The curve of the probability of activity *create* reflected the fact that the structure and available educational content of the e-learning course were almost unchanged and teachers actively participated in the e-learning course environment. Moreover, the activity *navigation* had its maximum during the working hours, what indicates, that the teachers used the e-learning course during their lessons.

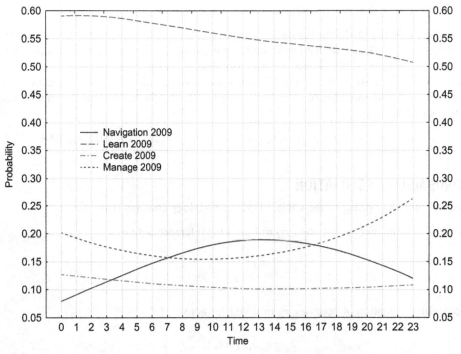

FIGURE 10.2

Probability visualization of accesses of teachers to the observed activities in 2009.

The probabilities of the accesses to the activities had the similar course in the academic years 2010 and 2011.

It is worth mentioning that the academic year 2012 (Fig. 10.3), in which the probability of activity *learn* decreased (from 0.6–0.51 to 0.4–0.33), and the probability of activity *create* slightly increased (0.3–0.23). The changes correspond to the fact, that the teachers modified the e-learning course content.

During the next 2 years the probability for activity *manage* continually increased.

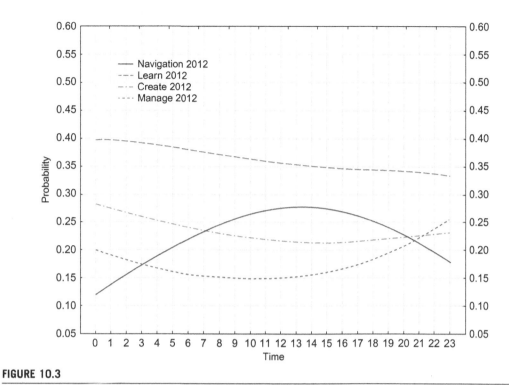

FIGURE 10.3

Probability visualization of accesses of teachers to the observed activities in 2012.

Fig. 10.4 visualizes the probability of teachers' accesses to the observed activities in the academic year 2015. We can summarize that the probability of accesses to the activity *manage* was highest at night. The maximum ($\pi = 0.59$) was around 11 p.m. and continually declined during the day. It reached the minimum at 11 a.m.

In contrast, the probability of accesses to the activity *navigation* was low at night. It increased during the day and culminated in the value of around 0.35. The probabilities of accesses to the activities *create* and *learn* were quite low during the day. However, probability estimations for activities *create* and *learn* were more stable timewise in the academic year 2015. The dramatic decrease in the probability of the activity *learn* and an increase in the activity *manage* had two reasons. The stabilization of e-learning educational content and structure of the interactive activities available in the course represents the first reason. The second reason, which is more serious from the institutional point of view, is the absence of the institutional e-learning strategy and insufficient support for teachers using e-learning courses in the blended learning form.

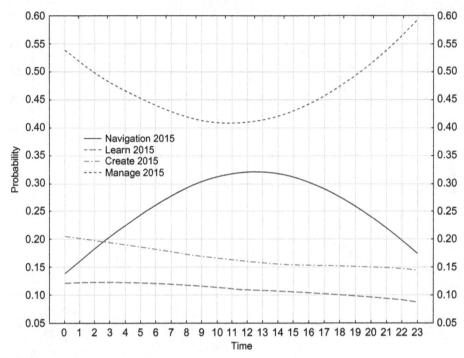

FIGURE 10.4

Probability visualization of accesses of teachers to the observed activities in 2015.

The results of the analysis showed that teachers managed the educational process mainly in the evening and at night. This finding was surprising because we supposed that the management of the educational process would be at its maximum during the working hours.

We also notice a general trend of teachers using the e-learning courses mostly for a presentation of study resources and navigation of students to the educational resources during the working day. They do managerial tasks predominantly in the evening or at night when they have more time to prepare forthcoming e-learning activities.

2. Visualization of individual teachers' activities during the observed period of academic years.

Visualization of particular teachers' activity during the observed period of academic years brings another perspective to the e-learning course life cycle. Furthermore, this view confirms our previous claims. Figs. 10.5 and 10.6 stressed the changes in the preferred activities of teachers during academic years 2009–15. We can see an increase in the probability of the activity *manage* (Fig. 10.5) and a significant decrease in the probability of the activity *learn* (Fig. 10.6).

Both figures provide another benefit to the academic coordinator or managers. The shape of individual curves has not changed during the observed period. It means that the teachers of these e-learning courses preferred managing course activities, actively participating in the course environment or using educational resources during a day.

This information obtained from the different e-learning courses can significantly contribute to the development of an online teaching guide of the educational institution. Moreover, comparison of the students' and teachers' behavior during the day shows the optimal conditions for better "visibility" of teachers in the course, and the right time for videoconference meetings or to chat with students.

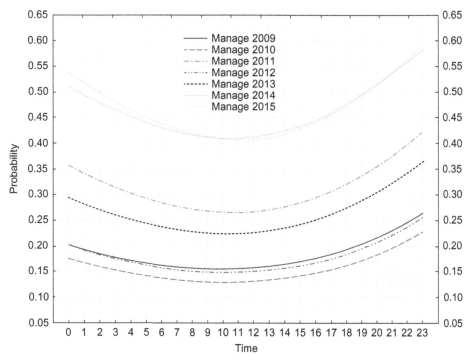

FIGURE 10.5

Probability visualization of the activity "manage" during the academic years 2009–15.

The probability visualization of the activity *learn* during the academic years 2009–15 (Fig. 10.6) indicates that the teachers were used to modifying the content of the e-learning course at night.

It is evident that the e-learning course reached its maturity in the last academic year. The teacher probably found the optimal structure and content of the e-learning course. For that reason, the probability of the activity *learn* significantly declined.

3. Visualization of students' behavior in individual academic years.

Figs. 10.7 and 10.8 visualize the probability of accesses of students to the observed activities in the academic years 2009 and 2015. The probabilities had a very similar course in the other academic years.

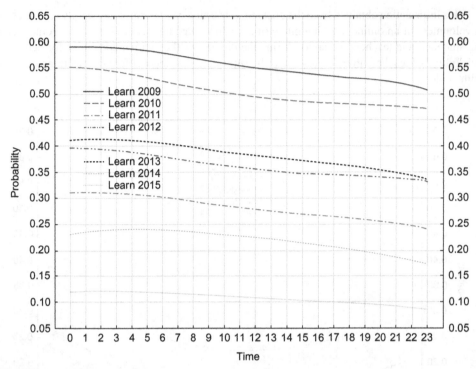

FIGURE 10.6

Probability visualization of the activity "learn" during the academic years 2009–15.

It is natural that the most preferred activity of the students should be *learn*. An interesting finding is that the probability of accesses to this activity declined during a day (from 0.83) and reached its minimum at 11 p.m. (0.57). At the same time, the activities *manage* and *navigation* reached their maximal probabilities. This means that the students were used to browsing the e-learning course at the end of the day with the aim of reading the news or new posts in discussion forums. If there was any deadline for tasks or assignment, they were also able to work towards it after the midnight. This confirms the curve *learn* of the course.

Figs. 10.7 and 10.8 provide surprising information about the students. The similar shape of the curves uncovers the fact that the students' behavior in e-learning courses is harder to change than teachers'.

While the probability of teachers' accesses to the activities changed over the years, the behavior of the students remained unchanged.

4. Visualization of individual students' activities during the observed period of academic years.

Figs. 10.9–10.11 confirm the fact that the students used the e-learning course in the same manner during the observed period.

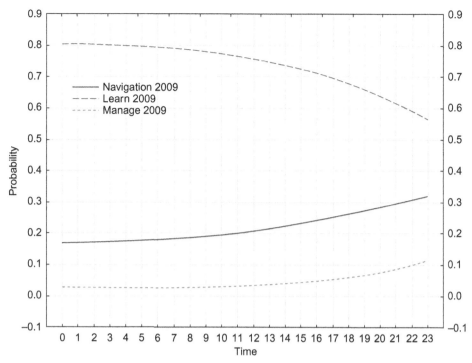

FIGURE 10.7

Probability visualization of accesses of students to the observed activities in 2009.

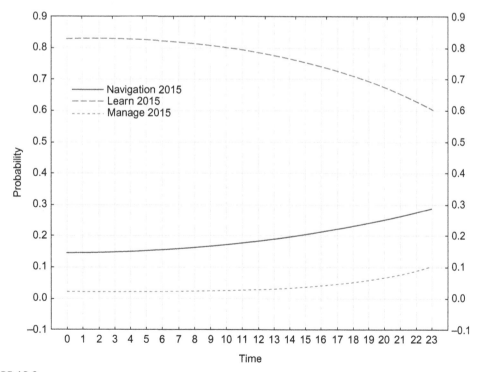

FIGURE 10.8

Probability visualization of accesses of students to the observed activities in 2015.

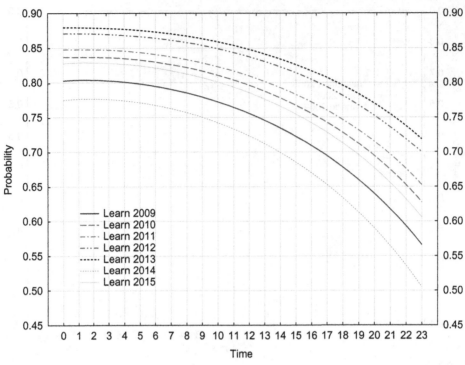

FIGURE 10.9

Probability visualization of the activity "learn" during the academic years 2009–15.

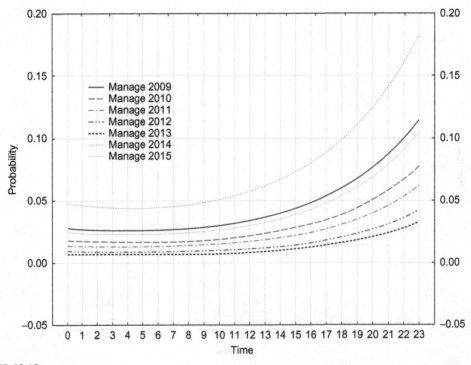

FIGURE 10.10

Probability visualization of the activity "manage" during the academic years 2009–15.

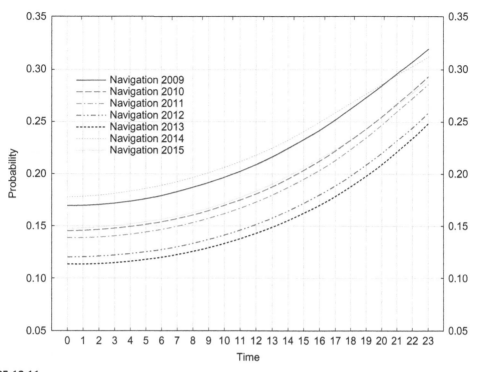

FIGURE 10.11

Probability visualization of the activity "navigation" during the academic years 2009–15.

3.10 EVALUATION

The last phase of the CRISP-DM methodology used in this chapter is an evaluation. We went through several steps of this phase:

1. Empirical counts determination,
2. Theoretical counts estimation,
3. Visualization of differences in the empirical and theoretical counts of accesses,
4. Extremes identification,
5. Calculation of relative empirical counts of accesses,
6. Comparison of the distribution of the relative empirical counts of accesses with the estimated probabilities of selecting the web part j in hour i,
7. Calculation of empirical logits,
8. Visualization of empirical and theoretical logits for individual web parts except the referential,
9. Further evaluation methods of MLM.

We marked several important aspects in our case study.

We specified empirical counts of accesses y_{ij} as a first step. We determined theoretical counts estimation

$$\hat{y}_{ij} = \hat{\pi}_{ij} \sum_j y_{ij}.$$

Subsequently, we visualized differences in the empirical and theoretical counts of accesses

$$d_{ij} = y_{ij} - \hat{y}_{ij}.$$

In the next step, we identified extremes $d_{ij} > \bar{d}_j \pm 2s$ by visualizing the differences between empirical and theoretical counts of accesses to the examined activities in the e-learning course. In other words, we found an hour in which the forecast was overestimated or underestimated (Munk and Drlík, 2014; Munk et al., 2011a). In the presented case, the suitability of the model was confirmed by the means of differences, which was approximately equal to zero. We identified extremes using the application of 2σ the rule.

After that, we calculated the relative empirical counts of accesses

$$p_{ij} = \frac{y_{ij}}{\sum_j y_{ij}}.$$

Finally, we compared the distribution of the relative empirical counts of accesses with the estimated probabilities of selecting a particular web part j in hour i

$$r_{ij} = p_{ij} - \pi_{ij}, \text{H0}: F(-r) = 1 - F(r).$$

Considering the fact that the distribution of pairs was symmetrical around the zero value, we used the Wilcoxon pair test for testing zero hypothesis.

In this step, we could calculate empirical logits

$$h_{ij} = \ln\left(\frac{p_{ij}}{p_{iJ}}\right), j = 1, 2, ..., J-1, i \in \{0, 1, ..., 23\}.$$

Finally, we visualized empirical and theoretical logits for individual web parts except the referential. We visualized the empirical and theoretical logits of examined activities whether the theoretical logits fit to the empirical logits (Munk and Drlík, 2014; Munk et al., 2011a). At the same time, we could test if the logits compose a quadratic function of time.

Evaluation of the proposed MLM also can be realized using other evaluation methods:

1. Likelihood-ratio test (LR test),
2. Pearson's statistics chi-square,
3. Maximizing of logarithm likelihood function for model comparison,

Table 10.7 LR Test for a Model Student and a Model Teacher

Student	df	Stat.	Stat./df	Teacher	df	Stat.	Stat./df
Deviance	616,538	373,961	0.606550	Deviance	91,137	75789.9	0.831604
Pearson χ^2	616,538	618,097	1.002528	Pearson χ^2	91,137	91210.4	1.000805
Loglikelihood		−186981		Loglikelihood		−37894.9	

4. Chi-square goodness of fit test for comparison of theoretical and empirical counts for selected categories,
5. Cross-validation—training and test data (75, 25),
6. *m*-fold cross-validation (10-fold),
7. Classification of cases,
8. Residual analysis
   - Raw residuals,
   - Standardized residuals,
   - Cook's distances,
   - Pearson's chi-squared statistics.

For example, we used an LR test for comparison of the actual model with the saturated one providing that the expected counts were large enough, eg, there were not zero values, and no more than 20% of the expected counts were lower than 5

$$LR(\hat{\pi}) = 2 \sum_{i=0}^{23} \sum_{j=1}^{J} y_{ij} \ln \frac{y_{ij}}{\hat{y}_{ij}}.$$

We could consider the models useful because the values of the LR test were low in our case (Table 10.7).

Pearson's chi-squared statistics represents the alternative to the LR test statistics, which was used for Likelihood-ratio testing. For that reason, we could also use it for comparison of $\hat{y}_{ij}$ estimations with y_{ij}. We applied

$$\chi^2 = \sum_{i=0}^{23} \sum_{j=1}^{J} r_{ij}^2,$$

where $r_{ij} = \dfrac{y_{ij} - \hat{y}_{ij}}{\sqrt{\hat{y}_{ij}}}$ is a Pearson's residuum, which has $\chi^2(df)$ distribution.

The values of ratios were approximately one (Table 10.7). It confirmed the suitability of the models.

The condition for using the LR test and Pearson's statistics of chi-square is often interrupted in this application domain. The reason is that the examined variable usually has many levels representing the web parts of the VLE or website (web pages, content categories, activities …). It causes the violation of the condition for using the LR test or Pearson's chi-squared statistics. In other words, the expected counts are not sufficiently large.

For that reason, we used alternative techniques such as visualization of the differences between empirical and theoretical counts and identification of extremes.

The maximum of a logarithmic likelihood function (Table 10.7) is also suitable for a comparison of models. The lower the value is, the better model will be.

If it is not possible to test the quality of the whole model, we can verify the quality of selected categories. The only assumption to use a chi-square goodness of fit test is a violation of assumptions.

We can also use a cross-validation or *m*-fold cross-validation for verification of the accuracy of the classification of cases using the training and test data. The module STATISTICA, generalized linear/

nonlinear models, provides the possibility for verifying the selected classification using training data, test data and the whole dataset.

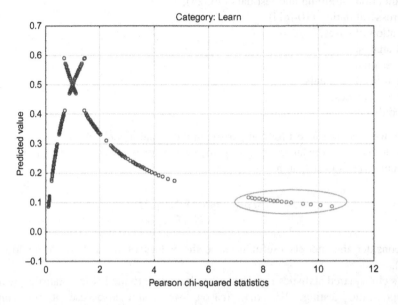

FIGURE 10.12

Residual analysis of the model Teacher.

The last class of evaluation technique for the MLM is based on the residual analysis. We can identify the extreme cases using a residual analysis. These extremes contribute to the model's inaccuracy. One extreme observation can significantly influence the final estimations. For that reason it is always suitable to evaluate these statistics and repeat important steps of analysis after removing extreme cases.

The main aim of all mentioned statistics is extreme cases identification:

- Raw residuals

$$residuals = relative\,counts - estimated\,probabilities.$$

- Standardized residuals

$$standardized\,residuals = \frac{relative\,counts - estimated\,probabilities}{standard\,deviation}.$$

- Cook's distance is another example of how to measure an impact of a given case on a regression. It indicates the differences between estimations of regression coefficients. All distances should have approximately the same size. If not, we can assume that the given case affected the regression coefficients.
- Pearson's chi-squared statistics. The cases with a large value of chi-square (Fig. 10.12) cause the inaccuracy of the model. Removing them can lead to different results.

4 DISCUSSION AND CONCLUSIONS

We modeled the probabilities of accesses of students and teachers to the particular activities of an e-learning course in the VLE during several academic years and in different hours of a day. We can utilize this knowledge to update, restructure, and personalize the content of the e-learning course, with the eventually aim of managing the maintenance of the VLE.

The MLM used to assess the probability of students' and teachers' accesses to the individual activities of the e-learning course in the VLE at different times, finds its application in various stages of the e-learning course's life cycle; generally in the VLE administration and in the management of the higher education institutions.

The structure of the e-learning course predetermines the probability of using individual activities in a particular period. Therefore, the greatest contribution of the MLM application does not lie in the process of designing a new course, but rather in the process of restructuring the existing e-learning course.

We researched the students' behavior in the e-learning course in great depth previously in Munk and Drlík (2014). Based on the results of this experiment, the author of the e-learning course content may change an original representation of the individual categories of activities in the course according to the students' behavior considering the determined probabilities. If some activity seems to have only a small probability of being used by the students, we can conclude that this method of the study was not attractive to them. In such cases, we should search for alternative activities with the same or similar learning outcomes.

In this chapter, we applied the MLM to research how the probabilities of accesses to the activities of the e-learning course change over the time. This application of the MLM can help teachers to fit their behavior to the students' behavior or modify the schedule of the course according to their learning preferences. Eventually, the teacher can observe the impact of the changes in the structure of the interactive activities on the students' behavior over several cycles of the e-learning course.

The personalization of the e-learning course content—not the content for every user but rather a personalization based on stereotyped users—can be considered as the next application of the MLM. Drawing on the determined probabilities, the teacher may adjust the period of study to the needs or, rather, habits of the student target group. The teacher can modify the schedule of study or rearrange the future deadlines, eg, submission of assignments or tasks, participation in discussion forums or the realization of tests and self-tests. For example, if the course supports blended and distance learning at the same time, it is possible to create separate groups of students. Consequently, we can adjust the activities and deadlines for the particular group according to the differences in the probabilities of accesses.

The obtained results can also be useful for the VLE administration and planning VLE maintenance. The fact that the stakeholders' accesses to the e-learning courses have different probabilities during the whole day should be taken into account during the planning of the VLE maintenance, and whilst backing up courses and ensuring an overall accessibility of the VLE. Searching for a suitable schedule for administrator activities, a particular compromise should be made, and teachers should synchronize deadlines for the submission of students' tests and assignments in their e-learning courses in order to determine a period with minimum accesses.

The proposed methodology can also be successfully applied at the institutional level, which closely relates to the LA research interests. The application of the MLM at the different levels (an e-learning course, several cycles of the e-learning course, courses of a particular study program) can help teachers, tutors, academic coordinators or managers to improve the feedback processes. For instance, they can combine the students' answers in the feedback surveys focused on their study preferences or usual period for study in a day or a week with the probabilities of accesses that have been discovered.

Furthermore, they can more precisely react to the changes in the frequency of the VLE visits, in students' learning preferences, and in students' study habits by adapting the deadlines of e-learning activities or predict the long-term engagement.

Academic coordinators can utilize the results of MLM application to evaluate the activity of teachers or tutors in e-learning courses over the several academic years. They can identify the teachers who exhibit similar behavior and approaches to the management of opened e-learning courses. Moreover, considering the students' behavior, the academic coordinators can propose or improve an e-learning methodology or a set of institutional recommendations, how and when should be the teachers more "visible" in the e-learning course to help students to reach better learning outcomes.

We identified several cases, how can the methodology of predictive modeling of students' behavior in the VLE contribute to better academic outcomes and improve students' satisfaction with the e-learning courses and the decision making of managers of an educational institution.

Future work should focus on research into how to utilize the obtained knowledge about the students' behavior efficiently to improve the learner's experiences or outcomes.

ACKNOWLEDGMENT

This paper is supported by the project VEGA 1/0392/13 Modelling of Stakeholders' Behaviour in Commercial Bank during the Recent Financial Crisis and Expectations of Basel Regulations under Pillar 3—Market Discipline.

REFERENCES

Anděl, J., 2007. Základy matematické štatistiky. Matfyzpress, Bratislava.

Baker, R., Siemens, G., 2014. Educational data mining and learning analytics. In: Sawyer, R.K. (Ed.), The Cambridge Handbook of the Learning Sciences. second ed. Cambridge University Press, New York, pp. 253–274.

Baltagi, B.H., 2007. Econometrics. Springer, Berlin Heidelberg.

Ba-Omar, H., Petrounias, I., Anwar, F.A., 2007. Framework for using web usage mining to personalise e-learning. In: Seventh IEEE International Conference on Advanced Learning Technologies, 18–20 July 2007 (ICALT 2007), pp. 937–938.

Ceddia, J., Sheard, J., 2005. Log files for educational applications. In: Kommers, P., Richards, G. (Eds.), EdMedia: World Conference on Educational Media and Technology. Association for the Advancement of Computing in Education (AACE), Montreal, Canada.

Ceddia, J., Sheard, J., Tibbey, G., 2007. WAT: a tool for classifying learning activities from a log file. In: Proceedings of the Ninth Australasian Conference on Computing Education – Volume 66. Australian Computer Society, Ballarat, Victoria, Australia.

Chapman, P., 1999. The CRISP-DM User Guide.

Cooley, R., Mobasher, B., Srivastava, J., 1999. Data preparation for mining world wide web browsing patterns. Knowl. Inf. Syst. 1, 5–32.

Dimopoulos, I., Petropoulou, O., Retalis, S., 2013. Assessing students' performance using the learning analytics enriched rubrics. In: Proceedings of the Third International Conference on Learning Analytics and Knowledge. ACM, Leuven, Belgium.

Dos Santos Machado, L., Becker, K., 2003. Distance education: a Web usage mining case study for the evaluation of learning sites. In: Proceedings of the 3rd IEEE International Conference on Advanced Learning Technologies, 9–11 July 2003, pp. 360–361.

Drlik, M., Skalka, J., Švec, P., 2014. Comparison of approaches to the data analysis in the virtual learning environments. In: 10th International Scientific Conference on Distance Learning in Applied Informatics, Štúrovo, Slovak Republic.

Fakir, M., Touya, K., 2014. Mining students' learning behavior in moodle system. J. Inf. Technol. Res. 7, 12–26.

Gaudioso, E., Talavera, L., 2005. Data mining to support tutoring in virtual learning communities: experiences and challenges. In: Data Mining in E-Learning. WIT Press, Southampton, UK.

Haig, T., Falkner, K., Falkner, N., 2013. Visualisation of learning management system usage for detecting student behaviour patterns. In: Proceedings of the Fifteenth Australasian Computing Education Conference – Volume 136. Australian Computer Society, Adelaide, Australia.

Hosmer, D.W., Lemeshow, S., 2005. Multiple logistic regression. In: Applied Logistic Regression. John Wiley & Sons, Hoboken, NJ, USA.

Hwang, W.Y., Li, C.C., 2002. What the user log shows based on learning time distribution. J. Comput. Assist. Learn. 18, 232–233.

Jensen, K., 2012. CRISP-DM process diagram. In: Diagram.png, C.-D. P. (ed.). Wikimedia Commons. https://commons.wikimedia.org/wiki/File:CRISP-DM_Process_Diagram.png

Kapusta, J., Munk, M., Drlik, M., 2012. Cut-off time calculation for user session identification by reference length. In: 6th International Conference on Application of Information and Communication Technologies (AICT), 17–19 October 2012, pp. 1–6.

Kleftodimos, A., Evangelidis, G., 2013. An overview of web mining in education. In: Proceedings of the 17th Panhellenic Conference on Informatics. ACM, Thessaloniki, Greece.

Kurgan, L.A., Musilek, P., 2006. A survey of knowledge discovery and data mining process models. Knowl. Eng. Rev. 21, 1–24.

Liu, B., 2011. Web Data Mining. Exploring Hyperlinks, Contents, and Usage Data. Springer, New York.

Macfadyen, L.P., Dawson, S., 2010. Mining LMS data to develop an "early warning system" for educators: a proof of concept. Comput. Educ. 54, 588–599.

Marquardt, C.G., Becker, K., Ruiz, D.D., 2004. A pre-processing tool for Web usage mining in the distance education domain. In: Proceedings of the International Database Engineering and Applications Symposium, 7–9 July 2004 (IDEAS '04), pp. 78–87.

Mazza, R., Bettoni, M., Faré, M., Mazzola, L., 2014. MOCLog – Monitoring Online Courses with log data. In: 1st Moodle ResearchConference, Heraklion, Crete-Greece.

Mor, E., Minguillon, J., 2004. E-learning personalization based on itineraries and long-term navigational behavior. In: Proceedings of the 13th International World Wide Web Conference on Alternate Track Papers and Posters. ACM, New York, NY, USA.

Munk, K., 2011. Počítačová analýza dát. UKF, Nitra, p. 361.

Munk, M., Drlik, M., 2011. Influence of different session timeouts thresholds on results of sequence rule analysis in educational data mining. In: Cherifi, H., Zain, J., El-Qawasmeh, E. (Eds.), Digital Information and Communication Technology and Its Applications. Springer, Berlin Heidelberg.

Munk, M., Drlík, M., 2014. Analysis of stakeholders' behaviour depending on time in virtual learning environment. Appl. Math. Inform. Sci. 8, 773–785.

Munk, M., Drlik, M., Vrábelová, M., 2011a. Probability modelling of accesses to the course activities in the web-based educational system. In: Murgante, B., Gervasi, O., Iglesias, A., Taniar, D., Apduhan, B. (Eds.), Computational Science and Its Applications – ICCSA 2011. Springer, Berlin Heidelberg.

Munk, M., Vrábelová, M., Kapusta, J., 2011b. Probability modeling of accesses to the web parts of portal. Procedia Comput. Sci. 3, 677–683.

Munk, M., Drlík, M., Kapusta, J., Munková, D., 2013. Methodology design for data preparation in the process of discovering patterns of web users behaviour. Appl. Math. Inform. Sci. 7, 27–36.

Peña-Ayala, A., 2014a. Educational Data Mining: Applications and Trends. Springer, Cham (ZG), Switzerland. http://www.springer.com/us/book/9783319027371.

Peña-Ayala, A., 2014b. Educational data mining: a survey and a data mining-based analysis of recent works. Expert Syst. Appl. 41, 1432–1462.

Rodríguez, G., 2011. Generalized Linear Models. http://dl.acm.org/citation.cfm?id=1223659.

Romero, C., Ventura, S., 2007. Educational data mining: a survey from 1995 to 2005. Expert Syst. Appl. 33, 135–146.

Romero, C., Ventura, S., 2010. Educational data mining: a review of the state of the art. IEEE Trans. Syst. Man Cybern. Part C Appl. Rev. 40, 601–618.

Romero, C., Ventura, S., García, E., 2008. Data mining in course management systems: Moodle case study and tutorial. Comput. Educ. 51, 368–384.

Romero, C., Ventura, S., Pechenizkiy, M., Baker, R.S.J.D., 2010. Handbook of Educational Data Mining. Chapman & Hall/CRC, Boca Raton, Florida, USA. http://www.crcnetbase.com/isbn/978143980458.

Romero, C., Romero, J., Ventura, S., 2014. A survey on pre-processing educational data. In: Peña-Ayala, A. (Ed.), Educational Data Mining. Springer International Publishing, Cham (ZG), Switzerland. https://link.springer.com/chapter/10.1007/978-3-319-02738-8_2.

Sheard, J., 2011. Basics of statistical analysis of interactions data from web-based learning environments. In: Romero, C., Ventura, S., Baker, R.S.J.D. (Eds.), Handbook of Educational Data Mining. CRC Press, Chapman & Hall, Boca Raton, Florida, USA.

Spiliopoulou, M., Mobasher, B., Berendt, B., Nakagawa, M., 2003. A framework for the evaluation of session reconstruction heuristics in web-usage analysis. INFORMS J. Comput. 15, 171–190.

Talavera, L., Gaudioso, E., 2004. Mining student data to characterize similar behavior groups in unstructured collaboration spaces. In: Workshop on AI in CSCL, pp. 17–23.

Tobarra, L., Robles-Gomez, A., Ros, S., Hernandez, R., Caminero, A.C., 2014. Analyzing the students' behavior and relevant topics in virtual learning communities. Comput. Hum. Behav. 31, 659–669.

Wei, W., Jui-Feng, W., Jun-Ming, S., Shian-Shyong, T., 2004. Learning portfolio analysis and mining in SCORM compliant environment. In: 34th Annual Frontiers in Education, 20–23 October 2004 (FIE 2004), T2C-17-24 Vol. 1.

Yan, L., Bo-Qin, F., 2009. The Construction of Transactions for Web Usage Mining. In: International Conference on Computational Intelligence and Natural Computing, 6–7 June 2009 (CINC '09), pp. 121–124.

A REVIEW OF EMOTION-AWARE SYSTEMS FOR e-LEARNING IN VIRTUAL ENVIRONMENTS

11

M. Feidakis
University of Aegean, Mytilene, Greece

1 INTRODUCTION

Emotions and affective factors, such as confusion, frustration, shame and pride, are acknowledged as major influences in learning (Immordino-Yang and Damasio, 2007). However, despite major advancements in fields such as artificial intelligence, human-computer interaction, and sensorial technologies, e-learning platforms are still struggling with incorporating emotion awareness into this context (Calvo and D'Mello, 2012). The limited-to-null adoption of emotional analysis tools and affective feedback prevents both learners and teachers from reaping the benefits of emotion-aware learning management systems (LMSs).

The integration of emotion awareness can greatly advance the frontiers of educational technologies and provide an added value to enhance and improve the overall distance learning experience as well as discovering new opportunities for the cost-effective delivery of training programs.

In literature, *emotion awareness* is defined by knowing one's self (*self-awareness*) and others emotions (*empathy*) (Salovey and Mayer, 1989). However, so far *emotion awareness* has been little investigated in e-learning. In this work, *emotion awareness* is defined by the *implicit* or *explicit collection of emotion data* and the *recognition* of *emotion patterns*. In the above definition, the following should be clarified:

- *Implicit detection of emotion data*: Physiological signals or the motor-behavioral activity of emotions, that is, heartbeat, facial expressions, voice intonations, etc.
- *Explicit input of emotion data*: First-person subjective report of feelings.
- *Recognition* of *emotion patterns*: Identification of the respondent's emotions based on computer intelligence.

The necessary insights into the social and knowledge-based value of emotion-aware tools for a greater ecosystem of effective e-learning systems remain skewed. Complicating matters even further in this field is a set of interrelated conceptual, methodological, technological, and application problems. In a nutshell these are (Calvo and D'Mello, 2010; Feidakis et al., 2014a; Hascher, 2010):

Formative Assessment, Learning Data Analytics and Gamification. http://dx.doi.org/10.1016/B978-0-12-803637-2.00011-7
Copyright © 2016 Elsevier Inc. All rights reserved.

(i) *Conceptual*: Though previous research initiatives have indicated that taking emotions into account can offer more effective motivation and engagement of learners, boosting their self-confidence, the jury is still out on lowering dropout rates and raising the engagement of potentially bored cohorts of students (Hascher, 2010). Indeed, while in the context of computer-supported collaborative learning (CSCL), the dynamic of learners' affective states can be assessed to determine key moments of the collaborative situation (by detecting if the learners are in conflict or if their collaboration is efficient from a socio-affective point of view), the patterns of emotions between learners that underlie social situation outcomes have yet to be modeled.

(ii) *Methodological*: Affective learning has usually been investigated from a general educational perspective with, to the best of our knowledge (Feidakis et al., 2014a), very few studies aiming at (a) exploring the impact of emotions in specific and complex learning situations and scenarios, such as collaborative and social learning; and (b) investigating students' profiles and attitudes towards problematic academic disciplines (eg, mathematics and programming) or special education.

(iii) *Technological*: Sign posting the learner's feelings in LMSs is still in its infancy while respective technological questions remain open-ended. For instance, multimodal user interfaces and the use of sensor technologies, have yet to be integrated in seamless, nonintrusive ways into LMSs (Calvo and D'Mello, 2010).

(iv) *Application*: Latest learning technologies and experiences gained in research projects, such as mobile learning, serious games for education, massive open online courses (MOOCs), and learning analytics have not been conveniently leveraged for augmenting learner's engagement and interactive behavior in the learning process. The potential use of these outcomes for affective learning has not been explored yet.

Taking the above issues and challenges into account, this research is about understanding the underlying mechanisms of socio-affective processes as well as how best to build multimodal emotional-awareness e-learning tools that are adaptive not only to learners' cognitive performances but also to their affective states and social interactions with peers and teachers. To this end, next we provide an extensive review work of the literature in the domain following a methodology for conducting systematic reviews, offering a starting point towards the integration of emotion awareness into e-learning systems.

2 METHODOLOGICAL STUDY

The chosen methodology for this review study is an adaptation of the process for systematically reviewing literature explained in Oates (2005). In this section we present the steps and tasks that comprise our methodology, which are applied sequentially but may overlap in time or even repeat iteratively as needed (see Fig. 11.1).

FIGURE 11.1

Steps and tasks in the chosen study methodology (Oates, 2005).

2.1 SEARCH AND RETRIEVAL

The process of creating a survey about the state of the art in our research field started with a search of publications on an initial set of topics of interest that we had defined at the beginning of the search. Published papers can be searched using some databases and search engines. To this end, we selected about 100 articles from the most commonly used search portals, that is, IEEE, ACM, Scopus, Springer, Science Direct and Web of Science. We also described the studies conducted over the past 10 years in the domain, highlighting the use of emotions in education.

The terms used for the search were related to the topic being searched, starting from generic phrases to more refined and specific terminology. For instance, for the topic "Use of emotions and affective learning in VLE" we first searched "emotions in e-learning" and "affective learning," and then we narrowed our search by combining both terms with other specific terms in this research field.

The search step needed to be iteratived along with the literature review because new search topics appeared during the review of the targeted papers. Once a potentially interesting publication was found we retrieved a copy of it for analysis and selection as pointed out in the next step of the process.

2.2 ANALYSIS AND SELECTION

In this step an initial analysis was performed of each retrieved publication in order to decide whether it fitted the topics in the review or not. Those papers not matching the research topic were archived for later use if needed. Typically this analysis was done by reading the paper abstract and conclusions. If this was not enough to determine if the article was useful or not, a more in-deep read was done.

2.3 REVIEW

The next steps included a careful review of the selected papers, identifying their structure, and distinguishing the main points. During this phase we took some notes to summarize the most important contributions commonly found in the core sections, and evaluated the benefits and drawbacks of the proposed solutions.

We also found interesting information in other sections of the paper, such as the background section, where discovered new related work (whose references we iteratively analyzed and reviewed). Also, in the conclusions and further work sections we found ideas to formulate suggestions for the future research work.

The outcomes of the review phase are developed in Sections 3 and 6.

2.4 DISCUSSION AND REPORT

The discussion step involves writing a report of the state of the art about the papers reviewed. For each paper reviewed, the main contributions were described and discussed, stating their benefits and weaknesses or drawbacks if applied, and in some cases purposing some improvement ideas that helped to guide our future investigative work. The result for the discussion phase is covered in Section 7.

2.5 CONCLUSIONS AND REFINE

The aim of this final step is to conclude the accomplished work and propose a set of improvement goals for the tools and technologies discussed in the review. The result of this phase is reflected in Section 8.

---

3 AFFECTIVE LEARNING

The study of emotions entails a multifaceted complex approach involving psychological, behavioral, cognitive, social, and neurobiological aspects (Marsella and Gratch, 2015). Davou (2000) has resembled the study of emotions with a chain that consists of six interdependent rings namely neuro-bio-cognitive (brain functioning as studied in cognitive neuroscience), emotional (the study of emotions in clinical psychology), and sociocultural (current social and cultural factors that affect human behavior). In line with this approach, this section presents a review of emotion theory with respect to learning, taking into account four different aspects: neurophysiological, educational, sociopsychological, and socio-emotional. Each of these aspects is developed next and will serve as a basis for proposing new models, methods, and tools for managing emotions in e-learning.

3.1 NEUROPHYSIOLOGY

In literature, the words *emotion, affect, feeling, mood* are often treated as synonyms. However, the deep understanding and definition of emotion entails the examination of different neurobiological functions and their interplay. If we wish to define emotions, we have to bear in mind that each human's "emotional repertoire" significantly develops in his or her very early years, from 3 months after conception, when a child's verbal system does not even exist, until 5 years old (LeDoux, 1996).

Findings from neurosciences uncovered neurological paths to the root of emotions in the brain, focusing on the emotional operations of autonomous and basal neural systems (limbic system). Above all, emotions belong to the very first, strong synapses that neurons create (Afzal and Robinson, 2011). Neurology provides us with a neurobiological approach to emotions, focusing on the emotional operations of autonomous and basal neurotic systems (eg, the limbic system).

Latest research findings point to activity in different brain areas, when positive, as well as negative emotions are experienced. Positive emotion areas are located in the ventromedial prefrontal cortex, ventral tegmental area, and ventral striatum, while negative emotion areas are located in the dorsal anterior cingulate cortex, thalamus, and insula. Positive emotions are also processed in the amygdala; in fact, it seems, negative ones are also processed here to a similar extent (Sergerie et al., 2008).

Based on the above findings from neuroscience, we refine our definitions published in Feidakis et al. (2014b):

- *Emotion* is the organism's reaction to any disturbance in the perceptual environment. This disturbance is "naturally" appraised as "suspicious" at first (milliseconds), triggering somatic changes (rapid heartbeat to produce more blood, ephidrosis to cool the body, eye blinking to protect the eyes, etc.) in an attempt to prepare the organism, as quickly as possible, to face a potential threat against the organism's survival.
- This motion/activity/alertness is *felt* or sensed by the organism, which also tries at first to appraise it cognitively according to the organism's subjective experiences and, then, to control the somatic changes.
- All the effects (cognitive processes, feelings) aroused by the specific emotion (ie, fear) constitute the *affect*, (ie, anxiety) the effect of the emotion that the organism is aware of.
- *Mood* (ie, sadness) identifies the feeling left in the organism, after the cause of the emotion has ceased, and is more cognitive and less emotive.

Although emotion, affect or feeling are used interchangeably, the perception of *affective state* is more often deployed in the learning domain (Afzal and Robinson, 2011; Arroyo et al., 2011; D'Mello and Calvo, 2013; Linnenbrink-Garcia and Pekrun, 2011) to attribute both emotions (for instance excitement, confusion, anger, stress) and other less emotive, and more cognitive states (for instance inspiration, interest, boredom, fatigue). The perception of mood (eg, very bad, good, very good) is also used to assign the respondent's feelings either a positive or negative classification (Zimmermann, 2008).

3.2 EDUCATION

For almost two decades, Pekrun and his team (Pekrun, 1992; Pekrun et al., 2011) examined the impact of so-called academic emotions, which classify enjoyment, pride, hope, and relief as positive valence and anxiety, anger, shame/fault, boredom, and hopelessness as negative valence. According to their findings, positive mood fosters holistic, creative ways of thinking. Harmful effects can only be expected in situations where students are in a good mood and the learning topics are of less importance to them. In this case the positive emotion might detach them from learning (Hascher, 2010). Negative emotions, on the other hand, direct students' attention to themselves, in most cases. Necessary attention to learning and task solving is lacking, because they are trying to find ways to get rid of the bad feeling (Hascher, 2010). When negative emotions create a pessimistic perceptual attitude, they divert the learner's attention to factors irrelevant to the task, which activate intrusive thoughts that give priority to a concern for well-being rather than for learning (Boekaerts, 2010).

However, negative mood proved to enhance an analytical, detail-focused way of processing information. *Curiosity* and *puzzlement* may lead to investigate problems and even *frustration* may lead to action, despite its negative valence (Heylen et al., 2005). The state of *confusion* is considered more positive than *frustration* because students are motivated to overcome the source of their misunderstanding, whereas in *frustration* they are more likely to disengage from learning (Robison et al., 2009).

In the literature, *uncertainty* is encountered as an opportunity to learn (Forbes-Riley and Litman, 2011). Op't Eynde et al. (2006) have reported that during a mathematical problem, students experienced negative emotions such as *worry*, *frustration*, and *anger*, which helped them to reorient their efforts to solve the problems, following different paths like starting from the end and then returning to the start.

With regard to emotion transitions, D'Mello et al. have shown that, students are more likely to remain in the same affective state if no intervention is provided (2008). This tendency appears to be particularly strong for students in negative affective states.

Robison et al. have shown that when transitions to alternate affective states did occur, they followed interesting patterns (2009). For instance, *frustrated* learners were very likely to transit to *confusion* or *fear* and were particularly unlikely to enter a positive state such as *flow* or *excitement*. Students experiencing the positive state of *flow* were likely to transit to *confusion*, which is still considered positive for learning and were unlikely to move to the more negative state of *frustration*. Interestingly, *confused* learners were equally likely to transit to *flow* and *frustration*. These findings suggest that the states of *confusion* and its antecedents and consequences are worth additional study to determine which factors contribute to a positive transition to *flow* or a negative transition into *frustration*.

In general, there are no adequate empirically proven strategies to address the presence of emotions in learning, especially the negative ones (Hascher, 2010). Theoretical background has been built upon theoretical foundations of pedagogy/affect or recommendations made by pedagogical experts (D'Mello et al., 2008). And despite the evidence of the positive effects of positive mood and emotions, there are no clear rules such as: positive emotions foster learning, and negative emotions are detrimental (Hascher, 2010). As Goleman (1995) aptly highlighted, a student with a positive disposition would see an F on a math test as a sign that he or she needs to work harder, while another may see it as evidence that he or she is "stupid."

3.3 SOCIAL PSYCHOLOGY

Socio-affective learning has strong roots in social psychology, whose concept representations are both intrapersonal and interpersonal (Davou, 2000). The person's thoughts are communicated through the channel of a social representation to another mind. The human brain is able to decrypt new information according to experiences that are being stored in its cognitive database. Whether the selected place for the new data is ecological (Davou, 2000) or not, whether new cellular synapses will strengthen or atrophy, is decided in the individual's everyday life by his or her social reality in a specific time and place. The frequent recall of a concrete piece of information to satisfy different needs, to resolve various problems, confirms its validity and ensures a place for it in long-lasting memory.

In theory, emotions highly correlate with learners' individual (Boekaerts, 2010) as well as social identity (Bandura, 1977). Humans learn through observing, imitating, and speaking with others, and they learn from sources of information that they pay attention to (Davou, 2000) because of their reflection of their inner needs. The socio-cognitive model takes into account, both the subjective influences that learners bring to a learning situation and the influence of emotion.

In recent years, the pedagogy of collaborative learning (Dillenbourg, 1999; Koschman, 1996) has become an active field, based on the theories of: constructionism (Papert, 1980), situated learning (Lave and Wenger, 1991), social development (Vygotsky, 1978), and social learning (Bandura, 1977). Dillenbourg (1999) described collaborative learning as "a situation in which two or more people learn or attempt to learn something together." There has been a variety of commonly used collaborative learning structures, for example, brainstorming, case studies, dyadic essays, jigsaw, problem solving, etc. Within this context, CSCL has been established as a fundamental pedagogical approach in e-learning, underpinned by the rapid advancements attained in computer technology and network telecommunications.

However, just because an environment makes it technologically possible, it does not mean that social interaction will take place. A main pitfall in CSCL environments is "the tendency to restrict social interaction to educational interventions aimed at cognitive processes, while social (psychological) interventions aimed at socio-emotional processes are ignored, neglected or forgotten" (Kreijns et al., 2003). Emotions strongly influence human behavior in social situations and must be seriously considered when forming collaborations. Just placing students together does not mean that they will collaborate. "Students need to trust each other, feel a sense of warmth and belonging and feel close to each other before they engage wilfully in collaboration and recognize the collaboration as a valuable experience" (Rourke, 2000, p. 1). Xolocotzin-Eligio (2010) has provided strong evidence that in collaborative learning, mental awareness (being aware of another's knowledge and ideas) cannot be considered irrespective of emotion awareness (being aware of another's affective state).

Students are known to effectively engage and learn in their favorite social networks, where they exchange information and experiences with peers. These experiences are predominantly emotionally colored. Social sharing of emotions occurs frequently in platforms such as Twitter and Facebook. People are compelled to share emotions shortly after they experience them, and find the sharing relieving (Kivran-Swaine and Naaman, 2011).

3.4 SOCIAL-EMOTIONAL LEARNING

Over the last three decades, there have been hundreds of school-based programs that have been developed to assist people in gaining control of their emotions (eg, *PATHs*,[1] *Resolving Conflict Creatively*,[2] *Self Science*,[3] *6Seconds*[4]). These programs are better classified under the more general label *Social and*

---

[1] http://www.prevention.psu.edu/projects/paths.html
[2] http://www.ncrel.org/sdrs/areas/issues/envrnmnt/drugfree/sa2lk16.htm
[3] http://www.selfscience.net/
[4] http://www.6seconds.org/

Emotional Learning (SEL).[5] Their main objective is to establish effective SEL as an essential part of education from preschool through to high school.

In the USA, *Collaborative for Academic, Social, and Emotional Learning (CASEL)*[6] programs have been reported to improve students' social-emotional skills, attitudes towards themselves and others, positive social behavior, as well as students' academic achievement. They reduce conduct problems and emotional distress. A similar approach has been adopted in the United Kingdom with the establishment of the *Social and Emotional Aspects of Learning (SEAL)*[7] program conducted by the Department of Education and Skills. The *National Framework of Values*[8] for Australian Schools has also initiated an interest in social and emotional well-being and learning in Australia.

From this point of view, *emotion learning* refers to the flourishing of social and emotional competencies such as *emotional awareness*, *empathy*, *self-efficiency*, and *self-motivation* that are crucial components of *emotion intelligence* (EQ). Goleman has presented convincing evidence that the emotional intelligence quotient (EQ) is just as important in academic success as cognitive intelligence that is measured by IQ or SAT scores (1995). The early emotional intelligence theory was originally developed during the 1970s and 1980s through the work and writings of psychologists Howard Gardner, Peter Salovey, and John Mayer.

In his visionary book *Frames of mind* (1983), Gardner acknowledges the "personal" forms of human intelligence: the *interpersonal* is concerned with the capacity to understand the intentions, motivations and desires of other people, while the *intrapersonal* entails the capacity to understand and to appreciate one's feelings, fears and motivations.

Salovey and Mayer (1989) combined the work of several researchers to define measures of effective use of emotion. They used five attitudes to determine emotional intelligence:

1. *Self-awareness* (knowing one's emotions)
2. *Managing emotions* (handling feelings)
3. *Self-motivation*
4. *Empathy* (recognizing emotions of others)
5. *Handling relationships* (the art of relationships).

4 AFFECTIVE LEARNING TOOLS TO COLLECT EMOTIONAL INFORMATION

In face-to-face situations, students communicate and exchange information, enriched with emotional cues like facial expressions, voice intonations, gestures, body positions, etc., in an attempt to transmit what the respondents really want (need, desire, love, etc.) or do not (afraid, dislike, hate, detest, etc.). These emotional signals are communicated, explicitly (first-person, subjective expression) or implicitly (the person is rarely aware of it), in an "automatic" way. In contrast, the exchange of emotion data in online learning environments is quite limited.

---

[5]http://danielgoleman.info/topics/social-emotional-learning/
[6]http://casel.org
[7]http://www.education.gov.uk/publications/standard/publicationDetail/Page1/DFE-RR049
[8]http://www.valueseducation.edu.au/values/val_national_framework_for_values_education,8757.html

Affective elements in the analysis of the interaction with the student, has become an increasingly prominent theme in recent years (Afzal and Robinson, 2011; Arroyo et al., 2011; Bevacqua et al., 2012; Calvo, 2009; D'Mello et al., 2011). Developers and designers are struggling to empower learning environments with usable interfaces, in an attempt to trace student emotions in an unobtrusive and non-invasive way, in parallel with their tasks, without extra cost or equipment and expertise, and without language barriers (Wong, 2006; Zimmermann, 2008).

This new research area is propelled by the advancements attained in *Affective Computing* (Picard, 1997). Picard and her team in MIT (*Massachusetts Institute* of *Technology*, Cambridge, MA, USA) have produced several systems and digital devices that recognize and express affect with high accuracy (MIT Media Lab: Affective Computing Group[9]). Similarly, the National Centre of Competence in Research "Affective Sciences – Emotions in Individual Behaviour and Social Processes" (NCCR Affective Sciences) exhibits significant studies on emotions and their effects on human behavior and society[10] (Chanel et al., 2013; Molinari et al., 2013).

Another relevant effort on affective computing for general purposes is the SIENTO project,[11] where they use a variety of means to detect emotions. However, still particularly scarce is the application of affective computing to e-learning and learning situations; in addition there is a the lack of ecological validity of the input channels used and effective emotion-awareness discourse in order to bring emotion awareness to where people's emotions happen, which is what really matters to them (Picard, 2010).

The embodiment of emotion awareness in learning environments is by definition a difficult issue that presupposes the confrontation of complex questions; *what* do we want to evaluate, *how* can we do it, *when* do we and *why* should we get involved in such a *sensitive* process (Feidakis et al., 2014b)? There have been remarkable attempts to detect and recognize students' emotional states with high accuracy that provide respective feedback aiming at a positive impact, not only on students' cognitive performance, but also on their affective state (Arroyo et al., 2011; D'Mello et al., 2011; Pekrun et al., 2011; Robison et al., 2009). All these studies are based on conceptual models and theories of *basic* and *secondary* emotions (Damasio, 1994; Ekman and Friesen, 1978; Ortony et al., 1988; Parrott, 2001), emotion *dimensions* (Hascher, 2010; Plutchik, 2001; Russell, 1980) or more *eclectic* approaches (Csikszentmihalyi, 1990; Kort et al., 2001; Pekrun, 1992), employing computer intelligence to model students' emotional behavior.

In most research studies, the explicit collection of the respondent's affective state is applied by conducting psychological first-person subjective self-reports in the form of verbal or pictorial scales, questionnaires, interviews, conductive chat, and logbooks, whenever we need to collect the respondents' subjective feelings, expressed either in their own words or by selecting pictorical images. Explicit emotion collection can take place before the task (register initial respondent's mood and disposition before accomplishing a specific learning task), in parallel with the task, or after the task (retrospective evaluation of the respondent's affective state after a quiz or test). The respondent's emotion or affective state is implicitly captured either by detecting physiological signals (electromyogram, EMG; electrodermal activity, EDA; electrocardiogram, EKG, ECG; blood volume pulse, BVP, etc.) (Arroyo et al., 2011; Picard, 2010), or by observing motor-behavioral activity (facial expressions, voice

---

[9]http://affect.media.mit.edu/
[10]http://www.affective-sciences.org/
[11]http://sydney.edu.au/engineering/latte/projects/siento.shtml

intonation, mouse movements, log files, sentiment analysis, etc.) (Arroyo et al., 2011; D'Mello and Calvo, 2013). The detected or observed signals are further analyzed in order to mine patterns of emotional behavior. Next, these input channels are further studied.

4.1 PSYCHOLOGICAL (SELF-REPORTING) TOOLS

Psychological tools originate from clinical psychology and employ verbal and nonverbal descriptions of emotions. They are inexpensive ways to measure the subjective experience of emotions in an unobtrusive and noninvasive way. This method measures user's subjective feelings, although users are often reluctant to disclose their inner feelings to researchers in order to avoid embarrassment (Wong, 2006). They cannot be easily used in parallel with the user task, only in very specific cases where mannequins and imaginaries are used for quick and short answers. Further classification includes:

- *Verbal self-reporting*: Subjects report on their emotions with the use of questionnaires with predefined, open-ended questions, verbal rating scales or verbal protocols. Also interviews, conductive chat and logbooks (like an emotion diary) are used, so that subjects could indicate their affective state in their own words. They can be assembled to represent any set of emotions or mixed emotions (Desmet, 2005). However, they can meet with language and cultural barriers (Wong, 2006).

Examples are (a) The Academic Emotions Questionnaire (AEQ) (Pekrun et al., 2011), (b) The Semantic Differential Scale (Osgood et al., 1975), (c) The Affect Grid (Russell et al., 1989), and (d) the Geneva emotion wheel (Scherer, 2005).

- *Nonverbal self-reporting*: This includes unobtrusive, language-independent tools that can be used in different cultures. These tools are claimed to be less subjective than verbal self-report instruments (Caballé et al., 2014), because they are not limited by student's vocabulary. On the other hand the range of emotions that they can assess is limited.

Examples are (a) Self-Assessment Manikin, SAM (Lang, 1980), and (b) PrEmo (Desmet, 2005).

4.2 BIO-PHYSIOLOGICAL TOOLS

Physiological sensors provide an objective measure of physiological signals. In comparison with other sources of emotional information (facial expressions, gestures, and speech), physiological signals offer substantial advantages; they are mostly involuntary and, as such, are quite insensitive to deception, they can be used to measure the affective states continuously, they can be observed as early as 200 ms after emotional stimuli in the case of neurophysiological signals and, usually, they are nondisruptive to task performance. A potential pitfall is that they are often obtrusive or even invasive, troubling user's experience with the interface. They also necessitate specialized and frequently expensive equipment and technical expertise to use the equipment (Wong, 2006). However, these drawbacks are alleviated with the development of new light physiological sensors, which are more and more user friendly (Liao et al., 2012).

Most of these measures based on recordings of electrical signals produced by brain, heart, muscles, and skin (http://www.mindmedia.nl) (see Fig. 11.2):

- EMG that measures muscle activity
- Electroencephalography that measures brain activity

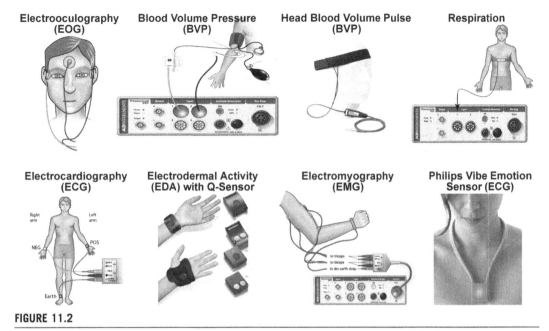

FIGURE 11.2

Bio-physiological signals (Respiration, Electrocardiography (ECG), Electromyography (EMG), Blood Volume Pressure (BVP), 2015; Electrooculography (EOG), 2015; Q Curve EDA sensor, 2015; Head Blood Volume Pulse Sensor, 2015; Vibe Emotion sensor, 2015).

- EDA or skin conductance that measures the hydration in the epidermis and dermis of the skin. It is typically recorded from the surface of the hand or wrists
- EKG or ECG that measures heart activity (heart rate, inter-beat-interval, heart rate variability)
- Electrooculogram measuring eye pupil's size and movement
- BVP measures blood pressure
- Respiration, where rate of respiration and depth of breath are the most common measures.

Emotion detection from physiological signals has been employed in several contexts, including in ecological settings like the adaptation of game difficulty to the player's emotions (Chanel et al., 2012). It has also been combined with other sources like facial expressions (Koelstra and Patras, 2013).

4.3 MOTOR-BEHAVIORAL TOOLS

Motor-behavior expression is the most common technique humans employ to evaluate each other's affective state in everyday life (Zimmermann, 2008). These tools measure behavioral expressions and physical changes in the body that communicate one's emotional experience. Their major asset is that they provide an opportunity to evaluate the subject's affective state by using traditional devices like a PC camera or a microphone, or the traditional mouse and keyboard, though special software is needed (Zimmermann, 2008). They can pick up emotional cues that cannot be measured by self-reporting or physiological signals.

However, they require experience and objectivity on the part of the observer. These methods are tested almost exclusively on "produced" affect expressions. Recognition accuracy would drop significantly in real-life situations (Wong, 2006), although there have been outstandingly successful results using complex user interfaces (Hoque et al., 2013):

- *Facial expressions*: For example, the Facial Action Coding System (Ekman and Friesen, 1978) analyzes 44 face muscles that are linked to 6 basic emotions: anger, disgust, fear, joy, sadness, and surprise.
- *Voice modulation/intonation*: Sound features like pitch, tempo-rhythm, volume, modulation, intonation, and vibration are used to differentiate affective states.
- *Hand tracking*: Body posture that can be analyzed through observation with the help of video-recording or by using special devices like the Body Posture Measurement System, developed by Tekscan (see Fig. 11.3).
- *Mouse-keyboard movements*: By recording data (mouse movements, buttons pressed, idle time, etc.) from log files or by using special devices like pressure-force-sensitive mouse and keyboard.
- *Corrugator's activity*: In combination with the activity of the zygomaticus muscle this can give us information about subject's valence.
- *Sentiment analysis/opinion mining*: This constitutes a special category of behavioral activity. Text is an important modality for sensing affect, as the bulk of computer-user interfaces remain textually based (Calvo and D'Mello, 2012). In sentiment analysis opinions, with regards to an entity, are classified on a scale similar to the valence used in emotion models (Feldman, 2013). This new trend in emotional research involves the lexical analysis of the text in order to identify words that are predictive of the affective states of the writers (Calvo and D'Mello, 2012). Text is classified by its overall sentiment, for example, determining whether a review is positive or negative.

Posture analysis seat

IBM Blue Eyes
video camera

FIGURE 11.3

Posture analysis seat and IBM BlueEyes video camera (Zheng and Morrell, 2013; IBM BlueEyes video camera, 2015).

5 AFFECTIVE FEEDBACK STRATEGIES

Once the learner's emotional state is detected or recognized, the obvious next step is what to do with this valuable information. The user needs to see some reaction from the system or adaptation to his or her feelings. For example, "if the learner is frustrated, the tutor would need to generate hints to advance the learner in constructing knowledge, and make supportive empathetic comments to enhance motivation. If the learner is bored, the tutor would need to present more engaging or challenging problems for the learner to work on" (D'Mello and Calvo, 2013).

Feedback is varied according to type (explanation, hints, worked examples) and timing (immediately following an answer, after some elapsed time) (Shute, 2008). Common tools include dialogue moves (hints, prompts, assertions, and summaries), immersive simulations or serious games, facial expressions and speech modulations, images, imagery, cartoon avatars, caricatures or short video-audio clips (D'Mello and Graesser, 2012). Affective feedback techniques also incorporate the knowledge of student group characteristics (eg, profile of cognitive skills, gender) to guide interference (Woolf et al., 2007). A relevant study (Robison et al., 2009) reports on the results of two studies that were conducted with students interacting with affect-informed virtual agents, evaluating the agents' response to both positive and negative affective states. The agents could respond to student affect with either parallel, reactive empathetic, or task-based feedback.

In some research studies, affect-adaptive computer tutors have been evaluated within a "Wizard of Oz" scenario, where a human "wizard" performs system tasks such as speech recognition, natural language understanding, and affect detection (Forbes-Riley and Litman, 2011). Machine learning optimization algorithms are applied in searching for policies for individual students, with the goal of achieving high learning and positive attitudes towards the subject. For instance, in AutoTutor (D'Mello and Graesser, 2012), the authors used a variety of heuristic policies to respond to student's emotion. Instructional feedback is varied according to type (explanation, hints, or worked examples) and timing (immediately following an answer or after some elapsed time) (see Fig. 11.4). The system adaptively manages the tutorial dialogue by providing feedback on the learner's answers (eg, "good job," "not quite"). The tutor also synthesizes affect via the verbal content of its responses and the facial expressions and speech of an embodied pedagogical agent.

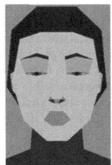

FIGURE 11.4

Affect synthesis by Virtual Agents (Feidakis et al., 2013).

Affective feedback techniques also incorporate knowledge of student group characteristics (eg, profile of cognitive skills, gender) to guide interference. In this work (Woolf et al., 2007), the authors developed an agent tutor that personalized the choice of hint type for individual students based on their cognitive profile, gender, spatial ability, and math fact retrieval speed. They also used heuristic policies to respond to student's emotion and they measured how feedback variables interact to promote learning in context (characteristics of the learner, aspects of the task).

In this study (Robison et al., 2009) the authors evaluated the agents' response to both positive and negative affective states. In both studies, agents' responses to negative emotions were rated significantly worse than agents' responses to positive emotions. They suggested that positive emotions (flow, delight, boredom) appear to be particularly susceptible to the quality of feedback given. In contrast, for particularly negative emotions such as frustration, the risk of inappropriate delivery is not large enough to warrant extreme caution when providing responses. They highlight the uncertainty with regard to delivering useful affective feedback.

Unfortunately, there are few studies that exploit computer-mediated affective feedback strategies and their impact on users' task performance or affective state. Furthermore, the number of tools and strategies for the design of expressive avatars in response to a learner's detected affective state is quite limited.

5.1 LEARNING TECHNOLOGIES APPLIED FOR AFFECTIVE LEARNING

5.1.1 Learning analytics

Learning analytics techniques (Romero and Ventura, 2013) provide a clear way of analyzing data and discovering the affective knowledge hidden in large volumes of well-structured text. Sentiment analysis and opinion mining (Feldman, 2013) are among the most relevant educational data mining and learning analytics techniques and can greatly improve the abilities of all the implicated actors in the learning process to increase their knowledge about others, in terms of the skills of the individuals and of the group as a whole in solving problems, individual and group effectiveness, social support and help, etc.

Within the context of e-learning, a very limited number of proposals that have been filed in scientific literature and/or released as actual platforms have tried to take advantage of functionalities based on sentiment analysis. Relevant examples often belong to the wider category of adaptive frameworks and include SentBuk (Forbes-Riley and Litman, 2011), Mi-iLMS (Martín et al., 2012), and the widely used Moodle (moodle.org), whereas other, more theoretical works like those of Kechaou et al. (2011), Mazlan et al. (2012), and Song et al. (2007) try to address the problem of extracting the learners' sentiment from related social networks. Nevertheless, the scope and pervasiveness of sentiment analysis in the aforementioned proposals is somewhat limited, either because it is restricted to comments and questionnaires within a specific learning platform, or because it lacks a fully fledged, cohesive integration between the results obtained from various social media and the affective profiles of the users of the learning platforms.

Moreover, the constant and updated presentation of this knowledge by recent developments in software for visualization techniques (Go et al., 2009) (see Figs. 11.5 and 11.6) can help show the results in a way that is easier to interpret and provides a clear picture of what is happening in the online classroom, which positively impacts on participant's motivation, emotional state and problem-solving abilities (Caballe et al., 2012).

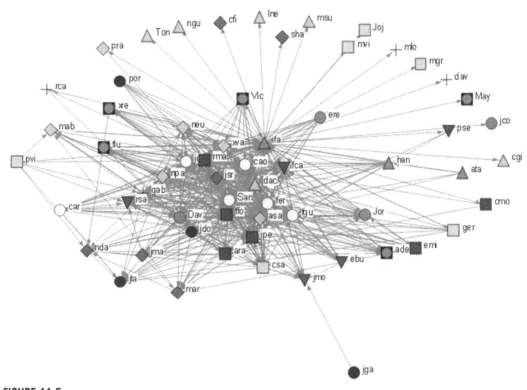

FIGURE 11.5

Sociogram representing indirect relationships at classroom-group level.

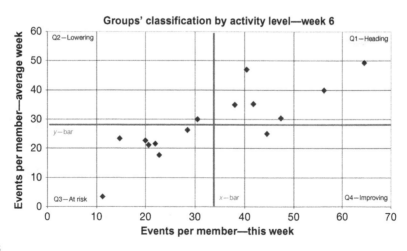

FIGURE 11.6

Classification of learners according to their activity level.

5.1.2 Serious games for education and storytelling

Serious games for education or educational games are a powerful way of developing SEL in young people. Playing games is where we work through emotions, learn to share, negotiate joining groups or ongoing play, experience the perspectives of others, learn to cope with our own emotions, and explore our self-perceptions (Caballé et al., 2011). Children with learning disabilities are often struggling not just with their disability, but also with labeling and social stigma, and often view themselves as less competent across multiple domains, such as intelligence, academic skills, behavior and social acceptance (Piaget, 1962).

In addition, previous research has claimed that a game's story or storytelling can motivate students to use an educational game (Bopp, 2007; Smith and Nagle, 1995). Within the field of game design, narration is beneficial to a learning environment (Arnab et al., 2014) and provides opportunities for reflection, evaluation, illustration, exemplification, and inquiry (Kelleher et al., 2007). A systematic literature review on computer games and serious games in regard to the potential positive impacts of gaming on users aged 14 years or above, especially with respect to learning, skill enhancement and engagement was conducted by a research group (Gee, 2009). The most frequently occurring outcomes and impacts were knowledge acquisition/content understanding and affective and motivational outcomes (Connolly et al., 2012).

5.1.3 Collaborative complex learning resource

Collaborative and social learning can be greatly enhanced by the latest educational technologies, such as Collaborative Complex Learning Resource (CC-LR) (Caballé et al., 2014) (see Fig.11.7), which virtualizes the knowledge elicited during the live collaborative sessions in order to alleviate the

FIGURE 11.7

A CC-LR showing a virtualized live discussion performed in a Web forum converted into an animated and interactive storyboard enriched with cognitive and emotional assessment.

isolation of online learners whilst providing them with social identity, empowerment and effective interactivity. The CC-LR approach supports complex types of interactions, such as emotional and cognitive, provides relevant knowledge from all possible sources, increases the interaction behavior, and eventually improves the quantitative and qualitative learning analytics processes and outcomes. As a result, online learners are provided with challenging and attractive resources that engage and promote self-motivation to collaborate during the learning process.

5.1.4 Massive open online courses

Similarly, the recently established MOOCs (Pappano, 2012), a mass educational and technology perspective to support large distributed organizations as part of their e-learning strategies, can support academic and corporate education with the aim of greatly increasing the amount of collaboration and networking interaction data collected from large audiences. MOOCs are defined as open, free, participatory, and distributed courses, representing a new generation of online education, easily and widely accessible on the Internet and involving a large or very large number of students (Siemens, 2013).

5.1.5 Mobile learning

Finally, mobile learning is seen by researchers and pedagogues as a new opportunity for education, since it provides more chances for learners to personalize their collaborative learning process, enhance their social interactions, learn more effectively and more autonomously, and collaborate with peers and teachers at any time and from anywhere, inside and outside the formal collaborative learning context (Sharples, 2005). Indeed, both the capabilities of mobile devices and their wide context of use contribute to their propensity to foster collaboration. Mobile devices can easily communicate with other devices of the same or similar type, enabling learners to share data, files and messages. They can also be connected from anywhere and at any time to a shared data network, further enhancing the possibilities for communication. These devices are also typically used in a group setting, and so interactions and collaboration will tend to take place not just through the devices, but also at and around them (Caballé et al., 2010).

The application of the above learning technologies and approaches (mobile learning, MOOCs, CC-LR, and learning analytics) to enhance affective e-assessment and feedback functionalities through increasing learners' interactive behavior, to the best of our knowledge, has not yet been explored. In addition, a technical challenge is posed by the costly adaptation of functionalities and contents to the particular features and limitations of mobile devices.

6 DISCUSSION

Based on the review work reported in the previous sections, we turn now to discuss how to potentially enhance and improve the application of emotion awareness to e-learning. Then, we propose a set of issues and open questions to be shared with the research community. We organize this section in a list of discussion topics.

6.1 MODELS AND METHODS FOR AFFECTIVE LEARNING

Innovative models and methods for affective learning should not only explore the impact of personal emotions in collaborative and social learning but also investigate how group emotions develop and how that impacts learning outcomes. New approaches and tools should provide both emotion awareness at an individual/group level and feedback aimed at enhancing students' motivation, engagement, self-regulation and learning outcomes, as well as their ability to cope with issues regarding social interaction and personality (eg, conflict and mutual understanding), which so far have been difficult to address. To this end, emotion awareness will be the base for building an efficient emotion management model which, together with an effective time-management approach, will lead to enhanced learning performance, self-motivation, self-regulation, cognitive engagement, empathy and effective handling of relationships.

6.2 AFFECTIVE LEARNING TOOLS TO COLLECT EMOTIONAL INFORMATION

The next generation of tools in the field will collect emotions from a variety of input channels and devices that are known to be relevant for emotion assessment, taking advantage of the latest technological advances and integration methods, including the combination of multimodal adaptive user interfaces and sensors, and from a variety of disciplines, so as to take an holistic approach to emotion recognition. Emotion detection and recognition should be applied transparently for the user, deploying both standard and new innovative devices without interrupting the learning process or disturbing the learner. Finally, the combination of several nonintrusive input channels will allow the collection of more objective and reliable emotion data than was possible using the previous methods.

6.3 AFFECTIVE FEEDBACK STRATEGIES

Innovative affective feedback strategies and tools should provide a positive impact on both the learner's own cognitive performance and emotional regulation in an integrated way, based on "emotion awareness," "time management," and the learner's "cognitive-emotional profile." Monitoring, regulation, and assessment of students' learning process will be greatly enhanced by a well-designed and focused feedback approach that takes emotional-affective aspects into account.

6.4 LEARNING TECHNOLOGIES APPLIED FOR AFFECTIVE LEARNING

The latest learning technologies are to enhance affective e-assessment and feedback functionalities through increasing learners' interactive behavior. In particular, system's input/output functionalities and representations (ie, databases, performance, and interfaces), as well as other integrated technologies should be adapted to mobile devices (smartphones, tablets, glasses, etc.). The existing applications of MOOC, CC-LR, and serious games are to be integrated into current affective learning tools and applications in a plug-and-play fashion in order to augment learners' engagement and participative behavior during the learning process, with the ultimate aim of providing more emotional data that enhance the reliability of the affective responses. Indeed, the simple and basic application of learning analytics will increase the effectiveness of these technologies to support and improve the whole chain of e-learning stakeholders. The combination of these technologies for affective learning has not yet been explored.

7 FINDINGS AND NEXT GOALS

In this last step of our methodology, we summarize and extract from the above discussion the main findings, which in turn set the goals that need to be achieved in order to improve the adoption of affective learning in VLEs. These goals will guide the next iteration of this review study (see Fig. 11.1):

- New forms of reporting will offer a consistent way of collecting the respondents' affective state in e-learning environments
- Advanced multimodal interfaces and nonintrusive sensor technologies for emotion-awareness will measure learners' affective state more objectively, thus providing a more effective cognitive response
- The use of artificial intelligence techniques (learning analytics) to analyze students' emotions and opinions from large amounts of text will extract and predict learners' affective states
- New approaches for making emotion awareness explicit both at individual and group level will increase students' motivation and engagement in learning
- New methods and tools of emotion awareness will improve students' self-regulation and learning outcomes
- Innovative visualization methods for reporting learners' emotional states will affect the way a teacher provides affective feedback
- New forms of affective feedback will enhance students' cognitive performances and emotion regulation in e-learning environments
- Increasing the ability of learners to manage emotions better and more effectively will positively influence their ability to manage the time allocated to the learning practice more productively, and, consequently, their learning performance, in terms of behavioral and cognitive engagement, self-regulation and achievement
- The use of interoperability principles and open standards to integrate multimodal emotion-awareness learning tools will speed up their adoption in smart learning environments and foster open education
- Introducing emotional education and awareness to students by unfolding the secrets of emotions and the motional brain will open the way to a healthier emotional life
- New affective e-learning practices and strategies will advance the pedagogy of emotions, especially in the sensitive field of special education.

In order to overcome the above problems and limitations, innovative emotional intelligent learning platforms are to be developed that will take into account the availability of resources in a real education context (ie, standard keyboard, mouse, monitor, web-camera found in the majority of classrooms and homes or students' PCs, mobiles, etc.) while combining this approach with multimodal advanced user interfaces and sensor technologies for emotion detection in an affordable and nonintrusive way. In addition, further implicit mechanisms, such as sentiment analysis and text mining, and explicit mechanisms, such as self-reporting, will complete the full picture for achieving the challenge to identify learners' affective state in an objective and effective way. Fig. 11.8 summarizes the different channels and mechanisms we will use for emotion detection.

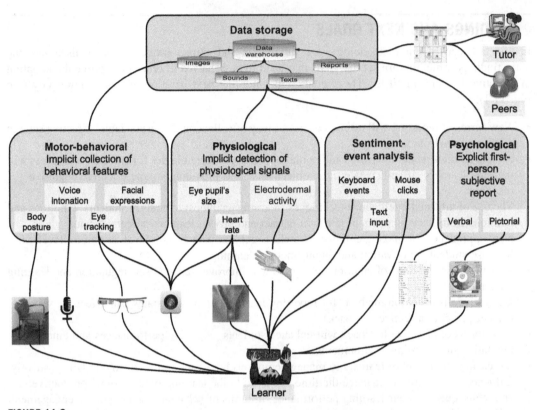

FIGURE 11.8

Channels and mechanisms for emotion detection. Emotion visualization is included (upper-right area) for tutors and peers in the form of emotional cartography.

Finally, once the learner's affective state is collected or recognized, what is the system's response to this emotion sharing? Is it possible to intervene and correct a negative emotion that blocks learning or reduces task performance? To answer these relevant questions, we will develop and evaluate affective e-assessment and feedback strategies aiming at emotion regulation and cognitive performance. This mediation will derive from both human and machine. The former will require effective visualizations of individual and group emotions so that instructors, tutors or peers make appropriate decisions on the affective feedback type they receive. The latter involves artificial intelligence algorithms, capable of supporting students emotionally.

To sum up, new affective, social and e-assessment strategies for personalizing and adapting the learning process to the learner's needs, including interindividual differences between learners, will be developed, resulting in innovative models for emotion detection and recognition, affective representation and emotional-affective e-assessment (see Fig. 11.9).

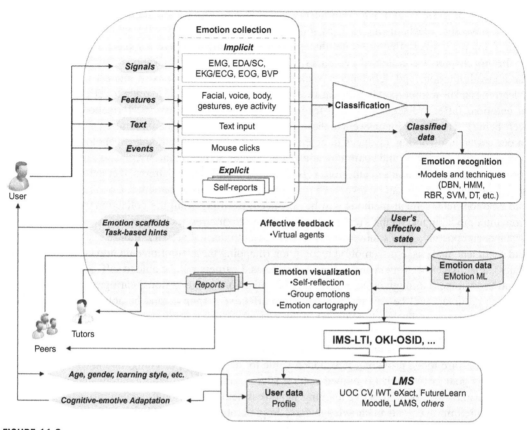

FIGURE 11.9

Conceptual model diagram: emotion collection mechanisms and affective response feedback representations are depicted along with the background models and techniques for emotion recognition and to produce the appropriate affective strategies response.

8 CONCLUSIONS AND FUTURE WORK

Despite the advancements of affective computing, research that addresses the presence of emotions and affective states is still lacking, especially in CSCL activities within LMS. One main reason is that understanding of the role of emotion/affect in learning is in its infancy, and we are far from being able to construct adequate empirically proven strategies to respond affectively to detected individual or group emotions. Although numerous studies are struggling to reliably collect information about students' emotions, the empirical evidence resulting from school-based research about the role of emotions in learning is still limited. In addition, the aforementioned systems often employ expensive sensors and complex computer intelligence for detecting behavioral activity and physiological signals requiring special expertise or extra resources, while they introduce obtrusiveness and invasiveness to the learning process. To avoid these problems, emotion detection usually depends on single, weak and highly subjective mechanisms, such as self-reporting, which becomes the main point of failure in identifying the correct affective state, thus providing a wrong affective response.

In this chapter, we collected evidences to respond to important questions that have arisen from the above limitations and deficiencies, such as "What are the emotions of interest in the context of e-learning and how important is emotion awareness?" and "Is it feasible to mine for effective sequences of emotions (affective sequences) that lead to both increased cognitive performance and emotional well-being?" The search for answers to these questions will drive further exploration and developments in our research, involving advances in neuroscience, pedagogy, educational psychology, sensor technologies and information and communication technologies. In particular, we plan to capture and model the exchanges and dynamics of emotions between learners, revealing patterns of emotions that underlie social situations, which can be leveraged to improve the learning experience. Cognitive performance and emotion management methods will be enhanced, resulting from the collection of emotions data from multimodal input channels (eg, psychological questionnaires, facial expressions, voice tone, body gestures and postures, eye's movement, heart rate, electrodermal activity, mouse events, text mining and sentiment analysis, etc.), emotion recognition (mapping these emotion data into targeted affective states), affective e-assessment and feedback strategies. Learners will be able to self- and peer-evaluate emotion awareness through effective emotion visualizations and emotional cartographies. Tutors and learning designers will benefit from insights into affective responses and be able to monitor in new ways the saliency of feedback achieved by human tutors using an innovative emotional-awareness dashboard.

The ultimate goal of our research is to expand the frontiers of educational technologies on emotional-aware tools, providing new added value to the learning, teaching, and assessment experience. This goal is twofold: (a) embed nonintrusive, module-based emotional-awareness tools into LMSs that allow for socio-affective learning and assessment of individuals and groups, and (b) validate and measure improvements in knowledge gain, dropout rate, learning analytics capacity, and affective profiling as measured by changes in socio-cognitive performance, motivation, collaborative and social interactions, in addition to managing the cost-effectiveness of the platform and the rate of adoption of these technologies in modernization of education and training.

ACKNOWLEDGMENTS

This research was funded by the Spanish Government through the project "ICT-FLAG" Enhancing ICT education through Formative assessment, Learning Analytics and Gamification (TIN2013-45303-P).

REFERENCES

Afzal, S., Robinson, P., 2011. Designing for automatic affect inference in learning environments. Educ. Technol. Soc. 14 (4), 21–34.
Arnab, S., Lim, T., Carvalho, M.B., Bellotti, F., de Freitas, S., Louchart, S., Suttie, N., Berta, R., De Gloria, A., 2014. Mapping learning and game mechanics for serious games analysis. Br. J. Educ. Technol. 46, 391–411.

Arroyo, I., du Boulay, B., Eligio, U.X., Luckin, R., Porayska-Pomsta, K., 2011. In the Mood for Learning: Methodology (D.O. Informatics, Trans.). In: Cognitive Science Research Papers. University of Sussex, Brighton.

Bandura, A., 1977. Social Learning Theory. General Learning Press, New York.

Bevacqua, E., Eyben, F., Heylen, D., ter Maat, M., Pammi, S., Pelachaud, C., Wöllmer, M., 2012. Interacting with emotional virtual agents. In: Intelligent Technologies for Interactive Entertainment. Springer, Berlin, Heidelberg, pp. 243–245.

Boekaerts, M., 2010. The crucial role of motivation and emotion in classroom learning. In: The Nature of Learning: Using Research to Inspire Practice. OECD Publishing, Paris. http://dx.doi.org/10.1787/9789264086487-6-en.

Bopp, M., 2007. Storytelling as a motivational tool in digital learning games. In: Didactics of Microlearning. Concepts, Discourses and Examples, pp. 250–266.

Caballé, S., Xhafa, F., Barolli, L., 2010. Using mobile devices to support online collaborative learning. Mob. Inf. Syst. 6 (1), 27–47.

Caballé, S., Daradoumis, T., Xhafa, X., Juan, A., 2011. Providing effective feedback, monitoring and evaluation to on-line collaborative learning discussions. Comput. Hum. Behav. 27 (4), 1372–1381.

Caballe, S., Demetriadis, S., Xhafa, F., 2012. Advanced knowledge-intensive approaches in support for social networks and learning. Int. J. Knowl. Learn. 8 (3/4), 185–187.

Caballé, S., Mora, N., Feidakis, M., Gañán, D., Conesa, J., Daradoumis, T., Prieto, J., 2014. CC-LR: providing interactive, challenging and attractive collaborative complex learning resources. J. Comput. Assist. Learn. 30 (1), 51–67.

Calvo, R., 2009. Incorporating affect into educational design patterns and technologies. In: Proceedings of the 9th IEEE International Conference on Advanced Learning Technologies, July 14–18, Riga, Latvia.

Calvo, R.A., D'Mello, S.K., 2010. Affect detection: an interdisciplinary review of models, methods, and their applications. IEEE Trans. Affect. Comput. 1 (1), 18–37.

Calvo, R., D'Mello, S., 2012. Frontiers of affect-aware learning technologies. IEEE Intell. Syst. 27 (6), 86–89.

Collaborative for Academic, Social, and Emotional Learning (CASEL) Project. Available in: http://casel.org.

Chanel, G., Kalogianni, K., Pun, T., Betrancourt, M., 2012. GamEMO: how physiological signals show your emotions and enhance your game experience. In: 14th ACM International Conference on Multimodal Interaction.

Chanel, G., Molinari, G., Cereghetti, D., Bétrancourt, M., Pun, T., 2013. Assessment of computer-supported collaborative processes using interpersonal physiological and eye-movement coupling. In: Conference on Affective Computing and Intelligent Interaction, Geneva, Switzerland.

Connolly, T.M., Boyle, E.A., MacArthur, E., Hainey, T., Boyle, J.M., 2012. A systematic literature review of empirical evidence on computer games and serious games. Comput. Educ. 59 (2), 661–686.

Csikszentmihalyi, M., 1990. Flow: The Psychology of Optimal Experience. Harper and Row, New York.

D'Mello, S., Calvo, R.A., 2013. Beyond the basic emotions: what should affective computing compute? In: CHI'13 Extended Abstracts on Human Factors in Computing Systems. ACM, New York, pp. 2287–2294.

D'Mello, S.K., Graesser, A.C., 2012. AutoTutor and affective AutoTutor: learning by talking with cognitively and emotionally intelligent computers that talk back. ACM Trans. Interact. Intell. Syst. 2 (4). 23:2–23:39.

D'Mello, S., Jackson, T., Craig, S., Morgan, B., Chipman, P., White, H., Person, N., Kort, B., el Kaliouby, R., Picard, R.W., Graesser, A., 2008. AutoTutor detects and responds to learners affective and cognitive states. In: Workshop on Emotional and Cognitive Issues at the International Conference on Intelligent Tutoring Systems, June 23–27, Montreal, Canada.

D'Mello, S., Lehman, B., Graesser, A., 2011. A motivationally supportive affect-sensitive AutoTutor. In: Calvo, R.A., D'Mello, S.K. (Eds.), New Perspectives on Affect and Learning Technologies, Vol. 3. Springer, New York, NY, pp. 113–126.

Damasio, A.R., 1994. Descartes' Error: Emotion, Rationality and the Human Brain. Putnam, New York. 352 pp.

Davou, B., 2000. Thought Processes in the Era of Information: Issues on Cognitive Psychology and Communication. Papazissis Publishers, Athens, Greece.

Desmet, P., 2005. Measuring emotion: development and application of an instrument to measure emotional responses to products. In: Funology. Springer, Netherlands, pp. 111–123.

Dillenbourg, P., 1999. Collaborative Learning: Cognitive and Computational Approaches. Advances in Learning and Instruction Series, Elsevier Science, New York, NY.

Ekman, P., Friesen, W.V., 1978. Facial Action Coding System: A Technique for the Measurement of Facial Movement. Consulting Psychologists Press, Palo Alto, CA.

Electrooculography (EOG), retrieved 12 Mar, 2015 from https://electrooculography.wordpress.com/.

Feidakis, M., Daradoumis, T., Caballé, S., Conesa, J., Gañán, D., 2013. A dual-modal system that evaluates user's emotions in virtual learning environments and responds affectively. J. Univers. Comput. Sci. 19 (11), 1638–1660.

Feidakis, M., Daradoumis, T., Caballé, S., Conesa, J., 2014a. Embedding emotion awareness into e-learning environments. Int. J. Emerg. Technol. Learn. (iJET) 9 (7), 39.

Feidakis, M., Caballé, S., Daradoumis, T., Gañán, D., Conesa, J., 2014b. Providing emotion awareness and affective feedback to virtualized collaborative learning scenarios. Int. J. Cont. Eng. Educ. Life-Long Learn. 24 (2), 141–167.

Feldman, R., 2013. Techniques and applications for sentiment analysis. Commun. ACM 56 (4), 82–89.

Forbes-Riley, K., Litman, D., 2011. Designing and evaluating a wizarded uncertainty-adaptive spoken dialogue tutoring system. Comput. Speech Lang. 25 (1), 105–126.

Gardner, H., 1983. Frames of Mind. Basic Books, New York.

Gee, J.P., 2009. Deep learning properties of good digital games: How far can they go. Serious Games: Mechanisms and Effects. Routledge Taylor and Francis, New York. pp. 67–82.

Go, A., Bhayani, R., Huang, L., 2009. Twitter sentiment classification using distant supervision. CS224N Project Report, Stanford. pp. 1–12.

Goleman, D., 1995. Emotional Intelligence. Bantam Books, New York.

Hascher, T., 2010. Learning and emotion: perspectives for theory and research. Eur. Educ. Res. J. 9, 13–28.

Head Blood Volume Pulse Sensor, retrieved 12 Mar, 2015 from http://www.iranhosco.com/en/our-product/accessories/sensors/blood-head.html.

Heylen, D., Nijholt, A., op den Akker, R., 2005. Affect in tutoring dialogues. Appl. Artif. Intell. 19 (3–4), 287–311.

Hoque, M.E., Courgeon, M., Martin, J.C., Mutlu, B., Picard, R.W., 2013. MACH: my automated conversation coach. In: Proceedings of the 2013 ACM International Joint Conference on Pervasive and Ubiquitous Computing (UbiComp '13). ACM, New York.

IBM BlueEyes video camera, retrieved 12 Mar, 2015 from http://forums.techarena.in/technology-internet/1093108.htm.

Immordino-Yang, M.H., Damasio, A., 2007. We feel, therefore we learn: the relevance of affective and social neuroscience to education. Mind, Brain, and Education 1 (1), 3–10.

Kechaou, Z., Ben Ammar, M., Alimi, A.M., 2011. Improving e-learning with sentiment analysis of users' opinions. In: Global Engineering Education Conference (EDUCON), 2011 IEEE. IEEE, Amsterdam, pp. 1032–1038.

Kelleher, C., Pausch, R., Kiesler, S., 2007. Storytelling alice motivates middle school girls to learn computer programming. In: Proceedings of the SIGCHI Conference on Human Factors in Computing Systems. ACM, New York, pp. 1455–1464.

Kivran-Swaine, F., Naaman, M., 2011. Network properties and social sharing of emotions in social awareness streams. In: Proceedings of the ACM 2011 Conference on Computer Supported Cooperative Work. ACM, New York, pp. 379–382.

Koelstra, S., Patras, I., 2013. Fusion of facial expressions and EEG for implicit affective tagging. Image Vis. Comput. 31 (2), 164–174.

Kort, B., Reilly, R., Picard, R.W., 2001. An affective model of interplay between emotions and learning: reengineering educational pedagogy-building a learning companion. In: Proceedings of the International Conference on the Advanced Learning Technologies. IEEE, Amsterdam, pp. 43–46.

Koschman, T., 1996. Paradigm shifts and instructional technology. In: CSCL: Theory and Practice of an Emerging Paradigm. Lawrence Erlbaum, Hillsdale, NJ, pp. 83–124.

Kreijns, K., Kirschner, P.A., Jochems, W., 2003. Identifying the pitfalls for social interaction in computer-supported collaborative learning environments: a review of the research. Comput. Hum. Behav. 19 (3), 335–353.

Lang, P.J., 1980. Behavioral treatment and bio-behavioral assessment: computer applications. In: Sidowski, J.B., Johnson, J.H., Williams, T.A. (Eds.), Technology in Mental Health Care Delivery Systems. Ablex, Norwood, NJ, pp. 119–137.

Lave, J., Wenger, E., 1991. Situated Learning: Legitimate Peripheral Participation. Cambridge University Press, Cambridge.

LeDoux, J.E., 1996. The Emotional Brain: The Mysterious Underpinnings of Emotional Life. Simon & Schuster, New York.

Liao, D., Lin, C.-T., McDowell, K., Wickenden, A.E., Gramann, K., Jung, T.-P., Ko, L.-W., Chang, J.-Y., 2012. Biosensor technologies for augmented brain–computer interfaces in the next decades. Proc. IEEE 100 (13), 1553–1566.

Linnenbrink-Garcia, L., Pekrun, R., 2011. Students' emotions and academic engagement: introduction to the special issue. Contemp. Educ. Psychol. 36 (1), 1–3.

Marsella, S., Gratch, J., 2015. Computationally modeling human emotion. Commun. ACM 57 (12), 56–67.

Martín, J.M., Ortigosa, A., Carro, R.M., 2012. SentBuk: sentiment analysis for e-learning environments. In: International Symposium on Computers in Education (SIIE).

Mazlan, M.A., Chyi, L.C., Selan, N.E., Lukose, D., 2012. Blended Learning With MIMOS Intelligent Learning Management System.

Molinari, G., Chanel, G., Bétrancourt, M., Pun, T., 2013. Increasing emotion awareness to improve collaboration in computer-mediated communication. In: Symposium "New Learning and Teaching Environments for the XXI Century" at the 28th International Congress of Applied Psychology, Paris, France.

Oates, B.J., 2005. Researching Information Systems and Computing. Sage, Thousand Oaks, CA.

Op't Eynde, P., De Corte, E., Verschaffel, L., 2006. Accepting emotional complexity: a socio-constructivist perspective on the role of emotions in the mathematics classroom. Educ. Stud. Math. 63 (2), 193–207.

Ortony, A., Clore, G.L., Collins, A., 1988. The Cognitive Structure of Emotions. University Press, Cambridge.

Osgood, C.E., May, W.H., Miron, M.S., 1975. Cross-Cultural Universals of Affective Meaning. University of Illinois Press, Urbana, IL.

Papert, S., 1980. Mindstorms: Children, Computers, and Powerful Ideas. Basic Books, New York.

Pappano, L., 2012. The year of the MOOC. The New York Times 2 (12), 2012.

Parrott, W., 2001. Emotions in Social Psychology. Psychology Press, London.

Pekrun, R., 1992. The impact of emotions on learning and achievement: towards a theory of cognitive/motivational mediators. Appl. Psychol.: Int. Rev. 41 (4), 359–376.

Pekrun, R., Goetz, T., Frenzel, A.C., Perry, R.P., 2011. Measuring emotions in students' learning and performance: the achievement emotions questionnaire (AEQ). Contemp. Educ. Psychol. 0361476X. 36 (1), 36–48.

Piaget, J., 1962. Play, Dreams and Imitation in Childhood (C. Gattegno & F. M. Hodgson, Trans.). W.W. Norton & Company, New York.

Picard, R.W., 1997. Affective Computing. The MIT Press, Cambridge, MA. pp. 167, 170.

Picard, R.W., 2010. Emotion research by the people, for the people. Emot. Rev. 2(3).

Plutchik, R., 2001. The nature of emotions: human emotions have deep evolutionary roots, a fact that may explain their complexity and provide tools for clinical practice. Am. Sci. 89 (4), 344–350.

Q Curve EDA sensor, retrieved 12 Mar, 2015 from http://web.media.mit.edu/yadid/.

Respiration, Electrocardiography (ECG), Electromyography (EMG), Blood Volume Pressure (BVP), retrieved 12 Mar 2015 from http://support.kuracloud.com/.

Robison, J., McQuiggan, S., Lester, J., 2009. Evaluating the consequences of affective feedback in intelligent tutoring systems. In: Proceedings of the 3rd International Conference on Affective Computing & Intelligent Interaction. IEEE, Amsterdam, The Netherlands, pp. 1–6.

Romero, C., Ventura, S., 2013. Data mining in education. WIREs Data Min. Knowl. Discov. 3 (1), 12–27.

Rourke, L., 2000. Operationalizing social interaction in computer conferencing. In: Proceedings of the 16th Annual Conference of the Canadian Association for Distance Education, Quebec City.

Russell, J.A., 1980. A circumplex model of affect. J. Pers. Soc. Psychol. 39 (6), 1161–1178.

Russell, J.A., Weiss, A., Mendelsohn, G.A., 1989. Affect grid: a single-item scale of pleasure and arousal. J. Pers. Soc. Psychol. 57 (3), 493–502.

Salovey, P., Mayer, J.D., 1989. Emotional intelligence. Imagin. Cogn. Pers. 9 (3), 185–211.

Scherer, K.R., 2005. What are emotions? And how can they be measured? Soc. Sci. Inf. 44 (4), 693–727.

Sergerie, K., Chochol, C., Armony, J.L., 2008. The role of the amygdala in emotional processing: a quantitative meta-analysis of functional neuroimaging studies. Neurosci. Biobehav. Rev. 32 (4), 811–830.

Sharples, M., 2005. Learning as conversation: transforming education in the mobile age. In: Proceedings of Conference on Seeing, Understanding, Learning in the Mobile Age, 2005.

Shute, V.J., 2008. Focus on formative feedback. Rev. Educ. Res. 78 (1), 153–189.

Siemens, G., 2013. Massive open online courses: innovation in education? Open Educational Resources: Innovation, Research and Practice. COL, Vancouver, BC, pp. 5–16.

Smith, D.S., Nagle, R., 1995. Self-perceptions and social comparisons among children with LD. J. Learn. Disabil. 28 (6), 364–371.

Song, D., Lin, H., Yang, Z., 2007. Opinion mining in e-learning system. In: IFIP International Conference on Network and Parallel Computing Workshops, 2007. NPC Workshops. IEEE, Amsterdam, pp. 788–792.

Vibe Emotion sensor, retrieved 12 Mar, 2015 from http://www.vhmdesignfutures.com/project/70/.

Vygotsky, L.S., 1978. Mind in Society. Harvard University Press, Cambridge, MA.

Wong, M., 2006. Emotion assessment in evaluation of affective interfaces. Neuron 65 (3), 293.

Woolf, B., Burelson, W., Arroyo, I., 2007. Emotional intelligence for computer tutors. In: Workshop on Modeling and Scaffolding Affective Experiences to Impact Learning at the 13th International Conference on Artificial Intelligence in Education, (AIED 2007), pp. 6–15.

Xolocotzin-Eligio, U., 2010. Emotion understanding during computer-supported collaboration. Doctoral Dissertation, University of Nottingham, England.

Zheng, Y., Morrell, J.B., 2013. Comparison of visual and vibrotactile feedback methods for seated posture guidance. IEEE Trans. Haptics 6 (1), 13–23. http://dx.doi.org/10.1109/TOH.2012.3.

Zimmermann, P.G., 2008. Beyond usability—Measuring aspects of user experience. Doctoral Dissertation, Swiss Federal Institute of Technology, Zurich.

GAMIFICATION

LudifyME: AN ADAPTIVE LEARNING MODEL BASED ON GAMIFICATION

F. Llorens-Largo, C.J. Villagrá-Arnedo, F.J. Gallego-Durán, R. Satorre-Cuerda, P. Compañ-Rosique, R. Molina-Carmona

Universitat d'Alacant, Alicante, Spain

1 INTRODUCTION

Huge progress has been made in information technologies (IT) in recent years, and the education systems cannot remain unaware of these changes. IT allows access to massive learning environments, as well as customization, enabling attention to the students' heterogeneity, favoring progressive, autonomous, and adaptive learning. But all this transformation in the educational world will require advances in both theory and technology. New innovative teaching proposals that make use of new technologies have emerged, although they are usually based on ancient pedagogical principles.

A comprehensive understanding of the teaching-learning process, and a clear analysis of the value of IT along with the application of gamification principles and techniques, can provide solutions to the current problems of the educational process. Some previous experiences present preliminary results that endorse this hypothesis and enable us to face this challenge with guarantees (Gallego and Llorens, 2011; Illanas et al., 2013; Llorens et al., 2013; Illanas et al., 2014; Llorens, 2014b; Villagrá et al., 2014a,b, 2015). The members of our team, whilst being researchers in the area of artificial intelligence (AI), are also computer science teachers. That is why we ask ourselves about the use of IT in education. And as far as possible we try to answer some of the following questions: Are there appropriate pedagogical models for the digital world? Are teaching the evolving paradigms keeping pace with technologies? Are we making full use of IT to improve these processes? Are we really achieving the goal of improving them?

In this sense, we propose an innovative gamified training model, *LudifyME*, with a strong technological component as support. The research focal point of this project is to develop a system that synthesizes the potential of gamification, that is at the essence of video games and that makes them powerful as learning catalysts. It is conceived as existing independently of e-learning platforms and being easy to embed into any of them. Its main contribution is focused on the heavy use of methodological teaching principles to enhance student's motivation, performance and satisfaction.

The chapter is structured as follows: in Sections 2 and 3 the relationship between the concepts of learning, gamification and technology is introduced. From our point of view they are the key to developing an instructional, customized and student-centered learning model. In Section 4 *LudifyME* is

Formative Assessment, Learning Data Analytics and Gamification. http://dx.doi.org/10.1016/B978-0-12-803637-2.00012-9

presented, our innovative proposal of an adaptive gamified learning model with a solid technical basis. In the fifth section, *PLMan* is detailed. It is a gamified online learning system that allows the gathering of data for experiments with *LudifyME*. In addition, the obtained results are shown and analyzed. Finally, the conclusions drawn and lessons learned from this research are indicated.

2 LEARNING AND TECHNOLOGY

In this section, the relationship between learning and technology is described. It is first shown that learning is a vital and human activity in which intrinsic motivation and learning by doing play a very important role. The goal is getting active, student-centered and immediate feedback learning methods.

Moreover, learning can be improved through technology. The possibilities of the new technologies must be exploited in the field of education, integrating or complementing different tools in order to create technological ecosystems for learning.

2.1 ACTIVE LEARNING

People learn from the moment of their birth, since learning is a vital ability. Although favorable environments for learning can be created, all modern educational theories agree on giving the active role to the learner. In this context, students' motivation and compromise are the key points in the learning process. Another aspect to consider is the fact that each learner has particular skills and learns in a different way, at different paces and could even have different intelligence styles (Gardner, 2000, 2011).

"One-size" teaching, coming from the industrial era and series production, is not appropriate for the digital world (Robinson, 2013). As Reigeluth (2011, 2012) explains it is necessary to define a new instructional paradigm for the Information Society. Reigeluth's instructional theory is learner-centered, and student progress is based on learning rather than time. This model is supported by Merrill's work, who proposed a set of five prescriptive instructional principles that enhance quality instruction (Merrill, 2007, 2009). These principles have to do with task-centeredness, activation, demonstration, application, and integration.

According to Csikszentmihalyi (1990), when the challenge is appropriate to learners' abilities, they get into a state known as "flow." If the challenge is too difficult, learners get into anxiety. And, finally, if the challenge is too easy, they get bored. Therefore, the way to overcome anxiety is by improving their skills; the way to overcome boredom is to face more difficult challenges. Learners should be placed in their flow state, and step by step, as long as their skills improve, the difficulty in challenges should be increased.

Some authors consider that all human activity is carried out taking into account the reward earned once completion is reached (motivation) (Rinaudo et al., 2003; Tapia, 1995). There are two kinds of motivation: extrinsic and intrinsic. Extrinsic motivation is present when the motives for action are external to the personal interests (for instance, there is a tangible reward), while in intrinsic motivation what it is that leads to the activation of a behavior are inherent to a particular person (in this case, the reward is just personal satisfaction). Enhancing intrinsic motivation is particularly important in the learning process. Some of the ways to achieve this is the inclusion of learning-by-doing activities within the learning methods, using interesting task for students and providing opportunities to collaborate. To sum up, task-based instruction is especially important (Markham et al., 2003; Llorens et al., 2013; Villagrá et al., 2014a,b; Compañ et al., 2014). This term is used in the widest sense, including learning based on projects, problems, topics, cases, and questions. Intrinsically motivated students choose and carry out activities just through curiosity or because of the supposed challenge; intrinsically motivated students are ready to make a significant mental effort during the task, to be committed to richer processing and to use deeper and more effective learning strategies. On the other hand, extrinsically motivated students are only committed to activities when they are externally rewarded (getting good marks, recognition of others, avoiding failure, etc.); in addition, it is also possible that these students choose easier tasks to assure the reward. Generally, extrinsic motivation is easier to induce than intrinsic motivation (Ryan and Deci, 2000). This is the reason why teachers work, mainly, on extrinsic motivation. But, ideally, the goal of an extrinsically motivated instruction should be to begin the transition to an intrinsically motivated instruction. This is the only way to make lifelong learning come true, taking into account that we live in an extremely changing and uncertain high-tech society.

All this transformation in the educational world will require advances in both theory and technology. New proposals for teaching methods have emerged, using new technologies, although they are usually based on old pedagogical principles. One example is the *flipped classroom* or *reverse teaching*, which emerges for blended learning systems where students gain knowledge by watching online videos at home and, later on, carrying out activities, tackling problems and taking part in debates in the classroom, with the help of teachers (Ronchetti, 2010). This is an integrated approach combining direct instruction with constructivism methods, helping students to be committed in the course and improving their conceptual comprehension. It is usually combined with just-in-time teaching (JiTT) (Novak et al., 1999) that allows teachers to get feedback from students the day before the lesson so that teachers can adjust the lesson flow preparing new strategies and activities centered on students' difficulties to understand the content. Therefore, before the lesson takes place, students are assigned videos and readings and they answer some online quizzes to know their actual situation. These techniques allow teachers to apply student-centered learning methods.

Another example of new methodologies is gamification. Gamification in education aims to customize the learning experience to student differences, increasing the students' responsibility for directing their own learning. These are some of the main features of the student-centered learning paradigm (Kapp, 2012).

2.2 TECHNOLOGY ENHANCED LEARNING

Technological progress, particularly in information and communication technologies (ICT), has led us to a digital world where we have tools that connect with others and foster collaboration, tools that make less hierarchical teamwork easier and, finally, tools that allow us to create social networks. In our every day we are used to receiving information from several different sources, in different formats and in different media and instantly. Nowadays, university cannot be ignorant of the constant technological evolution and, particularly, the learning-teaching process must directly reflect this technological evolution (Illanas and Llorens, 2011). Using technology in teaching offers new possibilities, complementary to traditional teaching. There are two key aspects to be considered in quality teaching using technology: teaching methodology and the technological platform. Some pedagogical points have already been addressed in the previous section. Now, we are going to study technological aspects.

The increasing complexity of ICT and the frequency of use in all areas, make it necessary for us to address the technological aspects from an integral point of view, understanding the problems and challenges, and paying attention to the increasing importance of ICT developing strategies, implementation and management. The main aim should be to improve the overall efficiency and profitability in the organization using ICTs. Switching to a digital world requires reengineering of all the process and even rethinking of the aims. Rogers (2003) analyzed why some ideas and products become new trends while others become out-dated quickly. He proposed his diffusion of innovations theory, where he outlines different user categories (innovators, early adopters, early majority, late majority, and laggards) following a normal distribution. According to Moore (2014) one innovation succeeds when crossing the chasm and it is able to reach majorities (early majority at the beginning and late majority afterwards). Another feature of technological innovations is that early users drop new products as soon as the mainstream accepts it and the new innovation appears. Gartner *hype cycle* (Linden and Fenn, 2003) provides a graphic representation of maturity and adoption of technologies, and how they are potentially relevant to solving real business problems and exploiting new opportunities. Each hype cycle drills down into the five key phases of a technology's life cycle. It starts with a trigger where a new technology breakthrough kicks things off reaching a peak of inflated expectations. Later on, interest wanes as experiments and implementations fail to deliver, falling toward disillusionment. Then, second- and third-generation products appear to get the slope of enlightenment. Finally, a plateau of productivity is reached. Forecasting the way a technology spreads, means foreseeing a high level of passing trends and social contagion, which may even be considered as not being useful from the objective point of view of the technology (information cascades) (Friedkin and Johnsen, 2011). Practices that rely on ICT in this global environment—connected and complex and increasingly recursive—are usually characterized by behaviors like the Black Swan (Taleb, 2007), not the normal distribution behavior we are used to. But changes in the world of education cannot depend on trends nor continuous changes since the effects can only be assessed in the long term. Therefore, serious research is needed into the use of the new technologies in education and their behavior.

An increasing number of projects with open educational resources and the strong "open" movement make creating open and collaborating systems easier (Llorens et al., 2010). Virtual campuses and learning management system (LMS) tools, although powerful and useful in the relationship between teachers and students, from the beginning have been basically aimed at teaching management. They are rigid with communication flow, limiting the interaction possibilities. Therefore, they are being increasingly complemented by other tools, in the internet or given by the institution, creating a technological ecosystem for learning. There is a long list of technological tools that can be used for learning (Top 100 Tools for Learning, Centre for Learning & Performance Technologies). But this is not a matter of focusing in learning with a technological tool; this is about teachers finding a tool that suits their way of teaching and creating a learning environment. The integration of different tools allows us to create technological ecosystems for learning, going beyond the mere accumulation of trendy technologies (Llorens, 2009, 2011). An ecosystem consists of a community of living organisms interacting with each-other and growing based on physical factors in the environment. Using this analogy, a technological ecosystem is defined as a community of educational methods, policies, regulations, applications, and work teams that coexist so that their processes are interrelated and their implementation is based on the physical factors of the technological environment (Llorens et al., 2014).

In the past, that is, at the beginning of using IT in education, automation led to the development of LMS. Nowadays, integration is the main aim: connecting and establishing relationships between the different emerging tools that are useful to us as teachers, creating what we call technological ecosystems. The analysis of the behavior of the technological innovations and the advances in cognitive science and education show that, in the near future, personalization and adaptability will be the main features in IT in education (Llorens, 2014a).

3 LEARNING AND GAMIFICATION

In this section, the benefits of gamification are presented. Games, and video games in particular, offer many features to enhance the learning process and improve students' performance: as a tool for teaching, as an object of learning project and as a philosophy when the training process is designed.

In addition, applying gamification to learning is currently one of the most explored areas of research. But in order to design a successful gamified learning experiences, gamification principles must be considered from the beginning.

3.1 GAMES, GAMIFICATION AND MORE

The continued development and strong penetration in society of technology in general and video games in particular, is unquestionable. Video games have changed the way our youth conceive of reality and interact with each other (McGonigal, 2011; Turkle, 2011). And in this context, the use of video games for educational purposes has become a booming area in recent years (Kapp, 2012). Much research has been carried out on its benefits in education, not only into its attractiveness and motivating properties for students, but also for the variety of fields and subjects that can be covered and skills that can be trained using this technology (Illanas et al., 2008; Gallego et al., 2014; Llorens, 2014b). According to Prensky (2001) computer games attract players for several reasons: they encourage participation, motivate users to gradually achieve small goals, offer immediate rewards or punishments, and allow the difficulty of each level to be adapted according to an individual player's ability, age or knowledge of the game. Video games are used in learning in what we call game-based learning and as learning objects in what we call serious games or educational video games (Prensky, 2006). Reflecting on this reality provokes clear questions: Can video games be used in the learning process to motivate students? And if so, how can it be done?

From our point of view, video games can be a very powerful tool in improving the learning process from three different and complementary perspectives: as a tool for teaching other contents or skills, as an object of the learning project itself, and as a philosophy to consider when designing the training process. Besides, as university professors, who, therefore, have research responsibilities, video games also provide researchers with a platforms to validate their research.

Numerous studies indicate that games encourage learning, since, when the fun impregnates the learning process, motivation increases and stress is reduced. As Koster (2004) says, immediate feedback reinforces through endorphins and dopamine the neuronal links involved in accurate prediction, which creates an atmosphere for the player commonly recognized as fun. In particular the use of video games increases satisfaction levels during learning and memorization ability is also improved (Moreno-Ger et al., 2009). This is because a complete immersion of the players in the task being carried out occurs (De Freitas and Neumann, 2009), allowing them to decide what to do at all times. It is important to add that during the game, immediately after each action, the player receives response information, enabling learning by trial and error.

Nevertheless, it must be noted that video games have different characteristics to the other means of knowledge transmission currently available (books, videos, and audios) (Gallego and Llorens, 2011). In this sense, video games in general and educative (serious) games in particular are a complement to what we have so far, not a substitute.

Furthermore, video games can also be the object of the learning process. While this aspect is better suited to some disciplines than others, there are more and more areas in which the study of video games is not only interesting but also convenient. This is clear in the case of computer engineering and other similar fields. From this perspective, a video game can be used as a project to be developed by students.

Finally, there is an aspect that has taken off in recent years, gamification. Gamification consists of applying the principles of video game design, the use of the mechanics and the elements of a game in any process, beyond the specific context of video games (Werbach, 2012). The aim is to take advantage of the psychological predisposition of people to participate in games to motivate and improve the performance of the participants. This approach applied to the educational world is a promising direction (Prensky, 2006).

Gamification was included in Gartner hype cycle about Emerging Technologies 2011. In 2012 it was included at the peak of inflated expectations, with the prediction of reaching a plateau of productivity in between 5 and 10 years. In 2013, gamification was considered to have reached the peak of expectations, but fell in 2014 into a trough of disillusionment. Gartner consultants (2012) in their report "Gamification 2020: What Is the Future of Gamification?," published in November 2012, were already predicting that the world would become disillusioned with gamification by 2013 and 2014, mainly because it is difficult to understand the design of video games and the strategies that motivate players, resulting in fake applications of gamification due to superficial applications of the concept. They even forecasted that by 2014 80% of applications based on this philosophy would fail to satisfy business needs due to bad design. However, the correct application of the video games principles will have a strong impact in many fields, becoming a transforming force together with other emergent technologies. As Anderson and Rainie (2012) of the Pew Research Center say: "if the enjoyment and challenge of playing can be embedded in learning, work, and commerce then gamification will take off."

3.2 GAMIFIED LEARNING

Education is one of the fields where gamification will become a disruptive innovation, mainly in tech-based learning (eLearning) and lifelong learning. NMC Horizon Report is a series of publications designed to help teachers and educational staff to understand emerging technologies and also the effects in learning, teaching and research; from a global point of view this takes into consideration the next 5 years. According to Horizon 2013 (Johnson et al., 2013), in education gamification is one of the two technologies experiencing growing interest in the mid-term (2–3 years). The report states that using gamification and games in a wider sense are two sides of the same coin. It also proposes the further refinement of learning analytics. Their impact will be even bigger if these approaches are used at the same time, that is, games and gamification as gathering information platforms that feed data systems analysis (educational data mining). Using the results of this analysis allows us to adapt the educational gamified proposal to learners' special needs and pace in learning. The new revolution of educational software will come from applications comprehending the learning needs of the user and, so, adapting their advance to a custom pace, what we call *adaptive learning*.

Therefore, as international referenced reports say, we can conclude that the following years are crucial worldwide to determine if gamification, particularly its correct application to different experiences, will be able to consolidate the great expectations of it, in general, but also in education in particular, where it is expected that these years are the key. This is why both high levels of research and clear justification for using gamification techniques are necessary, based on quality indicators. Analysis of a large quantity of experiences and reports reflects the interest in gamification, but for the experts it is perfectly clear from the evidence that we are facing merely the first steps, only isolated items that overlap, and not the core of gamification: gamifying all the learning process. The reengineering of the whole process is needed, taking into account the principles of gamification from the beginning in order to design a successful gamified experience. Nowadays, according to Kapp (2012), there are two types of gamification: structural gamification and content gamification. Structural gamification is the application of game elements to propel a learner through content with no alteration or changes to the content itself. The content does not become game-like, only the structure around the content (Pastor et al., 2015). Content gamification is the application of game elements and game thinking to alter content to make it more game-like.

For a discipline to be mature, the design methodology must be clearly defined and accepted. In gamification, nevertheless, many experiences fail because the solutions are just a mix of pieces from game components with no formal design process. There has been some effort to define design frameworks for gamification, and a complete review can be found in Mora et al. (2015). Some interesting experiences are those of González et al. (2014) who present a conceptual architecture for an Intelligent Tutorial System that includes gamification elements as key components, or the work of Domínguez et al. (2013) who describe a gamification plugin for an e-learning platform, collecting quantitative and qualitative data in the process.

4 LudifyME MODEL

As a result of the process of reflection about technology, gamification and learning illustrated in the previous paragraphs, *LudifyME*, our proposal of an adaptive and gamified learning model, was created and is presented in this section. First, its objectives and main features are described. Then, a more detailed description of the system is given. Finally, the core components of the model are defined.

4.1 OBJECTIVES AND MAIN FEATURES

LudifyME[1] is a cutting-edge gamified learning model, adaptable to provide new teaching-learning tools to experts, trainers, professionals, students, and other interested people, both online and in classroom training, which provides facilities for designing itineraries, experiences, scoring/assessment systems, and learning networks using activities as basic building blocks. We can pick out the following *LudifyME* features that make it an innovative system:

1. It is inspired by video games' characteristics: interactivity, real-time feedback, motivation, progression, rewards, levels, challenges, and so on.

---

[1]Ludify from latin root "Ludus" (play) and from "Ludificar," the recommended term for gamify in Spanish.

2. It integrates the education experts as a key component in creating gamified learning models: creating gamified systems is a creative process, not an automated one, where experts play an essential role.
3. It raises creation beyond the content, to methods and methodologies: the tools are thought to enable experts to directly experience new methods and learning methodologies.
4. It allows the design, creation, testing and evaluation of scoring/assessment systems: it allows experts to design the essence of feedback in a teaching system.
5. It promotes the process meta-evaluation and the improvement of the whole system: the information needed to assess whether gamifications fulfill the desired objectives or not is available and the aspects that should be redesigned or improved are easily detected.
6. It automates the assessment and the feedback to students: thanks to its design, all activities and itineraries give overall information of student learning process status.
7. It encourages integrated formative assessment: due to the automation of the assessment process, it is given enough flexibility to easily allow students to fail and retry activities without penalization or feeling of frustration.

4.2 DESCRIPTION

Taking into account these objectives and main features, we propose a new training model, gamified and with a strong technological component as a backup. It should be clarified that it is a training model independent of current e-learning platforms, which can be easily integrated into any of them, and whose main contribution focuses on the heavy use of methodological teaching principles to enhance students' motivation, performance and satisfaction. As the core of these principles we use gamification, because video games have shown tremendous ability to achieve our goals, as we explained before. Finally, the project will have a solid technological component because the computing capabilities and possibilities of universal access are those that allow the proposed model to become a real system.

The project's central point of research is to develop a system that encapsulates the strength of gamification, the core of video games, which will make it potent as a learning catalyst. The fundamental attributes of video games that encourage the gamification of other processes, in short, are:

- Experimentation or learning by doing: unlike traditional training, a game player learns directly by experiencing and testing. Testing, experimenting, observing what happens and learning from it to retry is the natural cycle of our brain functioning and the proof of this is the fun that it generates.
- Interactivity and immediate feedback: it is impossible to test, experiment and see the consequences if there is no immediate cause-effect relationship in the learning experience. This is the fundamental factor in any learning experience that seeks to get the most out of our brain functioning.
- Allow and naturalize the error: effective, deep and lasting learning is very difficult without being wrong. Any educational system tends to pursue, punish, and stigmatize committing errors. Video games teach us that this is not the way: you can go wrong as often as you want and repeat or try again without stopping to achieve mastery.
- Give control to the player: the main element of intrinsic motivation is the autonomy in decision-making. Games let players decide what they want to do or where they must continue at all time.

Moreover, it is essential to assume that any formative experience, gamified or not, should have experts in the field as the main actors. These experts must have the tools to design learning experiences, to implement them, to assess their viability and to constantly improve them.

Considering the above analysis, our proposal establishes three axes or starting concepts on which to build all the tools and the system itself:

- Activities: Activities are the core of learning. The sequence of tasks that lead to learning lies on them, ie, what students should do/practice to learn by doing. Our system generalizes the concept of activity, allowing them to be conceived as an external service, in order for experts and developers to create unlimited activities and different kinds of activities and adapt existing activities.
- Itinerary and dependencies: the activities themselves are the building blocks of learning, but it is necessary to join them together, creating networks of dependencies between them. Dependencies between activities allow the setting of precedencies, constraints, challenges, and itineraries in which students can make decisions that help them to achieve their goals. In addition, displaying these dependencies in an automatic and immediate way provides essential instant feedback that is rarely present for students.
- Integrated formative assessment: as video games are constantly evaluating their players through the challenges, constraints, difficulties, and different available itineraries, the proposed system gives the flexibility that the assessment is ongoing and not punctual. This is achieved by designing tools for the creation of scoring systems that properly assess the activities carried out by students constantly and not just at the end.

A platform with the architecture suggested in Fig. 12.1 will be developed on these three pillars.

In this preliminary technical design we anticipate an independent platform (*LudifyME*) to that experts and students will have direct access via the Internet, and also indirect access from any other community or learning platform/e-learning. The platform *LudifyME* integrates creation and management tools for experts as well as activities, itineraries and networks for students.

The platform *LudifyME* is developed in Software as a Service (SaaS) models. SaaS is a model for software distribution in which applications are hosted by a service provider and made available to customers over the Internet (Erl et al., 2013). In the context of our work, the portability and interoperability of this model is particularly useful. This architecture allows the easy communication and share of information between platforms that are internally different but are capable of transparently working together, as if they were integrated. As a result, it allows the creation of external activities to the platform. These activities may work in any medium—web, desktop, smartphone or tablets—as they integrate with *LudifyME* in the same way that communities and platforms do, through a service point.

This is the most currently used model of software, especially in large companies and developments, due to its versatility. We find the model in the large cloud platforms like Amazon WS, Microsoft Azure, Facebook, and almost all Google services, Forex, etc.

This design allows all services offered by *LudifyME* to be easily integrated into any existing and/or future platform; creating multiple activities for independent developers and easy evolution of the *LudifyME* platform itself, without affecting other developments. We can have a close reference to help us to visualize this building of the system in the running of games and applications for Facebook. These games and applications are not stored or managed internally by Facebook, but they are each stored in their respective external platforms, and communicate with Facebook via a service point. This allows for as many third-party developers as they want to adapt their existing applications/games to integrate with Facebook, or it makes new developments designed to integrate with Facebook from the first time.

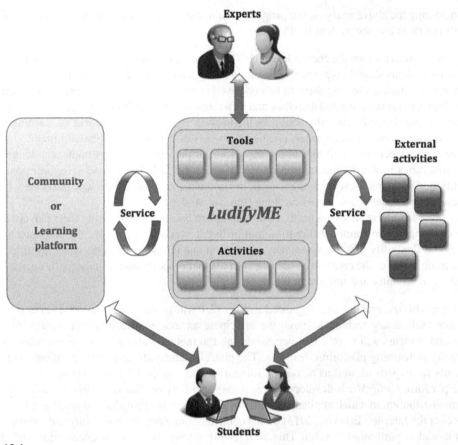

FIGURE 12.1

Architecture of *LudifyME* system.

4.3 COMPONENTS OF *LudifyME* SYSTEM

4.3.1 Tools

The tools created in *LudifyME* are aimed at giving the experts the ability to design itineraries, experiences, scoring/evaluation systems and learning networks using activities, such as a basic building block. They are oriented to customized and autonomous learning, from the needs of any type of education, lifelong learning, using gamification, automation and usability as the basis for improving the existing tools. A set of patterns is available, to develop gamified tools that allow extension of the model and facilitate the collaboration of third parties. These patterns are scalable, expandable to new tools proposals, modular and configurable. In addition, we have developed a set of gamified tools based on the proposed patterns, to specify the model, which results in a complete learning model.

4.3.2 Learning Networks or Itineraries

Networks or learning itineraries, along with the generalization of activities as a service, are the two most powerful concepts of *LudifyME*, so they allow experts to develop learning systems at a higher level of abstraction than those currently present in e-learning platforms. Thanks to this, experts will be able to create learning methodologies (they can also create content).

Experts may navigate between the available activities, test and configure them specifically for their interests and add them to a graph or itinerary of activities' diagram, similar to Fig. 12.2.

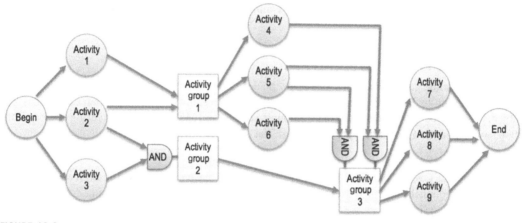

FIGURE 12.2

Diagram of activities' itinerary and activities' group.

The diagram in Fig. 12.2 shows a network of activities making up a training itinerary. The building components of this diagram are:

- Links: they represent the dependency relationships between activities, indicating what achievements are needed to get access to new activities and to progress in the itinerary.
- Circular nodes: these are specific activities to be carried out, preconfigured and prepared by the experts who have designed the activities' network. The system will allow configuring options, constraints, number of tries, score changes, achievements, efficiency schemes, and statistics to give maximum flexibility to the experts when designing the ways in which students can cope with the activities and the feedback received from them.
- Square nodes: they represent subgroups of activities. Each group of activities is, internally, another network with activities, groups and dependencies, with the same possibilities and design options as the main network of activities. Thus, larger and reusable building blocks can be created. For example, a network of activities designed to teach how to handle a surgical knife could be directly integrated as a subset of a larger network to teach surgery.
- Begin and end nodes: they represent where students begin and what is the ultimate goal of the learning network or specific itinerary they are following. Depending on scoring systems established by the experts, it may or may not be required that the student reaches the end node, as explained below.

- Logical connectors: they allow decisions as to how the preceding activities will affect one in particular. Thus, for example, they allow us to indicate that an activity may require that several previous activities be completed before it can be accessible (AND logic operator), or only anyone of a set (OR logic operator).

Itinerary diagrams are a basic tool of learning design for experts, as well as the visual scheme and the main point of feedback for students. Browsing the scheme, students will have an immediate knowledge of where they are on their path of learning, what options they have to continue, what assessments the options have and how they must work to achieve their goals. Moreover, the system always gives control to the student, who will decide where she/he wants to continue, how, when and where she/he wants to arrive.

5 CASE STUDY: PLMan

PLMan is an online gamified system that helps the development of logical thinking skills through the Prolog programming language. This system has allowed us to gamify the practical part of the first-year subjects that related to logic taught in the Computer Science and Multimedia Engineering degrees from 2008, with the aim of learning logic reasoning. The objectives of the subjects are:

- Develop the capacity of logical reasoning for problem solving.
- Experimentally verify the validity of rule-based logical reasoning for solving a given problem.
- Acquire, through the practical exercises, the ability to solve problems of increasing difficulty, using logical rules systems.

Practical exercises basically consist of solving a series of levels or mazes about *PLMan* game, a maze game, an adaptation of the famous "Pacman" game. Mazes (activities) are organized in stages (itineraries) of increasing difficulty, which require the acquisition of new skills to face them. Within each phase, mazes have different levels of difficulty, which can be chosen by the student. The more difficult, the higher mark they can get. When the students solve a maze, they submit it to the system and achieve a mark or score, which builds toward their final grade, allowing the release of successive mazes if the minimum established score is obtained.

This system represents a true formative assessment, because students have at any time the necessary feedback to let them know where they are and what chance they have to continue, without having to wait until the end to be evaluated. Moreover, control of the educational process falls into the hands of the student him- or herself, who is responsible and knowledgeable about his or her own progress. His or her motivation increases while the sense of obligation decreases, and it enhances autonomy and responsibility.

The system is constantly evolving and, above all, it has increased the intrinsic motivation of students for the practical exercises in the subjects in which it is used. Currently 336 students use it, and it allows us to collect data on *LudifyME* experimentation from the results obtained from students' interactions with the system (choice of difficulties, marks obtained and so on).

5.1 DESCRIPTION

As stated before, this research relies on a custom-made gamified learning system. This system gives support to a first-year subject whose aim is to introduce students to computational logic. Along with the practical lessons of the subject, students use Prolog (Sterling and Shapiro, 1994) as logics programming language. For this purpose, a game called *PLMan* (Castel et al., 2009) is used. In this game, students program the AI of a Pac-Man like character, using a Prolog knowledge base. Prolog is especially suitable for this purpose since it is a declarative language based on first-order logic whose statements are expressed in terms of facts, relations and rules, widely used in the field of AI.

Each exercise comes in the form of a new maze, for which students have to program an AI that is able to get all the dots whilst dodging the perils. They start by constructing bunches of simple rules in the form "*If you see an enemy to your right, move left*" (in Prolog rule :- see(normal,right,'E'), doAction(move(left)).), that lets them solve the first mazes. Mazes increase in complexity and programming requirements, encouraging students to learn more about Prolog and to be creative with the way they construct the AI.

More than 400 different mazes have been made for *PLMan*, with different layouts, objects to collect and use, enemies and obstacles to avoid, and even problems to solve. These mazes are organized into four main stages and five levels of difficulty per stage. All of them have been gathered into a gamified, automatic, web-based system that manages the progress of students in their practical assignments with *PLMan*.

Students have to beat the four stages and a checkpoint in the system to get the maximum grade. At each stage, students have to solve one to five different mazes (depending on the stage). For each new exercise (ie, maze), students pick up their desired difficulty level (from one to five) and they are presented with a random maze. Mazes can only be assigned once, so the same maze cannot be assigned to two different students. Then they use the *PLMan* software to construct and test their AI for the maze. When they think their AI is ready, they submit it to the system and get an automatic assessment in percentage. When they achieve more than 75% on a given maze, they unlock the next one and can continue.

In Fig. 12.3 the flow of *PLMan* system from the point of view of the student has been represented, which allows us to clearly see aspects of student autonomy, immediate feedback and system automation. The student chooses the difficulty (1) and the system assigns her/him a maze (2). At her/his local computer and after installing SWI-Prolog and downloading *PLMan*, the student programs the AI to solve the maze and tests it (3), showing the results and the necessary information to fix bugs (4). When the student is already satisfied with her/his he submits its to/he submits its to *PLMan* gamified web (5), immediately obtaining the correction and results (6).

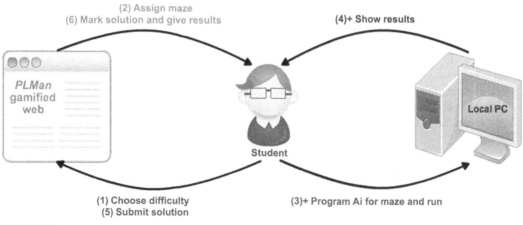

FIGURE 12.3

Student-centered information's flow of *PlMan* system.

The system is designed with the aim of formative assessment, considering that students need to learn from their own mistakes without being penalized for it. Because of this, students do not have a limit of submissions for a given maze. If they fail, they can continue developing and submitting solutions until they succeed. The system always considers the best solution they have submitted to give marks to. Partially solved mazes also contribute to their final grade proportionally to the percentage of the maze solved. Students can also follow their own path by selecting difficulty levels that make them feel more comfortable: the greater the difficulty level, the more the contribution to the final grade. They may also stop whenever they wanted: ie, if they got to the third stage and have accumulated marks of 6.5 over 10, they may stop solving mazes if they want.

5.2 *PLMan* AND *LudifyME*

PLMan was conceived as a first attempt to gamify just one concrete item of the syllabus of a subject: learning about Computational Logic. After years of experience and refinement, we have found out the potential of this platform. *LudifyME* is the generalization of the lessons learnt using *PLMan* and our proposal for a general gamification platform. Nowadays it is a theoretical model, whose structure is based on a concrete implementation, *PLMan*, that allows us to obtain some initial conclusions and to foresee its advantages.

Because of the bottom-up design of this experience (in the particular case of *PLMan* to the general model of *LudifyME*) some elements of *LudifyME* are not easy to be identified in *PLMan*. Nevertheless, the general philosophy of both models is concordant. It is possible to identify the main elements of the architecture of *LudifyME* in *PLMan* and to give some general guidelines for extending the *LudifyME* model to other contexts:

- *LudifyME* platform: the web-based gamified system of *PLMan* can be considered as a simplified version of the *LudifyME* platform. It allows the students to access every activity and to follow all the learning process. In the future, the gamified platform will be improved to add new functionalities and to generalize its features to other disciplines with other types of activities.
- Learning platforms: the LMSs are connected to *PLMan* by providing data about the student profiles (enrolment) and by receiving the learning results of every student (marks). The SaaS model will allow the generalization of the connections and the interoperability in a transparent way.
- *LudifyME* tools: they are aimed at giving the experts in general and the teachers in particular the capability of designing the learning activities. In the case of *PLMan*, there are not ad hoc tools but a set of existing tools that allow the teachers to create the mazes, check their correctness and evaluate their difficulty. They mainly comprise a text editor and a Prolog interpreter. In a general case, the tools should be selected or designed to assist the teachers in creating activities of the particular discipline. A total of eight experts (teachers) have participated in the design of the activities.
- Activities: they are the activities that the students must do to complete the learning process. They can be internal (specifically designed to be included in *LudifyME*) or external (not included in *LudifyME* but accessible thanks to the SaaS model). In the context of a complete *LudifyME* development, the case of *PLMan* may be considered as a unique large activity, to be complemented with other activities to obtain a whole learning process. However, this large activity is made up of a set of atomic activities arranged in itineraries that can be represented in a

graph. Each atomic activity is the resolution of a single *PLMan* maze, made up of a series of external tasks (offline resolution of the maze using the Prolog interpreter) and internal tasks (solution upload and system feedback). As was explained earlier, at each stage the student must select a difficulty level, so there are different ways of overcoming the stage. The possibility of selection is provided by the use of the OR logical operator (at least one of the possible itineraries must be completed). The stages, however, are consecutive and mandatory. Fig. 12.4 shows the characteristic itineraries graph of *LudifyME* with the *PLMan* activities (solving mazes).

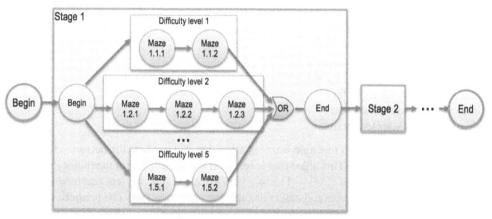

FIGURE 12.4

Activities of *PLMan* structured as a *LudifyME* graph. Circles represent activities; boxes represent groups of activities.

5.3 PROGRESSIVE PREDICTION SYSTEM

However, while designing, building, redesigning and maintaining a system like this, it becomes clear that the flow of data that goes in and out of the system is invaluable from the teaching/learning point of view. The main aim of our work is to transform these data into valuable information and advice for teachers about the progress of the students towards success in the early stages of the academic term. Then, using real-time student interaction data to predict the performance of the students by the end of term is the key idea here (Villagrá et al., 2015). Therefore, building some informative characteristics well correlated with student performance and evolution is the first step to obtaining accurate result predictions.

The idea of using data from learning platforms to help identify at-risk learners and provide intervention to assist learners in achieving success is not new (Macfadyen and Dawson, 2010). Kotsiantis (2012) wrote an interesting review of prediction in education. Another interesting example is found in Huang and Fang (2013), where authors compare four machine learning models for predicting student performance. Also, Lykourentzou et al. (2009) achieve an accurate prediction at an early stage of an e-learning course using feed-forward neural networks. We ourselves, have previous experience in predictive systems (Illanas et al., 2013, 2014), using a serious game to predict students' performance in foreign languages. Students data were collected while they were playing the game and then data were analyzed to predict the final marks in various items (average, quiz, oral, writing, and blog), obtaining very good accuracy. This previous work encouraged us to strengthen this research line and helped us to identify the key information needed to build a predictive system.

With this previous experience in mind, we started designing which information would be valuable to log. We considered a list of concrete events that occur during the interaction between students and the system. All these events (see Table 12.1) are logged in an event database, with their appropriate timestamp and related information.

This simple subset of events depicted in Table 12.1, along with the information about the status of a student (mazes solved, marks obtained and stages passed) is the primary matter to construct the following set of features that have been designed for their use in the predictive system:

- Number of front page visits
- Number of maze downloads
- Number of submissions by stage
- Average marks (percentage) by stage
- Time (secs) to finish each stage
- Time (secs) to finish each maze
- Difficulty levels selected by maze

These features are the input for a machine learning algorithm that predicts the performance the student is to achieve by the end of term. This algorithm is based on the support vector machines (SVM) method with pairwise coupling (Wu et al., 2004). This is a very effective and efficient machine learning algorithm that works very well for general datasets like the one under analysis. The prediction system classifies expected student performance in one out of three possible classes, depending on the expected final marks out of 10 points:

1. Great students (expected final mark > 8.05)
2. Normal students (expected final mark between 5.75 and 8.05)
3. Underperforming students (expected final mark < 5.75).

The main reason to split output in three big classes is to improve the performance of the classification algorithm. With a small sample (336 students in this first experience), making more than three classes would leave out very few examples of each class, undermining the possibilities of the algorithm.

After selecting the best set of parameters, 10 SVMs are trained, one for each week being considered. This improves expected performance by having specialized SVMs for each week. It is important to clarify that data used to train SVMs has to be from previous, closed terms, because knowing the actual

Table 12.1 Most Important System Events Logged

Event	It Happens When a Student...
show_frontpage	Enters in the system and sees the main status page
show_results	Sees their results on a concrete maze
select_difficulty	Picks up the difficulty they want for a new maze
maze_download	Download a maze
solution_submission_ok	Submits a solution which compiles and executes correctly
download_logs	Downloads execution logs (used to replicate AI bugs)
solution_submission_error	Submits a solution that does not work properly

final performance achieved by students is required to train SVMs. Once SVMs are trained, they can be used to carry out real-time predictions for a current term. These final predictions are added to the prediction stack, where all predictions for past weeks are stored. One this prediction step is finished, graphs and information are elaborated and presented to teachers for student evaluation, in the form of estimated performance progression of students over time. The last value in the weekly prediction stack always corresponds to the week in course, whose predictions are made using its corresponding SVM as if the week had passed.

This continuous cycling architecture is illustrated in Fig. 12.5. The relationship between students, teacher and system is observed in the diagram. The gamified web is accessed by students who are progressing and accumulating grades, generating events associated with such actions. The system records these events and processes them obtaining the features with which the predictive system operates. Thus, throughout the weeks the prediction is updated for each student, making this information available to students and teachers. Thus both, students and the teacher, can evaluate these data and take action accordingly.

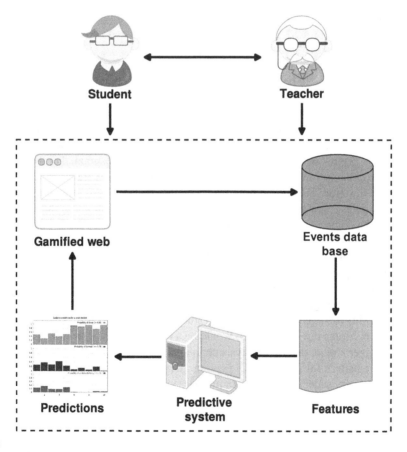

FIGURE 12.5

Architecture of predictive system.

The progressive way in which predictions are made and shown to teachers, together with the real-time processing system that makes this possible, are the main contributions of this system. During each term, new predictions are stored every week in an evolutional, performance-predicting graph. These predictions are always made using all the interaction data the system has collected, which is constantly growing. The first predictions are expected to be very weak in terms of accuracy, as there is very little evidence collected about students. But, as new data are collected, the accuracy of the predictions improves and, what is more, having four to five consecutive weekly predictions yields much more information than the mere probabilities: they show student evolution over time. This gives to teachers the ability of inducing student learning trends. Taking into account the very noisy, variable nature of data and prediction, this outcome is a considerable result. The next section shows up to what point this outcome has been achieved.

5.4 EXPERIMENTS AND RESULTS

The proposed system (Fig. 12.6) was implemented in the previous term starting at October, 2014, and ending in January, 2015. It was implemented at the University of Alicante (Spain), for a first-year subject "Matemáticas 1," which includes Computational Logic and Prolog in its practical lessons. There were around 400 students enrolled, 336 of which finally participated actively in the practical lessons and therefore used the system.

Although the complete term consists of 15 weeks, only 13 practical lessons are given. From these 13 lessons, only 11 turned out to be usable, as the first two were used to give students a general introduction to Prolog and *PLMan*. Consequently, 10 weeks of predictions are given to the teachers, and then the system closes giving final marks to students in week 11.

As mentioned before, the main idea of this experience is to provide teachers with information about the trend of students through progressive predictions. To achieve this goal, the system makes probabilistic evolutionary graphs such as Fig. 12.7. These graphs show the estimated probabilities that a student has a high performance (green; light gray in print version/above), average (blue; dark gray in print version/center), or low (red; medium gray in print version/down). These probabilities are calculated each week of the course and they are accumulated in the graphic showing the trends of students after 10 weeks of the course. Logically, each week shows the results obtained with the data collected up until that week.

The three students depicted in Fig. 12.7 are three typical examples of each class: (7.1) a great student (9.75 out of 10 points), (7.2) a normal student (6.4 out of 10 points), and (7.3) an underperforming student (1 out of 10 points). By analyzing the graphs of (7.1) and (7.3), it appears clear that there are two ascending and descending trends, on the top (green; dark gray in print versions) and the bottom (red; dark gray in print versions) boxes. These two students show very clearly where they are heading around weeks 4 to 6. Moreover, student (7.3) would be a nice example of an early detection of a problem that should trigger a more detailed analysis on the part of the teacher to try and find a solution. In contrast, grasping a pattern for student (7.2) is more difficult. Up to week 5, student status tends increasingly to normal but, suddenly, it changes to great and then continues deflating to normal again. It is probably due to the student solving a lot of mazes between weeks 5 and 6, and then getting comfortable with the global mark achieved and ceasing to put in additional effort. So, in the 6th week the system thinks that the student is going to make a lot of effort and become great, but this probability goes down as the effort is not sustained.

FIGURE 12.6

Web-based gamified system (up) and examples of a stage-2, level-5 maze (left), and simple stage-1 AI code for the *PLMan* game (right).

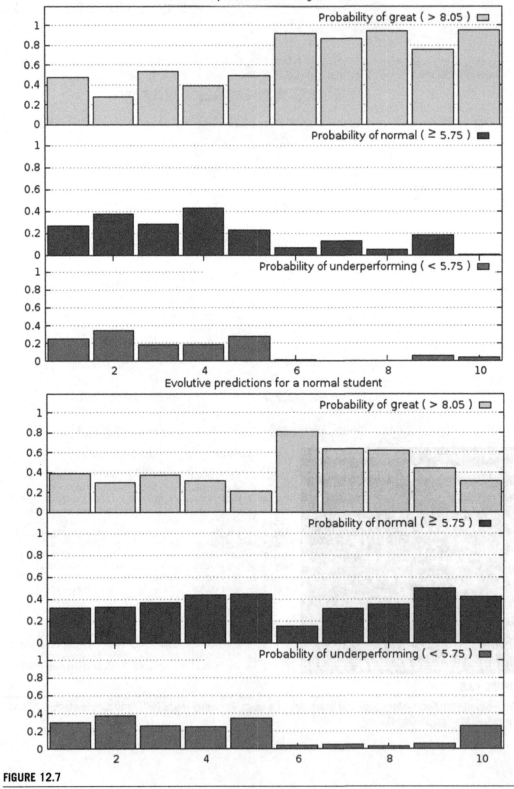

FIGURE 12.7

Evolutional probabilistic graphs for three typical students.

Continued

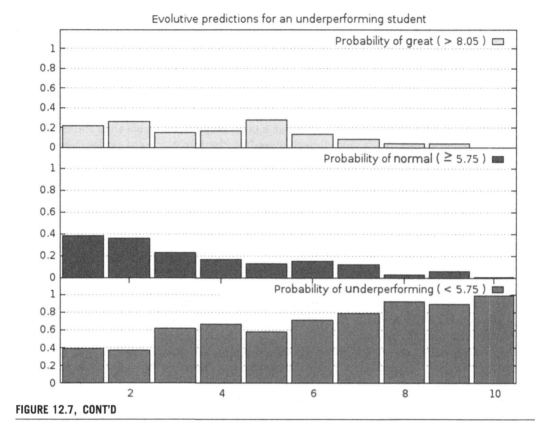

FIGURE 12.7, CONT'D

This last simple example of analysis represents an achievement with respect to the main goal of this experience: it shows the power that the progressive prediction graphs can give to teachers. With this tool, teachers can grasp trend patterns early from the activity of students and the predictions of the system. This discovery pattern means they are able to act on students' difficulties at early and middle stages of the learning process, greatly improving the probability of guiding students to success. The information is now given weekly both to teachers and students, as a graph with the probability of the student for achieving a great, normal or underperforming result. What actions are needed to put students back on track (the assignment of new activities, for instance) are now deliberated by the teachers. However, we plan in the future to obtain more elaborate graphs and an automatic guiding system to help students to improve their results.

6 LESSONS LEARNED AND CONCLUSIONS

From our experience we have learned some important lessons about the gamification of the teaching-learning process. This is not an exhaustive list, and certainly there are aspects that are subject to discussion. However, we consider it is a starting point for teachers who want to approach the world of gamification.

- *Fun*: Fun must have given humans some evolutionary advantage. One of the best analyses we can find about what fun is and how to manage it can be found in the work of Koster (2004). Fun occurs when patterns are recognized by the human brain. This recognition depends on prior knowledge of the individual and how new information is obtained and processed. This process triggers the release of dopamine, which is the substance that the brain uses to fix the successful adaptations. Precisely, the release of dopamine produces positive feelings in the individuals, what we call fun.
- *Motivation*: Psychological self-determination theory (Ryan and Deci, 2000) identifies which factors take part in the motivation of people to perform a task, setting a continuum from absolute lack of motivation to intrinsic motivation, through several intermediate degrees of extrinsic motivation. There are three key factors for a person to be in a state of intrinsic motivation: autonomy, competence and meaning. The conclusion is that in a gamified solution the mere combination of video game elements (dynamics, mechanics, and components) is worthless if they are not properly combined to produce intrinsic motivation (offering autonomy, having meaning and being adapted to the competence of our students).
- *Feedback*: The basis of any educational process is communication. An efficient communication strategy requires an immediate feedback.
- *Trial and error*: In traditional educational systems, errors are usually penalized. However, errors are a major source of learning and progress. The way humans naturally learn is by trial and error. We consider that error analysis and its perception as normal make individuals less fearful and more disposed to experiment. The aim of the learning process is to learn to be able, and mistakes are part of learning.
- *Experimentation and creativity*: We usually design exercises or tasks to have only one possible solution (the case of multiple choice tests is paradigmatic). However, the reality is not closed and usually has infinite possible interpretations. This feature is what allows experimentation and creativity. Good games also have this feature, so that succeeding in a game is often a matter of ingenuity and complex skills.
- *Autonomy*: In this context, autonomy is giving the students control over their learning process. Instead of following a strict and closed syllabus, why not allow students to choose the contents that really interest them and develop them autonomously? From our point of view the capability to acquire new knowledge is more important than content. Moreover, the extra motivation given by autonomy is a propellant for learning.
- *One size fits all gamification*: Precooked gamification systems typically offer a layer of standardized elements, such as badges, leader boards and medals. They also tend to allow the creation of missions or challenges as groups of goals or medals for completing these challenges. However, mechanics, dynamics and components are not the only elements of fun games. A fun and efficient gamified learning system will usually require a complex process of customization and, in most cases, a complete reengineering of the learning process.

Our proposal claims active and customized learning, promoting the intrinsic motivation of the students, who learn for their own satisfaction. New technologies may play an essential role in achieving this goal, complementing traditional teaching. We think that automation and integration of emerging tools are the keys to succeed, given the usually overcrowded classrooms.

We have also taken into account the benefits of gamification as an innovative emerging technology to improve the design of the learning process. A gamified strategy for learning is closer to students' interests and provides them with some autonomy thus getting the best from them, and considering that students have different abilities and learn at different rates.

From these considerations and from the lessons learned, we propose a model of adaptive gamified student-centered learning named *LudifyME*. It is a conceptual model that pursues the satisfaction, motivation and performance of students from the benefits of gamification and with a solid technological component for taking advantage of the potential of IT.

Finally, as a case study based on *LudifyME*, we have presented the *PLMan* system. This is an online gamified system aimed at introducing students to logical reasoning. We have also collected data from the students' interactions with the system that has enabled us to design a progressive prediction system of students' performance. This system allows the construction of evolutionary graphs representing trends that allow the guidance of students in the learning process, detecting early anomalies in their progress. The results have been promising and encouraging to further research and improvements of the system.

REFERENCES

Anderson, J., Rainie, L., 2012. The Future of Gamification. Pew Research Center, Washington, D.C.

Castel, M.J., Gallego, F., Pomares, C., Suau, P., Villagrá, C., Cortés, S., 2009. Real-time evaluation. In: International Conference on Education and New Learning Technologies (EDULEARN).

Centre for Learning & Performance Technologies. Top 100 Tools for Learning (http://c4lpt.co.uk/top100tools).

Compañ, P., Molina, R., Satorre, R., Llorens, F., 2014. Is teaching a fractal? In: 2014 International Symposium on Computers in Education (SIIE), pp. 7–12.

Csikszentmihalyi, M., 1990. Flow. The Psychology of Optimal Experience. Harper & Row, New York.

De Freitas, S., Neumann, T., 2009. The use of exploratory learning for supporting immersive learning in virtual environments. Comput. Educ. 52 (2), 343–352.

Domínguez, A., Saenz-De-Navarrete, J., De-Marcos, L., Fernández-Sanz, L., Pagés, C., Martínez-Herráiz, J.J., 2013. Gamifying learning experiences: practical implications and outcomes. Comput. Educ. 63, 380–392.

Erl, T., Puttini, R., Mahmood, Z., 2013. Cloud Computing: Concepts, Technology & Architecture. Prentice Hall, Upper Saddle River, NJ.

Friedkin, N.E., Johnsen, E.C., 2011. Social Influence Network Theory: A Sociological Examination of Small Group Dynamics. Cambridge University Press, Cambridge.

Gallego, F.J., Llorens, F., 2011. ¿Qué nos enseña Pacman? Lecciones aprendidas desarrollando videojuegos educativos. In: I Congreso Internacional sobre Aprendizaje, Innovación y Competitividad (CINAIC 2011), Madrid.

Gallego, F.J., Villagrá, C.J., Satorre, R., Compañ, P., Molina, R., Llorens, F., 2014. Panorámica: serious games, gamification y mucho más. ReVisión (Revista de Investigación en Docencia Universitaria de la Informática) 7 (3), 13–23.

Gardner, H., 2000. Intelligence Reframed: Multiple Intelligences for the 21st Century. Basic Books, New York.

Gardner, H., 2011. Multiple Intelligences: Reflections After Thirty Years. National Association of Gifted Children Parent and Community Network Newsletter, Washington, DC.

Gartner, 2012. Gamification 2020: What Is the Future of Gamification? Published: 5 November 2012. Analyst: Brian Burke.

Gartner, Gartner Hype Cycle (http://www.gartner.com/technology/research/methodologies/hype-cycle.jsp). (accessed 14 March 2016).

González, C., Mora, A., Toledo, P., 2014. Gamification in Intelligent Tutoring Systems. In: Proceedings of the Second International Conference on Technological Ecosystems for Enhancing Multiculturality (TEEM '14).

Huang, S., Fang, N., 2013. Predicting student academic performance in an engineering dynamics course: a comparison of four types of predictive mathematical models. Comput. Educ. 61, 133–145.

Illanas, A., Llorens, F., 2011. Los retos Web 2.0 de cara al EEES. In: En Suárez Guerrero, C., García Peñalvo, F.J. (Eds.), Universidad y Desarrollo Social de la Web. Editandum, Washington, DC, pp. 13–34.

Illanas, A., Gallego, F., Satorre, R., Llorens, F., 2008. Conceptual mini-games for learning. In: International Technology, Education and Development Conference (INTED).

Illanas, A., Calvo, J.R., Gallego, F.J., Llorens, F., 2013. Predicting student performance in foreign languages with a serious game. In: International Technology, Education and Development Conference (INTED).

Illanas, A., Llorens, F., Molina, R., Gallego, F.J., Compañ, P., Satorre, R., Villagrá, C., 2014. ¿Puede un videojuego ayudarnos a predecir los resultados de aprendizaje? I. In: Congreso de la Sociedad Española para las Ciencias del Videojuego (CoSECiVi).

Johnson, L., Adams Becker, S., Cummins, M., Estrada, V., Freeman, A., Ludgate, H., 2013. NMC Horizon Report: 2013 Higher Education Edition. The New Media Consortium, Austin, TX.

Kapp, K.M., 2012. The Gamification of Learning and Instruction. Game-Based Methods and Strategies for Training and Education. Pfeiffer, San Francisco.

Koster, R., 2004. A Theory of Fun for Game Design. Paraglyph Press, Scottsdale, Arizona.

Kotsiantis, S.B., 2012. Use of machine learning techniques for educational proposes: a decision support system for forecasting students' grades. Artif. Intell. Rev. 37, 331–344.

Linden, A., Fenn, J., 2003. Understanding Gartner's hype cycles. Strategic Analysis Report No. R-20-1971. Gartner, Inc.

Llorens, F., 2009. La tecnología como motor de la innovación educativa. Estrategia y política institucional de la Universidad de Alicante. ARBOR Ciencia, Pensamiento y Cultura CLXXXV EXTRA, 21–32.

Llorens, F., 2011. La biblioteca universitaria como difusor de la innovación educativa. Estrategia y política institucional de la Universidad de Alicante. ARBOR Ciencia, Pensamiento y Cultura 187, 89–100.

Llorens, F., 2014a. Campus virtuales: de gestores de contenidos a gestores de metodologías. RED, Revista de Educación a Distancia. 42. Número monográfico sobre "Experiencias y tendencias en affordances educativas de campus virtuales universitarios". September 15, 2014. (Accessed 14 March 2016 in http://www.um.es/ead/red/42).

Llorens, F., 2014b. Número especial: aprendizaje y Videojuegos. ReVisión (Revista de Investigación en Docencia Universitaria de la Informática) 7(2).

Llorens, F., Bayona, J.J., Gómez, J., Sanguino, F., 2010. The University of Alicante's institutional strategy to promote the open dissemination of knowledge. Online Inf. Rev. 34 (4), 565–582.

Llorens, F., Molina, R., Gallego, F.J., Villagra, C., Aznar, F., 2013. ABPgame: un videojuego como proyecto de aprendizaje coordinado para varias asignaturas. In: Congreso Internacional sobre Aprendizaje, Innovación y Competitividad (CINAIC).

Llorens, F., Molina, R., Compañ, P., Satorre, R., 2014. Technological ecosystem for open education. In: En Neves-Silva, R., Tsihrintzis, G.A., Uskov, V., Howlett, R.J., Jain, L.C. (Eds.), Smart Digital Futures 2014. In: Volumen 262 de Frontiers in Artificial Intelligence and Applications, IOS Press, Amsterdam, Netherlands, pp. 706–715.

Lykourentzou, I., Giannoukos, I., Mpardis, G., Nikolopoulos, V., Loumos, V., 2009. Early and dynamic student achievement prediction in e-learning courses using neural networks. J. Am. Soc. Inf. Sci. Technol. 60, 372–380.

Macfadyen, L.P., Dawson, S., 2010. Mining LMS data to develop an "early warning system" for educators: a proof of concept. Comput. Educ. 54, 588–599.

Markham, T., Larmer, J., Ravitz, J., 2003. Project Based Learning Handbook: A Guide to Standards-Focused Project Based Learning for Middle and High School Teachers, second Rev Spl ed. Buck Inst for Education, Novato, CA.

McGonigal, J., 2011. Reality Is Broken: Why Games Make Us Better and How They Can Change the World. The Penguin Press, New York.

Merrill, M.D., 2007. First principles of instruction: a synthesis. In: Reiser, R.A., Dempsey, J.V. (Eds.), Trends and Issues in Instructional Design and Technology, second ed. Prentice-Hall, Upper Saddle River, NJ, pp. 62–71.

Merrill, M.D., 2009. First principles of instruction. In: Reigeluth, C.M., Carr-Chellman, A.A. (Eds.), In: Instructional-Design Theories and Models: Building a Common Knowledge Base, vol. III. Routledge, New York, pp. 41–56.

Moore, G., 2014. Crossing the Chasm, third ed. Harper Business, New York, USA.

Mora, A., Riera, D., González, C., Arnedo-Moreno, J., 2015. A literature review of gamification design frameworks. In: 7th International Conference on Games and Virtual Worlds for Serious Applications (VS-Games).

Moreno-Ger, P., Burgos, D., Torrente, J., 2009. Digital games in e-learning environments: current uses and emerging trends. Simul. Gaming 40 (5), 669–687.

Novak, G.N., Patterson, E.T., Gavrin, A., Christian, W., 1999. Just-in-Time Teaching: Blending active Learning and Web Technology. Prentice Hall, Upper Saddle River, NJ.

Pastor, H., Satorre, R., Molina, R., Gallego, F.J., Llorens, F., 2015. Can Moodle be used for structural gamification? In: 9th International Technology, Education and Development Conference (INTED).

Prensky, M., 2001. Digital Game-Based Learning. McGraw-Hill, New York.

Prensky, M., 2006. Don't Bother Me Mom – I'm Learning! Paragon House, St. Paul, MN, USA.

Reigeluth, C.M., 2011. An instructional theory for the post-industrial age. Educ. Technol. 51 (5), 25–29.

Reigeluth, C.M., 2012. Instructional theory and technology for the new paradigm of education. RED, Revista de Educación a Distancia 32.

Rinaudo, M.C., Chiecher, A., Donolo, D., 2003. Motivación y uso de estrategias en estudiantes universitarios. Su evaluación a partir del Motivated Strategies Learning Questionnaire. Anales de Psicología 19 (1), 107–119.

Robinson, K., 2013. Finding Your Element: How to Discover Your Talents and Passions and Transform Your Life. Penguin, New York.

Rogers, E., 2003. Diffusion of Innovations, fifth ed. Simon & Schuster, New York, USA.

Ronchetti, M., 2010. Using video lectures to make teaching more interactive. Int. J. Emerging Technol. Learning (iJET) 5(2).

Ryan, R.M., Deci, E.L., 2000. Self-determination theory and the facilitation of intrinsic motivation, social development, and well-being. Am. Psychol. 55 (1), 68–78.

Sterling, L.S., Shapiro, E.Y., 1994. The Art of Prolog. Advanced Programming Techniques, second ed. The MIT Press, Cambridge, MA, USA.

Taleb, N., 2007. The Black Swan: The Impact of the Highly Improbable. Random House, New York, USA.

Tapia, J.A., 1995. Motivación y aprendizaje en el aula. Cómo enseñar a pensar. Santillana, Madrid, Spain.

Turkle, S., 2011. Alone Together: Why We Expect More from Technology and Less from Each Other. Basic Books, New York.

Villagrá, C.J., Gallego, F.J., Molina, R., Llorens, F., 2014a. ABPgame+: siete asignaturas, un proyecto. In: Actas de las XX Jornadas sobre la Enseñanza Universitaria de la Informática (JENUI 2014).

Villagrá, C.J., Gallego, F.J., Molina, R., Llorens, F., Lozano, M.A., Sempere, M.L., Ponce de León, P., Iñesta, J.M., Berná, J.V., 2014b. ABPgame+ o cómo hacer del último curso de ingeniería una primera experiencia profesional. In: XII Jornadas de Redes de Investigación en Docencia Universitaria.

Villagrá, C.J., Gallego, F.J., Molina, R., Llorens, F., 2015. Boosting the learning process with progressive performance prediction. In: Tenth European Conference on Technology Enhanced Learning (EC-TEL 2015).

Werbach, K., 2012. For the Win: How Game Thinking Can Revolutionize Your Business. Wharton Digital Press, Philadelphia, PA.

Wu, T.F., Lin, C.J., Weng, R.C., 2004. Probability estimates for multi-class classification by pairwise coupling. J. Mach. Learn. Res. 5, 975–1005.

κPAX: EXPERIENCES ON DESIGNING A GAMIFIED PLATFORM FOR SERIOUS GAMING

13

D. Riera, J. Arnedo-Moreno

Open University of Catalonia, Barcelona, Spain

1 INTRODUCTION

Games are something that all civilizations through time have in common. Even though the games themselves may vary, we all share the concept of play as a free activity outside of the "ordinary" or "serious" world. Nevertheless, in almost every case, they are conceived as greatly engaging activities. In fact, Huizinga defined human beings as *homo ludens* in 1955 (Huizinga and Hull, 1949). In recent years, the evolution of digital technologies and the rise of video-games as a medium has increased the prominence of the role of games in society, as well as their the recognition of capability to provide enjoyment and engagement (Brumels and Blasius, 2008). A new ecosystem has arisen, populated by the so-called Z generation (Prensky, 2001), people who have grown up playing video-games and feel at home in a society where games are prevalent in daily life. In a world with an increasing number of such citizens, the concepts of serious games and gamification arise almost organically. However, even though both concepts share several characteristics, and sometimes overlap in some parts of the literature, it is important to take into account that each one has its own meaning and goals.

On the one hand, serious games push entertainment into the background, looking for another focus, usually training or learning. It is very difficult to say precisely when serious games were born since, from ancient times, they have been a tool used to facilitate learning. From a formal standpoint, one of the first written references is Clark Abt's discussion of the term in his 1970s book, Serious games (Abt, 1970). There, he states "We are concerned with serious games in the sense that these games have an explicit and carefully thought-out educational purpose and are not intended to be played primarily for amusement", giving us a first attempt at a formal definition of the concept.

On the other hand, the goal of gamification is engagement. This concept has evolved considerably since its inception in 2002 (Pelling, 2011), Nick Pelling defined it as the application of a game-like accelerated user interface designed to make electronic transactions both enjoyable and fast. Nowadays, it also encompasses different aspects of a game experience, and has slowly started to encroach on playful experiences and anything game-related, such as serious games themselves. Nevertheless, the most

Formative Assessment, Learning Data Analytics and Gamification. http://dx.doi.org/10.1016/B978-0-12-803637-2.00013-0

widespread definition in the literature could be summarized as "the use of game design elements in non-game contexts" (Deterding et al., 2011).

In this paper, we present our experiences in the design and development of *κPAX*[1]: kudos, *Plataforma d'Aprenentatge en Xarxa* (*kudos — Network Platform for Learning*). This project was born from mixing the prevalence of social networks (eg, Facebook, LinkedIn, etc.), the rising number of electronic devices, portable and nonportable (eg, smart-phones, tablets, consoles, computers, etc.), and the entrance of serious games into the spotlight. The chosen means to join this triad is gamification, both as an engagement mechanic and, tracing back to the roots of its definition, as a video-game-like feedback mechanism. From here, the main goal has been twofold: (a) the design and implementation of an open source platform easily extensible by independent heterogeneous modules (including games, plugins, simulators, etc.), which can be the result of other research or innovation projects, or external developers contributions, and (b) the creation of a social network for games-based learning over the technological platform.

For a good understanding of the platform's purpose, it is necessary to introduce a bit on our institution, the *Universitat Oberta de Catalunya* (UOC, *Open University of Catalonia*)[2]. This is a public Internet-centered university created in 1994 in Barcelona. That makes it one of the first universities in the world to be completely online based, with more than 60,000 students and 50,000 graduates in fields like IT, psychology, education, law, management, communication and humanities, among others. The Internet-only nature of our institution and the digital literacy of our students makes it a good match for *κPAX*'s approach to e-learning.

The platform is built upon four ideas that take into account the idiosyncrasies of UOC:

1. Providing support for the training and assessment of certain skills or proficiencies
2. The current state of technology, which adds a new dimension to the spatial and temporal asynchronism of traditional online learning, thanks to the latest trends in mobile devices
3. Using tools based in ubiquitous technology, such as social networks, that allow people to be connected to others everywhere
4. An interest in applying the results of innovative projects across different fields, courses and studies.

In addition, the impact of this project goes beyond the UOC's campus, as *κPAX*, being a universal open learning tool, accepts internal and external users.

The result of our work has been the design and implementation of this technological platform and social network. The code of the platform has been published under the GNU General Public License (GPL) Version 2[3] so that any contributor can see, improve and complete the source code if so desired. Also, the addition of new games to the platform is fully open both to the UOC community (eg, faculty, management staff, students, designers, etc.) and to external programmers too. The main benefit of *κPAX* is that educators are provided with a platform that easily allows the distribution of serious games on different topics. Students get feedback on their skill mastery progress through their performance on all games in the platform.

---

[1]http://kpax.uoc.edu/elgg.
[2]http://www.uoc.edu.
[3]http://www.gnu.org/licenses/gpl-2.0.html.

This paper is structured as follows. First of all, Section 2 introduces the use of gamification and serious games as supports to the learning processes both from a conceptual and practical standpoint. *κPAX*'s conceptual design, based on the three pillars of system requirements, the specific gamification design and the website and interface definition, is presented in Section 3. Then, in Section 4, we discuss the decisions taken during the architectural design, mainly focusing on the services definition, the internal database and some key aspects on security. Finally, Section 5 concludes this work and provides some insights into our current and future work.

2 BACKGROUND

Serious games and gamification have many things in common, both being based on the application of a game design process to create a product that is not purely for entertainment. In this regard, they have been successfully applied in an educational context many times, their benefits have been tested and proved (Hamari et al., 2014).

Formally defining the designing of a "game" is a topic of contention in the literature. However, we consider Whitton's (2009) approach very useful. Instead of thinking in terms of "game/not game," it may be more useful to talk about game-like properties:

- *Competition*: There is a winner/loser scenario
- *Challenge*: The activity itself is not trivial
- *Fantasy*: There is and imaginary environment component
- *Exploration*: There is a simulated environment that can be investigated
- *Goals*: There is an objective that must be achieved
- *Interaction*: Actions change the state of play and have consequences
- *Outcomes*: Performance can be measured (scoring, success/defeat)
- *People*: Other individuals take part in the activity
- *Rules*: It is bounded by artificial constraints
- *Safety*: The activity has no consequences in the real world.

Therefore, serious games and gamification are design processes based on integrating properties from this list. The more properties that are taken into account, the more "game-like" an activity becomes. However, it is also very important to point out that, even though both gamification and serious games share their root in game design, they are conceptually different and have different goals.

On the one hand, serious games take the role of a discrete resource in a course, providing the students with understanding on a topic by directly transmitting knowledge or training skills, just like a book, a lecture or a hands-on lab. Therefore, serious games are learning resources that, by virtue of being consumed or interacted with, directly affect the student's learning. Briefly summarizing, one might say that, up to some point, serious games can be considered interactive simulations which include game-like properties. Their main advantage are their high levels of interactivity, capability of immediate feedback and sandbox nature. The student's decisions and actions play a fundamental role in how the resource is experienced, in such a manner that parts of the experience might even be different for each student, but outcomes within the game do not affect other aspects of the course. These characteristics benefit students by motivating experimentation and re-consumption of the game as a learning resource itself until the topic is mastered (ie, playing again and again).

On the other hand, gamification serves as a tool for course structure or content delivery, in such a manner that students become engaged with the topic by interacting with its new game-like properties. Between all these properties, probably the most important one in gamification would be "outcomes." Thus, the final product is not a discrete learning resource that is incorporated to the course, but a new version of the course itself. In this regard, game-like properties and mechanics are integrated into the kind of actions a student can usually perform during the course (eg, consume learning resources, deliver exercises, help fellow learners, etc.), or in the aesthetics or look and feel of course content, in such a manner that following the course becomes a motivating experience itself. A good gamification design will also slowly build a sense of accomplishment and progress for the student.

κPAX mixes both techniques to provide a set of learning resources (serious games) and then motivates students to consume them collaboratively, while also providing useful feedback on skill mastery (gamification). However, it must be noted that, as a platform, it is not directly concerned with the educational structure of such content beyond the purely technological aspects (ie, integration and deployment). Content itself is left up to the developers and educators. Therefore, the focus during the platform design process fell into the gamification aspects and how to integrate games as easily pluggable elements. How each serious game should be designed and created is out with of the scope of this project.

In order to better understand how gamification can be effectively used, we provide a brief background about how gamification works from a motivational standpoint and some relevant examples of existing platforms that rely on gamification to engage their user base in similar scenarios.

2.1 ON THE BASIS OF GAMIFICATION

Gamification pursues engagement. In order to achieve this goal, it relies on well-known game design techniques to shape user behavior through engagement and motivation. The psychology of motivation has raised several theories with different levels of complexity, even though, in the end, they all translate to the physiological level. When you are motivated, the brain emits the chemical signal dopamine, as anticipation to pleasure. Even though gamification feeds from different sources in the psychological and motivational literature, the self-determination theory (SDT) (Deci and Ryan, 1991) and Flow (Csikszentmihalyi and Csikzentmihaly, 1991) are its main foundations, and enough to understand its context. On one hand, in SDT, it is stated that there are three aspects which govern human motivation: autonomy, competency and relatedness. First of all, people are motivated when they are in control of their own choices and can create their own strategies. Second, the task at hand, even though challenging, should be perceived to be within reach of one's own skills. Finally, people are also motivated when their actions have an impact on their immediate environment, especially at the social level (eg, achieving recognition, helping other people, etc.). According to Flow, the optimal experience also requires that the difficulty of a task and the our skill mastery is perfectly balanced all the time. At the beginning, tasks should be very easy. As our skills grow, tasks should slowly become more challenging. An imbalance will lead to frustration (the task is too difficult) or boredom (too easy), and therefore, a lack of engagement.

In this regard, effective gamification requires that the different aspects of human motivation are taken into account when importing game properties and mechanics to a nongame context, such as in education. The mechanics need not be complex, but nevertheless need to account for motivational aspects. This is a delicate process that should never be performed in an *ad hoc* manner, but with the help of a gamification framework, understood as a formal process or guideline. Given the increasing interest in the topic, several such frameworks have been developed in recent years ranging from those fully defined to a loose list of pieces of advice with a few examples tacked on. For a more detailed comparison of them, a comprehensive literature review can be found in Mora et al. (2015). Even though the specifics may be a bit different between them, they usually agree on three basic steps: defining the expected behaviors, identifying player types and deploying the appropriate game mechanics, for the given player types.

By defining expected behaviors, the purpose of gamifying a process is set. Gamification operates at a motivational level, and, therefore, whenever it is applied, it is because the designer desires to shape the participant's behavior, so that they will perform some specific actions. For instance, in a learning environment, it could be attending class, delivering exercises or solving problems at class, among others. Usually, when deciding on the expected behaviors, the designer also decides a set of metrics that will help him or her to evaluate the degree of success.

The player type is the link that translates pure motivational theory into game design and gamification. At this stage, game players are classified into roles, each one considered to be motivated by different game mechanics. Again, different approaches exist, but the most well known, and the basis for *κPAX*, would be Bartle's (1996). The main roles are established by classifying players according to two axes: players vs world, and interacting vs acting. This results in four possible roles. The so-called "Killers" like competition against other players. "Socializers" enjoy having a sense of community with other players, as well as recognition. "Achievers" work towards a clear goal or obtaining some reward. And finally, "Explorers" like experimenting with the game rules and narrative. Usually, players do not belong to a single type, but have a "Bartle Quotient": they belong to all categories at once, each at a different degree. Given a player type classification, a gamified system may be designed so it will cater to a single type, by relying on a very focused set of mechanics, or to different types at once, by using a broader array.

The choice of game mechanics judges as suitable for the chosen types of player could be considered the core of the gamification process, as well as the most creative one. Again, just as with the term "game," there are different approaches to defining "game mechanic." We will go with Sicart's "methods invoked by agents, designed for interaction with the game state" (Sicart, 2008). There are many types of mechanics that can be extracted from the study of games. As far as the application of gamification in education is concerned, however, we can assess the most important ones from a representative survey in Nah et al. (2014). They are listed as:

- *Points*: A basic numeric performance measurement. It need not be tied to course evaluation (pass/fail)
- *Badges*: A token of recognition used a status symbols
- *Leaderboards*: Competitive ranking which displays each participant's position
- *Levels*: Indicator of overall skill mastery, attained by accumulating points
- *Storytelling*: The course encompasses a story or narrative
- *Customization*: Ability to customize some aspect, such as an avatar
- *Unlockables*: Content that is not accessible until the player has completed some task.

This is just a short summary extracted from some use cases in learning. There are many kinds of mechanics that could be extracted by studying games. The limit is in the designer's imagination, and, therefore, it is not possible to provide an exhaustive review in this section. Nevertheless, the most widely used mechanic by a very large margin, in all contexts, learning or not, is some variation of the Points, Badges and Leaderboards trio, often shortened as "PBL" (not to be confused with "Project Based Learning" in a learning context). Briefly summarized, whenever a participant acts according to the desired behavior, he or she is awarded either some points or a badge that can be used as a symbol of status (proving to others that he or she was able to do it). Points are used to rank all students in a public leaderboard, the one with the most points being at the top.

This simple combination is good enough to provide some satisfaction to each one of Bartle's player types: competition (Killer), social status (Socializer), concrete achievements and clear sense of progress (Achiever) and a sense of real system interaction with feedback (Explorer). More complex mechanics, such as the inclusion of storytelling or narrative also exist, like in Villagrasa and Duran (2013), but the effort required to properly design and deploy this kind of approach makes it less appealing. Nevertheless, other game mechanics can be found in the literature, but often included on top of a PBL system. For instance, using points as a form of virtual currency.

2.2 PLATFORMS BASED ON GAMIFICATION

Once the basis of gamification has been discussed, it is time to take a brief look at some relevant existing platforms that are conceptually similar to κ*PAX*. Namely, those able to integrate a broad set of educational resources while at the same time relying on gamification techniques to encourage users to consume them. In addition, even though not directly related to education, we think it is worth mentioning some examples of platforms which use gamification to persuade users to consume video games. It is important to note that, in this context, we define "consume" not as a synonym of "buying," but as experiencing, experimenting, tinkering, etc., with the video game content. This is an aspect very relevant to educational resources such as serious games, and, therefore, up to a point, what κ*PAX* is about.

Most mainstream platforms that act as a gamified learning management system (LMS) tend to be quite focused on corporate training. All of them incorporate the typical LMS resources: virtual classrooms with a calendar or scheduler and some method of web content delivery. However, resources tend to be simple ones, such as downloadable documents or HMTL, not complex ones such as virtual labs or simulations. They all also provide a highly polished graphic style. Given that, from an educative standpoint, they all share very similar basic functionalities; in this section we just focus on the gamification design aspects and chosen mechanics.

Between the most current platforms, Academy LMS (Growth Engineering, 2015) is a popular one. According to the creators, the system may also accommodate higher education, going beyond small-scale corporate training. Its application of gamification is based on three very basic game mechanics: points, badges and levels. As students interact with the system, they accumulate points, that allow them to gain levels, as a status symbol and feedback mechanism. In fact, the level number acts as a course progress indicator. Other very similar platforms can be found in Accord, ExpertusOne and Axonify (Accord, 2009, Expertus, 2013, Axonify Inc., 2014). In these cases, the points and badges dichotomy is expanded by incorporating leaderboards, thus fully embracing the model. Axonify also incorporates some other more social-network-oriented game techniques, such as "coaches," virtual avatars that will comment on the student's performance, and teambuilding.

With regard to platforms developed by the academia, and not the enterprise, the most relevant one would be Gradecraft (Holman et al., 2013). It is a project at a much lower scale, but directly designed with higher education in mind. Even though this platform was created for a specific subject, videogames and learning, it is implemented as a generic LMS, which could easily fit any other course

Table 13.1 Gamified Platforms

Name	Context	Game Mechanics
Academy LMS	Learning	Points, Badges, Levels
Accord	Learning	Points, Badges, Leaderboards
ExpertusOne	Learning	Points, Badges, Leaderboards
Axonify	Learning	Points, Badges, Leaderboards, Mentoring, Teambuilding
Gradecraft	Learning	Progress Bar, Badges
Steam	Gaming	Points, Badges, Leaderboards, Levels, Trading, Crafting
Gree	Gaming	Points, Badges, Leaderboards

subject. Gradecraft has a great focus on learning analytics, and, therefore, its main mechanics are related to providing video-game-like feedback: progress bars and badges based on assignment completion.

Moving to platforms that use gamification as a tool to encourage users to consume computer games, probably the most well know one is Steam (Valve Inc., 2003). Truth be told, this platform was the most influential during *κPAX*'s conceptual design process. Steam's gamification mechanics are based, again, on the PBL model. An API is provided for game developers so that they are able to update player high score leaderboards and award special badges when players complete a particular action in the game (for instance, successfully completing a stage). Developers also have the choice of letting their games drop trading cards during gameplay, which can be later exchanged with other players, or crafted into special badges. Finally, buying games and crafting badges award experience points to players, which allows them to increase their "player level." High level players have more options when customizing their user profiles, as well as a higher chance of getting some bonus trading cards each day.

A similar, but more simplistic approach, can be found in Gree (Tanaka, 2004), a Japanese social networking service focused on mobile games and applications. Gree offers an API too, which allows the development of over the platform providing leaderboards and badges to players. In contrast with Steam, this process is much easier and straightforward from a developer standpoint. Additionally, the platform allows the possibility of trading in-game items in order to customize the player experience. Some other minor game networking services exist, which are spread across various mobile developers, but they are conceptually very similar to Gree.

The main properties of the reviewed platforms are summarized in Table 13.1.

3 *κPAX* CONCEPTUAL DESIGN

Our main goal was to design and implement an online learning tool that exclusively relied on serious games as an educational resource, complemented with gamification as the engagement and feedback mechanism. The main idea would be to provide a set of core services that allow the community to publish the games.

The first step in the development was the conceptual design of the system; the description of how this process should work and meet its requirements. The basic capabilities were defined at an abstract level, before analyzing technological approaches. First, we started with the requirements definition and gamification mechanics design. From here, it was possible to create an initial mock up system that would provide the basis for the current one.

3.1 SYSTEM REQUIREMENTS

The approach for the system requirements definition process was twofold. In a first iteration, the minimum core expected functionalities were identified. We started with a minimalist approach, but having already in mind that *κPAX* would be modular and could be later easily extended by developers who wanted to improve it. In a second iteration, we then tried to collect the list of maximum possible future functionalities which would require the minimum number of changes in the core when incorporated. The result was a set of requirements which would allow a long-term incremental development, even when the system was already deployed, around a very stable core.

The list of *κPAX*'s core requirements follow:

1. The system must be open to and accessible from any operating system (Windows, Mac/iOS, Linux and variants such as Android, etc.) or device (mobile, tablets, videogame consoles, etc.).
2. There are three kinds of users: First of all, developers, who publish games as learning resources. It is possible that, in the real world, a developer may create a game at the behest of another entity (such as educators), but in the system we consider anyone who makes a game available within the platform and takes care of its management a "developer". Second, learners, who consume them. Finally, the administrators, who manage the system and approve game submissions, among others.
3. Developers can publish games, making them available to the platform's user base. This process should be as simple as possible.
4. Learners must be able to search for games related to a specific skill and freely play them.
5. Learners have a personal profile they can edit.
6. The system must provide feedback mechanisms on the evolution of learner skills, as they progresses through different games. As the system considers that a user becomes an expert in a subject/skill, labels on the levels of competence are incorporated in the personal profile.
7. *κPAX* should allow both on-line and off-line playing. It should be possible to download the game, play and reconnect to synchronize high scores, achievements, etc.

The role of *κPAX* admins is to guarantee that the games, as learning resources, will aim to promote learning (this includes theory, skills, etc.) and take advantage of the platform to facilitate distribution. Therefore, the administrators should comprise the educators at the institution deploying *κPAX* (in our case, lecturers at UOC). Developers request publication of their games via the platform interface, providing a description and some basic information about the game (topic, related competencies, genre, etc.). Each submission is then reviewed by the administrators, who then decide whether to approve it and incorporate the game into the platform, or not. Which characteristics must be taken into account in order to approve a submission are up to the admins. *κPAX* just provides the technological means to manage this process. Some of the technological requirements will be discussed in Section 4.3.2.

Games should offer incentives and awards due to partial successes, and some recognition can also exist for specific tasks, such as completing a game level, a set of games, achieving a set of skills, etc. Overcoming levels/stages should be directly related to the achievement of competencies. However, it is worth mentioning that these details of game design are beyond the scope of the system definition, and up to the developers. Again, κ*PAX* just behaves as the distribution channel. Nevertheless, games must be able to relay on the system to track the learning progress and offer a recognition scheme (see core requirement 2).

From the basic requirements, we also defined a set of possible functionalities that, even though not considered necessary for the initial versions of the platform, would be taken into account when designing the system core as probable additions:

- The system should support the potential for a game to be paused or saved and recovered, enabling it to be played at any time. Furthermore, it should be possible to resume games from any platform, upon synchronization with the previous machine.
- The system may incorporate a "teaching" mode that provides the player with digital resources that could be learning support.
- The system should allow interaction between users and groups: challenges, partnerships, groupings, etc. There are games that can be played individually or in groups. Competitions or "leagues" can be promoted, or simply teams of like minded players. Thus, players can join teams, according to the offers/demands of participants, for a specific game/league. In addition, it is possible to make regular tournaments, weekend leagues, etc., proposed by administrators or by users themselves.
- Players should know the connection status of their friends, for example, to allow requests for help if the game allows it.
- It should be possible to compare/correlate goals or achievements among friends and/or the community. Users should also be able to publish this information on games, results, etc., in other social networks (eg, Twitter, Facebook, etc.).

3.2 GAMIFICATION DESIGN

The design of the gamification elements in κ*PAX* needed to be included at the very initial stages of the project, since this would have big implications in the system development, acting as the structure that gives cohesion to the whole. Furthermore, offering a feedback mechanism is considered a very important part of the platform (see Section 3.1). Gamification was chosen as the means to fulfill this requirement. In order to create the gamified approach, we reviewed current gamification frameworks and followed the steps broadly described in Section 2.1: defining expected behaviors, identifying player types and, finally, choosing game mechanics that motivate the player types.

The expected behavior of users in κ*PAX* is quite straightforward: that they play the different serious games that developers make available through the platform. Even though the use of gamification to inspire this behavior may seem redundant with the use of serious games as an educational resource, it must be taken into account that a serious game is not unquestionably engaging just by virtue of being a video game. The goal of serious games is, first and foremost, learning, not entertainment, even though being fun is a highly desirable property. Nevertheless, even when a game has been correctly designed to be enjoyable, different people may like different kinds of games. For instance, some people may like triva games, but dislike logic puzzles. A student will not be directly engaged in a game from a disliked genre. In addition, as a user becomes used to a game and the novelty wears off, interest wanes. Given that playing the game has an educational purpose and is not a choice completely left up to students, there are cases where gamification may help, motivating the users into playing a broad set of instructional games.

κ*PAX* does not focus on a single player type, and its gamification design tries to cater to each of Bartle's roles. Therefore, we opted for the tried and tested PBL approach which many platforms already integrate (see Section 2.2), providing mechanics that can be adapted to all player types. Using this system, we also wanted to keep the gamification mechanics simple and straightforward, since the core focus of the platform is learning through serious gaming. Nevertheless, we have included some twists of our own. In this regard, Fig. 13.1 summarizes how the gamification mechanics work in κ*PAX*.

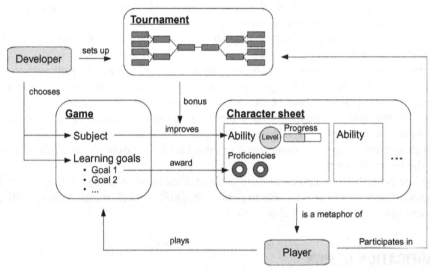

FIGURE 13.1

κ*PAX* gamification mechanics summary.

First and foremost, gamification is used as a method of personal feedback, heavily inspired by tabletop role-playing games (TRPG), and especially Advanced Dungeons&Dragons (AD&D) [Cook (1989)], in format and nomenclature. In this regard, each user has a *character sheet*, or profile, that acts as a metaphor for the learning progress. The character sheet contains a set of *ability scores*, each one representing the student's degree of mastery on different general subjects (eg, math, language, history, etc.). Abilities slowly increase as users interact with games within that subject. However, the higher the current ability score, the longer it takes to increase it. In addition, each ability score has a linked set of *proficiencies*, discrete indicators of specific skills students have demonstrated (eg, solving a very difficult equation, knowing some amount of vocabulary, etc.). Each proficiency can be earned up to three times (bronze, silver, and gold levels).

When a developer creates a game that will be included in the platform, a subject of study and a small (2–3) set of goals, that players should accomplish, are chosen. Every time a user plays a game, the impact on the character sheet is twofold: on the one hand, progress towards increasing an ability score increases according to user performance in the game (for instance, in the final score). A user may play the game many times, with no limit, in order to successively increase the ability score on the subject. On the other hand, any time one of the game's learning goals is achieved, a proficiency is awarded. Therefore, a user's ability score and linked proficiency list may be influenced by performance in different games on the same subject.

In addition to all the inputs and outputs related to the character sheet, the system also incorporates the functionality to create tournaments in different formats (league, single-elimination, etc.). This goes one step ahead of current approaches, which exclusively rely on course-long leaderboards. κ*PAX* is able to deploy much more flexible competition scenarios. Given these game mechanics, the system may engage "Killers" (tournaments), "Socializers" (status by level), "Achievers" (proficiencies) and "Explorers" (playing different games to increase abilities).

Finally, it is important to point out that we never explicitly present the gamified system as a game itself, but just as a form of performance feedback. In fact, the use of PBL seems almost natural, since students are used to being graded on their performance. Therefore, the system can be presented as an effective method for tracking their progress toward subject mastery. This approach transmits a sense of purpose and meaning to the system.

3.3 WEBSITE AND INTERFACE DESIGN

Once the basic system requirements and the gamification mechanics have been established, it is possible to proceed to the initial design of the system interface and web view. Initially, the design included the minimum parts of the system, the goal being a first release with basic features which would act as a wireframe prototype. From this version, the system could easily grow, step by step, by slowly adding new capabilities, or creating a more complex interface, that could be easily tested. This first release contained the following parts, using a very simple design:

- The presentation page (portal), which was very simple and provided validation of existing users and registration of new ones
- Log in capabilities, relying on a local user database
- The activity tab, visible once logged in, where internal communication between a users connected as friends is possible. Here it is possible to find the user's published results, achievements, messages, challenges, etc.
- The games tab, which allows a user to view and search through all available games in κ*PAX*. Different searches can be performed, changing several criteria
- For each game in the platform, a page containing all its related information (ie, game properties tab). This page includes both static data and specific space for future dynamic data (eg, current best results, the competitions and challenges set on it, etc.)
- A network tab that allows users to search for friends and chat with them
- Finally, the user profile tab, which contains all the personal information and progress in the system (the "character sheet", see Section 3.2)

In successive iterations, the web pages have been evolving in complexity beyond the prototype stage. Additionally, as functionalities are added as plugins, new interfaces become necessary. Examples of such evolution are shown in Figs. 13.2 and 13.3.

FIGURE 13.2

Evolution of interface: main page.

FIGURE 13.3

Evolution of interface: game properties.

4 *κPAX* **ARCHITECTURAL DESIGN**

From a technological standpoint, in order to simplify the system's architecture we decided to base it on W3C[4] standards, also based on CSS3 and Javascript, which should be exportable to different platforms. It should be accessible both from client applications and via web browsers. After a study into possible open social network platforms, we finally chose *elgg*[5] as a basis to implement *κPAX*.

κPAX has got a "core" architecture based on services, which in turn has a library that implements these services and allows the development of games and external applications that interact with the core. The services is available for use in any possible target platform, with an easily extensible data model to include future expansions. This keeps the inner workings of *κPAX* completely transparent to developers. The platform includes the services, forming a set of independent logical modules for users and groups, security, registers, publication, network, games and resources management. Fig. 13.4 shows a diagram of the platform core, depicting how it works.

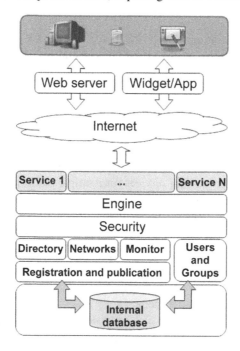

FIGURE 13.4

Platform schema.

The internal services engine is based on *Apache/Tomcat*, *Axis* or any other applications server which that allows communication mechanisms, such as sockets and/or XML and channels that allow secure encrypted transmissions (for everything concerning users, games and social networks).

---

[4]http://www.w3.org/.
[5]http://elgg.org/.

Developed games will be connected with the core by means of a set of calls to services provided by *κPAX*. These services and the corresponding documentation are available online for those developers wanting to add games or extend the platform.

4.1 SERVICES DEFINITION

Services make the internal *κPAX* code transparent to external developers. Thus, they only need to know which services to call and which parameters to use. Services allow mainly to validate a user or a game (validation is used to avoid fakes, inappropriate content or games that are not considered to be educative), to inform *κPAX* about a new game, a new result of a game, a new badge/competence level for a player, etc. The rest of the work is done by the platform itself. From a technical viewpoint, these are implemented in Java, use hibernate to access the *κPAX* (mySQL) database, and pass information using JSON. Finally, as a part of the platform architecture, all are served by a jBoss[6] server.

In general, these are the services the platform should implement (at the moment it does not support all of them):

- New users and games registration
- Access to dynamic information (eg, activities, users, social activity, etc.)
- Games interaction (services provided to the games information pass and retrieving)
- Social networks, bridge or publication in external networks
- Authorization (eg, of users to form groups, or participate in games, or join, etc.)
- Specific services for developers, including management and publication of games, monitoring their activity, etc.
- Services for statistics, platform global monitoring, etc.
- Resources (services to access and present internal and external resources available for the games)
- Visualization, information processing services for multiple platforms
- Security (for users, games, internal communications, etc.)
- Internal services for modules intercommunication
- Groups-users management (eg, user authentication, group membership, etc.).

In the platform's current state, a number of services from the previous list have been implemented, but many of them have not been integrated as yet. As an example, the main basic services for a typical scenario are introduced below. They are presented in a tentative chronological order to show how an external user and developer might use them.

A serious game has just been completed, so it is registered in *κPAX*. To publish it the developer fills in and submits all the required information. This implies that some services need to be called, but they are already in the *κPAX* core code and are kept invisible to the developer. Once the *κPAX* administrators validate and accept the game, players can see it in the games tab. As an accepted game, it is stored in the internal database. The service definition that allows adding a game is as follows:

```
+ addGame(idSession, name, gameInfo):idGame
```

On the other hand, players are also registered using some of the following services, depending on whether they are local *κPAX* users or use an external network (ie, Realm) password (eg, UOC, Facebook,

---

[6]http://www.jboss.org/.

twitter, etc.). Thus, when a new user registers, a service stores the information in the database. Notice that even when the player does not register as a *κPAX* user, an internal logical user is added to the database.

```
+ addUser(login, pwd, realm):idUser
```

From this moment, the player can log onto the platform (or external apps, webs, etc. connected to *κPAX*) triggering the corresponding services and receiving a session id. Then, the player can look for a specific game under a certain criteria, see all the information about a few games in order to choose one, etc.

```
+ login(login, pwd):idSession
+ listGamesByCategory(session, idCategory):listGames
+ listGames(session):listGames
+ getGame(session,gameId):gameInfo
```

After browsing and finding our developer's game, if the player is playing it (for instance, on a smart-phone), this will send the results to the platform at the end of the game (or later in case of being offline).

```
+ syncStateGame(gameId, userId, state):Bool
```

This approach makes it really simple to keep all the information on the games, the players and the results of each player's games in the database. Furthermore, it only leaves to developers the easy task of adding a few calls to their code in order to keep the platform up to date with regard to a player's achievements.

4.2 DATABASE DEFINITION

Although elgg contains a database itself, we have decided to create a specific one for *κPAX*. We find this clearer both for us and for external developers, and it avoids complete system breakdowns.

The *κPAX* database stores all the necessary information for the proper functioning of the platform. A basic structure with the minimum information has been designed and implemented. The structure of this basic database can be seen in Fig. 13.5. Notice that the idea is to be as simple as possible in a way that it is easy to understand, so that it may be complemented and modified (if necessary) by new modules' developers. The database, together with the elgg part of the platform, is served by an XAMPP[7] server.

As said in the *κPAX* architecture section, *κPAX*'s database can only be accessed by the services provided, for both reading and writing information. Thus, the allowed operations are limited and new capabilities' developments may require the inclusion of modifications, or even new tables in the database, and the inclusion of new services.

The main tables appearing in the basic initial version of the *κPAX* database are:

Users. The system has a set of users, who can access the platform via their usernames and pass-words, or through external validation by other social networks. In that case, the necessary information about the connection to the external service is stored in the *Realm* table (see below). In that case, as said before, it is not mandatory for a user to have an account in the *κPAX* system, therefore, the *login* and *password* fields of the *User* table are empty. Anyway, a player will always have a logical *κPAX* user, even when a local account does not exist. Authentication is very important in order to associate each call made to the system with a corresponding user (ie, assign *idUser* to calls made to services).

---

[7]https://www.apachefriends.org/index.html.

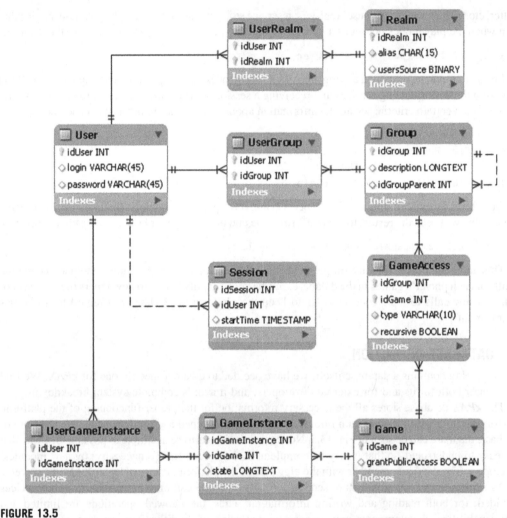

FIGURE 13.5

Platform database design.

Groups. To manage access to games, users can join groups. All groups must be registered in the *Group* table. Its structure is hierarchical and there are various root groups. Each group can only be part of another group (indicated in the attribute idGroupParent), although not necessarily be there. Root groups are limited to special system groups.

Users can belong to as many groups as necessary. Their affiliation to a group is in the *UserGroup* table. Attributes can be added to this table in order to specify types of membership, giving certain permissions within the group to some users (eg, manage users, create subgroups, etc.).

Games. Given a game, which is accessible through the *κPAX* platform it must be properly registered in the system. Only authorized games will appear in player searches. Thus, any developer can create an entry in the *Game* table, but it has to be accepted by the system administrators. Each game has a unique *idGame* within the system. In the *Game* table, all the necessary information to describe every game and even common properties can be added. For example, the field *grantPublicAccess* indicates that any user from *κPAX* can play this game (unless it is not specifically stated otherwise in a game later). Other properties might be, for instance: whether a game can be played by one or multiple players, whether it is collaborative or not, etc.

Games access. Since some games may be used for assessment purposes in academic environments, it is possible to restrict the access to certain users. For this reason, access rights can be assigned to the games for different groups. The table *GameAccess* contains information on access to games by different groups. To make the structure as flexible as possible, it contains not only the allowed accesses, but denied accesses to a game by certain groups (ie, blacklists). This information is encoded in the *type* attribute of the table *GameAccess* (values allow or deny).

Any order of refusal should outweigh more than the access ones to prevent someone who has been explicitly denied access to play the game. To know whether a user can play a game, we should firstly verify that no group for this user has got the access barred. In such a case, access will not be allowed. Since the structure of groups is hierarchical, a parameter *recursive* is defined in the *GameAccess* table. It indicates that the authorization must be made within the group tree. That means that if a group at a higher level of the hierarchy in the user's groups has access to some information, that will also apply.

Session. When a user logs in, a session associated with the connection is created. These sessions are recorded in the *Session* table, which contains the *idUser*, and are limited to a period of time (the *startTime* attribute has been defined with the creation date and time).

Game Instances. In order to play, users need to join an instance of a particular game, which should contain all the state information of that game. This information is stored in table *GameInstance*. Every instance has an unique identifier *idGameInstance* within the system. Since each game will have its proper information, a field has been created where the state of the game instance is stored using XML syntax, with the internal format and attributes decided by the game developers. In games allowing several users or collaborative gaming, this XML keeps the information needed to manage such a feature. Players who are playing a game are recorded in the table *UserGameInstance*.

Realm. As commented above, players in *κPAX* do not need to register on the platform and can be validated by third party networks. The *Realm* table contains a list of these networks validating those *κPAX*'s users.

4.3 SECURITY

Security is a key step in the architectural design process of any system, and should no longer be considered an add-on at a later stage of development. Even at the cost of some overhead, a minimum security baseline must be kept in order to ensure some degree of protection against attackers who want to intrude or disrupt the system. The security design model of *κPAX*'s architecture focuses on guaranteeing two basic capabilities.

- *User authentication*: To ensure that only authorized users can log into the system and they can only access and modify their own information.
- *Data integrity and trustworthiness*: To ensure that any information exchange between the platform and applications is correct and the result of an actual outcome from user actions.

In this subsection, we briefly explain how they are achieved.

4.3.1 User authentication

Being a multi-user system, ensuring that only legitimate users are able to log in, and constraining them to their account space, is a very basic functionality. As far as we are aware, every similar platform has some degree of user authentication. However, in addition to the ability to authenticate users with local accounts, κPAX is able to authenticate them through trusted third parties, such as UOCs virtual campus, or some social networks. Therefore, any user who already has an account with any of the trusted third parties need not have an additional local account, easing account management from the user's standpoint. In fact, the use of trusted third parties is the default behavior, since it is expected that every κPAX user has, at least, a UOC virtual Campus account. Local accounts should the used only as a last resort, for very special cases.

This part of the security model relies on a plugin that we implemented, based on OAuth 2.0 protocol (Hammer-Lahav and Hardt, 2011) integration for trusted third party authentication. Initially, only integration with UOC's OAuth 2.0 authorization server is supported, through simple Representational state transfer (REST) calls, based on the HTTP protocol. In order to ensure that only authorized applications may invoke the service, incoming REST calls require a client ID and secret API key provided by UOC beforehand. Otherwise, incoming REST calls are rejected. Therefore, κPAX has been assigned a client ID and secret key. Using this protocol, it is also possible to rely on UOC to obtain some additional information about the user, such as his or her username, e-mail address or role (student, instructor, etc.), even though the main goal is just user authentication.

The authentication process is summarized in Fig. 13.6. The process is initiated when a user connects via the browser to the login page, selecting authentication via his UOC account (a). Then, a message exchange begins between κPAX and the UOC OAuth 2.0 authorization server, using the secret API key to secure all messages. First, κPAX uses the client ID to identify itself and requests that UOC authenticates the user (b). Then, the user's browser is redirected to a UOC login page, where he or she can enter his or her username and password to authenticate him- or her self (c). It must be noted that this

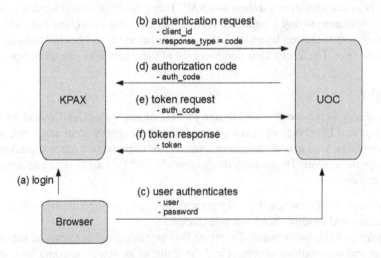

FIGURE 13.6

Authentication using OAuth 2.0.

communication is direct between the user and UOC, and, therefore, *κPAX* never has access to this sensitive information. After the user has been satisfactorily identified, a brief OAuth 2.0 message exchange follows (d) and (e). At the end, *κPAX* obtains a token that acts as proof of correct user authentication, and can also be used to access some of the user's data stored at UOC.

4.3.2 Integrity and trustworthiness

The integrity and trustworthiness security model of *κPAX* must take into account two kinds of adversaries. First of all, from an integrity standpoint, it must ensure that any information sent by a user cannot be modified in transit by an attacker. Second, from a trustworthiness standpoint, it must be ensured that a *legitimate user* is unable to send false information to the system in order to gain some advantage (ie, cheating). For instance, trying to force an update with an invalid score, higher than the one actually obtained by playing a game normally. This is a sometimes overlooked (or even outright ignored) problem. For instance, the highly popular game distribution platform Steam (see Section 2.2) takes into account the former, but does away with any kind of control for the latter. In contrast, Gree does take it into account. We consider that this security mechanism is very important in order to ensure the platform's reputation.

This part of the security model relies on the digital signature of data by each application, prior to transmitting. The fact that applications must have signed data requires some management on the part of the developers during the game registration process. But from the user's standpoint, it is completely invisible. The process description follows:

1. As part of the game registration process, it is required that the developer creates an RSA key pair: SK_{app} (the secret key) and PK_{app} (the public key). Such a key pair will be specific to that game and the only one, and it can be easily generated using open tools such as OpenSSL The OpenSSL Project, 1999). A step-by-step tutorial is provided to the developers.
2. The developer uploads PK_{app} to the system, which is stored in the database associated to that particular game. This upload process requires no extra security and can be done in plain text.
3. The developer integrates SK_{app} into the application's code. SK_{app} will be used to sign any service request to the platform. A timestamp is also added to any request prior to signature, countering replay attacks.
4. The platform validates any data received by applications using the associated PK_{app}, which is locally stored in the database and easily accessible.
5. At any time, developers may update SK_{app} and PK_{app} to new values, from their developer accounts. It must be noted, that when the update is finished the current instances of the application will stop working, since they contain the former private key in their code. Therefore, this method should be used, for instance, only when upgrading the application to a new version. This will also force users to upgrade.

The advantages of using a digital signature algorithm, instead of other simpler algorithms as an alternative, such as HMAC (Krawczyk et al., 1997), are twofold: first of all, no system manager can cheat, since SK_{app} is always in the developer's hand; and second, intruding the developer's *κPAX*'s account will also attain nothing, since the only retrievable information would be PK_{app}, which is not enough to execute the signature algorithm. The only point of failure is the developer, the only entity storing SK_{app}. Attackers could force an update with a new SK_{app} and PK_{app} of their choice. However, such an update would be easily detected, since all legitimate game instances would stop working after the change.

The main vulnerability of this approach is a reverse engineering code. SK_{app} should be somehow obfuscated to avoid this. Therefore, the method will avoid casual attackers, but not necessarily dedicated ones. Nevertheless, the technological level required for this kind of attack is not trivial, and the developer can always update the keys and the application. Highly sophisticated methods that could make the task much more difficult to attackers (but, unfortunately, which are never 100% effective) do exist (Subramanya and Yi, 2006), but we consider that, for this kind of platform, they are not really worth the costs (deployment complexity, monetary).

5 CONCLUSIONS

This paper presents our experiences in the design and development of a gamified platform to support learning through serious games. The project, born in the UOC (a fully on-line university), tries to take advantage of serious videogames as a resource to train a broad set of proficiencies. The learning process is framed inside a gamified social network in order to increase the engagement of players. Although the product has not been tested in a real environment, a first release is already completed and ready to be used. In the next semesters, it will be used to assess its efficiency within the UOC campus in a set of chosen subjects.

5.1 TECHNICAL DEVELOPMENT

In order to have a platform from an initial stage, we have made a global design and implemented only the core of it, ready for evolution. Thus, we have presented in this paper the main ideas and experiences of the complete design process, and the technology behind all the work that has been finished (and included in the release). Notice that *κPAX* is continuously being extended by final project students and external developers. The project has been developed under an open access license, making it accessible to any developer interested in participating in the project.

The design of *κPAX* takes into account three main aspects: a set of system requirements depicting our idea of the platform, the use of gamification and the interface design. These conceptual decisions imply taking into account four architectural focuses: the definition of the database, the services, the security, and the integrity and trustworthiness.

From a practical view, the core of the platform has been developed as an extension to elgg, an open source social networking engine, and mySQL as the database technology. These run on a XAMPP server. Furthermore, a set of services which mainly access the database are programmed in Java, and run in a jBoss server. Other technologies used in the project are JSON, hibernate, PHP, OAuth 2.0, and maven. An advantage of using elgg is that components can be easily added by developing new plugins. Thus, we have created the core development of the platform with a limited amount of capabilities and generated a first release. From this point, a number of new plugins have been developed and we are currently working on the integration, which is no easy task, since developers apply different changes to the database and create services.

The current situation is: after 4 years we have a first release ready to be tested. This is the result of a two months work on the part of a professional developer and around 15 students' final degree projects (250 h each). From now on, the results of every assessment will give us hints as to how to continue improving it. In order to do that we need specific games for the chosen skills. At the moment we have a trivia-like game, which will be used to prepare some of the lessons of chosen subjects. Furthermore, we will be working in two or more games to work with other learning aims. Altogether, *κPAX* should become a valuable new resource that will make students' learning a bit more engaging.

5.2 ACADEMIC IMPACT

From an academic point of view *κPAX* is mainly a tool for teachers who detect "gamers" among their students. It allows the inclusion of games and gamification in any education level subjects to promote work on competences and skills. The aim of gamification, in this case, is to engage students' and maintain motivation for learning. Educators using *κPAX* for their lectures need to choose the appropriate game (or games) for the competences/skills to work and set up the subject, including *κPAX* resources (eg, by generating a league on a game "X" and designing how the outcome can be included in the subject's global results). Feedback can be given to students both in the platform (where players can see their profile improving with every play) and in the classroom, depending on how the teacher has designed the whole activity. Thus, for the former, the feedback is automatic and for the later, it depends on the subject design. The teacher, as a creator of the specific competition regarding a game, can access some statistics and history to see who is more/less active, when and how much students are playing, what there achievements are at any given time, etc. This information can help students in the development of the learning process.

κPAX offers a set of services to help developers to include their serious games into the platform. The included games an be produced by anybody with the ability to develop (including from software companies to single developers). The use of services makes the integration of new games very easy, and involves only adding a few calls to *κPAX* in the game's source code. The game's quality cannot be ensured by construction, but the teachers and players will play and grade them. However, administrators perform a first filter by only accepting those games which are considered educative, and accomplish certain ethic terms. should an inappropriate game pass this first control, users can always denounce the contents and administrators will remove it from the available games in the platform.

5.3 FUTURE WORK

As of the current version, all the data collection is entirely geared towards the gamification engine, in order to generate the skill progression feedback via the character sheet. However, such a large amount of information could also be used from a learning analytics standpoint, in order to gauge other important information, such as which topics raise the most interest, which ones could be considered more difficult (learners consistently get poor scores), which topics are under- or over-represented, etc. But this would be a direction for a future version of the platform, or an auxiliary subsystem, under the umbrella of a spin-off project.

Further work includes analyzing the current feedback from the different tests in order to start refining the platform as well as including new plugins, so it can be upgraded from its current first release to a new version.

Finally, right now, developers and administrators act in a completely independent manner during the submission process. This is the nature of *κPAX* as a solely technological platform. However, we could consider going beyond the pure technological aspect and move towards a service-based approach in order to better coordinate the efforts of developers and administrators, or even other educators who just use published games, but do not directly participate in the platform. For instance, this could be carried out by creating special training sessions for developers as to how to create serious games, or by providing incentives for games in some of the under-represented skills/topics.

ACKNOWLEDGMENTS

This work was partly funded by the Spanish Government through the project TIN2013-45303-P "ICT-FLAG" (Enhancing ICT education through Formative assessment, Learning Analytics and Gamification). Moreover, we would also like to thank the following collaborators to the κPAX project, even though they are not paper authors: Àgata Lapedriza, Xavier Bar, César Crcoles, Josep Jorba, David Masip, Juan Francisco Sánchez, Francesc Santanach and Alicia Valls.

Last but not least, we thank a number of students who have been developing new functionalities as a part of their degree final projects. Part of their work (eg, Fernández, 2013; Farrerons i Herrero, 2014) has already been integrated into the platform and the rest will be in the near future.

REFERENCES

Abt, C., 1970. Serious games. Viking press, New York.

Accord, 2009. Accord LMS. http://www.accordlms.com.

Axonify Inc., 2014. Axonify. http://www.axonify.com.

Bartle, R., 1996. Hearts, clubs, diamonds, spades: Players who suit MUDs. J. MUD Res. 1 (1), 19.

Brumels, K., Blasius, T., 2008. Comparison of efficacy between traditional and video game based balance programs. Clin. Kines. J. Am. Kinesiother. Assoc. 62 (4), 26–31.

Cook, D., 1989. Advanced Dungeons & Dragons, second ed. TSR Inc., Lake Geneva, WI.

Csikszentmihalyi, M., Csikzentmihaly, M., 1991. Flow: The Psychology of Optimal Experience, vol. 41 Harper Perennial, New York.

Deterding, S., Khaled, R., Nacke, L., Dixon, D., 2011. Gamification: toward a definition. In: Chi 2011, pp. 12–15.

Deci, E.L., Ryan, R.M., 1991. A motivational approach to self: integration in personality. Perspect. Motiv. 38, 237.

Expertus, 2013. Expertus one. http://www.expertus.com.

Farrerons i Herrero, J., 2014. Perfil complet d'usuari per a la xarxa kpax.

Fernández, S.M., 2013. Tema per elgg. Master thesis, Universitat Oberta de Catalunya.

Growth Engineering, 2015. Academy LMS. http://www.growthengineering.co.uk/academy-lms.

Hamari, J., Koivisto, J., Sarsa, H., 2014. Does gamification work? — a literature review of empirical studies on gamification. In: 47th Hawaii International Conference on System Sciences (HICSS), pp. 3025–3034.

Hammer-Lahav, D.E., Hardt, D., 2011. The OAuth2.0 Authorization Protocol.

Holman, C., Aguilar, S., Fishman, B., 2013. Gradecraft: what can we learn from a game-inspired learning management system? In: Proceedings of the Third International Conference on Learning Analytics and Knowledge. ACM, pp. 260–264.

Huizinga, J., Hull, R., 1949. Homo ludens. A study of the play-element in culture [trans. by rfc hull.].

Krawczyk, H., Bellare, M., Canetti, R., 1997. HMAC: Keyed-Hashing for Message Authentication.

Mora, A., Riera, D., Gonzlez, C., Arnedo-Moreno, J., 2015. A literature review of gamification design frameworks. In: Seventh International Conference on Virtual Worlds and Games for Serious Applications: VS-Games, pp. 100–107.

Nah, F.F.-H., Zeng, Q., Telaprolu, V.R., Ayyappa, A.P., Eschenbrenner, B., 2014. Gamification of education: a review of literature. Yamamoto, S. (Ed.), HCI in Business, Springer, Heidelberg, pp. 401–409.

Pelling, N., 2011. The (short) prehistory of gamification. Funding Startups (& Other Impossibilities), Haettu. https://nanodome.wordpress.com/2011/08/09/the-short-prehistory-of-gamification/.

Prensky, M., 2001. Digital natives, digital immigrants part 1. On the Horizon 9 (5), 1–6.

Sicart, M., 2008. Defining game mechanics. Game Stud. 8 (2), 1–14.

Subramanya, S., Yi, B., 2006. Digital rights management. IEEE Potentials 25 (2), 31–34.

Tanaka, Y., 2004. Gree. http://product.gree.net.

The OpenSSL Project, 1999. OpenSSL: The Open Source toolkit for SSL/TLS.

Valve Inc, 2003. Steam. http://store.steampowered.com.

Villagrasa, S., Duran, J., 2013. Gamification for learning 3d computer graphics arts. In: Proceedings of the First International Conference on Technological Ecosystem for Enhancing Multiculturality. ACM, pp. 429–433.

Whitton, N., 2009. Learning with digital games: A practical guide to engaging students in higher education. Routledge, New York.

AN ATTRITION MODEL FOR MOOCs: EVALUATING THE LEARNING STRATEGIES OF GAMIFICATION

R.H. Rizzardini*, M.M. Chan*, C. Guetl[†]

Galileo University, Guatemala, Guatemala[*] Graz University of Technology, Graz, Austria[†]

1 INTRODUCTION

The current growth of massive open online courses (MOOCs) has gained the attention of the educational community. MOOCs provide many real learning experiences to students, from videos, readings, quizzes and activities, to opportunities to connect and collaborate with others through discussion and gamified forums and other Web 2.0 tools (Hernández Rizzardini et al., 2013). Originally inspired by connectivism cMOOCs (Siemens, 2005) and subsequently xMOOCs, which are based on the behaviorist approach, the teaching model for MOOCs has evolved since the foundation of Coursera and edX in 2012 (Cisel and Bruillard, 2013). In its recent review of key statistics and trends, Class Central (Class-Central Report, 2014) offers a summary of the rapid expansion of MOOCs over the past 3 years; the report showed that 400 universities offered MOOCs in 2014, with 2400 courses implemented and an average of 18 million enrolled students. An important point about the participation and involvement of universities is that 22 of the top 25 US universities listed in U.S. News & World rankings are now offering MOOCs. In 2013, Coursera offered nearly half of all MOOCs, but in 2014 its share had shrunk to one-third. It is still the largest, twice as large as edX, which had doubled its share over the last year (and now has close to 400 courses on its platform). No major providers launched in 2014. Other start-up companies, such as Udacity and Khan Academy, have also emerged. These online education companies offer hundreds of courses where students acquire real skills through a series of online courses and hands-on projects.

Initially, MOOCs were seen as providing better education for all, offering the opportunity to study with the best teachers for free and promoting the development and management of specific learning communities for people with limited access to education. However, the most recurrent criticism is the dramatic student dropout rates from MOOCs (typically 85–95%) (Parr, 2013; Jordan, 2013). Among the main reasons for student dropout are no real intention to complete, lack of time, course difficulty and lack of

Formative Assessment, Learning Data Analytics and Gamification. http://dx.doi.org/10.1016/B978-0-12-803637-2.00014-2

support, lack of digital skills or learning skills, bad experiences with user forums, poor quality or incorrect learning materials, and technical problems with the MOOC platform (Mackness et al., 2010; Yang et al., 2013). Three concepts are important in dropout research: (1) attrition is the "decline in the number of students from the beginning to the end" of the learning event; (2) retention is the "continued student participation in a learning event" and (3) persistence is "the result of students' decision to continue their participation in the learning event" (Berge and Huang, 2004). Because of the significance of research into attrition, retention and persistence, we present four perspectives introduced by Berge and Huang (2004): (1) social influences, (2) organizational characteristics and processes, (3) economic influences, and (4) psychological characteristics for extending the concept.

Koller and Ng rightly explained that the variety of intents of online course takers is very different from the traditional model. In the online framework, some students do, indeed, plan to complete the course and can be referred to as committed learners. However, others may just want to understand what the topic is about or find out more about a particular professor or even about MOOCs as a whole; these are the so-called browsers. Jordan (2013) found that though MOOCs still have as much content as before, the completion rates, in most cases defined by earning a certificate of accomplishment, have somewhat increased over this period (though the majority of them still have completion rates below 10% with a median of 6.5%). Jordan (2013) observes that across all course sizes, about half of all enrollees become active students and completion rates are negatively correlated with course length and are lower when the course requires relatively more assignments, especially those involving programming or peer assessment exercises.

Some publications, like the one from Hill (2013), have characterized students taking MOOCs, along with a large population of no-shows, as observers, dropouts, passive participants and active participants. Emerging data from a study by the University of Pennsylvania Graduate School of Education (Penn GSE) show that MOOCs have a small number of active users, user engagement usually falls in the first 2 weeks, and only a few students continue at the end (Stein, 2014). Kizilcec et al. (2013) investigated patterns of engagement and disengagement and found groups characterized as completing, disengaging, auditing, and sampling learners. The completing class comprises learners who completed a majority of the activities and finished the course. The disengaging class comprises students who initially take assignments but stop and leave the course completely or consumed some content without taking further assignments. The auditing class comprises students who infrequently took assessments but engaged by consuming learning content. The sampling class comprises learners who selectively consumed content.

Clow (2013) suggested the funnel of participation. There is a significant drop-off at any stage, from enrolment to course completion. Participants of traditional courses usually pass through four phases: awareness, interest, desire, and action. In the context of MOOCs, the analogies of these phases are awareness, registration, activity, and success. Each phase is characterized with a large number of dropouts. The funnel can be applied to the density of contributions in the activity phase. Perna et al. (2013) further explored the drop-off points for a set of Coursera courses run by the University of Pennsylvania. They defined the loss factor as the ratio of the number of students who accessed the lecture in the first course module to the number of students who accessed the lecture in the final module.

On the other hand, the initial finding from a MOOC experiment revealed that there was healthy attrition and unhealthy attrition (Gütl et al., 2014a). From the study, students who drop out due to healthy attrition have completed part of the course and some of the reasons they provided are that they have personalized their own learning by choosing relevant topics to study. Some of the main causes of unhealthy attrition relate to poor technical infrastructure, lack of support from employers, poor time management, lack of prerequisite knowledge and skills, poor learning experience, and lack of personalization, which created a feeling of isolation and disengagement. However, current research may determine the factors that are most likely to influence users and for which effective measures might be developed within the MOOC format. For example, among the main aspects considered to reduce unhealthy attrition, is motivation in the learning process; this element has been described as the "engine" that drives the teaching and learning (Harlen, 2006). Gamification strategies have been used in educational environments to engage students through their intrinsic motivation and typically make use of the competition instinct most people possess to motivate productive behaviors. Many authors have discussed different learning approaches to make education more attractive for students and to help them to "learn more, learn it earlier and more easily, and learn it with a pleasure and commitment" (DiSessa, 2000). Educational computer games have been promoted as being effective, powerful, and motivational learning tools. Papasterigiou describes the successful implementation of a digital game for learning computer memory concepts, which not only achieved better learning gains, but also enhanced student engagement (Papasterigiou, 2009).

The aims of this study are to understand and differentiate attrition reasons for a gamified MOOC, to analyze learner behavior and to measure the impact of the strategies used. This paper extends on a previous study using the Attrition Model for Open Learning Environment Setting (AMOES) (Gütl et al., 2014b) and compares the gamification strategies used to motivate and improve student participation. The rest of the paper is organized as follows: Section 2 overviews related work; Section 3 presents our research methodology; Section 4 presents the technological aspects and MOOC design; in Section 5, we discuss analytics for learner behavior in relation to the gamification strategies used in the learning experience; and in Section 6 we present conclusions and future work.

2 RELATED WORK

This section focuses on work relating to dropout rates and looks at two aspects. Firstly we show a previous study of the AMOES (Gütl et al., 2014a). Secondly, we present a general overview of the gamification strategies that exist in the education field.

2.1 ABOUT AMOES (ATTRITION MODEL FOR OPEN LEARNING ENVIRONMENT SETTING)

Inspired by various works in the literature, for example, Adamopoulos (2013), Chyung (2005), Clow (2013), Kizilcec et al. (2013), and Yang et al. (2013) on the attrition, retention, and completion rates of MOOCs, and our own research in the same field, we created the AMOES. This is shown in Fig. 14.1. It is used to understand and differentiate between the reasons for attrition.

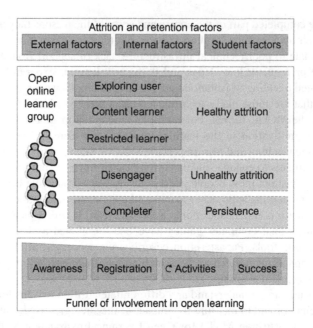

FIGURE 14.1

Attrition Model for Open Learning Environment Setting (AMOES).

From Gütl, C., Hernández Rizzardini, R., Chang, V., Morales, M., 2014. Must we be concerned with the massive drop-outs in MOOC?—An attrition analysis of open courses. In: International Conference of Interactive Collaborative Learning ICL, Dubai, UAE, December.

The AMOES model has three sections: (1) attrition and retention factors, (2) the open online learner classification, and (3) the funnel of involvement in an open learning setting. There are external, internal, and student factors, which influence whether a learner belongs to a healthy, unhealthy, or persistence group of learners. Examples of external factors include competing courses in the MOOC space, the local technological infrastructure and culture. As these factors are outside the control of a MOOC provider, institutions aimed to identify strategies to mitigate them. Examples of internal forces include aspects of the organization of the MOOC that are under the control of the MOOC provider. Student factors relate to a student's desire to study the MOOC and prior knowledge of the field. For example, some students enroll in a MOOC because of their job, some for general interest, some to gain a qualification and so on. The funnel of involvement in the learning setting has administrative aspects (awareness and registration) and pedagogical aspects (activities and success) of the MOOC. The final version of this model was based on a number of our own studies in MOOC uptake and dropout, and a deep analysis of attrition, retention, and persistence in MOOCs over recent years.

As the focus of attrition analysis is on the learners, AMOES has defined three groups: healthy attrition, unhealthy attrition, and persistence learners. Depending on the intention and motivation of the students, ultimately they can be divided further: exploring user, content learner, restricted learner, disengager, and completer, as shown in Fig. 14.1.

The healthy attrition group includes students who are exploring users who wanted a preview of the course to gain a quick understanding of the topic. Also included in this group are those who are eager to experience a new learning environment. These learners are usually trying to determine if this is a learning setting that they could adopt as an alternative to traditional face-to-face or online learning. The second class of the healthy attrition group comprises the content learners, who are selective learners and choose what they wish to learn from a list of topics. They deliberately choose to study content that interests them and do not intend to complete the entire course. Two external factors that contribute to their decision is the low or no entry barrier to enrolment in a MOOC and the free access. This gives learners a consumer advantage in gaining knowledge and skills that they may not otherwise have access to. The final class of the healthy attrition group comprises the restricted learners, who choose to audit the entire course and again do not intend to complete the course formally (or complete the assigned work or participate in gaining digital badges). All of the learners in these three classes are in the healthy attrition group since they have personalized their learning and they gain considerable knowledge and skills according to their learning requirements and needs. The attrition can be characterized as good attrition.

Learners in the unhealthy attrition group fail to continue the course for a variety of reasons. There are external factors, such as technology limitations, and their work or job commitments; internal factors, such as the institutional operation of the MOOC, the organization of the course itself and the lack of support services, and student factors, such as the lack of the prerequisite knowledge required for the course, and an inability to commit time to study the material or engage in online discussion forums.

The funnel of involvement in open learning is a funnel of participation modified from the work of Clow (2013). This last section of the AMOES model is closely linked with the external, internal and student factors, along with the groups. Awareness is affected by external factors in that the MOOC must exist. This is followed by registration, where students sign up and participate in the MOOC activities. At this stage, the MOOC provider (internal factors) plays a pivotal role in controlling the number of activities to achieve a balance of interactive, engaging and contributing participation that leads to a satisfying and ultimately successful experience. Implicit in the activities part of the funnel of involvement is dependency on the availability, compatibility, and reliability of the information technology, which has both external and internal factors. Finally, the measure of success is based upon contributing student factors and the healthy, unhealthy, and persistence groups of learners.

2.2 ABOUT GAMIFICATION STRATEGIES

Recently, gamification strategies have been used in educational models to engage students through their intrinsic motivation. Hamari et al. (2014) argued that gamification could be used to support user engagement and to enhance positive usage patterns of services, like the activity of the user, the sociability aspect of services and the quality of the user actions themselves. Gamification is defined as the use of "game design elements in non-game contexts" (Deterding and Khaled, 2011). Burke (2014) said that Gartner defines gamification as follows: "the use of game mechanics and experience design to digitally engage and motivate people to achieve their goals." Gamification is different from creating an educational or serious game. While the latter focuses on enriching the learning experience through computer simulation or virtual worlds, gamified application uses elements of games, such as leaderboards, badges, constant feedback, and points. The term "gamification" is quite recent: according to Deterding et al. (2011), the first documented use was in 2008, but it did not see widespread adoption before the second half of 2010.

Here, the distinctive element is to apply gamification in digital contexts, like a digital engagement platform. In New York City, Quest to Learn (Q2L) has an entire curriculum based on gamification strategies.

Instead of homework, Q2L promotes units with a mission and challenge. These quests involve game strategies such as collaboration, role-playing, or simulations. The learning experience focuses on hands-on problem solving (Augustine et al., 1990). Instead of frustrating and stressing students with exams, Q2L uses a point system where students are rewarded for applying extra effort to account for mistakes and they are not punished for failing an exam. They can constantly try to increase their level to master a course. The students focus on the course content instead of stressing over their grades (McGonigal, 2011).

Some organizations are leading the way in integrating gamification with learning processes. One of the most popular is Khan Academy, which has been using gamification mechanics more or less since its release. The participants collect points when they complete lessons and view videos. The platform provides statistics and analytics about their progress and improvement. Duolingo is another example of how gamification is used to assist learning. The Duolingo experience is designed like a game with trophies, characters and a scoreboard, where a student can see how they are doing in comparison to their friends who are using the platform. There are completion bars, a counter, badges, leaderboards and many other forms of recognition and feedback to promote engagement. With the identified dropout issues in MOOCs, gamification could be seen as a way to solve the engagement issues and improve the completion rate of MOOCs.

However, competitive gamification strategies do not inspire all learning types and can lead to student frustration instead of motivation. Studies comparing competitive, individual, and cooperative learning strategies report the most successful outcomes for cooperative strategies (Johnson et al., 1986). In the educational domain, it is important to integrate competitive game elements such as leaderboard information, with collaborative elements such as working together as a group to gain points and helping each other in achieving common goals.

The gamification concepts applied to learning processes, can become powerful motivators and support user engagement to achieve their goals; the gamification strategies are used in learning activities to build intrinsic motivation, these strategies are a combination of three concepts: autonomy, competence, and relatedness (Nicholson, 2015). These concepts are also known as psychological needs. External motivation like getting a good score is just one reason that people play games but using game elements such as exploring of narrative, making interesting decisions, and playing with other people (social engagement) increases intrinsic motivation. However there are two important considerations to have in mind, first, no one gamification strategy will benefit every user, and second every gamification activity needs to be built with the user's benefits at the center. We believe these gamification elements are powerful tools that can be applied in all sorts of educational contexts, and MOOC's are not the exception, we expect to validate their use in a MOOC implementation, specifically, we wish to prove their worth of use in learning environments.

3 RESEARCH METHODOLOGY

This analysis is based upon enrolment and completion data collected from the MOOC "Authoring tools for e-learning courses" implemented during 2015 in the Telescope Project. The course had a landing page with the syllabus, general description, methodology, and main course topics. Students can register by email or by using Facebook. The procedure for collecting data was: (1) students enrolled in the MOOC, (2) students completed an online survey that gathered demographic and other data, (3) students undertook a boot camp week to familiarize themselves with the learning environment and the assessment strategies (peer assessment and self-assessment), (4) students accessed 4 weeks of videos and learning activities with gamified strategies, participated in online collaboration groups and completed assessments and, finally, (5) the students who had completed the MOOC were asked to fill in a post-questionnaire to evaluate their overall MOOC experience. Our research had an additional questionnaire (the desertion test), which was sent to the students who did not complete the MOOC, with questions about why they did not finish the course. All questionnaires were sent through the Lime Survey tool and data processing was performed using SPSS.

4 DESIGN OF EXPERIMENTS

The Telescope Project was started in response to our previous experience of the development of online courses. It was influenced by the MOOC on "Artificial Intelligence" run by Stanford University, MOOC sites such as Coursera and Edx, and motivated by what this methodology could achieve. In 2012, we created the project with the aims of sharing knowledge in Latin America (Hernández Rizzardini et al., 2013), reaching out to a larger population that had not been reached by traditional education methods and increasing the visibility of our institution.

Considering the differences between xMOOC and cMOOC (Downes, 2005; Siemens, 2012), we chose to use xMOOC since this format promotes a teaching model that emphasizes cognitive behavior, which is a more traditional approach to virtual learning. The course is structured into five learning units. Each unit has between four and six short videos, with an average duration of 6–9 min, accompanied by a related presentation, an activity and an assessment associated with the topic. All units had a set of learning activities and assignments supported by a selection of cloud-based tools to give the students the skills and knowledge needed for real-life scenarios. We implemented the course in our learning management system. LRN (Hernández Rizzardini et al., 2013), with several adaptations to meet our needs for better visualization of the content. The Open Source Questions and Answers System (OSQA) was integrated to handle the massive forums, using a gamification approach in which users are given badges to highlight their main contributions (Hernández Rizzardini et al., 2013). A peer review system was integrated into the platform, which enabled students to evaluate one or more of their fellow students randomly and anonymously. For the evaluation, a criterion was presented for each activity as a rubric, which creates more objectivity when qualifying. The system was set up so that all students were rated at least once; if a student was rated by more than one person, the system automatically averaged the grades to calculate a final grade.

Our MOOC, "Authoring tools for e-learning courses," has an introductory unit, in which the general aspects and the methodology of the course are described to familiarize students with the learning environment, our platform, and the overall course structure and evaluation methods. General aspects of the course are presented in Table 14.1.

During the course, students accessed the video content, learning activities and assignments using different Web 2.0 tools as a new element in MOOC design, and three challenges were given special focus when implementing a MOOC, the first related to communication, because it is very difficult to obtain high levels of participation in students; we used gamified forums using badges (this is the first strategy). The second strategy used was evaluation, performed according to the quality of the delivered assignments; it was intended to motivate the participants by giving each a position within the learning group; and the last strategy is basically related to motivation for the delivery of tasks (two activities with a reward strategy for weeks 3 and 4), as seen in Fig. 14.2.

The main idea for our experimentation was to use different game mechanics that are typically used in MOOC forums. Each of these components will be described below.

Table 14.1 Description of the Course Design

MOOC "Authoring Tools for e-Learning Courses" General Information	
Course offered	Mar. 2015
MOOC pedagogical approach	xMOOC (cognitive behavioral teaching model)
Number of learning units	Four units (one unit per week, 5 weeks in total, including the boot camp week)
Number of learning activities	Eight activities
Video resources	24 video-contents and tutorials (duration: 6–10 min)
Collaboration type	Nonguided discussions. Question-and-answer (Q/A) forums
Teachers	Two teachers and two tutors

MOOC Learning Topics, Instructional Objectives, and Gamified Strategies			
Learning Topic	**Instructional Objectives**	**Activities/Gamified Strategies**	**Assessment Type**
Boot Camp Unit	Boot Camp Unit, meant for participants to get acquainted with the spaces, tools and services, as well as with the processes of work and communication that will be used in the course	Developing an essay about cloud-based learning in Google Docs	Peer assessment
Unit 1	Explore e-learning trends	Developing an essay about e-learning trends in Google Docs	Peer assessment Auto-grading
Unit 2	Presentation and documentation about eXelearning	Developing an eXelearning[a] content and implemented in Moodle[b]. Gamified activity (reward strategy)	Peer assessment Auto-grading
Unit 3	Characteristics, use and application of the proprietary authoring tools for e-learning. Storyline and Articulate	Developing a storyline[c] content and implemented in Moodle. Gamified activity (reward strategy)	Peer assessment Auto-grading
Unit 4	Main features about quiz maker	Developing a test with quiz maker platform	Peer assessment Auto-grading

[a]eXelearning (http://exelearning.org).
[b]Moodle (http://moodle.org).
[c]Storyline (https://es.articulate.com/products/storyline-why.php).

Badges and Leaderboard Forums: For the online discussion forum OSQA was used. This system is a free method of connecting people to information and to help them engage more deeply with topics and questions of personal relevance, allowing everyone to collaborate, answer queries, and manage learning. The online collaborative forums followed a gamification approach. Badges were used as electronic rewards for students based on their contributions to the course learning community. In our case, we use different badges to represent recognition within the community. For example, among the most awarded badges were "professor" for the first response with at least one positive vote, "collaborator" for the first positive vote, and

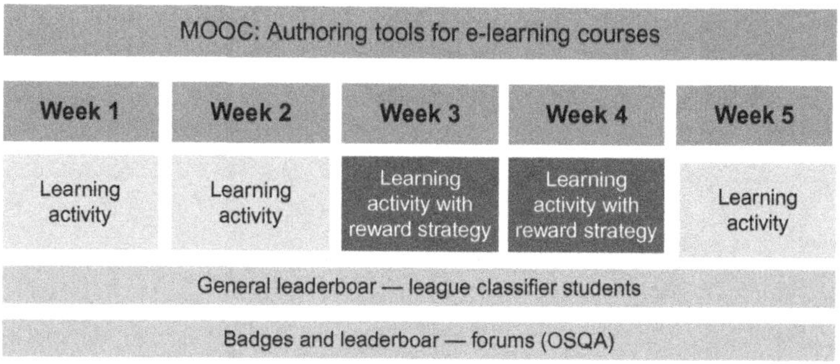

FIGURE 14.2

Gamified strategies massive open online course (MOOC).

"student" for the first question with at least one positive feedback. When using game elements and strategies in a MOOC, various implications must be considered. For example, when introducing games to teach content, it is important to identify which topics can and should be covered by a game, and which areas are either not suitable or would be too time- or cost-intensive for a game-based approach. We gave special focus to online collaboration through the discussion forum. Throughout the course, participants could propose topics for discussion, answer questions posed by teammates, vote, comment and exchange views and information with the rest of the participants.

Reward Strategy: During content weeks 3 and 4, a reward strategy was implemented to validate if these strategies increase student participation. All students who submitted their activities, received a template-authoring tool as a reward (in our case we send eXelearning and Articulate storyline, authoring tools template) through Mail Chimp. The template was offered as a reward, so that once they obtained a satisfactory grade there was a certain degree of expectation. For this activity the course team developed three templates for each tool, considering excellent visualization (graphic design) and a good level of interaction, because it needed to inspire considerable interest in enrolled students.

General Leaderboard—League Classifier Students: The purpose of the leagues was to avoid the negative effects of leaderboards (Werbach and Hunter, 2012). For this we developed a plugin to present an online leaderboard for the duration of the course, allowing the students to see their relative rank and progress over time in their league. We automatically classified students into leagues according to their accumulated grades. The leagues have three categories of student, based on their level of participation and knowledge (see Fig. 14.3). In the "Self-taught (Expert)" category are the students who have reached a good level of knowledge without support. The second category is "Curious (Intermediate)," for students who have asked many questions in class. The final category is "Passive (beginner)" for the students who do not have much knowledge and are not involved in the course.

5 EXPERIMENTATION FINDINGS

For the gamified MOOC, data were collected from a questionnaire passed to the students who completed the MOOC. They represented 38% of the total registered (1678 enrolled students and learners from 16 countries). In total, 40% of the learners were female and 60% were male. Their average age

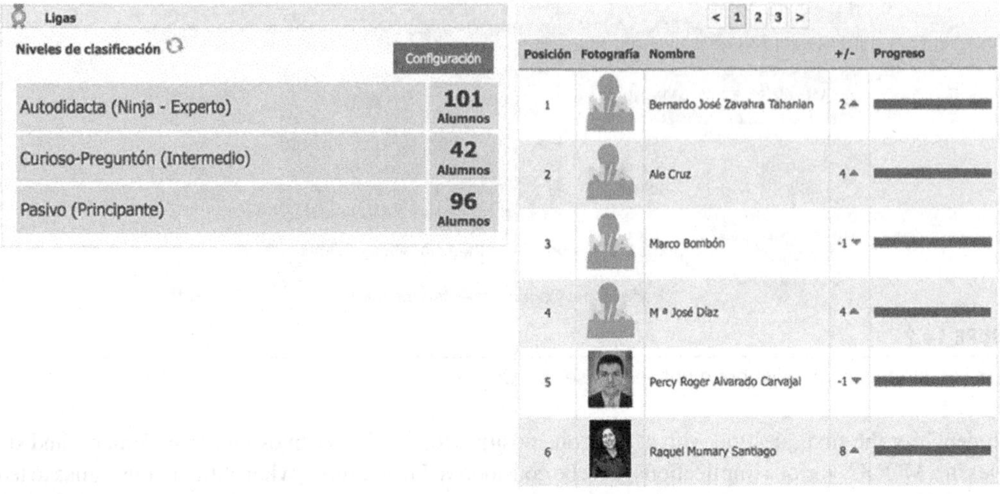

FIGURE 14.3

General leaderboard, league classifier for students with relative rank and progress bar for indicating how many positions the student has gained/lost.

was $M = 40$ ($\sigma = 11$) years. Among participants, 9% were pre-university students, 23% were university students, and 66% had professional backgrounds (requiring a bachelor's degree). Participants were from Spain (17%), Guatemala (17%), Mexico (11%), Peru (10%), and Colombia (9%); these represent 64% of the population. For 44% of the enrolled students, this was their first MOOC experience; they indicated that the main reason for their interest in the course was work related (62%). Of the 83% of participants who wanted to complete all the activities of the course, only 13% planned to watch all sessions and perform some activities. In total, 99% of participants wanted to complete the course successfully and they pledged to invest more than 3 h a week to realize all the assigned activities. Interestingly, 58% of the participants did not know about the gamification concept.

5.1 GAMIFIED MOOC: LEARNER BEHAVIOR ANALYTICS

To analyze the behavior of the students during the course, an analytics report was created to report throughout the course on the level of access to the MOOCs, the amount of learning tasks that were delivered and the number of views per video. The results for the participation of students in the MOOC "Authoring tools for e-learning courses" are summarized in Fig. 14.4. In this graph, we show the commitment of the students to deliver weekly assignments. Interestingly, for the first unit (week 1), only 8.76% of participants reviewed at least one video and completed the defined learning task. For this statistic, we calculated the average number of learning tasks delivered. In the second week, there was a decrease—only 7.51% of learners completed the tasks, while the third and fourth weeks showed similar behavior with decreased participation of 6.62% and 5.90%. Although 83% of participants surveyed at the beginning of the course, said they would complete all learning tasks; the average was $M = 7.69\%$ ($\sigma = 1.53\%$), which represents the commitment of the students to delivering weekly assignments; the graph (Fig. 14.4) shows that the behavior of learners for each assignment was similar.

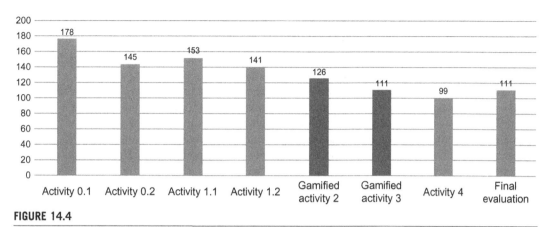

FIGURE 14.4

General behavior of the students regarding delivery of weekly assignments.

The gamified strategies used in our course did not increase the engagement of the participants with the delivered learning activities. However, based on an analysis of participants who completed the course and the questionnaire to evaluate their overall MOOC experience (58% of those who completed the course completed the questionnaire), it was determined that 80% of the students were completely motivated or motivated to finish the assignments to get the template-authoring tool reward. The majority of users, 33 (60%), indicated that the template-authoring tool would be very useful for creating their own resources or generating ideas for future work. In terms of the league of students (Fig. 14.5), 26 participants (47%) indicated that the use of these strategies motivated their participation and delivery of learning tasks in the course, and 17 (31%) participants indicated they were completely motivated.

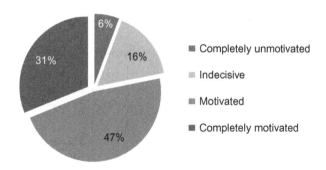

FIGURE 14.5

Motivation of the students in relation to the league classifier strategies used.

The analyses also show that earning badges in the gamified forums was neither important nor attractive to many students. However, badges can be used as positive reinforcement and to give students an overview of their results.

5.2 COMPARISON OF TRADITIONAL MOOC AND GAMIFIED MOOC: LEARNER BEHAVIOR ANALYTICS AND ASPECTS OF ATTRITION

In this section, we compare the previous study on the MOOC that was offered in Oct. 2012 (Hernández Rizzardini et al., 2013) and the gamified MOOC described in the previous section. The objective is to analyze learner behavior, specifically aspects of attrition such as the funnel of involvement (Table 14.2).

The dropout rates were very high for both the traditional MOOC (91.49%) and the gamified MOOC (93.98%). Like most other MOOC experiences, a high attrition rate and a low completion rate have been a major source of uproar and debate among institutional scholars and educators. The behavior of learners in relation to the stages of the funnel is very similar in both cases. However, the decrease of participation for the gamified MOOC is smaller than for the traditional MOOC. Although the average delivery of learning tasks is not similar, for the traditional MOOC $M = 13.78\%$ and the gamified MOOC $M = 7.69\%$, the standard deviation is superior for the traditional MOOC ($\sigma = 5.54\%$) compared to the gamified MOOC ($\sigma = 1.53\%$; Fig. 14.6). An important point is that in the first week of the traditional MOOC, 21.60% of the learners completed the learning activities, while for the gamified MOOC only 8.76% completed the learning activities. (Although the percentage or those with at least one login for the gamified MOOC (69%) is more than for the traditional MOOC (57%).)

In Fig. 14.6, a higher decrease can be observed in the learning tasks delivered for the traditional MOOC compared to the gamified MOOC.

5.3 COMPARISON OF TRADITIONAL MOOC AND GAMIFIED MOOC: DROPOUT ANALYSIS

The dropout analysis is based on data collected for both courses. For the MOOC "Introducing e-Learning," 1537 (91.49%) students dropped out in comparison to 1057 (93.98%) for the MOOC "Authoring tools for e-learning courses." For the dropout analysis, a desertion question was published

Table 14.2 AMOES Funnel of Involvement

Stages of Funnel	Activities				
	MOOC 2012—"Introduction to e-Learning" (Traditional MOOC)			MOOC 2015—"Authoring Tools for e-Learning Courses" (Gamified Approach MOOC)	
1. Awareness					
2. Registration	1680 registrants			1678 registrants	
3. Activities	Did not start the course	(722) 43%		Did not start the course	(520) 31%
	With at least one login	(958) 57%		With at least one login	(1158) 69%
	Week	Learning tasks	Forum discussion	Learning tasks	Forum discussion
	1	21.60%	33.00%	8.76%	3.75%
	2	13.80%	26.00%	7.51%	3.52%
	3	10.20%	18.10%	6.62%	5.54%
	4	9.52 %	12.74%	5.90%	2.38%
4. Success	143 (8.51%) completers			101 (6.02%) completers	
	1537 (91.49%) registrants, did not completers			1057 (93.98%) registrants, did not completers	

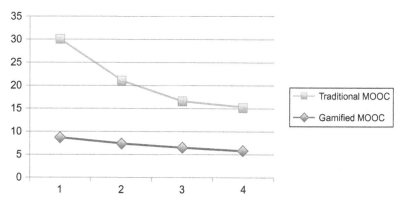

FIGURE 14.6

Comparison of delivered weekly assignments.

at the end of the course. All users were contacted by email and asked to participate in an online survey. This gave us general aspects of the people who did not complete the course and we could identify the main reasons for dropping out: personal reasons, academic reasons, support and interaction; and other influencing factors such as course quality and gamification strategies, workload and time management. The most cited reasons for dropout were personal and workload, such as an increased workload for their job, and also the academic workload was evaluated as too high in some cases.

In Table 14.3, we present general aspects of the participants and the dropout analysis for both courses. The findings are based on data collected from 134 students (8.72%) for the traditional MOOC and 68 students (6.43%) for the gamified MOOC who had not completed the course but answered the follow-up study questionnaire (desertion test). To get a better understanding of why the participants did not finish our courses, they were asked about personal, academic support, and learning environment reasons.

Among the personal issues for both courses, the main reasons students drop out were related to "job responsibilities changed during the MOOC duration" with an average $M = 68.52\%$ and "personal health problems" with $M = 17.02\%$. In terms of the academic reasons for leaving the MOOC, $M = 73.1\%$ participants indicated that it was "too hard to work full-time and complete all activities of online course." This was followed by $M = 14.82\%$ indicating, "not technically prepared for this program." For help and support reasons, $M = 39.97\%$ indicated the main issue was that they did "not get enough encouragement/support to continue from colleagues, family or employer." Finally, in the learning environment aspect, the category selected most often was "other," which included issues such as "the interactivity with the participants was very ambiguous and chaotic" and "too many forums which caused confusion."

In the above dropout analysis, we compared a traditional MOOC and a gamified MOOC in relation to the AMOES model and the classification of students in accordance with the learner types. Table 14.4 describes all the MOOC learners according to AMOES.

For the gamified MOOC, although gamified strategies were used (such as gamified forums and a league for students showing their relative rank and a progress bar indicating how many positions the student had gained or lost), the percentage of students classified as disengager is higher than for the traditional MOOC. This represents the unhealthy attrition of students who were disengaged. These

Table 14.3 Dropout Analysis

	Main Reasons	MOOC 2012—"Introduction to e-Learning" (Traditional MOOC) (%)	MOOC 2015—"Authoring Tools for e-Learning Courses" (Gamified Approach MOOC) (%)
Personal reasons for leaving the MOOC (multiple answers possible)	Family problems	8.21	16.18
	Financial difficulties	7.46	5.88
	Personal health problems	14.93	19.12
	Job responsibilities changed during the MOOC duration	69.40	67.65
	Program did not cover my expectations	13.43	11.76
	Other	2.99	5.88
Academic reasons for leaving the MOOC (multiple answers possible)	Course were poorly taught	6.72	5.88
	Course had been poorly created	3.73	2.94
	Academic program too difficult/demanding	8.96	8.82
	Academic program was not challenging	7.46	1.47
	Not academically prepared for this program	2.99	2.94
	Not technically prepared for this program	14.93	14.71
	Too hard to work full-time and complete all activities of online course	70.15	76.47
Insufficient support reasons for leaving the MOOC (multiple answers possible)	Not get enough encouragement/support to continue from colleagues, family, or employer	35.82	44.12
	Did not receive useful feedback on assignments and tests	32.09	19.12
	Did not receive the necessary training to use the technologies required in the course	22.39	25
	Not enough support from the technical staff	17.91	16.18
Learning environment reasons for leaving the MOOC (multiple answers possible)	Was too little interaction with other students	28.36	16.18
	Too little interaction with the instructors	24.63	11.76
	Typing skills were not sufficient enough to interact with the class	17.16	22.06
	Learning environment was not personalized	14.93	8.82
	Others	32.84	52.94

Table 14.4 MOOC Learners According to AMOES

Group of Learners	Class	Percentage Traditional MOOC	Percentage Gamified MOOC
Healthy attrition	Exploring users	51.50	23.53
	Content learner	3.37	7.35
	Restricted learner	8.96	19.12
Unhealthy attrition	Disengager	22.39	35.29
Persistence	Completer	8.51	6.02
Other Reasons		13.43	14.71

learners failed to continue due to a variety of reasons. The reasons may be external, such as personal factors. For example, in our case the main one was "job responsibilities changed during the MOOC duration." In relation to internal factors (such as the institutional operation of the MOOC, the organization of the course itself and the lack of support services) and student factors (such as the lack of prerequisite knowledge required to study the course and inability to commit time to study the material), the main reason was "too hard to work full-time and complete all activities of online course."

The good attrition (healthy attrition) group has three classes of learner. For the "authoring tools for e-learning courses" MOOC, 23.53% of the students were classified as exploring users and 7.35% were in the second class of content learners. The final class comprises the restricted learners, who choose to audit the entire course without intending to complete the course formally. For our MOOC, this was about 19.12% of learners. The attrition for the classes of exploring, content and restricted learners is classified as healthy attrition since these learners have personalized their learning and they have also gained considerable knowledge and skills according to their learning requirements and needs. Some reasons, such as "having a quick view of the subject," "deepening knowledge on a subject," "contributes to my job activities" and "refresh and update the knowledge in a subject," can easily be classified as healthy attrition.

About 35.29% of the learners in this MOOC indicated that they would have liked to complete the course but for a variety of reasons they were unable. In the data analysis, 14.71% selected "Other Reasons" for their inability to complete the MOOC.

6 CONCLUSIONS AND FUTURE WORK

Initial findings from our experiment revealed dropout rates were very high for both the traditional MOOC (91.49%) and the gamified MOOC (93.98%). The behavior of learners in relation to the stages of the funnel is similar in both cases. However, although we use gamified strategies in our course, this did not increase the learning activities delivered, but it is very interesting that the gamified strategies used reduced attrition of students and improved motivation; 78% students were more motivated with these kinds of activities. According to Fig. 14.6, we can deduce from this empirical study on the motivation of participants in weeks 3 and 4 that these gamified strategies allowed us to keep students more engaged.

Based on the study carried out, we compared traditional MOOC with gamified MOOC in relation to the behavior of learners according to AMOES. The model revealed different behaviors, showing a significant variation in the category of exploring users; in 2012 51.50% of exploring users utilized the MOOC "Introduction to e-Learning" compared to 23.53% for "Authoring tools for e-learning courses".

We can deduce that this behavior is a result of the ready availability of courses, people are now more familiar with the methodology and there is a greater diffusion of the principal characteristics that these courses offer. The difference is shown in the restricted learner percentage achieved in the MOOC implemented in 2015 in contrast with MOOC 2012.

Regarding the gamification strategies used in our course, the preliminary analysis shows that earning badges in the gamified forums was neither important nor attractive to many students; in many cases participants reported they did not understand the dynamics, found it very confusing when trying to have a conversation because of the huge number of messages and preferred using social networks, such as Facebook, for tool communication. In general, these gamification strategies had a good acceptance among enrolled students and provided motivation for the delivery of the different assignments and generated great expectation with regard to the rewards promised.

For new courses we proposed a change in the course design and methodology using more gamification strategies, more challenges, more rewards, and more activities that promote specific teamwork within the members of each league. These changes will improve the learner's experience and reduce the dropout rates.

REFERENCES

Adamopoulos, A., 2013. What makes a great MOOC? An interdisciplinary analysis of student retention in online courses. In: Proceedings of the 34th International Conference on Information Systems, ICIS Band.

Augustine, D.K., Gruber, K.D., Hanson, L.R., 1990. Cooperation works! Educ. Leadersh. 47, 4–7.

Berge, Z.L., Huang, Y.-P., 2004. A model for sustainable student retention: a holistic perspective on the student dropout problem with special attention to e-learning. DEOSNEWS 13(5).

Burke, B., 2014. Gamify: How Gamification Motivates People to Do Extraordinary Things, First published by Bibliomotion, Inc. p. 6.

Chyung, S.Y., 2005. Hoping to Reduce Attrition? Follow the SIEME Model and Investigate Motivation-Hygiene Factors. Retrieved July 7, 2012, from University of Wisconsin-Extension. http://www.uwex.edu/disted/conference/resource_library/proceedings/04_1063.pdf.

Cisel, M., Bruillard, E., 2013. Chronique des MOOC. Rev. STICEF. 19. Retrieved from, http://sticef.univ-lemans.fr/num/vol2012/13r-cisel/sticef_2012_cisel_13r.htm (accessed 18.09.13).

Class-Central Report, 2014. Available from, https://www.class-central.com/report/moocs-stats-and-trends-2014/ (accessed 19.02.15).

Clow, D., 2013. MOOCs and the funnel of participation. In: Proceedings of the Third International Conference on Learning Analytics and Knowledge (LAK '13). ACM, New York, NY, pp. 185–189.

Deterding, S., Khaled, R., 2011. Gamification: toward a definition. In: CHI'11 Gamificatoin Workshop. ACM.

Deterding, S., Sicart, M., Nacke, L., O'Hara, K., Dixon, D., 2011. Gamification: Using Game-design Elements in Nongaming Contexts. In: CHI '11 Extended Abstracts on Human Factors in Computing Systems (CHI EA '11). ACM, New York, USA, pp. 2425–2428.

DiSessa, A.A., 2000. Changing Minds: Computers, Learning, and Literacy. MIT Press, Cambridge, MA.

Downes, S., 2005. E-learning 2.0. eLearning Magazine. Accessed 15 Oct 2012 from http://elearnmag.acm.org/featuredcfm?aid=1104968.

Gütl, C., Hernández Rizzardini, R., Chang, V., Morales, M., 2014a. Attrition in MOOC: lessons learned from dropout students. In: Proceedings of the 3rd International Workshop on Learning Technology for Education in Cloud (LTEC), Santiago Chile, September.

Gütl, C., Hernández Rizzardini, R., Chang, V., Morales, M., 2014b. Must we be concerned with the massive dropouts in MOOC?—An attrition analysis of open courses. In: International Conference of Interactive Collaborative Learning ICL, Dubai, UAE, December.

Hamari, J., Koivisto, J., Sarsa, H., 2014. Does gamification work? A literature review of empirical studies on gamification. In: The 47th Annual Hawaii International Conference on System Sciences, Hawaii, USA, January.

Harlen, W., 2006. The role of assessment in developing motivation for learning. In: Gardner, J. (Ed.), Assessment and Learning. Sage Publications, London, pp. 61–80.

Hernández Rizzardini, R., Gütl, C., Chang, V., Morales, M., 2013. MOOC in Latin America: implementation and lessons learned. In: The 2nd International Workshop on Learning Technology for Education in Cloud (LTEC), Knowledge Management in Organizations. Springer, Netherlands, pp. 147–158.

Hill, P., 2013. Emerging Student Patterns in MOOCs: A (Revised) Graphical View. Online blog post retrieved from, http://mfeldstein.com/emerging-student-patterns-in-moocs-a-revised-graphical-view/ (accessed 12.06.13).

Johnson, R.T., Johnson, D.W., Stanne, M.B., 1986. Comparison of Computer-Assisted Cooperative, Competitive, and Individualistic Learning. In: American Education Research Journal 23(3), pp. 382–392.

Jordan, K., 2013. MOOC Completion Rates: The Data. Available from, http://www.katyjordan.com/MOOCproject.html (accessed 18.02.14).

Kizilcec, R.F., Piech, C., Schneider, E., 2013. Deconstructing disengagement: analyzing learner subpopulations in massive open online courses. In: Proceedings of the 3rd Conference on Learning Analytics and Knowledge, Leuven, Belgium.

Mackness, J., Mak, S., Williams, R., 2010. The ideals and reality of participating in a MOOC. In: Dirckinck-Holmfeld, L., Hodgson, V., Jones, C., De Laat, M., McConnell, D., Ryberg, T. (Eds.). Proceedings of the 7th International Conference on Networked Learning. University of Lancaster, Lancaster, pp. 266–275.

McGonigal, J., 2011. Reality is broken: why games make us better and how they can change the world. Penguin Press, New York.

Nicholson, S., 2015. A RECIPE for Meaningful Gamification. In: Wood, L., Reiners, T. (Eds.), Gamification in Education and Business. Springer, New York.

Papasterigiou, M., 2009. Digital game-based learning in high school computer science education: impact on educational effectiveness and student motivation. Comput. Educ. 52, 1–12.

Parr, C., 2013. MOOC Completion Rates 'Below 7%'. Available from, http://www.timeshighereducation.co.uk/news/mooc-completion-rates-below-7/2003710.article (accessed 13.01.14).

Perna, L., Ruby, A., Boruch, R., Wang, N., Scull, J., Ahmad, S., Evans, C., 2013. The life cycle of a million MOOC users. University of Pennsylvania, MOOC Research Initiative Conference, from http://www.gse.upenn.edu/pdf/ahead/perna_ruby_boruch_moocs_dec2013.pdf.

Siemens, G., 2005. Connectivism: a learning theory for the digital age. Int. J. Instr. Technol. Dist. Learn. 2. Retrieved from, http://www.itdl.org/Journal/Jan_05/article01.htm (accessed 18.09.13).

Siemens, G., 2012. MOOCs are really a platform. ElearnSpace. Available from, http://www.elearnspace.org/blog/2012/07/25/moocs-are-really-a-platform/ (accessed 15.02.13).

Stein, K., 2014. Penn GSE study shows MOOCs have relatively few active users, with only a few persisting to course end. Available from, https://www.gse.upenn.edu/pressroom/press-releases/2013/12/penn-gse-study-shows-moocs-have-relatively-few-active-users-only-few-persisti.

Werbach, K., Hunter, D., 2012. For the Win: How game thinking can revolutionize your business, 1st Edition. Wharton Digital Press, Philadelphia.

Yang, D., Sinha, T., Adamson, D., & Rose, C.P., 2013. Turn on, Tune in, Drop out: Anticipating Student Dropouts in Massive Open Online Courses. NIPS Data-Driven Education Workshop. http://lytics.stanford.edu/datadriveneducation/papers/yangetal.pdf.

CONVERSATIONAL AGENTS AS LEARNING FACILITATORS: EXPERIENCES WITH A MOBILE MULTIMODAL DIALOGUE SYSTEM ARCHITECTURE

15

D. Griol*, Z. Callejas[†]

Carlos III University of Madrid, Madrid, Spain[*] University of Granada, Granada, Spain[†]

1 INTRODUCTION

Information and communications technologies (ICT), especially the ones related to the Internet, have been developed and incorporated into our lives with dizzying speed. If we look around us, many changes can be observed in the way people communicate, organize, work, or have fun. This has been the origin of the new Information Society, which allows access to vast amounts of information and virtually connection with other groups with almost no space or time restrictions.

Within the education field, most educators acknowledge that ICT can lead to improved student learning and better teaching methods (Duta and Martínez-Rivera, 2015; Lakkala and Ilomaki, 2015; Boe et al., 2015). However, the main objective is not to teach about ICT, but to go a step further and use these technologies in the classroom not as a complement to traditional teaching, but as an innovative way to integrate technology into the curriculum, improve the teaching-learning processes, and adapt these processes to the specific progress of each student.

Gamification and virtualization are currently two of the most innovative trends in the effort to achieve these objectives (Kuo and Chuang, 2016; Seaborn and Fels, 2015). Gamification can be defined as the use of game mechanics to enhance motivation, concentration, effort, loyalty, and other positive that are common to the use of games. Games were introduced into the educative process several decades ago, but their application to achieve both the goals of entertainment and education is a more complex task. Also, the use of games as a motivation for learning has traditionally been incorporated at an early age, but may be stigmatized at older ages or even in adulthood.

The combination of gamification and virtualization is one of the main base of virtual learning environments (Songkram, 2015; Mikropoulos and Natsis, 2011; Lucia et al., 2009). From the educational, personal, and social points of view, there are a number of advantages to learning in these environments. Educational games benefit decision making, promote problem-solving abilities and creativity, improve the ability to cooperate with and respect others, increase motivation and arouse interest in learning, strengthen knowledge, and can also be used to propose roles and improve different skills (Urh et al., 2015; Pedreira et al., 2015).

Applications aimed at introducing ICT, and especially gamification, into education have mostly opted for the use of multimodal interfaces (O'Halloran, 2015; Salse et al., 2015). Multimodal dialogue systems (Heinroth and Minker, 2012; Pieraccini, 2012; Pérez-Marín and Pascual-Nieto, 2011; Griol et al., 2014a) can be defined as computer programs designed to emulate the communication capabilities of a human being including natural language and several communication modalities (such as speech, gestures, movements, and gaze, etc.). These interfaces employ a variety of techniques to engage students in learning. Using natural language in educational software allows students to spend their cognitive resources on the learning task, rather than on how to use the interface of the application (Beun et al., 2003). Also the dialogue and anthropomorphic characteristics of pedagogical multimodal systems may help support the social dimension of the learning activities, and the social context has been argued to help with the cultivation of, and motivation for, knowledge (Baylor and Kim, 2005; Fryer and Carpenter, 2006).

In addition, the widespread use of mobile technology implementing wireless communications such as smartphones and tablets enables a new type of advanced educative application. As a result, a combination of conversational interfaces and mobile devices can optimize interaction management and integrate different sources of information that make it possible to adapt the educative application to the users and the context of the interaction (McTear and Callejas, 2013).

Our chapter is focused on some of the most important challenges that researchers have recently envisioned for future educative multimodal interfaces. It describes current efforts to develop intelligent, adaptive, proactive, mobile, portable, and effective educative multimodal systems. We also describe the open-source architecture that we have developed to facilitate the building of interactive pedagogic conversational interfaces that can interact with the students in natural language (Griol and Molina, 2014). It provides a modular and scalable framework to develop such systems efficiently for Android-based mobile devices. Android, the most popular alternative among developers of mobile Apps, offers libraries to build interfaces including different resources for graphical layouts as well as speech recognition and text-to-speech (TTS) synthesis. Our architecture integrates the facilities of the Android API in a modular architecture that emphasizes interaction management and context-awareness to build sophisticated, robust, and maintainable educative applications.

In addition, the chapter describes two educative systems that we have developed by means of this framework, a mobile conversational system with an interactive chatbot that helps children to appreciate and protect with their environment and a conversational metabot developed to provide academic information and complete ICT learning activities in immersive virtual environments like Second Life[1] or OpenSimulator.[2]

The chapter addresses very important topics and guidelines corresponding to the main axes of the book, describing a proposal for developing systems for formative assessment that:

- provides a more natural and user-adapted human-machine interaction with educative applications;
- shows the benefits and challenges of using gamification techniques in academic contexts;
- generates immediate feedback by means of an automatic assessment and personalized selection of the different learning activities;

---

[1]http://secondlife.com/
[2]http://opensimulator.org

- improves the interaction and visualization of learning data in educational environments;
- employs learning analytics that consider the student's preferences using the system, their previous uses, and their specific evolution in order to process them and decide the next decisions to be taken;
- motivates students using gamification activities and learning scenarios;
- increases student participation and performance;
- has been applied to show and assess practical implementations in very different educative domains.

The remainder of the chapter is organized as follows. Section 2 describes related research in the development of educative systems that integrate conversational functionalities. Section 3 describes the main characteristics of our framework to develop educative conversational interfaces. Sections 4 and 5 show a practical implementation of the framework to develop the *Geranium* educative system and a practical conversational metabot interacting in the Second Life virtual world. These sections also present an evaluation of the described systems with teachers and students. Finally, conclusions and future work are presented in Section 6.

2 STATE OF THE ART

According to Roda et al. (2001), educative technologies should (i) accelerate the learning process, (ii) facilitate access, (iii) personalize the learning process, and (iv) supply a richer learning environment. These aspects can be addressed by means of dialogue systems through establishing a more engaging and human-like relationship between the students and the system.

The design, implementation and strategies of the dialogue systems employed in e-learning applications vary widely, reflecting the diverse nature of the evolving speech technologies. The conversations are generally mediated through simple text-based forms (Heffernan, 2003), with users typing responses and questions with a keyboard. Some systems use embodied dialogue systems (Graesser et al., 2001) capable of displaying emotion and gesture, whereas others employ a simpler avatar (Kerly and Bull, 2008). Speech output, using TTS synthesis is used in some systems (Graesser et al., 2001), and speech input systems are increasingly available (Litman and Silliman, 2004; Fryer and Carpenter, 2006).

The advances of the technologies required to develop these systems have made it possible to meet a wide range of applications in education, including tutoring systems (Pon-Barry et al., 2006), question-answering applications (Wang et al., 2007), conversation practice for language learners (Fryer and Carpenter, 2006), pedagogical agents and learning companions (Cavazza et al., 2010), dialogue applications for computer-aided speech therapy with different language pathologies (Saz et al., 2009), and dialogues to promote reflection and metacognitive skills (Kerly et al., 2008a). In some systems the student also must teach the conversational agent (Munoz et al., 2015), interact with agent peers or co-learners (Dillenbourg and Self, 1992), or face troublemakers intended to provoke cognitive dissonance to prompt learning (Aimeur et al., 1992).

Dialogue systems as personal coaches integrate information about the domain into the application. Systems of this kind are characterized by the possibility of representing and continuously updating information that illustrates the cognitive and social users' state. The main objective is to guide and monitor users in the learning process, providing suggestions and other interaction functionalities, not only with the developed application, but also with the rest of students. In order to achieve this goal, these applications usually integrate realistic and interactive interfaces.

For example, Grigoriadou et al. (2003) describe a system where the learner reads a text about a historical event before stating their position about the significance of an issue and their justification of this opinion. The answers are classified as scientific, towards-scientific or nonscientific, and a dialogue generator produces "appropriate reflective diagnostic and learning dialogue for the learner." Similarly, in the CALM system (Kerly et al., 2008b) the users answer questions on the domain, and state their confidence in their ability to answer correctly. The system infers a knowledge level for the student based on their answers, and encourages the learner to engage in a dialogue to reflect on their self-assessment and any differences between their belief and that of the system about their knowledge levels.

Dialogue systems may also be used as role-playing actors in simulated experiential learning environments. In these settings, the dialogue system carries out a specific function in a very realistic way inside a simulated environment that emulates the real learning environment. However, perhaps the most popular application of dialogue systems to education are tutoring systems.

Kumar and Rose (2011) shows that agents playing the role of a tutor in a collaborative learning environment can lead to an improvement of more than one grade. Also some studies (Rosé et al., 2001; Wang and Johnson, 2008; Graesser et al., 2005) have evaluated the effect of task-related conversational behavior in tutorial dialogue scenarios; whereas the work in the area of affective computing and its application to tutorial dialogue has focused on the identification of student' emotional states (D'Mello et al., 2005) and using the results to improve on the choice of tasks by tutors.

For example, the AutoTutor project (Graesser et al., 1999) provides tutorial dialogs on subjects including university level computer literacy and physics. The tutoring tactics employed by AutoTutor assist students in actively constructing knowledge, and are based on extensive analysis of naturalistic tutoring sessions by human tutors. The technology behind the system includes the use of a dialogue manager, curriculum scripts, and latent semantic analysis. This system was demonstrated to provide an important improvement in gains in learning and memory when compared to control conditions.

Another example of natural language tutoring is the Geometry Explanation Tutor (Aleven et al., 2004), where students explain their answers to geometry problems in their own words. Additionally, the Oscar conversational intelligent tutoring system (Latham et al., 2012) aims to mimic a human tutor by implicitly modeling the learning style during tutoring, personalizing the tutorial to boost confidence, and improving the effectiveness of the learning experience. The system uses natural language to communicate with the users about specific topics with the users and dynamically predicts and adapts to a student's learning style.

Other systems provide a visual representation through an animated bot with gestures and emotional facial displays. These bots have been shown to be a good interaction metaphor when acting in the role of counselors (Gratch et al., 2002; Marsella et al., 2003), personal trainers (Bickmore, 2003), or healthy living advisors (de Rosis et al., 2005), and have the potential to involve users in a human-like conversation using verbal and nonverbal signals (Cassell et al., 2012).

Due to these features, they can be successfully employed in the pedagogical domain (Johnson et al., 2004) and in other domains where it is important to create a long-term relationship with the user (Bickmore and Picard, 2005), as they have been shown to be successful in creating an emphatic relation with the user (de Rosis et al., 2005; Cassell et al., 2012; Ai et al., 2006; Bailly et al., 2010; Edlund et al., 2008). However, it is difficult to communicate with these agents whenever it is needed (ie, when the user is not in front of a computer but he/she has the need of suggestions and advice). Therefore, if we want to support student in a continuous way the personal advisor should be available and accessible also on a mobile device.

Multimodal dialogue systems are also a natural choice for many human-robot applications (Sidner et al., 2004; Dowding et al., 2006) and are important tools for the development of social robots for education and entertainment applications (Gorostiza and Salichs, 2011). A mobile robot platform that includes a spoken dialogue system is presented in Theobalt et al. (2002), which is implemented as a collection of agents of the Open Agent Architecture. The dialogue component uses discourse representation structures from discourse representation theory to represent the meaning of the dialogue between human and robot.

Li and Wrede (2007) describes an interaction framework to handle multimodal input and output designed for face-to-face human interaction with robot companions. Authors emphasize the crucial role of verbal behavior in a human-robot interaction. A spoken dialogue interface developed for the Jijo-2 mobile office robot is described in Matsui et al. (2003). A microphone array system and a technique of switching multiple speech recognition processes with different dictionaries are introduced to achieve robust speech recognition in noisy office environments.

Chatbots trained on a corpus have been proposed to allow conversation practice on specific domains (Abu-Shawar and Atwell, 2007), such as Immersive Virtual Worlds. These environments provide a number of advantages for the development of intelligent learning environments (Gardner and Horan, 2011). As software, they are portable and so can be used in/from multiple locations. They can be quickly adapted to suit an experiment or demonstration and reduce the time and costs required to modify the real environment.

Virtual worlds also allow the creation of multiple instances that can be run simultaneously to compare the effects of different technologies, agents or initial conditions. They are also not limited to the constraints of the physical environment and can show information that would be otherwise invisible. They can be used not only as a way to prototype some processes and methods that in the real world take a long time (weeks, months, or even years), but also to slow time down and allow the observation of processes that in the real world occur too fast for human perception.

In addition, virtual worlds provide a combination of simulation tools, a sense of immersion and opportunities for communication and collaboration that have a great potential for their application in education. However, the lack of interaction modalities in these environments may have a negative impact on the students' learning outcomes.

Recently, Mikropoulos and Natsis presented a 10-year review on the educative applications of virtual reality covering more than 50 research studies, and have pointed out that, although virtual worlds support multisensory interaction channels, visual representations predominate (Mikropoulos and Natsis, 2011). Unfortunately, there are a number of barriers that limit user interaction with computers when interfaces are only visual, as the users must have at least a minimum training in order to use the devices (mouse and keyboard) and must not be handicapped by visual or motor disabilities. In order to address these limitations, conversational agents can be designed to engage students in a conversation that aims to be as similar as possible to that of one between humans.

3 OUR FRAMEWORK TO DEVELOP EDUCATIVE MULTIMODAL CONVERSATIONAL INTERFACES FOR MOBILE DEVICES

Fig. 15.1 shows the framework we use for the development of educative multimodal conversational agents for mobile devices (Griol and Molina, 2014). Spoken dialogue systems integrate five main tasks to deal with a user's spoken utterances: automatic speech recognition, natural language understanding

(NLU), dialogue management (DM), natural language generation (NLG), and TTS synthesis. Multimodal dialogue systems require additional components to deal with the fusion and fission of the multimodal input and output. Our framework considers an additional module for the integration of the multimodal input to process the context of the interaction.

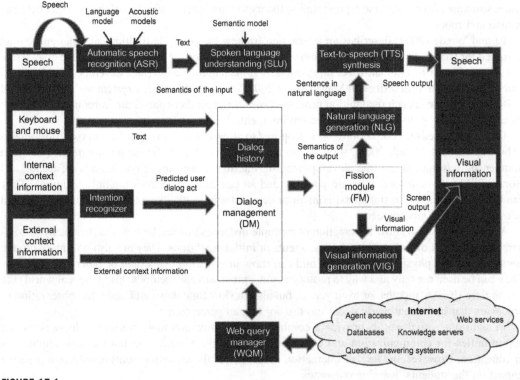

FIGURE 15.1

Proposed framework for the generation of educative conversational interfaces in mobile devices.

During the communication process, the system initially generates a welcome message and informs the user about the features and functionalities of the system. Then, the system must perform a basic set of actions that are cyclically repeated after each user utterance:

- Recognize the sequence of words mentioned by the user
- Extract the meaning of these words (ie, understand the information that is useful for the system domain)
- Access web services and databases to extract the information required by the user
- Adapt the interaction to the interaction context
- Decide what action or actions should be performed after each user request
- Play a spoken message to provide a response to the user

We suggest to use the Google Speech API to include the speech recognition functionality in a multimodal agent. Speech recognition services are available on Android devices to send messages, call contacts, show maps in Google Maps, visit a website, start route with Google Navigation, complete a Google search, write a note, send an email, or listen to music, to mention a few. Besides the recognition capabilities that are implemented within the Android operating systems, there is the possibility of building Android apps with speech input and output using the Google Speech API (package *android.speech*). Once the conversational agent has recognized what the user has uttered, it is necessary to understand what he or she has said. We propose the use of grammar in order to perform the semantic interpretation of the user inputs (Kaufmann and Pfister, 2012).

The statistical technique that we employ to model user's intention is described in Griol et al. (2013). External contextual information is usually measured by hardware or software-based sensors integrated in the mobile device (such as accelerometers, multi-touch screens, and compasses). Typically, sensors rely on low-level communication protocols to send the collected context information or they are tightly coupled within their context-aware systems.

The dialogue manager deals with different sources of information such as the NLU results, database queries results, application domain knowledge, and knowledge about the users and the previous dialogue history to select the next system action. We envisioned a statistical methodology that combined multimodal fusion and DM functionalities (Griol et al., 2014a).

The modality fission module receives abstract, modality independent presentation goals from the dialogue manager. The multimodal output depends on several constraints for the specific domain of the system, for example, the current scenario, the display size, and user preferences like the currently applicable modalities. This module applies presentation strategies that decompose the complex presentation goal into simpler presentation tasks. It also decides whether an object description is to be uttered verbally or graphically. The result is a presentation script that is passed to the Visual Information and NLG modules.

The visual generation module creates the visual arrangement of the content using dynamically created and filled graphical layout elements. An android provides a wide variety of controls that can be incorporated into the user interface, such as buttons, text fields, checkboxes, radio buttons, toggle buttons, spinners, and pickers. The View class provides the means to capture the events from the specific control that the user interacts with.

Once the dialogue manager has selected the next system action, the NLG translates the nonlinguistic representation into one or several sentences in natural language. The simplest approach for NLG consists of using a predefined text messages (eg, error messages and warnings). Finally, a text-to-speech synthesizer is used to generate the voice signal that will be transmitted to the user. We propose the use of the Google TTS API to include the TTS functionality in an application. The *android.speech. tts* package includes the classes and interfaces required to integrate TTS synthesis in an Android application.

4 THE GERANIUM PEDAGOGICAL SYSTEM

The *Geranium* pedagogical system (Griol et al., 2014c) has been developed with the main aim of making children aware of the diversity of the urban ecosystem in which they live, the need to take care of it, and how they can have a positive impact on it. The system has a chatbot named *Gera*, a cartoon that resembles a geranium, a very common plant in the Spanish home.

Fig. 15.2 shows two snapshots of the system. As can be observed, it has a very simple interface in which the chatbot is placed in a neighborhood. There are several buttons to select the type of questions,

FIGURE 15.2

Snapshots of the response of the *Geranium* system to a correct and an incorrect answer.

the chatbot has a balloon that shows the text, image or videos corresponding to the questions and possible answers, and there is a "push-to-talk" button that enables the oral input. As the chatbot changes its expressions, the background also changes. For example, Fig. 15.2 shows the response of the system to an incorrect response, as can be observed, *Gera* is "sad" and the background has a *gray* color.

The chatbot poses questions to the children that they must answer either orally or using the graphical interface. Once an answer is selected, the system checks if it is correct. In case it is, the user receives a positive feedback and *Gera* shows a "happy" (usual case) or a "surprised" (in case of many correct questions in a row) face. If the answer selected is not correct, Gera shows a "sad" expression and provides a hint to the user, who can make another guess before getting the correct response. *Gera* has seven expressions: happy, ashamed, sad, surprised, talking, waiting, and listening, shown in Fig. 15.3, which can also be extended by adding new resources to the chatbot expressions database.

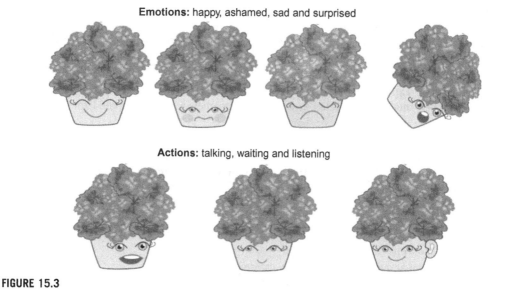

Emotions: happy, ashamed, sad and surprised

Actions: talking, waiting and listening

FIGURE 15.3

Facial expressions of the *Gera* chatbot.

The activities are grouped into four topics: "in the market," "animals and plants," "waste," and "water and energy." In the first topic, the children are asked about fruits and vegetables, the plants where they come from and the seasons when they are collected. The second topic comprises questions about animals and plants that live in the city, showing photographs, drawings and videos of birds, flowers, trees, and leaves and how they change or migrate during the year. In the third topic, the children are asked about recycling, differentiating between the different wastes and the suitable containers. Finally, the fourth topic deals with good practices to save water and energy at home. Currently, there are 20 questions per category (a total of 80 questions), although the system can be extended adding new questions with their respective answers to the database.

In the *Geranium* system, for each question type there is a grammar template with the usual structure of the responses, and new grammar is dynamically generated that makes use of the template and contains the exact response options for the actual question. Each of the options has an assigned code, which is used also in the GUI and makes it possible to easily control the synchronization between the different modalities employed. In addition the template makes it possible to maintain the same structure for the responses to similar questions (eg, to ask for the name of a bird, a plant, or a fruit in a photograph) even when they belong to different categories (eg, birds are in the category "animals and plants" and fruits are in the category "in the market"). This facilitates the system usage, as it is easier for the users to know what the system expects.

A preliminary evaluation of the *Geranium* system has been completed already with the participation of six primary school teachers for 8-, 9-, and 10-years-old children, who rated the naturalness and pedagogical potential of the system. Teachers were told to bear in mind that the system was aimed at children of the same age as their students. The questionnaire shown in Table 15.1 was defined for the evaluation. The responses to the questionnaire were measured on a five-point Likert scale ranging from 1 (strongly disagree) to 5 (strongly agree). The experts were also asked to rate the system from 0 (minimum) to 10 (maximum) and there was an additional open question to write comments or remarks.

Also, from the interactions of the experts with the system we completed an objective evaluation of the application considering the following interaction parameters: (i) question success rate (SR)—this is the percentage of successfully completed questions (system asks—user answers—system provides appropriate feedback about the answer), (ii) confirmation rate (CR)—it was computed as the ratio between the number of explicit confirmations turns and the total of turns, and (iii) error correction rate (ECR)—the percentage of corrected errors. These parameters were computed for a total of 30

Table 15.1 Questionnaire Designed for the Evaluation of the *Geranium* System

Technical quality

TQ01. The system offers enough interactivity

TQ02. The system is easy to use

TQ03. It is easy to know what to do at each moment

TQ04. The amount of information that is displayed on the screen is adequate

TQ05. The arrangement of information on the screen is logical

TQ06. The chatbot is helpful

TQ07. The chatbot is attractive

TQ08. The chatbot reacts in a consistent way

TQ09. The chatbot complements the activities without distracting or interfering with them

TQ010. The chatbot provides adequate verbal feedback

TQ011. The chatbot provides adequate nonverbal feedback (gestures)

Didactic potential

DP01. The system fulfills the objective of making children appreciate their environment

DP02. The contents worked in the activities are relevant for this objective

DP03. The design of the activities was adequate for children of this age

DP04. The activities support significant learning

DP05. The feedback provided by the agent improves learning

DP06. The system encourages continuing learning after errors interactions of the recruited professors with the described system. For these interactions, the professors used the described functionalities of the application without no restrictions.

The results of the questionnaire are summarized in Table 15.2. As can be observed from the responses to the questionnaire, the satisfaction with the technical aspects was high, as well as the perceived didactic potential. The chatbot was considered attractive and adequate, and the teachers felt that the system was appropriate and the activities relevant. The teachers also considered that the system succeeds in making children appreciate their environment. The global rate for the system was 8.5 (in the scale from 0 to 10).

Although the results were very positive, in the open question the teachers also pointed out desirable improvements. One of them was to make the system listen constantly instead of using the push-to-talk interface. However, we believe that this would cause many recognition problems, taking into account the unpredictability of children behavior. Also, although they considered the chatbot attractive and its feedback adequate, they suggested creating new gestures for the chatbot to make transitions smoother.

The results of the objective evaluation for the described interactions show that the developed system could interact correctly with the users in most cases, achieving a question SR of 96.56%. The fact that the possible answers to the questions are restricted made it possible to be successful in speech recognition. Additionally, the approaches for error correction by means of confirming or re-asking for data were successful in 93.02% of the times when the speech recognizer did not provide the correct answer.

Table 15.2 Results of the Evaluation of the *Geranium* System by Experts

	Min/Max	Average	Std. Deviation
TQ01	3/5	4.17	0.69
TQ02	3/4	3.67	0.47
TQ03	4/5	4.83	0.37
TQ04	5/5	5.00	0.00
TQ05	4/5	4.67	0.47
TQ06	4/5	4.83	0.37
TQ07	4/5	4.83	0.37
TQ08	4/5	4.50	0.50
TQ09	4/5	4.83	0.37
TQ10	4/5	4.67	0.47
TQ11	3/5	4.50	0.76
DP01	5/5	5.00	0.00
DP02	4/5	4.67	0.47
DP03	4/5	4.83	0.37
DP04	5/5	5.00	0.00
DP05	4/5	4.67	0.47
DP06	4/5	4.83	0.37
	SR	CR	ECR
	9.6.56%	13.00%	93.02%

5 CONVERSATIONAL METABOT PROVIDING ACADEMIC INFORMATION

Following the framework described in Section 3, we have also developed a conversational metabot (see Fig. 15.4, Griol et al., 2014b) that facilitates two main purposes in the Second Life and OpenSimulator-based virtual worlds: provide academic information and carry out test and questionnaires. The developed conversational metabot makes it possible for the students to have permanent additional support in their study, and helps the teachers to leverage their workload in tasks like academic information providing, as well as automating evaluations by posing questionnaires and tests through the metabot.

FIGURE 15.4

Conversational metabot (left) developed to interact in virtual worlds.

For the first task, the functionalities are based on a previously developed dialogue system that worked over the telephone (Callejas and López-Cózar, 2008). We defined a semantic representation in which one or more concepts represent the intention of the utterance, and a sequence of attribute-value pairs contains the information about the values given by the user. In the case of user turns, we defined four concepts related to the different queries that the user can present to the system (Subjects, Lecturers, Doctoral studies, and Registration), three task-independent concepts (Affirmation, Negation, and Not-Understood), and eight attributes (Subject-Name, Degree, Group-Name, Subject-Type, Lecturer-Name, Program-Name, Semester, and Deadline).

A set of 150 dialogues was acquired with the conversational metabot by means of its interaction with students and professors of our university. Fig. 15.5 shows an example of a dialogue extracted from this corpus and translated from Spanish to English. Turns with S refer to system turns, and turns with U refer to user turns.

S_1: Hi! You can ask me for information about subjects, lecturers, doctoral studies and registrations.
U_1: I want to know information about subjects in Computer Science.
S_2: Which subject do you want to consult?
U_2: Language Processors.
S_3: What do you want to know about Language Processors?
U_3: Can you tell me about the schedules of Group D?
S_4: The schedule of the Group D of Language Processors is: Monday 9:00-11:00, Wednesday 11:00-13:00. Anything else?
U_4: Can you tell me the name of the lecturer?
S_5: The lecturer of the Group D is David Griol. Anything else?
U_5: No, thank you.
S_6: Bye!

FIGURE 15.5

Example of a dialogue acquired with the conversational metabot.

The second task of the metabot was to interact with the students by presenting them a set of test questionnaires about the described subjects, including questions concerning theoretical contents as a review of methodologies and concepts. A total of 150 questionnaires were implemented using Sloodle.[3]

The participants in the evaluation of the metabot designed for the Second Life virtual world were 56 students attending to the Language Processors and Formal Languages and Automata Theory described courses of the Computer Science Degree at the Carlos III University of Madrid. These subjects cover theoretical and practical contents about Finite Automata, Push-Down Automata, Turing Machines, and the design and analysis of programming languages. Each student had at his/her disposal a computer and was invited to interact with the other students and with the teacher through the virtual world.

Before the lectures started, the tutors guided the students through the virtual campus and provided them with a little training session on the available communication features and avatar basic movements. The students had a basic knowledge of 2D computer graphics, and image and video editing. The teacher gave the initial lectures in a virtual classroom of the virtual campus. To perform collaborative sessions the students were aggregated into small groups of two or three members, each of whom had at his or her disposal a separate environment where it was possible to discuss, visualize, and record information. The conversations and decisions were automatically saved for later reference in a database using the Moodle plug-in.

We have carried out a subjective evaluation through an opinion survey based on the evaluation methodologies for educative virtual environments proposed in Lucia et al. (2009), which were adapted from Witmer and Singer (1998) and Kreijns et al. (2007). Three main aspects have been evaluated: perception of presence, communication and perceived sociability, and specific evaluation of the virtual environment. The responses to the questionnaire were measured on a five-point Likert scale ranging from 1 (for nothing/strongly disagree) to 5 (very much/strongly agree).

[3]http://www.sloodle.org/

The questionnaire related to the evaluation of communication, awareness, and perceived sociability is shown in Table 15.3.

Table 15.4 shows the results obtained for these questions. Also in this case, the median is high, but higher data variability denotes a heterogeneous perception of the communication features. A deeper analysis confirmed that a lower average score was obtained by the last question, which concerns the avatar's gestures. This indicates that the students had some difficulties in communicating by using the avatar's gestures. On the whole, students felt the offered communication favored discussion with others and speech communication improved the interaction with other students. Let us note that, even if the median is 3.9, a very good result, there were some negative judgments by users who found it more difficult to figure out what was happening at some moments.

Table 15.3 Adaptation of the Witmer and Singer (1998), Kreijns et al. (2007), and Lucia et al. (2009) Questionnaires for the Evaluation of Communication, Awareness, and Perceived Sociability

Communication, Awareness, and Perceived Sociability
Communicating with the other participants was easy COM
The system increased the opportunity of discussing with the others COM
Conversation has been properly managed COM
Nonverbal communication (gesture) was adequate COM
I have been immediately aware of the existence of the other participants AW
I was aware of what was going on AW
I was aware of the participant roles (teacher, tutor, and student) AW
This environment enabled me to easily contact my team-mates AW
I did not feel lonely in this environment AW
This environment enabled me to get a good impression of my team-mates PS
This environment allows spontaneous informal conversations PS
This environment allowed for nontask-related conversations PS
This environment enabled me to make close friendships with my team-mates PS

COM, communication; AW, awareness; PS, perceived sociability.

Table 15.4 Results Related to Communication, Awareness, and Perceived Sociability

	COM	AW	PS
Mean score	4.1	3.9	3.8
Std. deviation	1.3	1.1	1.0
Maximum value	5	5	4
Minimum value	2	3	3

6 CONCLUSIONS

In this chapter we have discussed the rich variety of applications for multimodal dialogue systems in education, covering a number of objectives and strategies that include tutoring, second language learning, learning companions, pedagogical agents, etc. The benefits reported for students include an improvement in their evaluations, enhanced motivation, strengthened compromise, and deeper training of metacognitive skills. Teachers can also benefit from the ability of these systems to assist them in their tasks and scaffold the students' learning thus helping them to cope with the diversity of learning styles and rhythms in their class. We have also covered different topics related to the development of multimodal dialogue systems addressed to solve these challenges, paying special attention to aspects related to their design.

We have described our own efforts towards providing a general framework for the development of conversational systems for education, and we have illustrated how it can be used to develop two conversational agents of different nature: a web-based chatbot for children, and a conversational avatar in a virtual world for university students. The evaluation results indicate that both agents were perceived as easy to use and have a high pedagogical potential. Their heterogeneous nature also shows the possibilities of our framework to develop pedagogical conversational agents targeted at different populations and pedagogical contents. We want to conduct a more comprehensive evaluation of the system's functionalities with regard to the students and professors.

In recent years, some experts have dared to envision what the future research guidelines for the application of multimodal dialogue systems for educative purposes would be. These objectives have gradually changed to accommodate ever more complex goals, such as providing the system with advanced reasoning, problem-solving capabilities, adaptiveness, proactiveness, affective intelligence, and multilinguality. These concepts are not mutually exclusive, as for example the system's intelligence can also be involved in the degree to which it can adapt to new situations, and this adaptiveness can result in better portability for use in different environments.

As can be observed, these new objectives refer to the system as a whole, and represent major trends that in practice are achieved through joint work in different areas and components of the dialogue system. Thus, current research trends are characterized by large-scale objectives that are shared out between different researchers in different areas.

Proactiveness is necessary for computers to stop being considered a tool and become real conversational partners. Proactive systems have the capability of engaging in a conversation with the user even when he has not explicitly requested the system's intervention. This is a key aspect in the development of ubiquitous computing architectures in which the system is embedded in the user's environment, and thus the user is not aware that he is interacting with a computer, but rather he perceives he is interacting with the environment. To achieve this goal, it is necessary to provide the systems with problem-solving capabilities and context-awareness.

Adaptivity may also refer to other aspects of speech applications. There are different levels in which the system can adapt to the user. The simplest one is through personal profiles in which the users have static choices to customize the interaction. Systems can also adapt to the user's environment, for example, ambient intelligence applications such as the ubiquitous proactive systems described. A more sophisticated approach is to adapt to the user's knowledge and expertise. This is especially important in educative systems to adapt the system taking into account the specific evolution of each of the students, the previous uses of the system, and the errors that they have made during the previous interactions.

There is also an increasing interest in the development of multimodal conversational systems that dynamically adapt their conversational behaviors to the user's affective state. The empathetic educative agent can thus contribute to a more positive perception of the interaction.

Portability is currently addressed from very different perspectives, the three main ones being domain, language, and technological independence. Ideally, systems should be able to work over different educative application domains, or at least be easily adaptable between them. Current studies on domain independence center on how to merge lexical, syntactic, and semantic structures from different contexts and how to develop dialogue managers that deal with different domains.

Finally, technological independence deals with the possibility of using multimodal systems with different hardware configurations. Computer processing power will continue to increase, with lower costs for both processor and memory components. The systems that support even the most sophisticated multimodal applications will move from centralized architectures to distributed configurations and thus must be able to work with different underlying technologies.

REFERENCES

Abu-Shawar, B., Atwell, E., 2007. Fostering language learner autonomy via adaptive conversation tutors. In: Proceedings of Corpus Linguistics, pp. 1–8.

Ai, H., Litman, D., Forbes-Riley, K., Rotaru, M., Tetreault, J., Purandare, A., 2006. Using systems and user performance features to improve emotion detection in spoken tutoring dialogs. In: Proceedings of Interspeech'06-ICSLP, pp. 797–800.

Aimeur, E., Dufort, H., Leibu, D., Frasson, C., 1992. Some justifications for the learning by disturbing strategy. In: Proceedings of 8th World Conference on Artificial Intelligence in Education (AI-ED'97), pp. 119–126.

Aleven, V., Ogan, A., Popescu, O., Torrey, C., Koedinger, K., 2004. Evaluating the effectiveness of a tutorial dialog system for self-explanation. In: Proceedings of 7th International Conference on Intelligent Tutoring Systems (ITS'04), pp. 443–454.

Bailly, G., Raidt, S., Elisei, F., 2010. Gaze, dialog systems and face-to-face communication. Speech Comm. 52, 598–612.

Baylor, A., Kim, Y., 2005. Simulating instructional roles through pedagogical agents. Int. J. Artif. Intell. Educ. 15, 95–115.

Beun, R., de Vos, E., Witteman, C., 2003. Embodied dialog systems: effects on memory performance and anthropomorphisation. In: Proceedings of the International Conference on Intelligent Virtual Agents. LNCS 2792, pp. 315–319.

Bickmore, T., 2003. Relational agents: effecting change through human-computer relationships. Ph.D. Thesis Media Arts and Sciences, Massachusetts Institute of Technology.

Bickmore, T., Picard, R., 2005. Establishing and maintaining long-term human-computer relationships. ACM Trans. Comput. Hum. Int. 12, 293–327.

Boe, T., Gulbrandsen, B., Sorebo, O., 2015. How to stimulate the continued use of ICT in higher education: integrating information systems continuance theory and agency theory. Comput. Hum. Behav. 50, 375–384.

Callejas, Z., López-Cózar, R., 2008. Relations between de-facto criteria in the evaluation of a spoken dialogue system. Speech Comm. 50, 646–665.

Cassell, J., Sullivan, J., Prevost, S., Churchill, E., 2012. Embodied Dialog Systems. The MIT Press, Cambridge.

Cavazza, M., de la Camara, R.-S., Turunen, M., 2010. How was your day? A companion ECA. In: Proceedings of AAMAS'10, pp. 1629–1630.

D'Mello, S., Craig, S., Gholson, B., Frankin, S., Picard, R., Graesser, A., 2005. Integrating affect sensors in an intelligent tutoring system. In: Proceedings of the Workshop on Affective Interactions: The Computer in the Affective Loop at IUI, pp. 7–13.

de Rosis, F., Cavalluzzi, A., Mazzotta, I., Novielli, N., 2005. Can embodied dialog systems induce empathy in users? In: Proceedings of AISB'05 Virtual Social Characters Symposium, pp. 1–8.

Dillenbourg, P., Self, J., 1992. People power: a human-computer collaborative learning system. In: Proceedings of the Intelligent Tutoring Systems (ITS'92), pp. 651–660.

Dowding, J., Clancey, W., Graham, J., 2006. Are you talking to me? Dialogue systems supporting mixed teams of humans and robots. In: Proceedings of the AIAA Fall Symposium "Annually Informed Performance: Integrating Machine Listing and Auditory Presentation in Robotic Systems", pp. 22–27.

Duta, N., Martínez-Rivera, O., 2015. Between theory and practice: the importance of ICT in higher education as a tool for collaborative learning. Proc. Soc. Behav. Sci. 180, 1466–1473.

Edlund, J., Gustafson, J., Heldner, M., Hjalmarsson, A., 2008. Towards human-like spoken dialog systems. Speech Comm. 50, 630–645.

Fryer, L., Carpenter, R., 2006. Bots as language learning tools. Language learning and technology. Comput. Speech Lang. 10, 8–14.

Gardner, M., Horan, B., 2011. Using virtual worlds for online role-play. In: Proceedings of 1st European Immersive Education Summit (iED'11), pp. 1–6.

Gorostiza, J., Salichs, M., 2011. End-user programming of a social robot by dialog. Robot. Auton. Syst. 59, 1102–1114.

Graesser, A., Wiemer-Hastings, K., Wiemer-Hastings, P., Kreuz, R., 1999. AutoTutor: a simulation of a human tutor. J. Cogn. Syst. Res. 1, 35–51.

Graesser, A., Person, N., Harter, D., 2001. Teaching tactics and dialog in AutoTutor. Int. J. Artif. Intell. Educ. 12, 23–39.

Graesser, A., Chipman, P., Haynes, B., Olney, A., 2005. AutoTutor: an intelligent tutoring system with mixed-initiative dialog. IEEE Trans. Educ. 48, 612–618.

Gratch, J., Rickel, J., Andre, J., Badler, N., Cassell, J., Petajan, E., 2002. Creating interactive virtual humans: some assembly required. In: Proceedings of the IEEE Conference on Intelligent Systems, pp. 54–63.

Grigoriadou, M., Tsaganou, G., Cavoura, T., 2003. Dialog-based reflective system for historical text comprehension. In: Proceedings of Workshop on Learner Modelling for Reflection at Artificial Intelligence in Education, pp. 238–247.

Griol, D., Molina, J., 2014. A framework to develop adaptive multimodal dialog systems for android-based mobile devices. In: Proceedings of International Conference on Hybrid Artificial Intelligence Systems (HAIS'14), pp. 25–36.

Griol, D., Carbó, J., Molina, J., 2013. A statistical simulation technique to develop and evaluate conversational agents. AI Commun. 26, 355–371.

Griol, D., Callejas, Z., López-Cózar, R., Riccardi, G., 2014a. A domain-independent statistical methodology for dialog management in spoken dialog systems. Comput. Speech Lang. 28, 743–768.

Griol, D., Molina, J., Callejas, Z., 2014b. An approach to develop intelligent learning environments by means of immersive virtual worlds. JAISE J. 6, 237–255.

Griol, D., Molina, J., Sanchis, A., 2014c. The Geranium system: multimodal conversational agents for e-learning. Adv. Intell. Syst. Comput. 290, 219–226.

Heffernan, N., 2003. Web-based evaluations showing both cognitive and motivational benefits of the Ms. Lindquist Tutor. In: Proceedings of International Conference on Artificial Intelligence in Education, pp. 115–122.

Heinroth, T., Minker, W., 2012. Introducing Spoken Dialogue Systems into Intelligent Environments. Kluwer, New York.

Johnson, W., Labore, L., Chiu, Y., 2004. A pedagogical agent for psychosocial intervention on a handheld computer. In: Proceedings of AAAI Fall Symposium on Dialogue Systems for Health Communication, pp. 22–24.

Kaufmann, T., Pfister, B., 2012. Syntactic language modeling with formal grammars. Speech Comm. 54, 715–731.

Kerly, A., Bull, S., 2008. Children's interactions with inspectable and negotiated learner models. In: Proceedings of International Conference on Intelligent Tutoring Systems, pp. 132–141.

Kerly, A., Ellis, R., Bull, S., 2008a. CALM system: a dialog system for learner modelling. Knowl.-Based Syst. 21, 238–246.

Kerly, A., Ellis, R., Bull, S., 2008b. Dialog systems in e-learning. In: Proceedings of Conference on Artificial Intelligence (AI'08), pp. 169–182.

Kreijns, K., Kirschner, P., Jochems, W., van Buuren, H., 2007. Measuring perceived sociability of computer-supported collaborative learning environments. Comput. Educ. 49, 176–192.

Kumar, R., Rose, C., 2011. Architecture for building dialog systems that support collaborative learning. IEEE Trans. Learn. Technol. 4, 21–34.

Kuo, M., Chuang, T., 2016. How gamification motivates visits and engagement for online academic dissemination—an empirical study. Comput. Hum. Behav. 55, 16–27.

Lakkala, M., Ilomaki, L., 2015. A case study of developing ICT-supported pedagogy through a collegial practice transfer process. Comput. Educ. 90, 1–12.

Latham, A., Crockett, K., McLean, D., Edmonds, B., 2012. A conversational intelligent tutoring system to automatically predict learning styles. Comput. Educ. 59, 95–109.

Li, S., Wrede, B., 2007. Why and how to model multi-modal interaction for a mobile robot companion. In: Proceedings of AAAI Spring Symposium on Interaction Challenges for Intelligent Assistant, pp. 71–79.

Litman, D., Silliman, S., 2004. ITSPOKE: an intelligent tutoring spoken dialog system. In: Proceedings of the Human Language Technology Conference: North American Chapter of the Association for Computational Linguistics, pp. 5–8.

Lucia, A.D., Francese, R., Passero, I., Tortora, G., 2009. Development and evaluation of a virtual campus on second life: the case of second DMI. Comput. Educ. 52, 220–233.

Marsella, S., Johnson, W., Labore, C., 2003. Interactive pedagogical drama for health interventions. In: Artificial Intelligence in Education: Shaping the Future of Learning Through Intelligent Technologies. IOS Press, Amsterdam, The Netherlands, pp. 341–348.

Matsui, T., Asoh, H., Asano, F., Fry, J., Hara, I., Motomura, Y., et al., 2003. Spoken language interface of the Jijo-2 office robot. STAR 6, 307–317.

McTear, M., Callejas, Z., 2013. Voice Application Development for Android. Packt Publishing, Birmingham.

Mikropoulos, T., Natsis, A., 2011. Educational virtual environments: a ten-year review of empirical research (1999–2009). Comput. Educ. 56, 769–780.

Munoz, A., Lasheras, J., Capel, A., Cantabella, M., Caballero, A., 2015. Ontosakai: on the optimization of a learning management system using semantics and user profiling. Expert Syst. Appl. 42, 5995–6007.

O'Halloran, K., 2015. The language of learning mathematics: a multimodal perspective. J. Math. Behav. 40, 63–74.

Pedreira, O., García, F., Brisaboa, N., Piattini, M., 2015. Gamification in software engineering—a systematic mapping. Inf. Softw. Technol. 57, 157–168.

Pérez-Marín, D., Pascual-Nieto, I., 2011. Conversational Agents and Natural Language Interaction: Techniques and Effective Practices. IGI Global, Hershey, PA.

Pieraccini, R., 2012. The Voice in the Machine: Building Computers That Understand Speech. The MIT Press, Cambridge.

Pon-Barry, H., Schultz, K., Bratt, E.-O., Clark, B., Peters, S., 2006. Responding to student uncertainty in spoken tutorial dialog systems. IJAIED J. 16, 171–194.

Roda, C., Angehrn, A., Nabeth, T., 2001. Dialog systems for advanced learning: applications and research. In: Proceedings of BotShow'01, pp. 1–7.

Rosé, C., Moore, J., VanLehn, K., Allbritton, D., 2001. A comparative evaluation of socratic versus didactic tutoring. In: Proceedings of Cognitive Sciences Society, pp. 869–874.

Salse, M., Ribera, M., Satorras, R., Centelles, M., 2015. Multimodal campus project: pilot test of voice supported reading. Proc. Soc. Behav. Sci. 196, 190–197.

Saz, O., Yin, S.-C., Lleida, E., Rose, R., Vaquero, C., Rodríguez, W.-R., 2009. Tools and technologies for computer-aided speech and language therapy. Speech Comm. 51, 948–967.

Seaborn, K., Fels, D., 2015. Gamification in theory and action: a survey. Int. J. Hum. Comput. Stud. 74, 14–31.

Sidner, C., Kidd, C., Lee, C., Lesh, N., 2004. Where to look: a study of human-robot engagement. In: Proceedings of 9th International Conference on Intelligent User Interfaces (IUI'04), pp. 78–84.

Songkram, N., 2015. E-learning system in virtual learning environment to develop creative thinking for learners in higher education. Proc. Soc. Behav. Sci. 174, 674–679.

Theobalt, C., Bos, J., Chapman, T., Espinosa-Romero, A., Fraser, M., Hayes, G., et al., 2002. Talking to Godot: dialogue with a mobile robot. In: Proceedings of IEEE/RSJ International Conference on Intelligent Robots and Systems, pp. 1338–1343.

Urh, M., Vukovic, G., Jereb, E., Pintar, R., 2015. The model for introduction of gamification into e-learning in higher education. Proc. Soc. Behav. Sci. 197, 388–397.

Wang, N., Johnson, L., 2008. The politeness effect in an intelligent foreign language tutoring system. In: Proceedings of Intelligent Tutoring Systems (ITS'08), pp. 270–280.

Wang, Y., Wang, W., Huang, C., 2007. Enhanced semantic question answering system for e-Learning environment. In: Proceedings of 21st International Conference on Advanced Information Networking and Applications (AINAW'07), pp. 1023–1028.

Witmer, B., Singer, M., 1998. Measuring presence in virtual environments: a presence questionnaire. Presence-Teleop. Virt. Environ. 7, 225–240.

Author Index

Note: Page numbers followed by *f* indicate figures, and *t* indicate tables.

Soler, J., 55, 57
Song, D., 230
Songkram, N., 313–314
Sorebo, O., 313
Soulie, F.F., 29
Spiliopoulou, M., 195
Spratt, C., 49
Srivastava, J., 192, 194
Stamatatos, E., 29
Stasko, J.T., 139
Stathacopoulou, R., 30
Steckelberg, A.L., 8
Steffens, K., 5
Stein, K., 296
Steinberg, L.S., 52
Sterbini, A., 10
Sterling, L.S., 256–257
Sterling, S., 172
Stewart, M., 139
Stocker, J., 30
Stone, R., 55–56
Storey, V.C., 171–172
Strickland, N., 57
Suau, P., 256–257
Subramanya, S., 290
Sullivan, J., 316
Sumithra, M., 29
Sun, J., 29
Sung, S., 6–8, 18
Suthers, D., 118–119, 121–122, 127t
Sutinen, E., 56
Suttie, N., 232
Švec, P., 188
Swan, K., 117

T

Tada, M., 122, 127t
Talavera, L., 189, 192
Taleb, N., 248
Tall, D.O., 91
Tallent-Runnels, M.K., 110
Tamassia, R., 140
Tanaka, Y., 277
Tang, A.Y., 41
Tangorra, F., 173
Taniar, D., 189, 195–196, 210
Tapia, J.A., 246–247
Tappert, C., 29
Tardy, C., 3, 8, 18
Telaprolu, V.R., 275
Tempelaar, D.T., 121, 127t

Temperini, M., 10
ter Maat, M., 225
Terzis, V., 121, 127t
Tetreault, J., 316
Theobalt, C., 317
Thern, T.C., 110
Thomas, J.A., 110
Thompson, S., 55
Thomson, A., 3, 5–7, 18–19
Ths, H., 35
Thurston, W.P., 91
Thüs, H., 118, 123, 173
Tibbey, G., 189
Timmers, C.F., 112
Tobarra, L., 189
Toledo, P., 251
Torrente, J., 249–250
Torrey, C., 316
Tortora, G., 313–314, 325, 326t
Touya, K., 189
Triantafillou, E., 55, 117
Tsaganou, G., 316
Tsakalidis, A., 27
Tselonis, C., 56
Tsihrintzis, G.A., 248
Tsolis, D., 27
Tsoukalas, V., 30
Tudevdagva, U., 65–84
Tulloch, I., 57–58
Turkle, S., 249
Turunen, M., 315
Twiner, A., 121, 129t
Tyler, R.W., 65

U

Ueno, M., 30
Urh, M., 313–314
Usener, C.A., 50, 55, 57
Uskov, V., 248
Uz, T., 29

V

Valor, J., 167, 171
Valtcheva, A., 135
Valve Inc, 277
van Barneveld, A., 174–175
van Buuren, H., 325, 326t
van de Vrie, E., 121, 127t
van den Boom, G., 3
Van der Kleij, F.M., 112
van der Kooij,, H., 121, 127t

Subject Index

Note: Page numbers followed by *f* indicate figures, and *t* indicate tables.

Printed in the United States
By Bookmasters